A Celebration of
Young Poets

East – Fall 2007

Creative Communication, Inc.

A Celebration of Young Poets
East – Fall 2007

An anthology compiled by Creative Communication, Inc.

Published by:

CREATIVE COMMUNICATION, INC.
1488 NORTH 200 WEST
LOGAN, UT 84341

Copyright © 2008 by Creative Communication, Inc.
Printed in the United States of America

ISBN: 978-1-60050-146-3

Foreword

The poets between these pages are not famous...yet. They are still learning how language creates images and how to reflect their thoughts through words. However, through their acceptance into this publication, these young poets have taken a giant leap that reflects their desire to write.

We are proud of this anthology and what it represents. Most poets who entered the contest were not accepted to be published. The poets who are included in this book represent the best poems from our youth. These young poets took a chance and were rewarded by being featured in this anthology. Without this book, these poems would have been lost in a locker or a backpack.

We will have a feeling of success if upon reading this anthology of poetry each reader finds a poem that evokes emotion. It may be a giggle or a smile. It may be a thoughtful reflection. You might find a poem that takes you back to an earlier day when a snowfall contains magic or when a pile of leaves was an irresistible temptation. If these poems can make you feel alive and have hope in our youth, then it will be time well spent.

As we thank the poets for sharing their work, we also thank you, the reader, for allowing us to be part of your life.

Thomas Worthen, Ph.D.
Editor
Creative Communication

WRITING CONTESTS!

Enter our next POETRY contest!
Enter our next ESSAY contest!

Why should I enter?

Win prizes and get published! Each year thousands of dollars in prizes are awarded in each region and tens of thousands of dollars in prizes are awarded throughout North America. The top writers in each division receive a monetary award and a free book that includes their published poem or essay. Entries of merit are also selected to be published in our anthology.

Who may enter?

There are four divisions in the poetry contest. The poetry divisions are grades K-3, 4-6, 7-9, and 10-12. There are three divisions in the essay contest. The essay division are grades 4-6, 7-9, and 10-12.

What is needed to enter the contest?

To enter the poetry contest send in one original poem, 21 lines or less. To enter the essay contest send in one original essay, 250 words or less, on any topic. Each entry must include the student's name, grade, address, city, state, and zip code, and the student's school name and school address. Students who include their teacher's name may help the teacher qualify for a free copy of the anthology.

How do I enter?

Enter a poem online at:
www.poeticpower.com
or
Mail your poem to:
    Poetry Contest
    1488 North 200 West
    Logan, UT 84341

Enter an essay online at:
www.studentessaycontest.com
or
Mail your essay to:
    Essay Contest
    1488 North 200 West
    Logan, UT 84341

When is the deadline?

Poetry contest deadlines are August 14th, December 4th, and April 8th. Essay contest deadlines are July 15th, October 15th, and February 17th. You can enter each contest, however, send only one poem or essay for each contest deadline.

Are there benefits for my school?

Yes. We award $15,000 each year in grants to help with Language Arts programs. Schools qualify to apply for a grant by having a large number of entries of which over fifty percent are accepted for publication. This typically tends to be about 15 accepted entries.

Are there benefits for my teacher?

Yes. Teachers with five or more students accepted to be published receive a free anthology that includes their students' writing.

For more information please go to our website at **www.poeticpower.com**, email us at editor@poeticpower.com or call 435-713-4411.

Table of Contents

States included in this edition:

Connecticut
Delaware
Maine
Maryland
Massachusetts
New Hampshire
Rhode Island
Vermont
Virginia
Washington D. C.

Fall 2007 Poetic Achievement Honor Schools

* Teachers who had fifteen or more poets accepted to be published

The following schools are recognized as receiving a "Poetic Achievement Award." This award is given to schools who have a large number of entries of which over fifty percent are accepted for publication. With hundreds of schools entering our contest, only a small percent of these schools are honored with this award. The purpose of this award is to recognize schools with excellent Language Arts programs. This award qualifies these schools to receive a complimentary copy of this anthology. In addition, these schools are eligible to apply for a Creative Communication Language Arts Grant. Grants of two hundred and fifty dollars each are awarded to further develop writing in our schools.

Alma E Pagels Elementary School
West Haven, CT
Anita Girasuolo*

Beacon Middle School
Lewes, DE
Mrs. Johnston
Emily Lehne*

Belfast-Elk Garden Elementary School
Rosedale, VA
Christy Bowman
Janette Miller

Blackrock School
Coventry, RI
Michaela L. Wells*

Blue Ridge Middle School
Purcellville, VA
Lee Martin*
Virginia Walker

Boonsboro Elementary School
Boonsboro, MD
Suzanne Sullivan
Jeremy White

Brookside Elementary School
Dracut, MA
Laurie Fahey
Allison Looney*
Mary Ellen McCarthy

C Hunter Ritchie Elementary School
Warrenton, VA
Mary Cicotello*

Clark Avenue Middle School
Chelsea, MA
Leeann Plona*

Clover Street School
Windsor, CT
Pauline Reale
Lisa Thomas*

Cranston-Johnston Catholic Regional School
Cranston, RI
Judy McCusker*

Davenport Ridge School
Stamford, CT
Mrs. Gasporino
Mrs. P. Mould
Pam Woodside

Dr Charles E Murphy Elementary School
Oakdale, CT
> Paola Bellabarba
> Michelle Manke
> Tracy L. Wigfield

E Ethel Little Elementary School
North Reading, MA
> Nancy Badavas
> Ellen Devecis

E Russell Hicks School
Hagerstown, MD
> Tracy Bambrick
> Julie Slivka*
> Mrs. Wingerd

Floyd T Binns Middle School
Culpeper, VA
> Cathleen Stocktill*

Good Shepherd Catholic School
Woonsocket, RI
> Constance Gardner*

Grace Episcopal Day School
Kensington, MD
> Ann Beirne*

Graham Middle School
Bluefield, VA
> John Crist*
> Sandy Kegley*

Greylock School
North Adams, MA
> Susannah Warren*

Highland Park School
Manchester, CT
> Nola Barrett
> Grace DeAngelis

Homeschool Plus
Norfolk, VA
> Carol Martin-Gregory*

Immaculate Heart of Mary School
Wilmington, DE
> Ms. Clark
> Marianne White*

Infant Jesus School
Nashua, NH
> Elaine Hebert*

Irving School
Derby, CT
> Joseph E. Benedetto*

Jack Jackter Intermediate School
Colchester, CT
> Linda Kurczy*

John J Flynn Elementary School
Burlington, VT
> Karen R. Paquette*
> Dave Weissenstein

John Ward Elementary School
Newton Centre, MA
> Brad Hammer
> Naomi E. Singer

Juliet W Long School
Gales Ferry, CT
> Nancy Hartz
> Catherine Holdridge*
> Mrs. McNabney*
> Santo Silva*
> Lisa Tedder*

Kenmore Middle School
Arlington, VA
> Mrs. Fraker
> Nancy Tiernan*

Learning Center-Children's Home
Cromwell, CT
> Ms. Dauer*
> Ms. Ray
> Ms. Sponzo

Long Meadow Elementary School
Middlebury, CT
Joan Kelly
Susan Shaw
Noel Siebern*

Main Street Middle School
Montpelier, VT
Mrs. Farrar
Lisa Moody*

McCleary Elementary School
New Castle, VA
Karen Jones*

Melwood Elementary School
Upper Marlboro, MD
Mr. Collins
Karen Daniels
Erica Daniels
Mrs. G. Gutrich
Mr. Hartling
Pia Jones
Mrs. C. Richmond
Ms. Tucker
Mrs. C. Walker

Memorial School
Bedford, NH
Courtney Hannah
Tara Shortt
Miss Wroblewski

Middlebrook School
Wilton, CT
Connie Block*
Susan W. Graybill

North Star Elementary School
Hockessin, DE
Mrs. Becker
Margo Miller*

Old Saybrook Middle School
Old Saybrook, CT
Mary Eileen Fillion
Joanne Giegerich
Mrs. Marshall

Old Saybrook Middle School
Old Saybrook, CT (cont.)
Danielle Watts-St. Germain*
Eric Yale

Pemberton Elementary School
Richmond, VA
Ann M. Ballinger*
Katie Schmid

Perrywood Elementary School
Largo, MD
Amy Louden
Ms. Schiery

Pollard Elementary School
Plaistow, NH
Lisa Kennedy*
Sue Lander*

Riverfield School
Fairfield, CT
Marcia Aliberti*

Rosemont Forest Elementary School
Virginia Beach, VA
Beverly Wooddell*

St Augustine Cathedral School
Bridgeport, CT
Susan Gulyas*

St Brendan Elementary School
Dorchester, MA
Siobhan M. Maguire*

St Brigid School
Portland, ME
Lorilee Newman*

St Joseph School-Fullerton
Baltimore, MD
J. Delores Keefer*
Barbara Owens*
Peggy Radziminski*
Helena K. Scher*

St Mary of Czestochowa School
    Middletown, CT
        Brenda J. Vumbaco*

St Patrick School
    Chicopee, MA
        Julie M. Leonard*

St Rocco School
    Johnston, RI
        Judy Carroccio*

St Rose School
    Newtown, CT
        Eileen Kirk*
        Mrs. L. Spina*

Village School
    Marblehead, MA
        Mr. Angelopolus
        Stephanie Trainor-Madigan*

Wakefield Forest Elementary School
    Fairfax, VA
        Karen M. Hickman*

Wapping Elementary School
    South Windsor, CT
        Karrie Noble
        Daria Plummer

Western Middle School
    Greenwich, CT
        Valerie Bolling*
        Mrs. Drumm

Zervas Elementary School
    Waban, MA
        Rebecca Deeks
        Kathleen Eakin
        Michael Stern

Language Arts Grant Recipients 2007-2008

After receiving a "Poetic Achievement Award" schools are encouraged to apply for a Creative Communication Language Arts Grant. The following is a list of schools who received a two hundred and fifty dollar grant for the 2007-2008 school year.

Acadamie DaVinci, Dunedin, FL
Altamont Elementary School, Altamont, KS
Belle Valley South School, Belleville, IL
Bose Elementary School, Kenosha, WI
Brittany Hill Middle School, Blue Springs, MO
Carver Jr High School, Spartanburg, SC
Cave City Elementary School, Cave City, AR
Central Elementary School, Iron Mountain, MI
Challenger K8 School of Science and Mathematics, Spring Hill, FL
Columbus Middle School, Columbus, MT
Cypress Christian School, Houston, TX
Deer River High School, Deer River, MN
Deweyville Middle School, Deweyville, TX
Four Peaks Elementary School, Fountain Hills, AZ
Fox Chase School, Philadelphia, PA
Fox Creek High School, North Augusta, SC
Grandview Alternative School, Grandview, MO
Hillcrest Elementary School, Lawrence, KS
Holbrook School, Holden, ME
Houston Middle School, Germantown, TN
Independence High School, Elko, NV
International College Preparatory Academy, Cincinnati, OH
John Bowne High School, Flushing, NY
Lorain County Joint Vocational School, Oberlin, OH
Merritt Secondary School, Merritt, BC
Midway Covenant Christian School, Powder Springs, GA
Muir Middle School, Milford, MI
Northlake Christian School, Covington, LA
Northwood Elementary School, Hilton, NY
Place Middle School, Denver, CO
Public School 124, South Ozone Park, NY

Language Arts Grant Winners cont.

Public School 219 Kennedy King, Brooklyn, NY
Rolling Hills Elementary School, San Diego, CA
St Anthony's School, Streator, IL
St Joan Of Arc School, Library, PA
St Joseph Catholic School, York, NE
St Joseph School-Fullerton, Baltimore, MD
St Monica Elementary School, Mishawaka, IN
St Peter Celestine Catholic School, Cherry Hill, NJ
Strasburg High School, Strasburg, VA
Stratton Elementary School, Stratton, ME
Tom Thomson Public School, Burlington, ON
Tremont Elementary School, Tremont, IL
Warren Elementary School, Warren, OR
Webster Elementary School, Hazel Park, MI
West Woods Elementary School, Arvada, CO
West Woods Upper Elementary School, Farmington, CT
White Pine Middle School, Richmond, UT
Winona Elementary School, Winona, TX
Wissahickon Charter School, Philadelphia, PA
Wood County Christian School, Williamstown, WV
Wray High School, Wray, CO

Young Poets
Grades 4-5-6

Note: The Top Ten poems were finalized through an online voting system. Creative Communication's judges first picked out the top poems. These poems were then posted online. The final step involved thousands of students and teachers who registered as online judges and voted for the Top Ten poems. We hope you enjoy these selections.

Top Poem Grades 4-5-6

Autumn

What is Autumn?
    Leaves dancing in the wind.
    A strip of color out of the rainbow.
    A beautiful view for everyone.
    A gift from mother nature.
    Warm, bright colors.
    The crunching of leaves on the ground.
    Coldness setting in.
    Frost on the trees.
    Snow just beginning to fall.
That is Autumn!

Emma Barry, Grade 4
Memorial School, NH

Top Poem Grades 4-5-6

Autumn

Red, orange, yellow, brown, all the leaves are tumbling down!
Herbst, otoño, automne, in any translation, autumn brings fascination!

Inhale the sweet crisp air, watch the leaves fall, this is autumn and I love it all!
Apple picking, rake the leaves, the allergies can make you sneeze!
Back to school, pumpkin pie, colder weather we cannot deny!

Red, orange, yellow, brown, all the leaves are tumbling down!
Herbst, otoño, automne, in any translation, autumn brings fascination!

Time to play football, time to wear sweaters, time to pluck the turkey's feathers!
Leaves sparkle, glisten, and glow in the sun, fall is tons and tons of fun!

Red, orange, yellow, brown, all the leaves are tumbling down!
Herbst, otoño, automne, in any translation, autumn brings fascination!

Beautiful decorations for all to see, these fall sights are always free!
Scarecrows, pumpkins, cornstalks galore, chrysanthemums, haystacks, and so much more!
Halloween is a time for pranks, at Thanksgiving, we all give thanks!

Red, orange, yellow, brown, all the leaves are tumbling down!
Herbst, otoño, automne, in any translation, autumn brings fascination!

Melanie Bigos, Grade 5
Lincoln Central Elementary School, RI

Top Poem Grades 4-5-6

Running

Running,
Through the golden fields of wheat,
My buckskin mare beneath me,
As we gallop forever.
My chocolate brown hair,
Thrown behind me,
Floating,
Just there.
My bare feet,
Dangling at her sides,
Tingling in excitement,
While we move onward.
My horse,
As golden as the wheat,
We are one together,
When we're gone,
All that is left,
Is a cloud of dust,
Then nothing.

Sunny Drescher, Grade 5
Hinesburg Community School, VT

Top Poem Grades 4-5-6

Friends

I hear all the secrets
That are whispered in my ear
My job is to keep them
Not let anyone hear

Laughter is our specialty
It happily rings inside my head
And even after a long day
I still hear it as I'm snuggled in bed

Without a helpful friend
Always standing by your side
You're without feelings
Neither hope nor pride

Friends are forever
So never let one go

Kira Fahmy, Grade 4
Memorial School, NH

Top Poem Grades 4-5-6

Gorgeous, Summer's Day

The warm summer's breeze gently danced through my hair
A wonderful smell of pine filled the air
The cool grass felt soft beneath my toes
Then a colorful butterfly landed lightly on my nose
Beyond the eye could see was all sunny and bright
Sun poured through the trees' branches making lots of gorgeous light
It was the tiny lake's waves that lulled me to sleep
As I dreamed of this summer and its memories to keep

Emily Gagne, Grade 5
Jordan Small School, ME

Top Poem Grades 4-5-6

Dear Star

You're a twinkle in my eye
Your glow is like a flashlight in the distance
I know when you're shy because you hide behind the sun's ray
You dance across the midnight sky gracefully
Your gleam is like a blazing fire
You warm me with your lovely light
You make me want to burst like a volcano
Stars

Michael Grinnell, Grade 4
Potter Road Elementary School, MA

Top Poem Grades 4-5-6

In My Path of Wonder

Ice flakes flowing in the wind
that sweep over the mountains.
White covers the miles of what
was once green.
Glistening blankets
stand
before
me.
The snow is my path of wonder
waiting.
My mind turns back —
to the fear of where I once stood,
five years ago
gripping the sharp poles,
that secured my confidence.
Inhaling the cool crisp air
I push off.
I rocket down into the depths
of not only the trees
but of my
      soul.

Kelsey Houlihan, Grade 6
Mystic Middle School, CT

Top Poem Grades 4-5-6

Anniversary of a Lifetime: To Mom and Dad

You watch children grow, and flowers bloom
And the sunset fade to black
You chop a tree, you count to ten,
You follow your children's tracks
Your birthday is your enemy, you're feeling down and low,
The crystal cracks the bubble bursts and then it starts to snow.
You spin the wheel, you break the ice, the ball falls to the ground.
The windows smash, the lights go out and still there is no frown.
All these things don't cost a thing not a dollar not a dime,
And here you have it folks, an anniversary of a lifetime!

Addisyn Kendall, Grade 4
George R Austin Intermediate School, MA

Top Poem Grades 4-5-6

The Prairie Breeze

Silently, gently rustling everything touched
Rustling tree by tree, blade by blade
Approaching ever so silently
Whipping the greenish-brown region hastily without mercy
Rattling, roaring, until the sky is sealed with darkness
A massive cyclone ripples through the prairie
Disturbing everything in its path
Suddenly an absurd silence sprints through the air
A great wave races through the grasses
A gust springs to life knocking the blades aside as if they were nothing
Rustling tree by tree, blade by blade
Silently, gently rustling everything touched

Shan Siddiqui, Grade 5
North Star Elementary School, DE

Top Poem Grades 4-5-6

Snow

The snow sparkles as the moonlight strikes it
dancing snow twirls its way down
the wind howls through the bitter night
other snowflakes leap down behind each other
as the night's light touches it
snowflakes leap, twirl as they drift downward
wolves howl as they race through the snow
the wind whispers as it whirls snowflakes around and around
the snow crunches under their black paws
the moon brightens its light in reply
snowflakes swoop down like they were parachuting
down from the black night sky covering the trail leaving no trace

Samara Spence, Grade 5
Amherst Middle School, NH

Winter

S is for snowboarding
in the day.
S is for Santa flying
on his sleigh,
S is for the sun that
heats the bitter air,
S is for the stars
that glow and glare,
S is for snowflakes that
fall all night,
S is for snowmen that
are sparkling white,
Winter
Chris Nagy, Grade 5
Pollard Elementary School, NH

Little Butterfly

Little butterfly,
Floating in the breeze.
Little Bumblebee,
Buzzing with her friends.
Sweet Flower,
Growing with ease.
All is beautiful.
You are beautiful.
W. Paul Miller, Grade 4
Boonsboro Elementary School, MD

Chocolate Strawberry Mountain

Right in the afternoon
I was floating in the air
It seemed like underwater
My hair was everywhere.
I saw chocolate strawberries,
On top of a mountain,
I couldn't believe my eyes,
It's Chocolate Strawberry Mountain!
I went inside the cave,
Chocolate was everywhere,
Strawberries were on the floor,
and chocolates in my hair.
Allyson Sikes, Grade 4
Boonsboro Elementary School, MD

Boys Rule

B oys
O ld
Y oung
S pecial

R espectful
U nique
L oving
E ducated
Juan I., Grade 6
Learning Center-Children's Home, CT

Manny

Home run hitting, Manny
Kicks the other teams fanny
When he's not hitting a home run
He's in the monster having fun
Kyle Maulden, Grade 6
Village School, MA

The Giant Twister

I twist in circles in the air.
I move fast on flat ground.
I suck up houses and vehicles.
I am the thrilling scary tornado.
Jonathon Koch, Grade 4
Greylock School, MA

The Future

The future not the present
The future not the past
Moving forward, not looking back
The future not the present
The future not the past
Not knowing what's in store
It'll be a surprise that's for sure
The future not the present
The future not the past
The future has opportunities
That'll sometimes make you laugh
The future not the present
The future not the past
Your dreams lie in the future
They'll make you reach for the sky
The future not the present
The future not the past
Dreaming of the future
While enjoying the present
The future not the present
The future not the past
Bryona Brooks, Grade 6
Melwood Elementary School, MD

There's A...

There's a monster in my house
I think it frightened a mouse

There's a monster in my closet
It kind of gives me a fright
I wish I could deposit him
Because he keeps me up all night

There's a ghoul in my pool
I think it has a tool
It's going to hit me in the eye
Oh no I'm gonna die!
Matthew Proulx, Grade 4
Brookside Elementary School, MA

Gold 'N' Blue

Mountains so high,
Rivers so blue,
Everyone knows about the gold 'n' blue.
Morgantown's where they are.
Anyone's a star —
If they're a fan of The Gold 'N' Blue.
Nick Shoemaker, Grade 4
Graham Intermediate School, VA

My Old Dog

A dog should never leave
Your life for good
Like the sun sliding across the sky
And the drifting clouds
There forevermore
But dogs live a life
With us for only so long
My old dog is soon to be gone
Too soon for me
Her life ran by
Like a subway in a tunnel
A car on the road
Soon to be gone from my world
Alex Daley, Grade 6
Canton Intermediate School, CT

One Window Is All I Need

To see the world
To hear sounds
To imagine the world around me
To know when someone is near
Carly Brennan, Grade 6
St Rose School, CT

Beautiful Fall

The season when the leaves
fall from the trees.
The smell of burned wood, pine,
and hot chocolate makes me feel
like I'm in another state of mind.
Jasmine Gordon, Grade 6
Floyd T Binns Middle School, VA

The Ocean

A splash a curl
The ocean
The twist the twirl
The ocean
The graceful sunset high tide
The ocean
The smooth sand that touches my toes
Low tide
The night the day the sun the sway
The ocean
Michaela Carrieri, Grade 6
Thomas Blake Middle School, MA

Black Like Night

Black looks like night, never being bright
Black smells like raisins, or sun-dried grapes
Black tastes like a blackberry you pick for a feast
Black sounds like a hawk, screeching at its food
Black feels like nowhere in a very deep sleep

James Toombs, Grade 4
Boonsboro Elementary School, MD

My Special Place

My bedroom is peaceful.
My bedroom is mine.
It's just for me and no one will ever know why.
I keep all my secrets locked up in my room,
and they will never get out.
I wake up in this very special room
and at night when I am drifting off to sleep
I know that when I wake up I will be in my very special room.

Isabella Pontbriand, Grade 6
Southbrook Academy, MA

A Dancer's Time

Spinning, twirling, and flying leaps.
Dancing on stage I'm in the spotlight
A thousand eyes looking at me.
Scared and fun beautiful outfits.
Practice and practice time to perform time flies.
I'm a graceful dancer.

Taylor Gregware, Grade 4
North Star Elementary School, DE

Peaceful Beach

On this peaceful beach you feel the sun's rays
Rays that make you want to praise
You may sit in the clear blue water
As blue as the sky
When you wish, you can fly
You may hear waves crashing
Like two boys smashing
You can smell the fresh air
That flows through your hair
This beach makes you happy
Because no trees are sappy
You may see the palm trees hanging over blue seas
There's nowhere I'd rather be
Than here at the sea

Parker DaCosta, Grade 4
Cranston-Johnston Catholic Regional School, RI

Love

Looks like a field of flowers
Smells like roses on their first bloom
Feels like making a new friend
Tastes like the sweetest thing in the world
Sounds like the beautiful sounds of nature

George Livingston, Grade 5
C Hunter Ritchie Elementary School, VA

Circle of Seasons

Bees buzzing, birds chirp
Bright sun rays seeping through trees vibrant air blossoms

Blazing suns shimmer
Gorgeous scarlet sunsets glow bright horizons POP

They are part of one helplessly plucked from their nest
Heaps of timid leaves

Timid trees rustle
Ivory crystals plummet down snow white blankets fall

Calm winds, bright suns smile
Warm flowers flow in the breeze cheerful happy sounds

Flowers wilt from heat
Fish jump and splash happily trees sweat and droop down

Dry grass, bitter wind balding branches weep and cry
Melancholy life

Landscapes are naked
Clouds turn gray and start to boom flakes fall quietly

Sophie Collender, Grade 6
Middlebrook School, CT

The Wonders of Winter

The snowflakes swiftly drip through the
Cold crisp air.
As the wind rapidly whirled around the
Midnight sky causing the clinging wind chimes to
ring in my ear.
The stars dance around the sky
Making the most beautiful pictures I'll always treasure.
The lights on some houses still remain bright
But some are dim and quiet.
The wolves howl at the large spherical moon
As the small field mice search
For a safe shelter to multiply.
Winter makes people wonder where all of the life
goes at night but to me…
It's still a wonder and a treasured sight.

Angelie Monique Santos-Haase, Grade 6
Juliet W Long School, CT

Colors

Blue is the color of the sky on a hot summer day.
Green is what makes you have fun and play.

Pink is the color of a fresh spring rose.
Gold is the color of sand between my toes.

Black is the color of my old, ugly cleats.
Purple is the color of my pretty bed sheets.

Anna Henley, Grade 5
C Hunter Ritchie Elementary School, VA

Dog/Cat

Dog
Fast, strong
Running, eating, licking
Nelsons, bed, poop, Andersons
Scratching, purring, jumping
Annoying, useless
Cat

Julian Nelson, Grade 6
Wakefield Forest Elementary School, VA

The Rock

I sit
On a
Rock
Nice And
Smooth
As hard
As a rock
Why does
It move?

Elizabeth Pawul, Grade 5
Hinesburg Community School, VT

Football

Football, football, football
C's football
B's football
A's A's A's football
Juniors, seniors game time football
Rough football
Flag football
Friday, Saturday, Sunday football
Blue, gold, uniforms, football
Those are just a few!
Leather footballs
Plastic footballs
Grip football
And don't forget street football
Last of all
Best of all
I like physical football

Joseph Mellor, Grade 6
Juliet W Long School, CT

Sun, Come Out!

Oh, little sun come out,
come out, come out!
I would like to see you shine.
Oh, come on,
don't make me shout
don't make me whine
you're making me pout.
Come on,
and give me some warmth!!!

Olivia Schrader, Grade 5
Litwin Elementary School, MA

Greece

The Parthenon was built strong by the ancient Greeks so it would never fall,
The present day Greeks built a 6 story mall.
The city of Athens was named after the Greek goddess, Athena,
I myself have seen many ancient Greek Olympic arena.
The Acropolis is a Greek rock formation,
It is a symbol of the great Greek nation.
In a museum the great god Zeus sits atop a golden throne,
No other god could match up to him and be his clone.
The Filopappos hill is marked from a battle,
Many brave men were lost as they sat upon their saddle.
In Greek history they went through many eras of art,
If you look very closely you can tell these eras apart.
My brother, sister, and I have run an Olympic stade,
Our tour guide was my brother and he never got paid.
Greece has so many things to do and historical sites to see,
Here, right now, that is where I wish I could be!

Megan Middlemiss, Grade 6
Infant Jesus School, NH

Nature

Nature is the sun above the horizon
The soft green grass beneath your feet
The creatures that share this wonderful wilderness with us
For what is happiness, or beauty, if there's no one to share it with?

Nature is every creation of the universe
Whether it's beautiful or not

The rain that trickles down,
The sun that melts the snow
That has just tucked in the ground beneath.

It's all nature.

Rebecca Marks, Grade 5
Weston Intermediate School, CT

Big Beautiful Beetle

Hi, my name is Herbie the Herculean Beetle
I have huge horns that look like curved needles

I am seven to nine inches long
But I fail to sing a pretty song

Harmless am I and my sisters and brothers
Born innocently, we are from our fathers and mothers

You can find me in the evening eating tree sap
Or catch me in my favorite place in Central America on the map

We scatter around very actively at night
We have big black spots not small white

As coleopteran soldiers, we aid in controlling the population of pests
Warning! This fun fact will pop up on your next science test

Christopher Curcio, Grade 6
Immaculate Heart of Mary School, DE

My Cousin

My cousin
is two and Reece
is her name. She
is fun and very cute
too. I love her a
lot and she loves
me too. We look
a lot a
like and
people we meet think we are sisters
but that is
not true for
when my mother
was little she
looked just like
me and when my

aunt was   now I
little my   must go
cousin looks   but I'll
just like   see you
her for   again soon

Alexis Wagner, Grade 4
Portsmouth Christian Academy, NH

Ireland

I am from a place full of compassion,
Galway, Kerry, Clare, and Antrim,
All these beautiful sights,
Nice farms, rich soil, green fields of Ireland.

Cows, sheep, and many other animals,
Cover this beautiful land.
Many people beside you,
Help you along the way.

Beautiful noise passes day by day,
Everyone together can sing along the way.

Leprechauns dancing,
Birds fly high in the sky,
Angels singing,
Now and all night long.

Now that I have told you of Ireland,
It's time for me to go,
I always want you to remember,
All of us together should all be heard in one voice.

Ashley Ford, Grade 5
St Brendan Elementary School, MA

Homework

This homework is so fun I can't wait to get more.
I love homework more than anything in the world even TV.
I can't wait to tell the teacher that my cat ate my homework.

Megan Dzen, Grade 4
Wapping Elementary School, CT

Just Because I'm Different

Just because I'm different
Don't be mean to me
Don't hurt my feelings
Treat me fairly
Just because I'm different
Don't talk behind my back
Don't make fun of me
It doesn't give you the right to tell me who I am
Just because I'm different
Don't make me feel bad
Don't make me sad
Don't treat me differently

Ellie Doering, Grade 6
St Rose School, CT

Lone Soldier

High above the billowing clouds
I catapult towards the ravine
My eyes tear up
Not from the pack pressing into my shoulder blade
But from the cold fear
moving its way down my throat and
spreading into my chest.
I am well into enemy lines now.
It will be a loss of life if
I encounter someone.
But whose life?
His or mine.

Anthony Caruso, Grade 6
Beacon Middle School, DE

Thank You Lord for This Day!

The sun lights the sky,
the moon ends they day.

We come together to light a candle this day.

When we come together we always sing a song of praise,
and a song of meaning.

When we sing we always say,
thank you Lord for this day.

We are thankful in many ways,
like in May He let us say "yea"

In life we remember God's grace,
mostly when we don't see his face.

I see Him in my dreams,
but sometimes I do not know what they mean.

Always remember to say,
thank you Lord for this day.

Tatiana Golditch, Grade 6
St Rocco School, RI

Icicle

The icicle in the sun,
melts away until there's none,
so the icicle will drip away,
and come on another cold day.

George Aldrich, Grade 6
Main Street Middle School, VT

Leaf

L ucky leaves stay on trees.
E xcellent colors fly above.
A utumn is finally here, cheers.
F lying leaves go everywhere?

Andrew Royes, Grade 4
St Gregory Elementary School, MA

Hungry Fox

A fox crept across a field,
trying not to be seen
in the dark grey mist.
Off to the hen house
at the crack of dawn,
to get some breakfast

Alexandre Fall, Grade 6
Kenmore Middle School, VA

Snow Days

Snow days!
Oh snow days!
White as the clouds.
Snowballs fly.
Snowboard down the hills,
feel like you took flight.
Come in for some cocoa.
Enjoy playing video games
cause there's no school.
Too bad I have to wait till
next winter for one!

Patrick Korzeniowski, Grade 5
Southbrook Academy, MA

Sky

The stars the moon
They shine so bright
It's just a dream
About the night
Until I wake
There will be more
About the moon
About the storm
Now I wake
We say good-bye
Until the next day
That I cry.

Kayla Nault, Grade 5
Good Shepherd Catholic School, RI

Halloween

H appy kids
A ll
L aughing
L icking
O val lollipops
W ith
E verybody
E ating candy
N o worries this night

William Villamayor, Grade 5
St Joseph School-Fullerton, MD

My Brothers

My brothers are confusing
Like comedians sometimes funny,
sometimes not
Like the only tissues
left in the box
Like a contest you lose
But win in
Like wrestlers
attack you almost every day
Like teddy bears you love,
but only have one eye
Like basketballs,
out of air you still play with
Like rain
you love but sometimes don't
Like my confusing brothers

Nicole Pierpont, Grade 4
Riverfield School, CT

Bomb

It's coming way down, down, down.
Almost about to hit the ground
KABOOM! It just exploded.
BOOM!
Like a pooping balloon.
People running for their lives.
Women, girls, boys, and guys.
BOOM! There goes another one.
It's all set and done.
A bomb,
The tragedies of a war,
Mourning, vengeance, and sadly more.

Franchesca Pena, Grade 6
Greenwich Country Day School, CT

Limerick Writer

Once when I ate a brick
I felt as though I was sick
I had an idea
I wanted to be a
Writer of limericks.

William Lynch, Grade 5
John J Flynn Elementary School, VT

Thanksgiving

I love Thanksgiving!
Having a great time.
Being with my family.
Making delicious food.
Playing lots of games.
Is there anything better?

KiJana Pollard, Grade 4
Valley View Elementary School, MD

Skating

They said I would like it
They say I've done it twice
I wore rollers
They meant ice

Molly Kephart, Grade 4
Portsmouth Christian Academy, NH

Chickens

Chickens rule other birds drool!
Chickens are the essence of beauty.
Chickens in Hawaii eat the kukuinut.
Chickens I love more than a dove.
Chickens are great
There's no chicken I hate.

Zachary Lorance, Grade 5
St Mary's School, MA

Tonight

Out of sight tonight
In the middle of the night,
I have a little fright
It is not very bright,
How I wish I was out of sight
Tonight

Bailey White, Grade 4
Brookside Elementary School, MA

A Football's Dream

I'm lying on the grass
right before the pass.
It's always been my dream
to hear the crowds' scream.

As I'm spinning in the air
the autumn wind rushes by.
I'm like an arrow getting ready
to meet the bull's-eye.

Into the hands I am squeezed.
I cannot feel any breeze.
A signal, a sign, is it good?
Yes,
Touchdown!

Robert Doherty, Grade 5
Cunningham School, MA

Skitty

Skitty is my little cat
A little cat that is awfully fat
He's my best friend in the whole wide world
He lays in my arms at night all curled

Skitty is so cute and big
But he'll always be my baby
I love him to death I want to hug him lots
I love my kitty whose name is Skitty

Cheyenne Sheedy, Grade 5
Boonsboro Elementary School, MD

I Miss Him

I miss your purring in the night
Your white and orange caught my eye.
You ran away I couldn't find you.
Meow, meow, is what I always use to hear.
Now all I hear is wind blowing in the air.

Tyiesha Tibbs, Grade 6
Floyd T Binns Middle School, VA

The Mysterious Beetle

I am the Hercules Beetle so strong and bold
When I go to sleep, my wings will fold.

You will never know where I will be
Even though I am so big and bulgy.

My color is as bright as stars
You would be able to see me from Mars.

Sometimes I fly and fly as fast as I can
It is very hard to detect where I am.
Although I am eight inches long,
My puny legs are very strong.

I've had the best time hiding from you
But now it is time to go to round two.

Joseph Stockburger, Grade 6
Immaculate Heart of Mary School, DE

Fried French Fries

French fries are fried
They taste so delish
They have pool parties
First they dive in Ketchup
Then they dive in my mouth
"Help," they say. "Don't eat me!"
I reply, "It's not my fault You taste so good!"
French fries are fried
As you can see
Crunch crunch so crispy in my mouth
Let's pig out on some
FRIED FRENCH FRIES

Jake Wood, Grade 6
Canton Intermediate School, CT

Creepy Crawly Creatures Called Earwigs

There is an insect that crawls through your sink,
Although you better know that it is not pink.
In fact the color is brownish to black,
Not really the color of plaque.
Earwigs may destroy fruits and flowers,
But that doesn't mean that they have special powers.
They use their pincers to capture small prey,
Especially arthropods that get in their way.
Earwigs are not suited for crawling very far,
They would be much faster riding in a car.
In the winter they nest underground,
And while they are there, there isn't a sound.
It is a myth that earwigs crawl through you ears,
So just relax and put away your fears.
Sometimes they like to be in places moist and dark,
But you might find them on picnic benches at the park.
I hope that you enjoyed my poem with fact and rhyme,
I wonder what I will talk about next time!

Ashley Abrams, Grade 6
Immaculate Heart of Mary School, DE

A White Day

Hooray! Hooray! It's a snowy day,
Come out come out and let us play,
Keep your jacket on really tight,
For we are going to have a snowball fight.

There are lots of Christmas trees,
But which one is right for me?
Hanging lots of candy canes,
Jingle bells coming down the lane.

Snowflakes falling day and night,
Hoping winter will be all right,
Snowing one or two inches high,
Wishing Christmas won't fly by.

Iqra Razzaq, Grade 4
Graham Intermediate School, VA

A Storm

I sit by my window, watching the rain
it drips then pours down like a waterfall
Lightning and thunder shake the Earth
Puddles build up high, drip by drip
Wind so powerful the trees blow down
Birds search for shelter, for protection
Darkness falls upon the sky,
That is covered with gray clouds all around,
It starts to drip again, drip drop
Wind dies down, the Earth is quiet
Clouds fade away while a rainbow shows upon the world,
The colors of the rainbow shine
With nature's beauty of the planet,
Then I go outside and splash in the puddles.

Madison Zammarelli, Grade 5
Lincoln Central Elementary School, RI

The Last Season of the Year
Winter is white
Winter tastes like fresh fallen snow
Winter sounds like snow ball fights
Winter looks like pure fun
Winter makes me feel happy
Elizabeth Ott, Grade 5
Pemberton Elementary School, VA

Basketball
Running down the court
With the ball or not.
Defense, defense, defense
The coach yells.
Your teammate steals
You smile to congratulate.
You get the pass
And think okay, offense.
After, flip your wrist and release.
You score the winning point.
Last, have team sportsmanship
And say good game.
Katie Harper, Grade 5
Pemberton Elementary School, VA

A Rare Calm Experience
I listen
to the rustling
of the trees.
I listen
to the caw
of the seagulls.
I see the dark
gross muddy ground.
Even though
I can't see it
I know
there are plankton
of every size
in the green algae
swaying side to side
because of the rippling water.
My friends and I laugh as we
breathe in the rare
moments of this learning experience.
Samara Singer, Grade 6
Kenmore Middle School, VA

Thankful
I am thankful for
My cousins
My parents
My brother
My pets
I'm thankful.
Drew Dixey, Grade 6
Village School, MA

My Thanksgiving Trip
For Thanksgiving I'm going to Alabama
and we are going to my aunt's house.
We are leaving Wednesday
when we get to my aunt's house we
are going to watch the parade and football too.
Then we are going to cook the turkey and then eat it.
Then when we are done we are going to bed.
Tomorrow we are going back to my house to celebrate Thanksgiving.
Matthew Sherdel, Grade 5
Boonsboro Elementary School, MD

Bull
There is no animal as powerful, as a huge raging black bull
You look so big and strong, like you know you must belong.

Everyone thinks you are mean, your senses are very keen.
You stand alone in the field to no one do you yield.

When everyone is wearing red, why do you run into them with your head?
You paw the ground before you charge. This is scary because you are so large.

There must be a reason that you snort I hope you have one to report.
It makes me think you might explode and end up in a new zip code.
What do you do in your dream other than make people want to scream?
Why are you so large and big? Do you use your paws to dig?

There is no animal as powerful, as a huge raging black bull
You look so big and strong, like you know you must belong.
Kyle White, Grade 5
Hinesburg Community School, VT

The River
As I rush I crush things my own way,
As I flow I go slow and I run another day.
And when I am calm, I am more delicate than a new born baby's palm.
When I am still, I gleam and when it's hot, I bubble and steam.
Christine Wood, Grade 5
Four Seasons Elementary School, MD

I Am a TV
I am a big box.
People love me.
They are attracted to me.
I am funny.
I am fun.
I get tired I the middle of the night when people watch me sometimes.
I don't have batteries so you could watch me all the time.
I am small.
I am seen almost everywhere.
I get some sleep at night.
People can fall asleep by watching me.
People also get interesting stuff from me.
Sometimes people put the volume too loud.
I have dark and bright lights.
Samir Cecunjanin, Grade 5
Old Saybrook Middle School, CT

Maddie

Three year old white lab
Cutest when she is sleeping like a bear
Runs around the yard
Nobody can stop her
Sheds until our carpet looks
Like a fresh blanket of snow.
Golden "zipper" down her back
Is very cuddly and lays right up
Against me
Doesn't like to be alone
We take hikes together
She's on a leash when she sees
Other dogs,
She runs toward them
Wags her tail while jumping up and down

Olivia Rood, Grade 5
Highland Park School, CT

Welcome Back

As I sit alone, in my room.
Wondering and thinking BOOM!
A blast fills my ears with gloom.
As I remember what is happening outside
I remember how you lied
You said everything would be all right
But now I hear the fight.
Soldiers running all around
And someone falls to the ground
A boom, a crackle of guns everywhere
And I remember our loved ones are there
They should cut the soldiers some slack
And let my loved ones come back
When everyone soon returns
The people will soon learn
That this was a bad choice
So let us all rejoice
That it is over never to return
And my stomach starts to churn
I am happy they have learned.

Elena Kidwell, Grade 6
Floyd T Binns Middle School, VA

My Dog

My little pain is mischievous
Wake up as early as you want
He will always hear you
Thinking everything is a game
The fun may never stop
My little glow worm will fill your heart with
Love that can never escape
Whenever you think of him
You will always get the warmest feeling in your heart
My dog will give you the most adventurous day
Along with a few sloppy kisses on your face

Sally O'Donnell, Grade 5
North Star Elementary School, DE

Painted Sky

The cars were so loud
I could not fall asleep
So I softly got up and walked to the window
To my surprise
A fuzzy feeling came to my mind.
Does the sky play?
Then something came to my mind.
Did the angels paint the sky?
Does the moon say hi to the sun?
Slowly
Drifting!

Madeleine K. Clark, Grade 5
John J Flynn Elementary School, VT

Cows

My favorite animal is the cow
They moo so loud it makes me say wow!

I went to the barn to get some fresh milk
It was so smooth it felt like silk

I went to the bull's pen to get some daisies,
I had to watch out, those bulls are crazy!

I went to the barn to pet the calves,
They are just like cows, only they're halves!

Now my trip to the farm is done,
Can't wait 'till the cows moo at the sun.

Sophie Warren, Grade 5
E Ethel Little Elementary School, MA

Summer

In the fridge, there's always lemonade,
And I'm sitting in the shade, underneath a tree.
While I read, and write some poems.
Don't want to go home.
But it's dinner time, the choice is mine.
Don't have to go home, could stay here alone.
But my stomach rumbles, I must be hungry.
There's something that's missing.
Not only in my stomach, in my summer poem.
I'm still alone, I didn't go home.
But I am now.
There's still something missing, I don't know what it could be.
I must wait and see, if it is something I overlooked,
or maybe it is something I should wait for.
Summer is over.
After many times alone, and many poems.
But now there can't be anymore Summer poem,
It's not summer.
But ah ha! I should have known
What's missing is the end.
But now it's here.

Eden Garcia Thaler, Grade 6
Simpson Middle School, VA

Seasons

Falling leaves down, down
Falling, falling to the ground.
Squirrels looking for a treat
Animals ready to eat.

Now wind's blowing colder air
It's getting colder there.
Animals trying to get home
But get scared by a groan.

Winter getting closer now,
Summer passed very fast.
Piles of leaves getting tall
There are only four seasons in all.

Amanda Lee, Grade 4
Memorial School, NH

Virginia Tech

V ery good
I mpossible to beat
R eady to play
G enuine
I mportant to me
N ew talent
I love them
A mazing

T oo good
E xcellent
C reamed Florida State
H igh in rank

Jake Tibbs, Grade 6
Graham Middle School, VA

Summer Mornings

Mary and I
stood in the squishy mud
and felt the algae
seep through our toes.
We found some good stumps
to watch the sunrise.
We listen to the birds chirping,
and the waves crashing on the shore.
Then Mary falls off her stump
and breaks out in laughter,
shattering the silence.
We laugh and race off to the docks.

Katie Atkins, Grade 6
Kenmore Middle School, VA

Rain

Sizzling with energy
droplets of fiery rain,
splashes the hot bubbling water.

Emily Clayton, Grade 5
Zervas Elementary School, MA

Be Bright

It's a day
A very good day
Everyone shines
But I look all over
I see that I am not shining
I say to myself
Be Bright
So I could help other people
Be Bright
That is what Bright is all about
If you see someone who is not Bright
You know what to do!

Jenesis S., Grade 4
Learning Center-Children's Home, CT

Wild Horses

Peaceful and quiet
Their bodies long and streamline
Coats soft and glossy

Wind blowing their manes
Crazy as breathtaking bulls
Running every day

Trotting through nature
Stomping over rocks and streams
Keeping nature same

Devin Heron, Grade 6
Beacon Middle School, DE

You're Glowing Bright

I look up
As I'm sitting here
I see the moon
Ever so clear

I looked the moon straight in the eye
And asked him how he learned to fly
All he did was just stand there
He didn't answer
It's not fair

He just sits there glowing bright
That's no different from other nights
I don't blame him
He has work to do
Just answer me
Tell me the truth

The moon looks brightly at the night
I can't keep guessing til I'm right
But if you can ever answer me
I'll be right here with my family.

Rachael Barbaresi, Grade 6
Thomas Blake Middle School, MA

The Sea

Waves
In the sea.
They swerve about
With me.
Waves are so fun
To splash in.
You should really
Dash in.
So if you would like to see
The sea.
You should come
With me.

Gabe Haddad, Grade 5
St Mary's School, MA

My Feelings of Fall

When I see the golden sun rise
And smell crispy apple pie
I know it's time for fall
When the crickets are chirping
On Halloween night
I feel as happy as can be
At the end of autumn
I wonder —
Why do the seasons change?

Amila Semic, Grade 4
John J Flynn Elementary School, VT

An Ode to Life

Life seems so long but ends so quick
are you strong or are you sick
make friends make enemies
live life to the fullest, don't be shy
will you live long or will you die
do not pretend or live a lie
you can't find out the reason why
people live and people die.

Brandon Chesnut, Grade 6
Juliet W Long School, CT

Paintball Fun

P ain
A thletic
I
N ight
T ight position
B arrel
A thlete
L oser
L ight of day

F alse fire
U sed gun
N othing left

Dillon Harrell, Grade 5
Linville-Edom Elementary School, VA

Beautiful Sky

B alloons are always floating up there
E specially ones with hot air
A irplanes fly high in the sky
U p where the clouds are soaring high
T wo birds fly together
I f they are friends forever
F lying kites is very fun
U ntil it gets stuck in a tree
L eaving it there until it comes free

S unshine lights the way
K issing the dark and stormy day away
Y esterday was a sunny day and I went out to play

Dariel Akins, Grade 5
Davenport Ridge School, CT

Cheese Cheese Everywhere

I am a little mouse named Sunny
And I know where to find cheese and honey
Go to 14 Light Bulb Circle to get the good snack
Make sure there are no huge bees to whack
Another place is the grocery store
Where you can find cheese galore
On the floor there is a fare amount of crumbs
There is enough for some
Cheese is better than ice cream
It is like a distant dream
You can go to so many places to get it
So go lickety-split

Abigail Lennon, Grade 4
Infant Jesus School, NH

K.T.'s Soundscape

The growls of Jumper and Fluffy during a wrestling match
Alarm clocks ringing and singing
Small chirps from the birds outside
Grasshoppers rubbing their legs together
The screech of a car pulling into the drive way
The scream of girls when the boys scare them
Fluffy's small paws beating on the floor
The pitter patter of rain on the windowpanes
The eerie yelps of coyotes
Creaking of rocking chairs in the dead of night
A soft snore coming from Fluffy's mouth
The mysterious footsteps of other animals outside

Sarah Baseler, Grade 5
Jack Jackter Intermediate School, CT

Beach

The wind howls against the waves, shaking its fist
Water demolishes the sand mercilessly
The rocks struggle against the raging current never giving up
And a child giggles while carving designs with a prickled stick
This is a normal day at the beach

Mary Dolan, Grade 6
Wakefield Forest Elementary School, VA

Angels

Angels, angels, oh so bright,
God sent them down from heaven one night,
They will stay by you every day,
They will stay by you every night,
When you get hurt, they will be there.

But you will not see them,
What counts is if they can see you,
Don't be afraid; they will not hurt you,
They will protect you from danger,
You never know when they are there,
Each kid has a special angel,
So we all should thank God!

Emma Thompson, Grade 5
Linville-Edom Elementary School, VA

Katydids

I am a katydid, I live in a tree,
My beautiful song is all you'll hear from me.

I use my song to attract a mate,
You'll hear me sing until the night is late.

My antennae may be twice the size of my body,
I don't take care of my offspring 'cause they're naughty.

I usually use my camouflage to protect me,
However, I can also jump very quickly.

I am lucky, I can live almost anywhere,
So look on a tree, you might find me there!

Kelly Tibbetts, Grade 6
Immaculate Heart of Mary School, DE

Protecting Earth

When I wake up in the morning I stare at the trees
and then the sky
and I think to myself, "What if this were all to die?"

Then I hear the cars and trucks trudging along
polluting the air
and it seems that to what I stare
soon will not be there.

Bobby O'Reilly, Grade 6
Thomas Blake Middle School, MA

Skateboard

I fly off of ramps.
I also get to drop in off of quarter pipes.
Kids get to ride me.
When I get spun around, I get dizzy.
My wheels get hot when I go fast.
I was made by a company called Warship.
I get hyper when people skate with me.

Spencer Saracina, Grade 5
Old Saybrook Middle School, CT

Ice Cream

Ice cream, ice cream
All different kinds,
chocolate, vanilla, strawberry more!
Eat it all up and…
my tummy's full.
Ice cream, ice cream
with hot fudge on top.
Eat it all up and…
I go plop.
Sprinkles, M&M's
tasted so good.
Now that I ate all the ice cream
BLAAAAAA!
I'm full!

Nina Martucci, Grade 5
Osborn Hill Elementary School, CT

Winter Forest

Trees blow in the breeze
Birds fly silently away
Sun rises at dawn

Snowflakes gently fall
Owls hoot all day long. Hoo! Hoo!
Hear crunching footsteps

Ground covered in white
Animals hibernate. Zzzzz!
For winter is here.

Kayla Doud, Grade 6
Beacon Middle School, DE

Blue Sea

I know every night
it is not so bright
when it gleams on the sea
it is just like
your deep blue eyes
going through my mind.
I see a lot of blue in my sight.
I also feel it through the night.

Robert Swope, Grade 5
Boonsboro Elementary School, MD

Birthday

Birthdays are the best
Way better than the rest
Birthdays are fun for anybody
But you're not just somebody
You're my sister
From the same mister
I hope your day is filled with joy
Maybe you will meet a cute boy
HAPPY BIRTHDAY!

Pitch Riley, Grade 6
Village School, MA

Poetry

I love poetry and it's my favorite thing to write
sometimes I write it all loose by hand or type it so it's nice and tight.
Some poetry is sad and slow
other happy poetry has a flow.
Poetry is an ingenious thing
it just makes me want to sing.
What to me is poetry
to me poetry is sad sentences or thoughts that are crazy.
I love these silly words
and to me it's 'bout as easy to write as eating hot hors d'oeuvres.
And now, as sad as it is, it has to be
the end, for today, of my poetry.

Eliza Funk, Grade 6
St John Regional Catholic School, MD

Friesian

A horse of blackness, beauty and perfection which graces the Earth
and sways his head at all that pass by.
An animal who has the power of flight.
Who flies with his feathered hooves above all their eyes
and they love it as his flowing mane and tail blow in the wind
as he gallops over the fields of America, into our hearts.
Perfection.

Julia Driscoll, Grade 6
Juliet W Long School, CT

Me

My hair is blonde seaweed getting tossed around in the ocean
My eyes are two black holes in space that you can't see anything for miles after miles
My teeth are shiny white pearls on display when I smile
My friendships are a cozy shelter for life's rainy days
My personality is a shaken up bottle of soda with fizz coming out endlessly
My heart is a soft blanket that you can cuddle up to on a blue day
I live in the real world and eat my problems

Ana DeCrosta, Grade 6
Tolland Middle School, CT

Water Dog

On your marks,
get set,
go!
We race to the pool.
Suddenly Mary Jane is a turbo booster
blasting right past me.

She jumps in the pool with so much excitement it could power up New York.
She hits the target, a green spongy raft,
and sets off like a rocket going to space,
sliding to the center of the pool.

Calmly drifting
in circles,
she enjoys the sun beams.
What a luxurious life she has!

Jefferson Donath, Grade 6
Mystic Middle School, CT

The Hen Named Ben

There once was a cat named Ben.
He thought that he was a hen.
When the owner found out,
He had to shout.
Now he knows Ben is a hen!

The owner had to change his house,
Because his hen does not chase a mouse.
He moved to a farm,
And Ben lived in a barn.
So now Ben does not live in a house.

Sierra Butler, Grade 5
Clover Hill Elementary School, VA

Dodge Durango Truck

I run on diesel fuel.
I drive really fast.
I park in a bay.
Tools lay in my bed.
I'm big, broad, and bulging.
I like to get dirty when mud splashes up onto me.
My wheels have shiny chrome spinners.
I have hydraulics that make me go up and down.
I have big shocks.

Dylan Smith, Grade 5
Old Saybrook Middle School, CT

Feelings in My Day

When I wake up in the morning,
My eyes are full of sleep.
I'm grouchy, grumpy,
And everything but neat.

In the afternoon,
My eyes pop out of my head.
I dance. I sing.
I feel so wild.

In the night, I feel so loved.
I hang out with my mom, dad, sisters, and pets.
Now it's back to bed again.
I feel so left alone.
I sleep, I dream, I think.
Thank God we have all these feelings and emotions.

Maureen McCarthy, Grade 4
Mitchell Elementary School, CT

Colors

Blue is rain falling from clouds.
Black is shadows scaring little kids.
Orange is the sun burning your skin.
Purple is paint splattered all around.
Green is the grass eaten by cows.
What do you think of colors?

Daniel Beran, Grade 5
C Hunter Ritchie Elementary School, VA

Life

Birds are in the tree,
Oh look there's a very busy bee,
Another beautiful day,
And people are fishing in the bay,
Life is great,
But not for the worms,
They're bait,

There's life here,
And there's life there,
Oh my goodness there's a grizzly bear,

What do you know life everything's living,
And everything knows life's about giving!

Trisha Bevan, Grade 6
E Russell Hicks School, MD

Love at First Sight

It was love at first sight when he saw her.
A maid and a man at first sight.
It was precious time.
For all had seemed right on that bridge.
On that bridge at love's first sight.

The angels rejoiced in the heavens.
Hand by hand down the street.
In Paris they went, together they spent in the night.
In night at love's first magical sight.

It was the greatest day of their lives.
When they both had said "I do."
As they went out the door they both knew it was love.
It was love at its most gracious sight.

Denny Gephardt Jr., Grade 6
Parkville Middle School and Center of Technology, MD

Christmas Day

C arols are being sung all through town,
H ear those bells ringing,
R eindeer fly with Santa's sleigh,
I t's the Christmas time of year,
S tars at the top of the tree,
T he lights are shining, bright as can be,
M others are trying to calm their children,
A gift is a way to give your heart away,
S now is falling, what a sight to see.

Gregory Ford, Grade 6
Floyd T Binns Middle School, VA

Fire

F lames leaping into the air
I s very hot to the touch
R eally makes me want marshmallows
E mbers and ashes

Kelsey Garonzik, Grade 5
C Hunter Ritchie Elementary School, VA

Strength

Strength is not muscle, but heart.
Strength is not lifting weights, but in your community, doing your part.
Strength is not running for praise, but running to help.
Strength is not putting down others, but having kind things to tell.
Strength is not always who is strongest, but who plays fair.
Strength is not who only listens to people who compliment them, but those who are there
To swim in some sadness, to swim in some joy
Not swimming in compliments, but helping every girl and boy
Feel that they have strength just as much
As people who run laps, have muscle, and such
If you really look inside, you will definitely see
That even if you have muscles, if you don't care, you're wimpy!
So, my good friends, this poem will tell
Even if you are "strong," you definitely fell
In the pool of sadness, failure, and hate
But if you help out, you're doing great
With life itself, now remember, all
Always answer the helping call!

Cassie Martin, Grade 5
Old Saybrook Middle School, CT

Mexico

Come with me to Mexico
where the air is clear and smells of salt and fresh grass, as sweet as the aroma of honey.

Come with me to Mexico
where the sound of running water and rain linger in the air and crickets sing their songs
bursting with sorrow and joy, as dark and empty as the crisp night air.

Come with me to Mexico
where vibrant shades of orange, green, yellow, and red dance around a dazzling diamond sea.

Come with me to Mexico
where the air is clear.

Jacob Schwartz, Grade 5
Zervas Elementary School, MA

The Lost Key

I heard a little buzz. It was a bee pulling the covers off of me telling me to find my key. I lost it when I went to school, people think that I'm a fool. My friend is as silly as a mouse, she said I might of lost It in my house. When I told my mother, she was as mad as my brother, now you see the kind of responsibilities I need!

Anjelica Scott, Grade 6
E Russell Hicks School, MD

Miraculous Treasures of the Beach

The exquisite shimmering rays off of the turquoise ocean moves with the sun blazing down on it.
The sun's rays are also beating bright down on the burning Aztec sand.
Sand is like little specs of dust lightly flying within the air.
Colorful spirals of umbrellas and chairs are as hot as the daring sun.
Crowds of people are bustling by to find a perfect spot to enjoy the fun.
Splashing salt water and babies crying so cacophonously are as clear as the indigo sky.
Incredulous multicolored various shapes and sizes of seashells are scattered everywhere.
Sometimes a cool breeze comes and blows the sand in your face while the water flows back and forth.
Sizzling sun, brilliant salt water, cool breeze and beautiful seashells are all treasures of the magnificent beach.

Renee Cooper, Grade 5
Davenport Ridge School, CT

What Am I?

My color is black and white.
I have a pair of wings but cannot fly.
I enjoy fish, squid, krill, and rock crabs.

I live in Antarctica
I can swim up to 50 mph.

I am a peaceful diver.
I slide on my stomach.

My predators are humans, leopard seals,
Killer whales and sharks.
Penguins

Aaron Rose, Grade 4
Pleasant Valley Elementary School, MD

Pencil Sharpener

I am a pencil sharpener.
People poke me.
People drop me.
When I'm unplugged, I die.
But when I'm plugged back in, I'm up and about.
I eat the same thing all the time.
When I'm empty, it feels like my heart has been ripped out.
I love being a pencil sharpener.

John (Jack) Messina, Grade 5
Old Saybrook Middle School, CT

Midnight Crows

Crows look like they came from a dying fire
With all the simmering ash and smoke
At night they fly toward the moon
And glide like night riders
It seems as if they're wearing a black cloak
When the day comes, they are ready to go
That's why they are called the midnight crows.

Miranda Couture, Grade 5
Heron Pond Elementary School, NH

Fenway Park

Babe Ruth was a very famous person.
He played on the Red Sox for a long time.
And then the Red Sox sold him to the Yankees
And they called that the curse of the Bambino.

Next, there is a red seat out by right field.
That was the longest homerun hit at Fenway Park.
That was hit by Ted Williams.

Another thing out in right field
Is the foul pole that is a very special pole
It was dedicated by Johnny Pesky.

And that is the history of Fenway Park.

Shaun Bradley, Grade 4
Portsmouth Christian Academy, NH

Dragons

Fire roars above the sky
where dragons sleep and never cry.
Heat rises above the earth
where dragons come and have their birth.

Jacob Gentry, Grade 4
Boothbay Region Elementary School, ME

My Dog

A very special member of my family
N ow for a morning walk
G ive a squeaky toy and we'll have fun together
E mpty food bowl, fill it up
L ove my little dog so much

Jonelle Parker, Grade 5
Rosemont Forest Elementary School, VA

Gymnastics

The fun of gymnastics.
Flipping in the air,
Doing vaults and flatbacks on the spring board,
The excitement of jumping to one bar,
Then to the other,
And landing in a dismount.

Kayla N. Andrews, Grade 4
Dr Charles E Murphy Elementary School, CT

Halloween

Cool wind blowing in the night
Pumpkins glow by candle light
Falling leaves touch the ground
all kinds of noises and scary sounds

Little kids dressed up in the streets
from door to door yelling "trick or treat"
Bright burning colors that used to be green
it's so much fun on Halloween!

Tony Asaiante, Grade 6
Village School, MA

The Nightmare of Tomorrow

The moon is up. The sun is down.
No noise for about a mile.
Except for the sound of snoring
That only lasts for a little while.
You are awoken by a bad dream.
You worry if you are too sad.
So you lay awake until you just can't take it.
You try to go back to sleep
But all you can really do as fake it.
The clock is ticking it is 9 past 1.
Your eyes are growing heavier and heavier.
Soon the sun will flow up through the sky
And shine it's warmth all over the world.
For everyone to know it is the growth of a new day.

Bianca Little, Grade 6
Irving School, CT

Caribbean Shore

I walked along the sandy beach,
The Caribbean water inches from reach.

The magnificent sunshine
Was
Just
Fine.

I walked along the watery world,
And all around me water swirled.

The radiant colors of the reef
Relieved
My
Grief.

I walked along the sandy beach.
Once more,
Once more.

The great Caribbean shore,
The great Caribbean shore.

Jamie Bonan, Grade 6
Hoover Middle School, MD

The Launch

A lone human
steps onto the platform.
he is about to launch
into the outer worlds
away from the inner ones.
He does not wish
to go
but,
the human race
called out to him.
There is no way out
as the shuttle leaves
into the inky depths
of the universe.

Thomas Muir, Grade 6
Kenmore Middle School, VA

9/11

The bad men took the plane down,
Everybody had a frown.
So many people died,
The pain will never subside.
To the bad men it was no bother,
A little girl just lost her father.
That day will go down in infamy,
Oh yes it will you see.
On that day it was a fright,
But our flag was still in sight.

Alexander Robinson, Grade 6
Everett Meredith Middle School, DE

Christmas

C ookies in the oven, watching, waiting, to be done,
H eavenly scents fill my nose, for the cookies are finished,
R unning through the snow, sliding down a hill,
I come inside and sit by the fire, sipping a mug of warm cocoa,
S melling the peppermint and chocolate scent of the holidays,
T he time has come to go to bed, waiting for tomorrow to come,
M erry Christmas to all, and to all a good night,
A s I lie down and close my eyes, I dream of gifts,
S lowly awaking, for today is Christmas day!!!

Katie Meixel, Grade 5
Rosemont Forest Elementary School, VA

I Am

I am a young girl who loves karate.
I wonder if I will succeed in class.
I hear my classmates punching and kicking in the corner of the room
with black punching bags.
I see my Sensay teaching kids their punching and kicking.
I want to get my next belt in the next six months.
I am a young girl who loves karate.

I pretend to be like my Sensay.
I feel that the more I practice my karate I will get much better.
I touch the cold rubber mat.
I worry that when I wrestle I will get hurt badly.
I am a young girl who loves karate.

I understand the steps to Temi Waza one.
I say the code of conduct.
I dream to get my black belt.
I try really hard in class.
I hope to never sit out of class and miss practice.
I am a young girl who loves karate.

Briana McGee, Grade 5
Blackrock School, RI

I'm Somebody

I am a cardinal, soft and light;
I'm usually the color green,
natural and flexible,
And a lot of the time I am the color purple,
curious and very creative;
I am snow falling pleasantly onto the ground for hours at a time;
I am the feeling of happiness,
always thinking of nice thoughts and barely ever of bad ones;
I am the sound of birds chirping outside in the morning;
I am the smell of whipped vanilla ice cream,
sweet and thin;
I am the taste of spaghetti with tomato sauce and parmesan cheese;
I am the texture of a plant,
always growing and blooming;
I am the son of a star, glowing and bright,
And I am the dream of magic,
powerful and supernatural.

Yair Mordfin, Grade 5
Melvin J Berman Hebrew Academy, MD

My Daredevil Brother

My brother loves to do crazy stunts.
He does whatever somebody dares him to do.
Even if the dangers are high.
He forgets about his tests.
I hope someone dares him to study.

Alison Frye, Grade 5
Wakefield Forest Elementary School, VA

The Soccer Field

There are three
rectangles.
There are certain
fields you play on.
There are 7
defenders.
There are 4
Offense.
There are certain times
to play.
There are regular
games and play
offs and championships
but they're all hard to
win.

Andrew Lehne, Grade 5
Friendship Valley Elementary School, MD

Colors

White makes me feel pale.
Green is like running on grass.

Yellow is as bright as the sun.
Blue is the cold water in the summer.

Red is the burn on your skin.
Gold is the goldfish on Mrs. Cicotello's cabinet.

Black is the night sky.
What color are you?

Adam Nibecker, Grade 5
C Hunter Ritchie Elementary School, VA

Cookies

My mom's cookies are very, very sweet,
On Halloween, they are a good treat.

My nose was surprised to smell cookies baking,
They were so grand, I was shaking.

I was so loud you could hear me munching,
You could also hear my brother crunching.

On Christmas my mother's cookies are tasty,
They seem like they were made from pastry.

Kyle Apicelli, Grade 4
Dr Charles E Murphy Elementary School, CT

I Love Jackie

Puppy
Loving, cute
Playing, yipping, sleeping
She loves me so
Jackie

Rebecca L. Taylor, Grade 4
Dr Charles E Murphy Elementary School, CT

Amazing Castles

Castles, oh what a marvelous sight,
Most are built all with great might.
There is one castle though that stands out from the rest,
I personally think it's enchanted, it's the best!

From the tree out front to the carpeted floors,
To the engraving on the walls to the great wooden doors.
It's blanketed with snow all over the roof,
It's the best looking castle and I'll give you proof.

There are four or five chimneys and windows galore,
Just how it looks from outside makes you want to explore.
If you really do want to know more,
All you have to do is walk through the great wooden door.

Eleanor LoConte, Grade 5
Infant Jesus School, NH

My Grandpa

My grandpa
I love him to the farthest star and back.
But he was sick
He was in the hospital
But on Thanksgiving he came out
Because I prayed.
I still do even though he is out of the hospital.
I love my grandpa to the farthest star and back.
My grandpa

Anna Leatherwood, Grade 4
Riverfield School, CT

My Brother

This is my brother
He is so cute
He likes to dance
Never is mute

This is my brother
He likes to sing
He loves to run
He plays with rings

This is my brother
He is very, very lovable
Loves clowning around
Can get into trouble

Kiara Walker, Grade 5
C Hunter Ritchie Elementary School, VA

A Night at Camp

In the evening
When the sun goes down
The moon comes up
And shows us the sky
Full of bright stars.
What else is happening?
Some animals take a
Nighttime stroll
You can hear the gentle
Breeze of the wind
Blowing in the trees.
The animals Shift tonight
They are happy.
Some come out to hunt
I am calm as I hear the howl
Of wolves at camp
And I fall asleep.
Christian Holway, Grade 5
John J Flynn Elementary School, VT

Halloween!

It's time for Halloween
Go ahead and scream

There're goblins, witches
Frankenstein's stitches

Witches flying on their brooms
Vampires stuck in a tomb

Skeletons, bats
Even black cats

OH NO!

There went the lights
Dancers are in their pink tights

I hear screaming
Oh well

I love Halloween!
Chairsh Brooks, Grade 6
Graham Middle School, VA

Broken Clock

I think the clock is broken.
I bet it is quarter past 3
but it says it's 8 in the morning.
The clock is dead to me.
The clock is so broken, it thinks
one hour is a minute. It's not right!
Oops, it's just me.
Ben Williams, Grade 5
Southbrook Academy, MA

Harvest Time

It is harvest time
So we gather our crops
Hoping to eat them
Kristina Roy, Grade 4
Brookside Elementary School, MA

Dreams

Dreams are simple
They happen all the time,
No matter what you think of it
You'll always find it stuck in your mind!

Dreams can be good
Dreams can be bad
They can be about friends
Or Mom and Dad!
Megan Rule, Grade 5
Davenport Ridge School, CT

Different Colors

Yellow like the stars in the sky
White like the moon that shines high

Orange like the inside of a flower
Black is like the highest tower.

Silver like the front of my math book
Brown like the chess board rook.
Nick Burrell, Grade 5
C Hunter Ritchie Elementary School, VA

Ode to a Cold Day

Oh! A cold day
Leaves, sticks, and sometimes even snow
The wind is cold
And the sky is bold
The taste of brisk air
In your mouth
Birds chirping
Spring is lurking
Leaves crunching on the ground
Snow falling from the sky
All we eat is apple pie
It must be a cold day…
Jordan Kowalski, Grade 6
Juliet W Long School, CT

Flowers

Flowers they're pretty flowers
You can watch them for hours
In all types
They're really nice
Beautiful and great flowers
Christina Nguyen, Grade 5
John J Flynn Elementary School, VT

The Road Toad

A man walked down the road,
hoping to catch a toad.
But what he forgot to get,
was his grand old net.
So he walked back up the road.
Madison Dumas, Grade 5
Good Shepherd Catholic School, RI

Cranky the Clown

A clown at the circus
Named Cranky the clown
On his face always
Had a big frown.

But Cranky the clown
Decided to bring
A big green parrot
That could talk and sing.

When he came to the circus
And he brought in the bird
Laughing and shouting
Was all Cranky heard.

With tricks and flips
Cranky got a new name.
Cranky the clown became
A clown that rose to fame.

Now that the clown
Enjoys the circus place,
Every day you'll see him
With a smile on his face!
Laura Iliescu, Grade 6
St Bridget School, CT

Swinging

I like to swing
way up high,
sometimes it feels like
I'm touching the sky.
I touch the leaves,
on the nearest trees —
swinging is fun,
believe me.
You don't need to have
a lot of knowledge,
to learn how to swing —
there's no need to go to college.
Swinging is fun,
I enjoy it a lot.
Maybe you'll try it,
on swings in a vacant lot.
Adella Carlson, Grade 4
Mitchell Elementary School, CT

My Sister

Not long ago,
When I was just three.
My mommy told me,
"We're getting a new baby!"

We didn't know
What it would be.
But I was going to love it,
Maybe.

The day finally came,
And I could see.
This new little baby
Looked just like me!

We brought her home
So warm and so tiny.
She smelled so good,
And she was almost shining!

I love my sister
Even when we fight,
Having her with me,
Makes everything else all right!

Makayla Eden Ball, Grade 5
Belfast-Elk Garden Elementary School, VA

Life

Dawn. The orchard awakes.
The spider sits, spinning its sticky lace.
The cricket chirps, looking for a mate.
The butterfly sits, drying its wings in the breeze.
The world is alive.

Tyler Wilson, Grade 5
Wakefield Forest Elementary School, VA

Mother Nature

On a cold winter night,
I felt it,
there alone,
Mother Nature
I saw her in a shaft of moonlight,
wearing a dress shimmering like pale starlight
shining in the night
glowing
She raised her magic wand and,
all of a sudden,
a little brisk air,
frost everywhere
I could feel it in the air
As dawn approached,
I heard a sound,
And Mother Nature was
Nowhere to be found

Arianna Conte, Grade 6
St Rocco School, RI

Chocolate

Chocolate
Crunchy, creamy, delicious, and sweet
It is my favorite type of treat.
Carmel, walnut, I love them all.
But Hershey's chocolate makes me want to fall!

Alexandra Haley, Grade 5
C Hunter Ritchie Elementary School, VA

Christmas Is Here

Christmas is here everywhere.
Christmas is here if you care.
Birthday and gifts come.
We give joyful love to everyone.
If you give then you receive
Fall is gone, so no more leaves.
Christmas is here.
Christmas is not all about gifts.
It's about helping people and the spirits who left
Let there be a group of family spending time
Instead of robbing malls and doing crimes
Christmas is here.
Give care to everyone.
Christmas is not done, but Christmas is here

Keiara Myers, Grade 6
Melwood Elementary School, MD

My iPod

This is my iPod.
It has lots of tunes.
But when my sisters have it
They act like buffoons!

This is my iPod.
I love it so much
Some of the songs on it
Are spoken in Dutch

This is my iPod.
I never leave it alone
I even listen to it
When I'm on the phone.

Nate Swift, Grade 5
C Hunter Ritchie Elementary School, VA

Beach

The beach is so beautiful with sand
The beach is so beautiful with palm trees down the line
The water is so blue and so clear
You can see your reflection in the warm afternoon water
The salty sea air calms
It lets me know that I am safe
As I sit there smelling the salty sea air
I wonder on this beautiful day
If I'll just stay.

Timothy D. Hennigan, Grade 6
Grace Episcopal Day School, MD

Autumn Leaves

I love the smell of mom's apple crisp
I hear the fireplace crackling
Owls hooting in the night
Halloween goblins are such a sight!
Children playing among the leaves
Leaves are falling each tree to tree
This is what autumn means to me.

Sarah Heon, Grade 4
Alma E Pagels Elementary School, CT

Valentine's Day

On Valentine's Day
You make a heart,
For a person who's special.
You write something sweet,
Maybe give some candy.
Then put your name on it
Or put "Your Secret Admirer."
Slip it in the box
Then you must wait
Until Valentine's Day.

Olivia Darveau, Grade 5
Good Shepherd Catholic School, RI

For So Long

Wishing you were here,
Let me make this clear,
You shouldn't have gone,
I haven't seen you for so long,
Now my eyes are filled with tears,
And all of my happiness disappears,
So why did you go?
Why are you gone?
I am left to wonder,
For so long.

Brandy Conatser, Grade 6
Floyd T Binns Middle School, VA

Things About Winter

Happy, excited.
Snowballs, snowmen.
In the breezy wind.
The snow sparkling, the ice shining.
Will I see my friends?
Snow falling.

Samuel Albertus, Grade 4
John J Flynn Elementary School, VT

The Beach

The waves swish smoothly
The people walk on the smooth sand
The sun shines brightly
Crabs snap like clapping hands
The water hitting the ground

Isaiah Nieves, Grade 5
Highland Park School, CT

My Life

I am from a sweet smelling room.
Friends and family eating plenty of food
Cats filled with envy, wanting food themselves.
People talking nicely while cooking great meals.
I am from home.

I am from a place loud with fasts cars.
From cats everywhere you look running, jumping, having fun.
From all aged kids talking, playing, walking.
Sirens going by, sometimes loud, sometimes quiet.
I am from Dorchester, a great place to live.

I am from pubs filled with hearty beer.
Men with hair colored flaming red.
From fields of livestock, wheat, and beautiful daffodils
Towns newly built, shining brightly, with old towns never far.
But friends always near by.
I am Ireland.

I will be a video game designer.
Having a family of six with four children running, playing, having fun.
Being rich with a nice, beautiful wife,
A shining, great, big house with many pets.
Running, hopping, swimming, flying, and moving, but always pleasant.

Kierran Pierce, Grade 6
St Brendan Elementary School, MA

My Family's Foods

Crunchy, hard, taste shell with dark dry meat
and red ripe tomatoes with a little bit of cheese,
sour cream, and the little bits of sauce that I love,

The little strawberries and the other ingredients that go with it
make it the best little strawberry smoothie in the world,

Warm, hot, melted cheese on the thick piece of pizza
with sauces that burn my tongue, and then shredded parmesan cheese on top,
with Ranch dressing for my hard crunchy crust,

Tasty, thick, warm cheese with the big hot steaming
tomato sauce and white slippery noodles,
I love lasagna sooooo much!

Green lettuce and red, slippery ripe tomatoes
with black olives and crunchy hard croutons, with bacon bits
and Ranch dressing dripping down on the plate, YUMMY!

Brittany Hicock, Grade 5
Long Meadow Elementary School, CT

The Bright, Blue River

From airplanes I watch as a blue snake comes curving,
Crushing rocks as it goes by.
The blue snake curls around mountains, canyons, and through forests
Until it disappears into the bright, blue body of the sea.

Shirin Ludwig, Grade 5
Four Seasons Elementary School, MD

Like the Ocean

My life is like the ocean,
Cause the ocean is so wide.
Staying away from the frightening motion,
And trying not to get caught in the tide.

There are so many fish in the sea,
Being as the friends I meet.
My life is more than just a myth,
Cause I get more than just a treat.

The ocean takes up most of the world,
Which means it's more like me.
As in my life being so curled,
My life is as big as history.

I have to work harder to succeed,
Cause I'm so small in the great big sea.
I'm like a tiny little seed.
It seems as if I'm only with me.

KayLeigh McHale, Grade 6
Blue Ridge Middle School, VA

The Tree

I am a tree
Covered in leaves
I live in the forest
With all the other plants
Animals live on me
Other trees live beside me
They are my friends
People climb on me
And build houses on me
They stay on me for a long time
Then they move out of the forest.
When winter comes, I lose my leaves
I am cold and black
People hide behind me
And throw snowballs at me.
I want to leave the forest and get out of my roots,
But I am just a tree
Covered with leaves

Isel Fitzgerald, Grade 6
Grace Episcopal Day School, MD

Growing Up

When growing up
The time flies by.
You don't even notice,
As it runs to the sky.

You wish you were older
Then you can't enjoy today.
Before you even look up,
The time is flying away.

Leah Postilnik, Grade 5
Marblehead Community Charter Public School, MA

Summer Is Great

On a breezy fall day seventy degrees feels like May
I am raking the leaves feeling the breeze
The leaves are changing color I miss summer
Fall is great I am playing with a mate
I call fall now it is winter living the life
Taking long naps good healthy snacks
Drinking hot chocolate staying up late
Half a year until summer
Here is spring leap up and sing
The birds are chirping it is getting hotter
Watch out here comes summer
Summer is here school is out go to the pool
Enjoy the sun and just have fun

Andrew Rater, Grade 5
St Joseph's Catholic School, MD

I Love to Relax

My life is a cloud because I love to relax.
When I do relax I feel as weightless as a cloud.
I relax at my house, and when I do I collapse.
When I get settled I make sure it's not too loud.

A cloud floats where the wind blows
And I follow where my parents take me.
I don't care where I go, but if it's a bad place I know.
When I float where the wind blows I feel free.

I cry like a cloud rains.
I hold in sadness like a cloud holds in precipitation.
Sometimes my eyes slowly let that water drain,
And sometimes my eyes pour with great acceleration.

When I'm angry I shoot lighting bolts.
I execute anything in my way,
So I have a powerful charge that makes people revolt.
Please don't get in my way!

Rachel Reese, Grade 6
Blue Ridge Middle School, VA

Inside a Forest

Inside the trunk, thick and tall
Are insects and bugs, hiding from fall

They swim in sap, they sleep in leaves
They crawl under the house's eaves

While they visit, they chomp on bark
And crawl through the tree in the dark

Then, in the winter, when the tree creaks in the breeze
They curl up and hibernate so they don't freeze

So, you see, though a tree is a tree
It is really an apartment house for bugs and bees

Aoife Troxel, Grade 6
St Brigid School, ME

Friends

F ull of care
R eally fun to play with
I admire them
E veryone is your friend
N ice
D o so many things for you
S tick up for you

Jason Guerrero, Grade 4
Marsh Grammar School, MA

Dear Apples

When I go to pick you,
You're so high,
Hanging from your tree,
Way up in the sky.

Your past makes you famous.
Your past makes you delish!
You have an amazing smell,
Unlike a smelly, rotten, fish!

I won't see you in the winter,
When it is oh so cold.
Also, your unknown presence
Has a mystery to hold.

It's unknown how you got here,
And how you got your taste.
But I know you'll always be here,
And never be a waste.

Darian Kianfar, Grade 4
Potter Road Elementary School, MA

Homework

The outside is now unknown to me
because
Homework is all I see.

Homework is like an electricity bill,
I want it
DONE
so I can just chill.

Just when it seems like homework's at its
maximum —
I get some more!

And when I'm done,
guess what hurts?
My thumb.

Now it's time to go to bed,
arithmetic
waiting to RIDDLE my head.

Peter Dutton, Grade 6
St Brigid School, ME

Snow

I wait all year
For the first snow fall
It makes me feel like I'm at a winter ball
I dance around
By and by
Watch it fall from the sky
Watch the wind make it fly
I see the specks coming to me
It always makes me feel so happy

Haley Sheets, Grade 6
Graham Middle School, VA

Fifth Grade

F ailed
I n school
F ound out I got an F
T he teacher yells at me
H elp

G raduating is impossible
R eturned to school
A gain
D etermined to get out of
E lementary School

Rives Worsham, Grade 5
Pemberton Elementary School, VA

St. Brigid School Rules

St. Brigid School Rules
the teachers are all jewels.

The students have maximum tools,
To help them learn what's cool.

We work all day,
just like slaves.

We have faith
this will pave the way,
to a great future for us
one day.

Ariana Russo, Grade 6
St Brigid School, ME

Cold

The cold is very old
But it is really bold

And the wind moves along
Like a strange song

And the rain falls down
In any different town

Mitchell Otey, Grade 6
Graham Middle School, VA

I Am Fire

I feel red hot
I blow blazes, high as the sky
I turn red,
And yellow
And orange
I begin, unpredictably
I glow at night
Lightning kick-starts me
I burn as if to have storms inside me
You get smoke in your face
Hear me *CRACK as* I blaze on
Water cannot stop me
Flames arise
Piercing as a hundred swords
I turn blue from time to time
I burn like chili peppers in you mouth
I AM FIRE

Bennett Collins, Grade 5
Wakefield Forest Elementary School, VA

Leaves

Colorful leaves die
Gently falling to the ground
They all go sadly.

Isabel Negron, Grade 4
St Augustine Cathedral School, CT

Happy Mother's Day

Mom
busy, yelling
cleaning, washing, cooking
always giving me love
Parent

Andrew Denkewicz, Grade 4
Eldredge Elementary School, RI

Halloween Night

It's Halloween night
What a scary fright!
Pumpkins glow in my sight.
Tricker treaters
Running around
Making a lot of scary sounds!

Brenna Jagodzinski, Grade 5
St Joseph School-Fullerton, MD

When It's Fall

Colored leaves
Red, orange and yellow
Leaves falling everywhere
People raking
Leaves rustling
I'm excited
When will it be winter?

Alicia Breen, Grade 4
John J Flynn Elementary School, VT

Tiger Sea

Tiger sea, eating down ships.
Leaping waves, pushing side to side.
Sleeping when calm, ferocious when awake.
Dragging down all the people.

Kristen DeLosh, Grade 4
Boonsboro Elementary School, MD

Thanksgiving Day

My mother cooks the kosher turkey
Getting so brown
The pumpkin pie is in the oven
Getting warm and
Ready to be eaten
I watch the Macy's Day Parade
Watch the huge floats and all of the actors do their acts
My cats scarf down turkey
As the cookie monster would scarf down a cookie
The sweet potatoes with toasty warm marshmallows
Taste like ice cream on a hot summer day
My mom's once a year
Homemade
Chunky cranberry sauce
Blends in perfectly with
The delicious taste of the turkey
The chocolate mousse pie
So light
And fluffy
And the family
Is the best of all.

Shira Steinberg, Grade 5
Wakefield Forest Elementary School, VA

Help

I see
smoke rising all around me
the wall I cuddled up against
flashes of red and orange everywhere

I feel
the heat that is making me sweat
and the smoke that is trying to get in my eyes

I hear
police officers outside
and loud cracking and snaps coming from the flames

I taste
ash in my little mouth
and potent fear

I smell
fire rising very high
and things I came to love are now burning
so that I will never get to see them again

Maggie DiMarco, Grade 5
Zervas Elementary School, MA

NASCAR

NASCAR is the best sport because
They have wrecking, they have smoke
And one of the sponsors is coke
They have cautions, they have pit stops
You can't hear a thing when the flag drops
I hate it when Hendricks Motor sports wins them all
And that's why I love NASCAR.

Kyle Abbott, Grade 6
E Russell Hicks School, MD

Bunny

My mom bought me a bunny that is fluffy,
Its tail was very, very puffy.

She likes when I give her fresh carrots,
But she did not like when I brought home a parrot.

Her ears are so big and floppy,
When she eats, she gets really sloppy.

My bunny's fur is so, so white,
I saw her sleeping and she was curled up tight.

Reese Burgess, Grade 4
Dr Charles E Murphy Elementary School, CT

Donald Trump

How about that Donald Trump,
Where he lives it ain't no dump,
At night he sleeps in a massive bed,
And most people think the same of his head.

Angelo Massaro, Grade 6
Village School, MA

The Sky

I love to look at the sky
It helps me to calm down

The sky is a beautiful sight
And very, very bright

It gets dark at night
But in the morning I see light

The stars in the sky are very, very beautiful
And also very pretty

What I like about stars is that
They don't move at all they're just steady

I love to fly my kite
When there is light outside

The sky calms me down
I love to look at the peaceful sky

Olakunmi Ogun, Grade 5
Perrywood Elementary School, MD

Kittens

Kittens are lazy,
And sometimes crazy.
Some like cheese.
Others sneeze.
They catch mice,
And lick ice.
Some watch TV,
But some can't see.

Maggie Wilcher, Grade 5
McCleary Elementary School, VA

Always Wild

I went to the
valley
to see Millie,
a wild horse.
I see love and affection
in her
baby blue eyes.
She holds
beauty in her heart.
I will always
love
Millie.

Kylie Bach, Grade 6
Kenmore Middle School, VA

Out the Window

Out the window is where they are,
From underground, to above the stars.
There isn't that much that we can do
Except hear the owl go Hoo-Hoo.
While we are inside making a curl,
People are out there finding a pearl.
Out the window is where they are,
From underground, to above the stars.

Jamey Miller, Grade 4
Potter Road Elementary School, MA

The Candle

My soothing forest smell
But no appreciation
Always shunned away for a switch
So mean and cruel to not want my wick
Oh why can't I be something
Nice and cute
Rather than a hunk of wax
Nothing more
And when my wax starts to dribble
I know my time is limited
I give my last bit of light
And start to fade
Now all that is left of me
Is a puddle of wax and a speck of ash

James Maniscalco, Grade 5
Cunningham School, MA

Who Knows

Days set in, I wonder still what there is to life or is it to say in my will.
I know it might happen today, or tomorrow; who knows?
I might drown in a pool of water or in the sea or die by being just plain me.
A clumsy fall or brave undertakings.
Dying, who knows, how it will be.
Age, or a hurricane or maybe poisoning.
No one knows how they will die.
Wouldn't it be nice to live forever?
No, that's not possible, never.
I know I'll die, but I'll not stop living nor quit.
Love life for now and look for the best.
I'll go on my own quest.
I hope my long years will be like the rest.
I'll have to wait, for my own fate.
Only God knows.
Will I die from old age; who knows?

Julia Parks, Grade 5
Shaftsbury Elementary School, VT

The Ultimate Grandpa

My grandpa spent most of his life helping
less fortunate people.
His agency fed the hungry,
found homes for the homeless,
taught children after school,
and helped many people get jobs.
He was one of the strongest leaders for civil rights.
He retired, but every day he kept doing the job he loved so much.
When my grandpa wasn't working he loved listening
to jazz while eating peanuts.
Even though he was busy with all of that stuff,
he still made time to be with me and my family.
We went on trips together
and he shared stories from his past with us.
He was the ultimate grandpa.
I am proud to be his grandson.

Trey Kearse, Grade 5
Rosemont Forest Elementary School, VA

Falling Leaves

As I walk down the road stepping on the brown and yellow leaves.
I see all around me there are birds, deer and bunnies.
It's warm outside a typical fall day,
pumpkins on people's porches.
As I look at them I notice all of their jack-o'-lantern faces
and they're all lit by candlelight.
I see people running around in excitement of Halloween.
As the light sky turns dark,
people are coming out in their Halloween costumes
all I hear is trick-or-treat.
Now it's time for the full moon to come out.
I look up in the sky
finally the moon is out.
And there's an end to a typical fall day.

Christine Mesnard, Grade 5
St Joseph's Catholic School, MD

Season Is Changing

The hot air is gone, now the cool air is here
Outside, the air smells like the fall season
That comes every year
The leaves are falling
Down to the ground
Summer is lost, fall is found
The birds have flown south
And the harvest is done
The children are ready for Halloween fun
The leafless trees
Looking like they are about to grab you
Swaying in the wind
Goblins, ghouls, and witches
Give us a fright
They will happily haunt
All through the night
Soon we'll be thankful
For all that we have
All our friends, family, and food
Fall is coming
We're all in the mood

Lisa Ghaffari, Grade 6
Greenwich Country Day School, CT

Lions and Tigers and Bears

Lions and tigers and bears, oh my!
Dangerous animals, please don't cry.
Come with me, don't be shy.
Lions and tigers and bears, oh my!

Today is the day we go camping,
By the creek with fish and bears!
Now let's get the tent ready,
And please don't be scared.

We're at the camping site,
THERE WAS NO BEAR!
All that we found was a trail,
Of panther hair.
We followed the hair to a mountain and
THERE WAS NO PANTHER THERE!

All is well that ends well,
That's what they say.
Well all was well because it ended well, I guess
Still I had fun today.

Kevin DeWitt, Grade 5
Perrywood Elementary School, MD

The Amazing Deer

I spring gracefully in the meadow.
I fight with the other bucks for does.
I have dark hazel colored fur.
I am the glamorous gigantic antlered deer.

Nathan Champagne, Grade 4
Greylock School, MA

Will Death Come as the Sun Sets

As the sun sets my blood runs cold,
evicted from my apartment,
I have no place to stay,
the cold of December is freezing my blood,
struggling to keep warm,
I have no place to turn to for comfort or warmth,
except this small cardboard box,
will I live till the sun has risen,
if I do it will be a painful journey in the course of my life.

Sarah Lambert, Grade 6
Auburn Village School, NH

Self Portrait

I am kind,
full of curiosity and attentive

My sister argues with me and she fights
She sometimes needs me

My dad encourages me so much,
fills me with laughter but sometimes nags

My mom says I'm unique
and she is full of questions

I am a bird flying all over the place
But I am gentle waves, calm as can be

I am quite talented and active and hardworking
I am patient, careful and love to hear jokes

I am half American, half Japanese
and like to play tennis and the trumpet

Noah Farrell, Grade 6
Middlebrook School, CT

Santa

It's Christmas Eve at Santa's shop
elves are busy making lollipops
now here comes Santa packing his sleigh
to all the bad kids Santa says "Nay"
he comes to your house putting toys under a tree
Santa's so nice he doesn't charge a fee
so he goes to people's homes one after another
now Santa should go take a break in the summer

Mary Kate Meunier, Grade 5
Litwin Elementary School, MA

The Sea

The sea's salty waves pull in and out.
A seagull's cries swift through the air and then fade away.
The footprints from the day are now gone and washed away.
The sun slowly sets being swallowed by the sea.
Now all is quiet and the sea sings its song.

Sofia K. Bonin, Grade 5
Osborn Hill Elementary School, CT

D'Vonya's Dream

D equals the determination which I have to succeed
V stands for the voice of which I speak
O is for the outstanding job I do at school
N stands for the nation in which I live
Y is for you, me, and my special family
A equals the attitude I always continue to improve

D'Vonya means everything that I set my mind to, all the things that I can and will do.
My future get brighter by the day and my mind is more powerful. That's why I want to learn more!

D'Vonya Johnson, Grade 5
Valley View Elementary School, MD

I Am From

I am from farming and trading from Illinois and Ohio valley,
I am from 200 B.C. to 500 A.D.,
I am from traveling great distances to the Rocky Mountains for bear's teeth and Obsidian arrow heads,
I am from turtle shells to sharks teeth from the Gulf of Mexico,
I am from alligator teeth from Florida to copper nuggets in the Great Lakes region,
I am from mounds that look like trapezoids to clothes sewn from animal hides,
I am from beautiful bark pipes that looked very much like animals,
I am from everyday items my mom used to have,
I was from all of those things, but now they are pieces of my past.

Austin Rhodes, Grade 5
Jack Jackter Intermediate School, CT

Tuesday Morning

When you wake up you think, "What will I do today?"
Like, "I have to give my teacher that note," or "I can't forget to give my second grade teacher a hug."

You get in the shower and then "write" yourself a personal note to get new shampoo.
You're almost out.

You get dressed and run downstairs for breakfast to find out that your favorite cereal is almost out.
You pour all that is left into the bowl, and add some other cereal to fill the bowl up!

You "wolf" down your breakfast and get up to brush your teeth.
An awesome commercial catches your eye on TV.

You get yourself out of shock and brush your teeth.

You get on the bus.
You laugh your guts out because the piece of paper you "flicked" landed in the bus driver's hair!

You get to school.
You prepare for a brand new school day.

But, that's…a different story.

Lee Farrish, Grade 5
Mary Walter Elementary School, VA

Candlelight

Candles, candles, flicker flicker. Wick oh wick you dare not sputter. All the candles different colors. Wax is dripping, little white
bells are merrily ringing. tinkle tinkle, by candlelight. All the candles pretty colors. Oh candles candles, flicker flicker. Wick oh
wick, you dare not sputter.

Kalina Lapenta, Grade 4
Litchfield Intermediate School, CT

Kitten
Cute, furry
Cuddling, sleeping, playful
Snuggles in my lap
Pet

Shannon O. Jeffords, Grade 4
Dr Charles E Murphy Elementary School, CT

Tears
I was sad, my Momma was blue,
As soon as my arms met his,
Tears started pouring down our faces
Making each other wet.
My Momma gave me tissues,
My brother gave me his ring
For safe keeping.
Jon was leaving for training.
I wouldn't be able
To see him again for 10 weeks.
When the time came to seem him,
I thought of that day,
When our arms met, tears came again,
I was happy now. It was time to leave again.
I still cried a little bit,
Though I'd see him tomorrow.
Time for him to leave for college.
I was awakened early to say
Good bye, but I did not cry,
I will see him soon,
Come December time!

Jillian Sower, Grade 5
Linville-Edom Elementary School, VA

Halloween
Halloween, Halloween, a scary night,
It's very creepy and gives a fright,
Halloween, Halloween, a spooky day,
Warning signs say "STAY AWAY,"
Halloween, Halloween, a haunted night,
Witches' brew is their delight.
Goblins ghosts and vampires too,
Creep out at night to startle you!

Halloween, Halloween flying bats,
Smashing mirrors and black cats,
Halloween, Halloween there's sticky candy,
Sour pops are surely dandy,
Halloween, Halloween a shrieking scream,
A sleepless night and bloodcurdling dream.
Halloween night is very scary,
Stay at home if you are wary,
Mummies, warlocks, ghosts too,
Creep out at night to haunt you!
Halloween, Halloween the candy is sweet,
Open the door, scream "Trick-or-treat!"

Stacey Mayer, Grade 5
Lincoln Central Elementary School, RI

The Meadow
Morning's cool air on a mountainside,
Peaceful, shimmering lake,
Dewy meadow filled with green grass,
A doe running gently by,
Her black tail shining in the sunlight so bright,
Never again have I seen such a sight.

James Hemphill, Grade 5
Rosemont Forest Elementary School, VA

The Sun
An orange
Suspended in midair
A tennis ball
Bounced too high
A daffodil
Planted in the wrong place
A goldfish
Never moving from it's position in the sky
A pumpkin
That never rots
A star
The biggest one of all
A rain coat
That never gets wet
This is the sun to me

Elizabeth Lanzilla, Grade 6
Thomas Blake Middle School, MA

Monkeys
Monkeys swing on vines,
They like to eat bananas,
Chimps are so cute.

Morgan MarcAurele, Grade 4
Dr Charles E Murphy Elementary School, CT

Blue Sky
B lue is the sky at noon
L ight in the morning
U kuleles playing at night
E is for early in the morning

S un that is bright
K ites flying at the beach
Y ellow sun.

Jillian Wise, Grade 5
C Hunter Ritchie Elementary School, VA

Cheese
C heese is Grant's favorite food
H is favorite type is cheddar
E veryone in the factory works together to make cheese
E eek! Is what some people say if they eat moldy cheese
S lices and slices of cheese is what Grant wants
E veryone should like cheese!

Adam Donaldson, Grade 5
C Hunter Ritchie Elementary School, VA

Gifts

G etting games
I Pod
F riends
T o play fun games
S pending money on gifts

Frankie LoBuono, Grade 4
Marsh Grammar School, MA

Midnight

Moonlight shines in my window
Star shine leaks in through the shades
Owls hoot
Mice scuttle
The house creeks
You hear an unknown noise outside
Are you scared?
You want to sleep
But feel it is not dark enough
Soon it will be morning
You feel safe and warm

Kathryn Winn, Grade 5
John J Flynn Elementary School, VT

Dogs

Sweet, loyal, loving
They're the puppies of the world
Dogs you want to meet.

Gina Bellassai, Grade 5
McCleary Elementary School, VA

Sunshine

The sunshine on me
Peeking through the trees
Bushes popping up

Nick Demers, Grade 4
St Brigid School, ME

I Am Earth

The plate-tectonics in my body move
Earthquake
Soil
7 continents I see
Oceans waves come up
The core burns me
Life is evolving as I live
Sphere shaped is the earth
Sharp crystals cutting rock

Jarod Golub, Grade 5
Wakefield Forest Elementary School, VA

Pine Cones

Pine cones, tiny things
They fall from the tall pine tree
Big, small fun to have

Mackenzie Hoglund, Grade 4
St Brigid School, ME

Winter Is Coming

The air is Crisp, the leaves are red.
As I walk down the cold path I hear my shoes crunching the old plants.
As the colorful leaves sway in the wind, I hear my name.
What is it?
I look behind me, I see nothing.
I hear someone whisper, "Winter is coming."
I keep on walking, I hear it again.
Why am I hearing it?
As the night falls, I am all alone.
the wind is whispering, "Winter is coming."
As I walk inside a bare cabin, I hear it again.
I start to get tired, so I lay down on a blanket.
I dream of Winter.
When I awake, I hear it again.
I walk outside, the air smells sweet.
I realized it was a sign.
I hear it again, "Winter is coming."

Alexandra Snell, Grade 6
Irving School, CT

Cats?

They come in many shapes and sizes different varieties too.
But one thing is for sure there up to no good.
They will attack you at night when nobody's watching and be very careful to.
Don't let them sneak up on you or they will be swift and quick about it.
They're like a friend in the dawn and a ninja at dusk.
A traitor to his friends and a warrior to his family.
So next time you see one keep a watchful eye.
So don't show shame or pity for this back stabbing person.
Rebel, attack, control, and defend.
Get revenge from this merciless horrible monster.
This fearless thing can tame anything.
They come to your house and tear up the place.
So don't act like nobody told you when you're the next victim of predator and prey.
What? I never told you the name of this devilish creature.
Well don't be surprised right before your eyes it's a Ca —
Meow! Milkshake! How did you get here? I love you because you wouldn't hurt a fly.
Trust me they're evil!

Ryan Rowe, Grade 6
E Russell Hicks School, MD

Thanksgiving

T hanksgiving was not always a
H oliday, until
A braham Lincoln said it would be on the 4th Thursday of
N ovember. It is interesting to
K now lots of presidents were involved
S uch as
G eorge Washington
I n time of the Revolutionary War.
F.D. Roose **V** elt moved:
I t to the 3rd Thursday of
N ovember to
G ive thanks

Elise Briody, Grade 5
The Burnham Elementary School, CT

Winter

I love winter
The sun that sparkles on the snow
Maybe school will be canceled you never know
The snow on the trees
And the cold winter breeze
Gone is the pollen that makes me sneeze
The skating is good but I fall on my knees
Now it is time for some zzzz.

Elizabeth Magee, Grade 5
Southbrook Academy, MA

My Shoes

These are my shoes.
They aren't that cool.
But I still wear them,
Even at school.

These are my shoes.
I've had them for a year.
If you try to throw them out,
You'll be screaming in fear.

These are my shoes.
They're a perfect fit.
If you try to take them,
You will get hit.

Tyler Weeks, Grade 5
C Hunter Ritchie Elementary School, VA

Light

What is the opposite of bright?
Maybe it is a candle that is alight.
Because it is something that helps you see,
It is something that I hold close to me.

Zach McNulty, Grade 6
St Rose School, CT

Richter Roo (My Puppy)

Soft, fluffy fur, that soothes my hands as I
rub up and down his back.
Big, bold, chocolate brown spots that make
him unique and give him an adorable look.
Long, fluffy ears that get drenched in his
water when he drinks.
His wet black nose sniffs at everything in sight.
His whiskers brush upon me, and give me
a tickling feeling.
He has a short stubby tail that wiggles back and forth.
It seems to never get tired.
Bushy eyebrows that look like fuzzy cotton balls
on his cute little face…
Long back legs that extend behind him when
he sleeps on the cold tile floor.
Muscular belly…he is such a beefy boy!

Cassidy Schod, Grade 5
Long Meadow Elementary School, CT

Lacrosse

This is the sport that I call lax.
Lax is such an amazing blast.
I play wing,
Or if on the sideline, I may just sing.

You need a stick, ball, and running legs, too.
These will help if you want to get through
The other girls who are standing and waiting,
I drive the ball down anticipating.

I keep on running, but I am in distress
As my opponent hitting my stick is making me stress.
I score the last goal and run to the coach with pride,
And my teammates quickly come to my side.

We win the game, and we jump for joy.
Lacrosse is not just a game for a boy!

Karissa LeMaire, Grade 6
Beacon Middle School, DE

Alaska

Alaska is a beautiful place
In the winter, the wind chills your face
Oh, the beauty of Glacier Bay
It makes you wish every place looked this way
As I see the eagle fly
It seems there is no end to the majestic sky
If you listen closely you can hear the whales
They seem to be telling you their secret tales
Oh, how this place is so grand,
There are not many places that are as beautiful as this land.

Tommy Barrett, Grade 5
Highland Park School, CT

Doomcoaster

Slowly moving up the track
Waiting for the drop
Looking down right under me
This feeling may never stop
We're sitting in the last car
Looking behind our doom
I feel I might be imaging
But then I know it's true
The urge to scream and the wind in my face
Holding on real tight
Billy having the time of his life
It might be the end of mine
Then I dare to let go and scream at the top of my lungs
Billy and I laughing together
Though our eyes are as dry as our tongues
The whole thing is now over
And we are all well
It's ok were disappointed right now
We have a great story to tell

Alison Fox, Grade 6
Thomas Blake Middle School, MA

The K 9*

Emerges with wiggly tail,
The dog.
Don't laugh — it has a really furry coat.
His four legs are moving about.
Barking really loud there is no doubt.
Why not love him?
He is one of a kind.
Also does tricks.
Well this K9
Is friendly
Only dogs
Shall bark with me.

Shaneisia Bloomfield, Grade 5
Clover Street School, CT
*Inspired by Marianne Moore

The Old Man!

There was an old man with a beard,
Who said it is just like I feared!
Two owls and a hen,
Four larks and a wren,
Have all build their nests in my beard!

Jose Zunig Ramirez, Grade 6
Floyd T Binns Middle School, VA

Mr. Man the Snowman

Mr. Man the snowman was
Made by Fran and Stan
He woke up one day
In the cold winter snow

Mr. Man, Stan, and Fran
Played outside and
Had fun all day long

Until the sun went down
And the children went inside
Mr. Man was all alone and bored
The next day was bad

The sun came up and
So did the temperature!
The moon went down and
So did Mr. Man the Snowman

Kevin McCarthy, Grade 6
Juliet W Long School, CT

Taylor Twellman

Taylor Twellman
Nice, fast
He loves soccer
Fun, agile, and athletic
Forward

Ryan Lynch, Grade 5
Pemberton Elementary School, VA

Break Dancing

Sean loves to break dance,
So he tried out for the competition.
He set his mind on the gold.
The next day was the competition,
I would say Sean was pretty good,
But the judges didn't think so.
Even though Sean didn't
Get the gold he still kept
On doing what he loved.

Shannon Gerke, Grade 6
Kenmore Middle School, VA

Fall

Trees come big and small
The leaves change color
Then it's fall
Flowers get duller
But fall is the best of them all
The boats still go out into the sea
While we are home peacefully
The fall is still the best if you ask me
When we go outside to play football
We slip and fall you see
But we have fun because it's fall
It starts to get chilly
So we sometimes may crawl
Can't you see the breath come out of me
Truly fall is the best of them all.

Connor Lanoie, Grade 5
Lincoln Central Elementary School, RI

Pumpkin Pie-Loving Squirrels

Ovens open wide
Nutty squirrels running for some
Creamy pumpkin pie

Kacey Price, Grade 5
McCleary Elementary School, VA

Maddison Samons

M arvelous
A thletic
D arling
D ramatic
I ronic
S mart
O utstanding
N ervous

S aviour
A ttending
M usician
O ptimistic
N ice
S erving

Maddison Samons, Grade 5
St Joseph School-Fullerton, MD

Memories

Looking back at the photographs
Brings back fond memories
When I was young
I miss those days
But I love these day better
Even though I am far away
From my Sister and Dad
I can still sense their presence
At times I wake up
To the sound of their voices
It feels like
They are right next to me
My Sister and Dad
Left a piece of themselves with me
And I hope I did too
I will always remember
The fun and the bad times
The happier and even the sad times
For some memories are simply fantasies
But mine is the foundation
Of what and who I am today

Vanisha Vinit, Grade 5
CT

The Future

In the future,
I see cars
Flying
Up ahead…
Nothing is a dread.
I fly to school,
But there's a twist…
It's way too far and high.
Problem being…the school is in the sky!
I see my friends.
We go to class.
First period is best…History!
(But we have a test.)
After school,
I fly back home.
It's almost 6:00.
I eat dinner,
Walk to bed…
Then the day is done.

Noelle Acaso, Grade 5
St Joseph School-Fullerton, MD

Leaf

L eaves are so lovely.
E ach one is unique.
A ll of them are beautiful.
F lying where the wind takes them.

Pascal Bernard, Grade 4
St Gregory Elementary School, MA

Nighttime

Nightie night,
sleepie tight,
say a prayer,
turn off the light.
I wish I may,
I wish I might,
dream of sweet dreams I dream tonight.
I dream of summers long gone by.
I dream of a winter snowman's coal black eyes.
I dream of meadows in the spring.
I dream of the brilliant colors that autumn brings.
Nightie night,
sleepie tight,
I dream of sweet dreams I dream tonight!

Alexis Weeks, Grade 5
Old Saybrook Middle School, CT

Socks

Socks, socks
I love my socks
So many bright colors all in a box.
Stripes, solids, polka-dotted blue
Lacy, holiday, and argyle too.
Wool ones and cotton
With toes and not
Favorite of all are bright purple
The socks Aunt Kathy got.
Some keep my feet warm on those cold winter nights
When I tiptoe down the hallway
The fuzzy bear socks are such a silly sight.
But the ones with the holes
Worn out in the soles
Are always left behind
Because the mate I cannot find
Where they go, I do not know!
Socks

Camille Logiudice, Grade 5
Old Saybrook Middle School, CT

My Snake

This is my snake.
It hides in my sock.
When my sister pokes it,
It slithers out in shock.

This is my snake.
It is green and red.
But it has a tendency to
Slither onto my mom's head.

This is my snake,
All covered in slime.
When it falls in the fruit basket,
It smells like a lime!

Ashby Thompson, Grade 5
C Hunter Ritchie Elementary School, VA

Weird Pig

There once was a weird pig that came from a goose
He once had a friend that's head was a little loose.

They like to drive a bike.
So they called themselves Mike.

They once went a little too crazy and had to wear a noose.

Jacob King, Grade 5
McCleary Elementary School, VA

When It's Cold Outside

When it's cold outside
and you can't get warm.
When there's
nothing to hold
and there's nothing but, snow as it falls
from the trees.
When it's cold outside
and there's a
BIG breeze.
Shivering and
shivering is all
I do now.
As I wait and
wait to try and
find a sweater.
It snows, it snows.
I SHIVER!

Samantha Stinson, Grade 5
Friendship Valley Elementary School, MD

The Poem

I wonder what my poem will be about.
It could be sad with lots of crying.
Maybe a sad story would be cool.
But there are many different poems.
Let's look at a few.

It could possibly be scary,
Very scary at that!
Maybe not very scary.
Some smaller children may read,
So let's not make it scary.

Maybe happy with a chuckle or two.
Like that funny little mouse Walt Disney made.
But I think funny would be too short,
Don't you.

I have no clue what to write about.
Could someone give me an idea?
Leave me to my thinking.
I need to decided.
Hopefully I will finish in time.

Jacob Jennelle, Grade 6
Graham Middle School, VA

Pigs

Oink!! Oink!!
That's my sound.
When I roll in the mud.
I've played all day!
Whew!!! I'm tired!
I take my nap in the hay.
When I wake it's time to play!
Oink!! Oink!!

Whitney Horne, Grade 6
Graham Middle School, VA

A-Rod Curse*

May your house be struck by lightning,
May your game be very frightening,
May you strike out with bases filled,
May your home-run dreams be killed,
May your fans break your heart,
May your Red Sox fears start!

David Bolognese, Grade 6
Village School, MA
*Written by a Boston Red Sox fan

The Rain

It drips from the sky
Soaking my silky, white wings
Rain falls to the ground

Amy Koch, Grade 6
Main Street Middle School, VT

The Spooky Night

Bats flying and scooping down,
Witches riding and spooking around.

Ghosts appearing everywhere,
Goblins dancing here and there.

Spiders crawling in your hair,
A black cat is over there.

The full moon is shining very bright,
Jack-o'-lanterns are very spooky tonight.

Jessie Gagnon, Grade 4
Brookside Elementary School, MA

Halloween

H aunting time
A gain
L onely spirits come
L onely streets are spooky
O nly ghosts and goblins scare
W olves are howling
E erie jack o'lanterns smile
E vening is quiet
N ow is Halloween

Patrick Gagliardi, Grade 5
St Joseph School-Fullerton, MD

My Sweet Beach House

As I came down the stairs from my beach house.
I took a step into the gold hot steaming sand.
I looked at the sun and I almost went blind.
So I walked down the street and smelt the stinky sea and I almost died.

Anthony Vollin, Grade 6
Kenmore Middle School, VA

Listen

Listen to the crunching of the huge pile of colorful leaves,
Listen to the thunder booming loudly in the dark sky,
Listen to the ocean and the seagulls soaring high above it,
Listen to the pages turning and turning in my favorite book,
Listen to the wind whistling in the cool Autumn breeze,
Listen to the splash in the refreshing pool under the warm Florida sun.
Listen, just listen.

Victoria Olaechea, Grade 5
Jack Jackter Intermediate School, CT

Walking on Greenwich Ave

Walking on Greenwich Ave
Hearing the clickity click of the high heels tapping the ground
Feeling the weight of all the new bags of clothes
Blanketing you so no one can see you
Seeing all the little kids saying, "Mommy, can we go to this store?"
Because of all the new Christmas toys
Tasting the hot chocolate burning your tongue
And feeling the moist smoke tickling your chin
Coming from the hot chocolate on your face
Jumping and prancing with joy from getting that cool new toy
Walking on Greenwich Ave

Cameron Kelley, Grade 6
Greenwich Country Day School, CT

The Light That Shines on a Summer Night

There's a light that shines on a summer's night.
I hope that light doesn't give you a fright!
For that light is I, the magnificent firefly.
Oh how I love to light up in the sky!
A lamp has a light bulb that produces heat.
I have a light, but it has no heat, isn't that neat?
I'm not creepy, crawly, sneaky, nor even harmful to you.
Hopefully I'm not the insect you'd like to shoo!
When two chemicals react my light can shine bright.
Isn't that neat it can shine with all its might!
All adult fireflies like me can glow!
But eggs, larva, and glowworms can glow too, did you know?
When I'm a glowworm I'm flat and small.
But as an adult, I am still not very tall!
I have four stages of my life that can all be such a sight!
If you could see them all it would probably be an amazing bright sight!
When you hear the word firefly you may think that I'm a fly!
But I am a soft bodied beetle flying high!
So now look closely on a humid summer's night.
And you may see a beautiful bright sight!

Kati Singley, Grade 6
Immaculate Heart of Mary School, DE

Halloween

Halloween is…
— Moaning mummies come to life
— Eating all the brains
— Frightening creatures scare us
— Creeping up the stairs
— Flying witches fly over houses
— Laughing with their evil voices
— Jumping skeletons clink-clack their bones
— Hitting them across the wall.
— That's what Halloween is about!

Leonora Torres, Grade 4
St Augustine Cathedral School, CT

Leaf

L ovely adventurous leaves.
E xcellent fliers of the sky.
A stonishing beautiful colors everywhere.
F abulous changing colors that makes fall beautiful.

Amira Corbett, Grade 4
St Gregory Elementary School, MA

Flag

This is how I feel hanging on a wall.
Sometimes I feel proud and feeling like a person.
On the Fourth of July, I get waved around.
Sometimes I get woozy.
Sometimes I'm afraid.
I feel famous for my stars.
I am really special, how about you?

Megan McNivens, Grade 5
Old Saybrook Middle School, CT

My Friend and I

The sun lowers itself in the sky.
Arrays of the sunset glisten up high.
Little crabs scurry here and there.
Gentle waves toss without a care.
The shore is desolate except for my friend and I.
We're looking for shells, but the tide is high.
Instead, we sit on the sand, gazing at the ocean.
Then we see a light, floating without motion.
My friend said, "See the light on the waters? What can it be?"
Then our imaginations were let free.
"It's a ship in distress. Call out SOS!"
"No, it's a falling star that came from the west."
We roll back in laughter getting sand in our hair.
Having such a good time, we don't stop to care.
After, we stand wiping sand off our pants.
We begin to look for shells again, just like little ants.
My friend finds a shell and hands it to me.
"It's yours. Keep it. It's a perfect Sand Dollar, see?"
Suddenly everything went blank and the beach was gone.
I woke up in my room and my house was calm.
I looked down and there was a shell in my palm.

Hope Cook, Grade 6
Cornerstone Christian School, VA

School

I wake up with the loud ring of the morning bell,
And the pitter patter of feet running through my hallways.
I always hear kids chatting away in the halls.
It's quiet during a test,
But the rest of the day is a pest.
I hear another ring of the bell,
And some more feet running through the halls.
That means it's time for me to have a rest.

Tyler Roberts, Grade 5
Four Seasons Elementary School, MD

The Flame

Fire redness through the night,
smoky blackness flying in fright
from flames so hot

The dirt had burnt the ground so hot
from the reddest flame,
on the darkest night

The wolf had ran from the flame so hot,
his paws burnt from the ground,
the heat that ran through his veins had made the wolf afraid

The fire split through the night and day,
racing through the trees that burnt at touch

The animals ran and left their homes to fall in ashes,
no mere animal can tame the flame

Man had made the flame,
the flame that burnt for miles and miles,
for they didn't know they couldn't tame the flame

The redness blinded at sight,
the only thing to stop it was the water that could tame the flame

Dylan Johnson, Grade 6
Litchfield Intermediate School, CT

Who Am I?

My scientific family name means ghost.
The oak and cherry trees are my host.

I do not move much in light.
I only move around at night.

I have two compound and three simple eyes.
My family lives for 18 months before it dies.

I am usually the color brown.
You cannot find me in a town.

I look like a twig; that is my trick.
You know me as a walking stick.

Jeff Waeghe, Grade 6
Immaculate Heart of Mary School, DE

Love Is All

Love is gratitude.
Love is truth.
Love is honest.
Love is giving.
Love gives life.
Love is what people long for.
Love is light.
Love is darkness.
Love turns to hatred.
Hatred turns to Love.
Love is done.
Love gives in.
Love is all.
Amber Nickerson, Grade 6
Monelison Middle School, VA

Fall

Fall is a season
Full of rainbow colors…
Red is maple,
The color orange is mums
And the pumpkins,
Yellow is elm, sugar maple
And sunflowers,
Green is the grass,
And evergreens,
Blue is the sky
And the blue jays,
Purple is thistle flowers
And dark oak leaves, too,
Now imagine
What fall is like,
With its rainbow.
Hannah Sonberg, Grade 4
Memorial School, NH

Family

What is a family?
A group of caring people
Very important people to me
Giving people I love
Friendly people to play with
Encouraging people to encourage me
Loving people
People I can trust.
That is my family.
Samantha Wallis, Grade 4
Memorial School, NH

Summer's Here

Since summer's here it's getting fun
I can't wait until we go in the sun
We won't have education
'Cause we're going on vacation
Madison Grover, Grade 4
Brookside Elementary School, MA

My True Friend

The one that I can go to
When life turns bright to black
The person who is always there
The one whose got your back

The sister that I wanted
But friends is good enough
So when you read this poem
Know that it's full of love
Jamie Downer, Grade 5
Craneville School, MA

One Window Is All I Need

To look inside the crystal ball
To dream an endless dream
To drift upon a cloud
To make my dreams come true
And be able to make a difference
Meagan Foy, Grade 6
St Rose School, CT

Husky

A husky is good on a dog sled team
To be in the Iditarod is its dream
A husky's fur is as white as snow
They also have shades of black though
They're always anxious to get going
Especially when it is snowing
They are able to follow the trail
Even through the blinding hail
Huskies move so very fast
And yet their legs can always last
This is the best dog ever
To me they can't be better
Jared Samost, Grade 5
E Ethel Little Elementary School, MA

Mystery in the Dark

Over the summer,
I went to a camp
called Adventure Links.
One day we went caving.
Inside the cave
without our lights on
it was like night,
totally black.
We didn't make an echo,
because we weren't allowed to shout.
Or talk.
The staff said
"It does something bad to the cave."
To me,
that is a mystery.
Ryan Szczerbinski, Grade 6
Kenmore Middle School, VA

I Wonder Why

I wonder why
a fish jumps high.
I wonder why
a bird can fly.
I wonder why
a deer is so shy.
I wonder why.
I wonder why.

Why can a fish jump to the sky?
Why can a bird fly so high?
Why is a deer so very shy?
I wonder why.
I wonder why.
Katherine V. Sublett, Grade 6
Floyd T Binns Middle School, VA

Me

Me
Fun, happy
Plays, runs, talks
Very happy and playful
Zachary
Zachary Mousseau, Grade 4
Brookside Elementary School, MA

Football

Friday nights when the sun goes down
Football comes to town

Passes are thrown through the air
The receiver catches them with care

The stands are filled with sound
When the Pioneers get a touchdown

The other team tries with all their might
But just can't win the fight
Jeffrey Mutter, Grade 5
Belfast-Elk Garden Elementary School, VA

Santa Claus

S anta brings presents on Christmas
A lot of Christmas goodies to eat
N orth Pole is where he lives
T hanking Santa for gifts
A lways wearing red on Christmas

C ookies are put out on Christmas Eve
L ots of goodies to eat and milk to drink
A lways listening to Christmas music
U nderneath the tree are presents
S aint Nick is what Christmas is all about
Kendall Beliveau, Grade 5
Litwin Elementary School, MA

Great Grammy

Old and forgetful in most eyes,
kind and wonderful in mine.
Then she is gone.
Tears spill, memories are discussed
but she is always there in my heart.

Trey Witter, Grade 5
West Woods Upper Elementary School, CT

My Instrument

I can still see the glimmering golden light,
reflecting off my instrument's plastic skin,
as if angels were touching it with their fingers.

When I play, there's a weird whimsical feeling…
The extraordinary noise it makes is a siren
singing in the wind.

I can perform on my instrument
with ease.
It's like making a pie
with all the ingredients
and time in the world!

When I rewind my mind's tape recorder
back to the day I gleefully held this smooth sound creator
for the first time,
an unmistakable grin appears on my face.
A blinding bolt of thunder
streaks through my body.
I truly feel alive!

Eric Zhang, Grade 6
Mystic Middle School, CT

Snow Storms

A windy January day
Snow races down
Trying to be the first snow of the New Year
"Ha! I win!"
"No! It was I!"
The gentle flurries now become a raging storm
The flakes attack a telephone wire
The electricity is now out
Little do the angry snowflakes know
Instead of making a fearful world
They are creating an adventure for the children
Suddenly they grow tired
"This is getting boring"
"Let's stop fighting"
So the wind takes over
Whoosh!
Bam!
Yikes!
The snow is now even madder
The storm rages on!

Madeleine Donohue, Grade 6
St Mary of Czestochowa School, CT

Legends Can Be

Legends can be
filled with monsters, animals
filled with maps, treasures
filled with sadness, happiness
filled with new worlds, new people
filled with fairies, magic
but you don't have to look in a book,
there might be lots of legends right in your family!

Sasha von Spakovsky, Grade 4
St John Neumann Academy, VA

What Is Christmas?

What is Christmas?
Christmas is a time of year
when everyone is jolly and gives a cheer.
When Mary and Joseph traveled far
following the holy star
that led them to a busy inn
where baby Jesus' life begins.
Three wise men came that night
following the star so bright.

Christmas is more than packages and bows
and things that Santa knows.
It's about joy, laughter, care, and fun
and Jesus' love for everyone!

Ryan Murphy, Grade 4
North Star Elementary School, DE

Snow

Snow comes in a drifting fall
Covers the ground with a white layer
The snowflakes descend to the ground
It comes down from heaven above
The world is like a magical snow globe
It leaves with a cold sensation that nobody will forget

Rachel Maguire, Grade 6
St Rose School, CT

The Evil Hornet

Look at me the hornet flying so free
I'm looking for a snack like a busy buzzing bee

Don't come near my nest or sting you I will
If you harm me, my nest will swarm and kill

I buzz like a bee, but surely I'm not
If you try to get honey from me I'll sting you a lot

When insects aren't around, I surely won't starve
I also like to eat fruit would you give me an apple to carve?

If you're searching for me just look in a tree
But don't come too close or you'll irritate me!!!

Chandler Smith, Grade 6
Immaculate Heart of Mary School, DE

At the Bird Feeder

On a late fall day
In a whispering kind of way
All the chickadees planned
While on the ground
The squirrels scatter around
In the cool crisp breeze
I found myself pleased
By the clever little job the birds did
They swooped above the crowd
Quite pleasantly and proud
Until the hawk came...
And they all hid

Delaney Maxell, Grade 5
Lincoln Central Elementary School, RI

Spring

Summer is next,
winter has passed.
I'm in the middle,
not first,
not last.

I am a kid,
not baby or teen.
I'm not an adult,
I'm in between.

The blossoms bloom,
the hummingbirds sing.
The weather is perfect,
I am spring.

Sunni Whitmore, Grade 6
Jared Eliot School, CT

Halloween

Halloween is...
— screaming girls being frightened
— haunting goblins spook the night
— moaning mummies come to life
— walking zombies give us a scare
— startling costumes scare the kids
— creeping creatures crawl the walls
— eating candy is so good
— scratching claws of creepy black cats
Halloween is...
spooking the night...BOO!

Angela Rivera, Grade 4
St Augustine Cathedral School, CT

The Truth

Celtics captain, Paul Pierce
On the court he's really fierce
If he starts screwing up,
The team will help him bounce back up

Chase Balayo, Grade 6
Village School, MA

Horses

A herd of horses stand in the meadow.
A cream colored mare lay in the meadow with her chestnut colored foal.
The wild jet black mustang looks me in the eye — a watchful glare.
The joyful foal fumbles in the leaves.
A mare chases her foal gracefully in a circle.
The mustang races around — bucking and rearing to show his excitement.
He is as wild as a fire spreading quickly through a village.
As the sun goes down, the herd settles and then runs off into the sunset.

Baylee Ports, Grade 5
Shaftsbury Elementary School, VT

Remember

Remember all the sticky clear tape wrapped around our fingers.
Remember all the candy cane and snowmen paper.
Remember all the exciting shopping for gifts.
Remember the glittering decorated tree.
Remember the ornaments hanging and the red and green bows tied on tight.
Remember all the gifts that hide below the amazing tree.
Remember the shimmering snow that drifts softly in the wind.
Remember the snowmen and snow women standing strong in the snowy storm.
Remember the sleds that slide down the slippery hill.
Remember the powerful snowball fights with your brother or sister.
Remember the snow angels that glitter so bright.
Remember the soft hats, mittens, and scarves that keep your neck snug and warm.
Remember the lights dangling from the roof on your house.
Remember the warm hot chocolate with the marshmallows or Cool Whip.
Remember the powdery snowball cookies.
Remember the delicious dinners with turkey and mashed potatoes and gravy.
Remember the screaming of Merry Christmas.
And always remember the mistletoe and the wreath.
Remember Christmas
Just remember!

Meghan Wood, Grade 5
Jack Jackter Intermediate School, CT

Myself

My hair is like a clump of yarn after a baby has knotted it tight
My lips are like a reddish-colored gate — opening and closing frequently
My eyes are like two buttons sewed on to my face, keeping my life together
My ears are two flying saucers, crashing down on Earth and abducting information
I live in an amusement park and eat cotton candy
My life is the biggest roller coaster with me in the front seat, having no
control over what happens

Kelly O'Connor, Grade 6
Tolland Middle School, CT

A Wolf's Soundscape

Birds fighting and the other footsteps of other pups wrestling.
A peaceful HOWL from the alpha wolf to say good night to other pack members.
A nearby river splashing calmly against the granite rocks.
A not so good sound of a rifle or shotgun shot in the distance.
Trees blowing viciously in the wind while leaves are CRACKLING.
Oh, to eliminate the sound of a GUN SHOT.
The nearby call of their favorite food — a moose!

Ian Donovan, Grade 5
Jack Jackter Intermediate School, CT

My Dogs

I have a dog named Star and she likes to run far
I have a dog named Cowboy and he ate my toy

Star and Cowboy are the best
And they always make such a mess

Star and Cowboy are a great pair
They are two of the best dogs you can find anywhere.

Troy Dixon, Grade 6
Melwood Elementary School, MD

The Chestnut Trees

We are the chestnut trees
Swaying majestically in the breeze
Extravagantly designed
To dance to the music of mankind

My chestnuts are plentiful and small
For those to pick, one and all
To intruder's hands they will not fall
I am indifferent to those who bawl

I see the boy's upturned face
And laugh merrily at his disgrace
If you would wait a moment or two
Mr. Weather will shake them down for you!

My chestnut bunches are growing thick
If you can reach them you may pick
My chestnuts bring mighty joy
To every single girl and boy

Rachael Dalton, Grade 6
St Brigid School, ME

Wild Like a Horse

My life is like a wild horse
Which roams around grounds
I can never stay on course
And never "in-bounds"

I let my mind wander
Being playful, yet careful
Never acting as plunder
I think freely and gracefully

I'm in the wild west
I'm free to think of myself
And am always on a quest
I want to do it and win just to prove myself

Curiosity is not a sin
But better yet to be sure
All I want is to win
But more and more, I'll become mature

Edka Wong, Grade 6
Blue Ridge Middle School, VA

Christmas

I heard a thump — he was on his way
Soon Santa will step from his sleigh
The elves have worked hard as they could
to make this Christmas jolly and good
I think I see Rudolph's red nose
Shining like a springtime rose.

Asia Santos, Grade 4
JF Kennedy School, CT

I Am a Poem

I am a poem
Sitting here on the paper
Waiting to be read by someone kind enough to do so
I am a poem
Waiting

Jenny McCann, Grade 5
Wakefield Forest Elementary School, VA

I Am a Football Player

I am a safety and linebacker on defense,
I wonder what the NFL is like?
I hear on every play the sound of helmets cracking
and the sound of my coaches whistle.
I see aggressive players ready to get the ball.
I want to do my best and hope for an NFL contract.
I am a safety and linebacker on defense.

I pretend I am the best NFL football player,
I feel that I play better football after I have had a good meal,
I touch a football at practice,
I worry about losing a game
without making a long touchdown.
I am a safety and linebacker on defense.

I understand how to tackle and to catch,
I say watch the pass defense,
I dream about winning the Super Bowl,
I try to get an interception.
I hope I will be the best football player in history.
I am a safety and linebacker on defense.

Brodie Murphy, Grade 5
Blackrock School, RI

Cheerleading Trophy

I close my eyes,
hold my breath,
I'm ready.
My friend yells, "one, two, full!"
The crowd goes wild.
I snap to success!
I cradle,
my skirt flows up as if an umbrella was inside out.
The crowd, a marching band, cheering in my ear!
Cheerleading is my passion!

Mia Henningsen, Grade 6
Mystic Middle School, CT

Christmas

Snowmen dance and bells ring.
Red doors open and black doors close.
Wreaths and icicles are hanging up, the signs of Christmas have come!
Ornaments and presents are being bought and put on and under green trees!
Happy voices ring from above, children are making their lists!
Snowy days are passing by, does St. Nicolas ring a bell?
Hats and mittens, scarfs and socks. Warm! Warm! Warm!
I see snow angels out on the lawn. Are you going to celebrate someone special's birthday?
Get out your best carrots and cookies, I think you know why!

Lauren Bialecki, Grade 4
North Star Elementary School, DE

Amazing Nature

Have you noticed how the dry leaves are swaying back and forth as the
wind gently blows across your wandering eyes?
As I carefully grazed the smooth feel of the bamboo it reminded me of a
slender panda cuddling with its mother in a dark, lonely cave.
Listen, there is a baby moth fluttering in the distance trying to find its peaceful home.
The creamy feel of the moss was like stroking your hand through a koala's soft, gray fur.
Can you see the little blue birds soaring through the air and how the tall,
thin trees are waving from side to side like someone saying good-bye to you?
I can see my blank face staring back at me in the clear river as a bright
orange fish happily flops away from my sight.
Watch as the terrifying bolts of lightning are flashing down before your still eyes.
In the distance you can see how a hungry leopard is chasing its prey then
leaping into the air and snatching it off the ground.
Think of a faithful dream that never ends and obtains a secret that no one knows about.
Hear a giant boulder falling from the top of an old, deserted cave and
closing the entrance forever as it pounds against the ground.

Justin Kohut, Grade 5
Pleasant Valley School, CT

My Mysterious Island

Welcome to my island.
Where blueberry water is as big as blue whale.
A monstrous size island like a dinosaur.
I have a hiding spot on this magnificent island where you can play in the crystal blue water.
Where you can sit on a broken piece of wood shaped like a bench.
Triangle shaped leaves cover you like a blanket.
Lay down and fall asleep near the crystal blue water with me near the sea.
Next time bring a friend.

Vincent Robert Volpe III, Grade 4
Cranston-Johnston Catholic Regional School, RI

Words

It's the words that zoom; they roar and screech…I'm 'mates with them, I wind them, I crash into them, I run them down, I ram into them, I lap them down…I race words so much…The damaged ones…The ones I wait for spin or crash until, suddenly, they drop…Racing them I love…They win at Daytona, they leap like Clint Bowyer in this year's Daytona 500, and they are lapping, passing, leading laps, winning…I run after certain words…They are so fast that it makes me want to win so bad at Daytona, as I drive past, I win $1,000,000+, hold the trophy, I set myself in front of the crowd, they cheer to me, screaming, shouting, even booing, like "The Big One," like improving positions fast, like spinning, like photo finishes…And then I race them, I lap them, I wreck them, I race them down the start/finish line, I beat them, I win them, I don't let them go in the races…I leave them in my poem like confetti and a huge check, like getting in the "Chase for the Sprint Cup," like being the new king of racing, winning over 200 races and over 7 championships, too…Everything exists in the word.

Jacob Boislard, Grade 5
Jack Jackter Intermediate School, CT

D.A.R.E.

Say no, don't say yes.
It's the worst, not the best.
It hurts, not helps.
It hooks, not frees.
Some say it's cool, but you know in your heart you'd be a fool.
It could land you in jail, if you don't prevail.
Friends say to chill, but the pill it can kill.
Do not accept one, you'll regret the deed.
Once you get started, it's tough to succeed.
Dare to be strong, when you know it is wrong.
Dare to deny, or you truly could die.
Dare to resist drugs.

Kristen Delzell, Grade 5
Jack Jackter Intermediate School, CT

In My Mirror

In my mirror, what do I see?
I know it's more than just a picture of me.
A person who looks to bring joy to many,
A seeks not to discourage any.
A nice person; I don't want to be mean at all,
I never want pride to be my fall.
A strong person, I put my faith in God.
Not any earthly thing or my iPod.
So in my mirror, that's what I see.
I'm not sure what you want to see,
But I hope you see God, reflected through me.

David Stump, Grade 6
Homeschool Plus, VA

Four Seasons

Golden daffodil petals,
which have shed like tears dancing in the breeze
The pitter patter lulling the willows asleep
Soon to leave fresh dew

Sweltering sunshine
Cosmic massage of hot beams, summer energy
The erosive straw battered my bare legs and feet
For this is her field

Serene autumn night lingering glow of sunset
Makes all picturesque
Jubilant colors enfold the land around me
Whispering hello

Snow covered house tops as if frosted little cakes
Glisten in the night
Pearly window panes
Eyelashes, milky with sleet, twinkle with delight

Rotating seasons
Golden, sunshine, autumn, snow
Nature's jungle gym

Lindsay Sheehan, Grade 6
Middlebrook School, CT

River

Watching the rain drip into the flowing peaceful river
Just watching the river carry away the rain like it's in charge
Water separating when rocks are in its way
The river growing when it's raining
The birds flying around like leaves in the wind
I'm inside bored waiting for the rain to stop

Ashlea Greenlaw, Grade 5
Bethlehem Elementary School, NH

The Pet Store

I went to the pet store to get a dog, either that or a hog.
But they said they've just sold their last hog, so I'll get a dog.
The dogs were yapping and lapping, lapping their water,
And with their thick fur, they can't get any hotter.
So, I'll settle for a cat, purring and stuff like that,
Lots of them are pretty fat and most don't like to be pat.
Maybe I'll get a bird; they're talkative, that's what I've heard.
When my mom said a bird is absurd,
I thought I'd take her word and not get a bird.
So I'll get a turtle and name it Myrtle.
When I remembered it lives a long while it made me smile;
I picked up the reptile and it immediately felt vile.
No, not a turtle, maybe a frog, for which I'll get a log.
They let me hold the frog, but it jumped out onto the log.
No more frog; I'll get a fish,
And no, I won't eat it for a fancy dish.
I wish for a fish, I'll buy it a tank,
And stuff so it won't be blank;
And food for when it's in the mood.
A fish, my very own fish Dude! YAY!

Karen Weinstock, Grade 5
Zervas Elementary School, MA

On the Way

A way of a path, a pathway.
A pathway can bring you anywhere if you really think about it.
When you go down a dark, shady path, you can probably
guess you are on the wrong path.
A man you never had met wearing all black will follow you.
You are on the wrong path.
The man tried to control your every move until suddenly —
a bright path grabs your attention!
You take the path, you look into a small puddle and see
Your reflection.
You will see next to you a girl.
She is younger than you,
and less experienced.
You walk the path and the girl runs ahead of you,
And you are left behind.
Suddenly you spot a path and take it.
This is the path of success.
Your journey can continue…or not…
But are you happy?

Cara Gannon, Grade 4
North Star Elementary School, DE

Soccer

S o much running
O utstanding passing
C an't live without it
C an't explain emotion when you score
E xtremely fun
R eally the best sport

Kristin Hartman, Grade 6
St Joseph School-Fullerton, MD

Summer to Winter

Summer
Awesome, fast
Swimming, relaxing, jumping
Pool, hot, frozen, cold
Shivering, shaking, freezing
Still, silent
Winter

Douglas Nguyen, Grade 5
Wakefield Forest Elementary School, VA

Who Is My Teacher?

Who is my teacher?
    Someone I learn from
    Makes class work fun
    Tests my knowledge
    She wins "teacher name that tune"
    Keeps me on task
    Gives us fun homework
    Wants me to pass
    Cares about me
    Sometimes gets mad
    Makes me want to learn
That is my teacher!

Devin McKenna, Grade 6
Charlton Middle School, MA

Mona Lisa

Something is missing
in her life.
She is looking,
But not looking.
She is happy,
But not that happy.
Hot on one side,
Cold on the other.
Maybe wearing her wedding ring,
Maybe not.
Happy and warm,
Sad and cold.
Fuzzy but clear,
Empty but full.
Soft music in the distance.
Something is missing
in her life.

Emily Jarka, Grade 6
Canton Intermediate School, CT

Lightning

Lightning comes with a flash of death like a cobra about to strike.
It kills all, it hunts all and no one has time to fight.
It creeps up slowly and then it gets faster until you don't know who you are.
It's been in your nightmares for years until now when it made you see your first star.
It leaves in fast slithers as if it never came.
And no one ever knows who there is to blame.

Juliana Sansonetti, Grade 6
St Rose School, CT

I Am

I am a lacrosse player and a mountain biker.
I wonder if there are really aliens.
I hear the wind blowing in the giant trees that are swaying.
I see the ocean waves crashing into the shore during the summer.
I want to become a professional lacrosse player.
I am a lacrosse player and a mountain biker.

I pretend to be a famous lacrosse player.
I feel the wave drowning me when I fall off the surfboard.
I touch the moon sand as I get out of the rocket ship.
I worry that I will crash in a plane.
I cry when I think about my dog.
I pretend I am a famous lacrosse player.

I understand that 5/4 people have trouble with fractions.
I say that there should be peace on Earth.
I dream that I will get a dirt bike for my birthday.
I try really hard in school.
I hope that there will be world peace.
I understand that 5/4 people have trouble with fractions.

Elliot Gordon, Grade 6
Amherst Middle School, NH

My Life

I am from a private place,
With a cluttered desk and a comfy bed.
With a big happy white dog, who sits upon my lap.
I am from a bedroom, a calm place where I nap.
I am from a calm place.
From dusk to dawn.
I rest each night and at morning I rise to the smell of molasses,
And freshly mown grass as noon slowly passes.
I am from Roxbury, on a peaceful street in town.
I am from a river of wine to go with good foods such as pasta or pizza.
Romantic music elegant dancing, shiny hair flowing in the light breeze
I am from Italy, a place of elegant life with romance and delicious cuisine.
I will be at Boston College, to find the voice and talent I have.
One day little children playing in the hall,
With a fluffy friend or two, and elaborate home and yard,
A calm neighborhood.
I will see Europe with family and friends.
I will have a peaceful life filled with joy and laughter.
I will live in a state with much history.
My life will be filled with happiness.

Sydney Smith, Grade 6
St Brendan Elementary School, MA

The Manatee

The manatee stuffs his tummy with seaweed
And he enjoys snapping on his feed
He has a veggie diet
But his weight does not reflect it
He is total fatness indeed

"You see," says the manatee
"I am too busy for having tea"
It sits and gobbles
While his bottom topples
You will find him sleeping in the sea

Paloma Bohanan, Grade 5
Southbrook Academy, MA

Falling into Winter

Leaves are falling, orange and red.
You can't help but hop out of bed.
Winter coats and mittens too;
It's like fall came right on cue.

Leaves are falling yellow and brown.
The grass is wearing a colorful gown.
Winter scarves and warm hats too;
Winter is coming. I'm ready! Are you?

Winter is coming around the corner.
No leaves, some frost, the chill sets in.
Wind is calling;
Snow is falling.
Fireplaces and hot cocoa, you'll always win.

A walk in the park;
The wind in your hair;
You can't possibly have one little care.
The snow is out.
The children shout.
Winter has come so soon!

Antonia Ciunci, Grade 6
St Rocco School, RI

In the Meadow

Surrounded by flowers — I am.
I see a ladybug on that one
And I wish that butterfly would come here
With its red and blue polka dots
And its purple stripes too!

This meadow is so beautiful
but now I have to go.
So goodbye butterfly, goodbye lady bug
I am off to my home,
And I will come back some day
but I will never leave you alone.

Briana DiNicola, Grade 4
The Pinecroft School, MA

Winter

Out the window I see the snow fall
Right before my eyes it covers it all
The roads are covered with snow and ice
Good reason to stay home where it's warm and nice

Kylie Rae Shope, Grade 6
Floyd T Binns Middle School, VA

Santa

Santa is a guy that makes lots of toys
On Christmas he gives them to good girls and boys
With his bag on his sleigh he's ready to take flight
Into the dark and cold starry night
He swoops down your chimney and under your trees
He spots some milk and Christmas cookies
He sits down the eat them on the couch, plump and fat
Then down to the ground falls his Santa Claus hat
The children hear him snoring and wake up with glee
They jump out of bed and race to their tree
But when they get there Santa is gone
They frown with heads down and let out an "Aww!!"
Then suddenly they hear a reindeer bell
They looked up at Santa when he let out a yell
He yelled "Merry Christmas!" that fateful December
And left his hat there so they could remember.

Amari Brown, Grade 5
Litwin Elementary School, MA

The Truth

You walk closer,
and closer,
    and closer.
My heart beats faster,
and faster,
    and faster.
Then you stop
and whisper in my ear
    three words I thought
Would never pass from you to me.
My heart skips a beat.
I fill with joy and love.
Right before I pass those words back to you,
    I blink
    and realize,
        it was only a dream,
that was too good to be true.

Virginia Villa, Grade 6
Canton Intermediate School, CT

The Creepy Halloween

Witches give *creeps*
We hear all the *weeps*
    Down goes the *sun*
Now begins the *fun*
    The creepy Halloween makes us *run*!!

Joseph Beaudoin, Grade 5
Good Shepherd Catholic School, RI

Wind

Wind blows
through fields of wheat
from dawn to dusk
wind blows
fast, slow, high, and low
all the way
through the lush fields

Lexi Tilton, Grade 4
Memorial School, NH

Utah

Come with me to Utah
with the white snow
the smell of hot coffee and cocoa
Come with me to Utah
we will run down the stairs
feeling the carpet on our bare
feet
We will go swimming in the
heated pool
we will roll in the snow
then jump in
we will feel the stinging
on our bodies
Then…we will go
skiing

Genevieve Ogden, Grade 5
Zervas Elementary School, MA

Precipitation

Tiny white crystals
Drop down to Earth
And make blankets of white
A beautiful sight

Tiny clear droplets
Flow down to Earth
Make huge dirty pools
With big fish schools

Big dents in cars
Loud noises on roofs
Made of rain that turns to ice
Sounds loud and not nice

Katharine Cusack, Grade 4
Memorial School, NH

My Parents

They have the strength to hold on to me.
They will take care of me with love
With all the love they have inside.
I love them and they love me
We will always be a happy family.

Kelsy Smith, Grade 6
Graham Middle School, VA

Going Down

Walking up and down the streets
Looking for some delicious eats
Looking, looking, hearing screams
Not everything is what it seems

Smoke is blowing in the air
Smoke is blowing everywhere
Looking, looking, hearing screams
Not everything is what it seems

Crashing, crashing, looking up
Crashing, crashing, I don't know what
Looking, looking, hearing screams
Windows shattering, what does it mean?

Aero planes going down
Screaming down through the town
People stepping into heaven
People, now it's 9/11

Hours and hours have passed by
Only birds are in the sky
People stepping into heaven
People, now it's 9/11

Nicholas McGrath, Grade 5
Salem Elementary School, VA

Winter

Everyone playing.
It will be snowing outside.
Today will be fun.

Vincent Protani, Grade 6
St Joseph School-Fullerton, MD

Determination

If you are determined
Then the whole universe is in
Your hands,
Open to all
Possibilities
And Impossibilities
That have yet to become
Possibilities.

Alyssa Resar, Grade 5
McDonogh School, MD

Mother Nature's Season

Birds returning from the South
Clear nights with planets glowing
When will the buds open up life?
Warm fires
Glistening winds
I know
It's spring

Josh Minor, Grade 4
John J Flynn Elementary School, VT

Dragons

Dragons, dragons, dragons
Scary dragons
Thorny dragons
Big, scaly, fat dragons
Small, skinny, smoking dragons
Those are just a few.
Chinese dragons
Japanese dragons
Fiery, fast, bad dragons
Swedish dragons too!
Healthy dragons
Old dragons
And don't forget young dragons!
Last of all
Best of all
I like my dragons!

David Moniz, Grade 6
Juliet W Long School, CT

I Have*

I have found
the Christmas Presents
that were in the attic.

which you
were probably saving
'til December 25th.

Forgive me
I was so anxious
I couldn't help myself.

Toriyonnah Lundy, Grade 5
Clover Street School, CT
*Inspired by William Carlos Williams

Hunter

Can't be apart
licking my face
like there's no tomorrow.
So dry, yet screaming red
playing some fetch,
with the fuzzy green ball.
Blue eyes
glowing at night
so very hyper
yet so very calm.

Nicholas Kieran, Grade 5
Zervas Elementary School, MA

Fall Fun

Leaves falling from trees
The sun is warming the air
Breeze blowing water

Thomas Courtney, Grade 5
Pollard Elementary School, NH

I Am

I am happy and exciting
I wonder if I'll get the new phone for Christmas
I hear my grandfather
I see his face
I want to be famous
I am happy and exciting

I pretend I'm rich
I feel wild
I touch the stars
I worry if I'll live long
I cry when I'm sad
I am happy and exciting

I understand people die
I say God watches over me
I dream to be with him in the clouds
I try to be strong
I hope I will grow to be a better person
I am happy and exciting

Essence Murray, Grade 5
Clover Street School, CT

Come Sail Away

Come sail away with me
We'll have fun
There will even be a beautiful sun
Crumb cake sand rubbing through your feet
Later today you'll want to sleep
Crystal blue sea with wrinkles creased between
As it seems like a dream
As palm trees blow in the air like they want to dance with me
Oh no, look there's a bumblebee
This place is so great
Don't run…
When the bumblebee stings you it's fun, fun, fun
So, come on…
Come sail away with me
I promise, it will be fun
Come on let's soak up the sun!!!

Max Derderian, Grade 4
Cranston-Johnston Catholic Regional School, RI

The Flag

This is what I feel like hanging by the ceiling.
Sometimes I feel lonely, like when your parents leave you alone.
I was adopted at the store when I was bought.
I feel proud about all the songs that people sing.
When they sing, I feel famous for my stars.
I think that I am freedom and independence.
I like being hung by the pole.
I hear the pledge and I feel mighty.
I feel proud for all of my 50 stars.
When everyone looks at me, I feel special.

Sabrina Diaz, Grade 5
Old Saybrook Middle School, CT

Alyssa

A lways wanted to be an actress.
L oves dogs and monkeys.
Y elling at my brother.
S pending time with my friends.
S pends time at school.
A lways loving, sweet and kind.

Alyssa Horsley, Grade 4
Dr Charles E Murphy Elementary School, CT

Turkey

T urkey is good to eat
U sually you eat it at Thanksgiving
R ejoice the huge turkey
K indness is brought at dinner by the turkey
E veryone loves it
Y ou eat it in a gobble

Greg Rasnick, Grade 6
Graham Middle School, VA

The Amazing Koala

T hey have two thumbs on each hand
H e or she is a climber
E xcellent climber and swinger

A n amazing animal
M any have lost their homes
A lmost endangered
Z oom! There it goes up a tree
I t is like it has spikes on its head
N ever eats meat
G oing up!

K oalas eat eucalyptus only
O cean isn't its home
A koala is a marsupial
L ike a climbing machine
A kangaroo is its relative

David Fowler, Grade 6
Lyman Moore Middle School, ME

The World Is Changing

The World is changing
   Right before our eyes
      Our climates are rearranging
         But some people have told lies
      They lie about pollution
   And they say they didn't do it
We need a huge solution
   Not another hypocrite
      So it is time we take a stance
         Help the world somehow
            This may be our one last chance
         Let's start it here and *NOW*

Lynn L. Chlumecky, Grade 6
Hinesburg Community School, VT

Memories

A memory is when
Someone in your family dies
But in your heart they are still alive
When you love them to death,
Remember they are just taking a rest
Paige E. Reynolds, Grade 5
Keene Elementary School, DE

The Big Tree

I love the blue sky
In my yard there's a big tree
Red yellow orange
Poeme Jimenez, Grade 5
Pollard Elementary School, NH

Autumn

Howling winds and autumn breezes
Crackling sounds of open fires
The sweet smell of homemade pie
Costumes on kids everywhere
Time for leaves changing colors
The air is cool
The skies are blue
Autumn is here.
Christopher Durost, Grade 4
Alma E Pagels Elementary School, CT

Fall

Red leaves everywhere
Tinted berries on the tree
Pretty fall is here
Caroline Ray, Grade 4
St Brigid School, ME

Woodchuck

Chuck, chuck, chuck, chuck,
What's that chucking sound?
Look, it's a woodchuck!
What has he found?
He's found a tree,
and he's chucking away!
Gosh, to chuck *that* tree,
will it take him all day?
No, look, he chucked the wood
all the way through!
A woodchuck chucked some wood!
Yay for you!
Tessa Keyes, Grade 4
Home School, NH

Winter

Snowmen all around
Snowballs flying through the air
Snowflakes falling down
Jacob Eisner, Grade 6
Wakefield Forest Elementary School, VA

Things to Do:

I have plenty of things to do!
First I'm going to soak up the sun,
go to the beach, or get my nails done.
Get a sports car soon,
get some clothes, and maybe go on a space trip to the moon!
I'm going to buy a carnival and have some fun,
buy some shoes, or buy a mansion!
Sometimes a person like me gets in trouble. My life can get hard,
especially when you have a mother in your ear yelling: "Stop using my credit card!"
Emily Blacker, Grade 5
Pasadena Elementary School, MD

Mother Nature

The fresh air smells crisp and clean.
Outside felt like winter, my legs felt like ice.
As I looked up I only saw the crystal blue sky.
As I walked forward I could feel the rough, grass beneath my feet.
Every time I turn around, I see a tree or a prickly bush.
I can always hear crunching beneath my feet
I see the soccer field and the kickball field
Empty as a desert
If I listen closely I can hear the
Whispering of the kids
If I was close enough
I could see the middle school
I can also see
A half faded moon

Pete Obey, Grade 6
Juliet W Long School, CT

Raccoons

Raccoon, Raccoon,
Why do you hunt under the moon?
No one is nice to you, no one thinks you are nice too

Why do you wear that mask?
Does it hide you when you are doing your task?
You're more around during the night is it that you don't like the light?

You can fit in trash cans
Is that because you have tiny hands?
Why do you like to play in the trash? Do you like all the mash?

Raccoons like to eat anything
Especially when it is spring
You have such a wacky mind with everything you may find

You were created as an animal that is very wild
You don't act very mild
Where did you get all your energy? You're busy as a bee

Raccoon, Raccoon
Why do you hunt under the moon?
No one is nice to you, no one thinks you are nice too
Erin Beaudry, Grade 5
Hinesburg Community School, VT

True Friends

No matter how far away,
True friends will always stay.
Age never matters,
Because we'll always have fun and play.
All our lives we've been apart.
But you've always been close to my heart.
Pauline and K.C. this is for you,
You are two friends that will always remain true.

Ali Dunne, Grade 6
Irving School, CT

Tomorrow's Dream

I am strong and brave
I wonder if I'll see tomorrow
I hear sounds telling me to do right
I see Jesus or the devil
I want to see many things that I could make right
I want to be famous and make a difference in the world
I am strong and brave

I pretend I am tough
I feel good and strong, but sometimes weak as a stick
I touch dreams and bring them close
I worry about my family
I cry when I'm not heard
I am strong and brave

I understand I'm not rich
I say I am okay and I really am
I dream of being in heaven
I try to be the best Christian
I hope for a better day
I am strong and brave

Lucinda Thomas, Grade 5
Clover Street School, CT

I Am a Kid Who Likes the Nature

I am a kid who likes the nature.
I wonder about the animals.
I hear the sound of people talking
I hear the sound of cars rumbling.
I see the birds fly up so high.
I want to reach them up high in the sky.
I pretend to be a flying bird.
I feel the wind go side to side as
I run through the breezing skies.
I touch the ground under my feet.
I worry if I'll trip on a stick and fall.
I understand I am very fast.
I say hello to the people that pass.
I dream to fly with the birds.
I try to run with the deer.
I hope I can catch up and run with them some day.

Isaiah J. Baker, Grade 5
Blackrock School, RI

Piñata

I love when everyone gathers around me.
I am thinking,
"When is anyone going to break me open?"
Boom!!!! I broke open.
Everyone likes when all my candy falls out!

Sophia D'Ambrosio, Grade 5
Old Saybrook Middle School, CT

Friends

A friend is someone who cares for you,
They're respectful, trustworthy, and truthful too.

But maybe you forget to do what is right,
And you get into a hurtful fight.

When you realize you've done wrong,
Say I am sorry and then get along.

You can have lots of fun together,
In all the different kinds of weather.

Having friends that last forever,
Is to me a great endeavor.

My friends are special to me in different kinds of ways,
They make me happy each and every day.

Kailyn Kreider, Grade 5
Linville-Edom Elementary School, VA

Nature

Oh! I love nature. I feel wonderful,
You have fresh air;
Mountains, trees, how lovely!
A brook near where you can splash!

An apple tree nearby,
Those apples are sweet and delicious,
Sun is shining and the brook is catching the light.
Flowers are blooming out!

When you look down, you can see the grass is green,
My hair swirls around and shines like gold,
I love nature; it's so beautiful!
It is wonderful, too!

Marsha Pozhilenko, Grade 5
Linville-Edom Elementary School, VA

Golden Twinkle

I am like a batch of twinkling eyes,
Glitter is me,
As I bathe the moon with my sparkle cloak.
What am I?

A star.

Shannon Au, Grade 5
Four Seasons Elementary School, MD

Bugs
Butterfly
Graceful, frolicsome
Flying, changing, blending in
Insect, colors, claws, arachnid
Sting, crawl, pinch
Poisonous, creepy
Scorpion
Jack Brubaker, Grade 6
St Rose School, CT

Fall
F reezing weather
A pple pies baking
L eaves falling
L eaves blowing
Nicole Parks, Grade 6
Juliet W Long School, CT

Baseball in September
As Bob goes up at bat,
the crowd is on their feet.
Bob is their worst hitter.
He hasn't hit a ball all season.
The pitcher winds up and fires!
It's across the plate.
Bob swings and hits it!
The crowd goes wild.
It goes to dead left centerfield.
It's over the fence.
It's a home run!
As he rounds the bases,
the crowd is going wild.
When he gets to home plate
the team crowds him and they cheer!
Michael Thompson, Grade 5
Perrywood Elementary School, MD

Penguins, Penguins, Penguins
Neat penguins
Dirty penguins
Happy, tall, helpful penguins
Fat, angry, short penguins
Those are just a few.
Slippery penguins
Stocky penguins
Tough, snappy, medium penguins
Thin, peppy, hungry penguins
Sloppy penguins too!
Tiny penguins
Big penguins
And don't forget famous penguins.
Last of all
Best of all
I like cuddly penguins!
Stephanie Correia, Grade 6
Juliet W Long School, CT

Snowfall
Snow
Drops in flakes
Covers the ground
Freezes your toes
It drops on the roof
Falls from clouds
It covers your hair
Again
Again
and Again
Jake Abell, Grade 4
Ballenger Creek Elementary School, MD

Puppies
They have big brown eyes,
And fluffy little tails.

They are faithful and cute,
And will brighten any day.

They love to play,
Any time any day.

In any breed or color,
They will bring you joy.
Kathryn Tighe, Grade 6
St John Regional Catholic School, MD

Falling Days
Watching leaves turn
To warm colors
Glisten of the sun
When are the leaves
Going to fall?
Rustling of the
Wind trees swaying
Side to side
Leaves fall
Crunch! crunch!
Crunch!
Moriah Lasker, Grade 5
John J Flynn Elementary School, VT

A Time to Give Thanks
The holiday is near
And so out of fear
Our turkey will run
When he sees the hunter's gun!

So let's wait and see
What our dinner will be
We'll give much thanks and praise
Whether turkey or take-out from "Kay's."
Edward Carroll, Grade 5
Good Shepherd Catholic School, RI

Why?
You see me,
I don't see you.
You don't know,
But I do.
I feel alive,
But you don't.
I hear you,
You don't hear me.
I wonder why?
Mimi Hull, Grade 5
Boonsboro Elementary School, MD

The Brown Dirt
The brown dirt layed on the ground,
It was still it made no sound,
The little ones walked barefoot over it,
And it hurt their feet not one bit.
The dirt.
Alliyah Morton, Grade 6
Floyd T Binns Middle School, VA

The Lonely Days of Winter
The wind sways
On cold winter days
When all that is out there
Is a fresh smooth blanket of snow,
Everything is frozen
And covered in snow
But still the wind blows
As the river flows.
Wesley Koshoffer, Grade 6
Juliet W Long School, CT

Bright Moon
The moon shines bright at night.
I see shadows from raccoons.
I can hear owls hooting.
Is the moon always so bright?
Time lingers every night.
I feel strange.
The night is dark and sometimes spooky.
It's okay. God is watching everyone.
Mesiah Miles, Grade 5
John J Flynn Elementary School, VT

Baseball
B aseball
A ctive
S tolen Bases
E ating Peanuts
B ats
A rizona Diamondbacks
L os Angeles Dodgers
L os Angeles Angels
Matthew Linz, Grade 5
St Joseph School-Fullerton, MD

Halloween

H aving cool costumes
A utumn fun
L ots of candy
L ollipops, Twix, and Hershey chocolate
O ctober 31st
W onka bars, Jolly Ranchers, and Swedish Fish
E vil vampires in the night sky
E xciting parties and haunted mansions
N ight that will scare your socks off.

Christian Mananghaya, Grade 5
St Joseph School-Fullerton, MD

The Kid That Never Stops Running

He swiftly springs throughout the house,
Dodging objects along the way
He is always in his basement doing something,
While the rest of the house is doing nothing

His room is very large,
Covered in dirty clothes and bouncy balls
He plays soccer year round
Always working hard and winning,
Although he can be friendly

In school he is quiet and focused,
Always thinking about his work
With his friends he is comical and energetic,
Mostly talking and ecstatic

He is somewhat short,
A little thin and skinny
His eye is always on the prize
He is demanding and tenacious in everything he pursues,
He will not stop until he gets what he wants

This kid's name is Mac
He is quite intelligent in fact

Mac Ross, Grade 6
Middlebrook School, CT

On the Ice

Whoosh, whoosh, whoosh.
I skate on my edge looking down onto the ice
just skating, skating, skating
Just skating full of sorrow, sadness, hatred, fear
just falling, falling, falling, boom.
Everyone sees me lying there on the ice and
gently drifting off into a distant land and
floating in air just floating in memories…
Wee ooh, wee ooh, wee ooh. I wake up in a
hospital being rushed to the ER.
On crutches I walk from here on out. No more
skating, no more coaching, no more walking, no
more hurting.

Enya Hughes, Grade 6
Main Street Middle School, VT

The Beach!

The beach is a lot of fun
You can play and relax in the sun.
I love playing in the sand
On the beach at night there might be a band.

You can also take a walk on the beach at night
With not a lot of seagulls in sight.
That's why I love the beach a lot
Everyone should go to the beach really you ought.

Lizzie Young, Grade 5
Pasadena Elementary School, MD

Snowflakes Everywhere

The snowflakes flutter down from the sky
They prance and they dance as they fly
They make a blanket of sparkling white
The snow seems so very very bright
I wish I could be out in the snow
Where all the snowflakes blow, blow, blow
Each snowflake is full of amazing things
Sometimes snowflakes make a soft ring
They always have a small jingle bell
And each is done very well
By the wonderful magical snow maker in the sky
And when winter is over the snow end
But then I know when winter comes again
The snow will be back and make a joyful snow again
And it will start all over again!

Andrew Alls, Grade 4
North Star Elementary School, DE

Flying

When I was born, I was very frail.
I could not fly. I could not eat.
I was the last one to fly.
My mother knew I was special.

When everyone flew away, to live on their own,
she helped me to know exactly how to start flying,
so I could join my brothers and sisters.

At first, I kept falling from the sky
into the pile of leaves mom had stacked in the middle of a field.

Finally, I DID IT!
I FLEW!
Mom was so proud of me, that I had actually DONE IT!

After saying "Goodbye," I lifted into the sky,
unfolded my wings and surrendered into the light,
watching my shadow follow me as I raced ahead,
ready to start
my new life!

Ashley Hadley, Grade 6
Kenmore Middle School, VA

Deeper Meanings

Love is like a bird.
Flies high, but does it get there?
We know when faith comes.
Megan Bollinger, Grade 5
St Joseph School-Fullerton, MD

Teachers

Teachers, teachers everywhere.
So kind, so smart, they always care.
They teach us things that we don't know,
And hopefully our writing will flow!
Madisyn Silva, Grade 4
Long Meadow Elementary School, CT

Christmas Wonderland

A Christmas wonderland is not just snow
It's the chilly wind
It's the thin cold air
It's the blissful sky
The ice over the lake
It's the footprints in the snow
Christmas Wonderland
Chris Williams, Grade 5
Pollard Elementary School, NH

Trees in the Breeze

Fruit falling down trees.
Fresh autumn settling leaves.
Breezy and cold ponds.
Jordan Oligny, Grade 5
Pollard Elementary School, NH

Snow

Snow to me is always near
It looks to me like a jeweled tear
It's so pretty and fine
It acts like a human so gentle and kind.

I hear it as it falls
I hear the echo in it's calls
It looks so clear
It is something I will never fear.

It's as white as a bunny
When it's out it's always sunny
When it glistens in the sky
You know it's from up high.
Mattie Soghikian, Grade 4
Memorial School, NH

Harvest

Pumpkins in a row
are bright orange and yellow
they look so happy
Lindsey Biron, Grade 4
Brookside Elementary School, MA

Looking in the Past

Looking into the past I can remember when I was just two years old.
I was waiting for my baby brother Steven to be born for he was the one
I was waiting to hold.
Five months later he came into the world so fast,
I was so happy that I knew it would be a blast.
More news a year later what can it be,
Mom and Dad said "two munchkins plus one equals three."
Oh Boy! Oh Boy! A new baby sister Mackenzie in November we will meet,
Now our family will be complete.
And there we were in two thousand one,
An unforgettable Christmas together was so much fun.
Looking in the past I now see,
How we all came about, starting with me.

Chastain Beardsley, Grade 5
Mary P Hinsdale Elementary School, CT

My Life

I am from a place with a lot of toys.
I have two cozy striped couches and a soft red rug.
I love to play fun games on my nice computer.
I am from a big cozy green house.

I am from a place with kids playing on the street.
I have a big pool in my backyard to swim in during the summer.
My street has a lot of birds, dogs, and other animals on it.
My street is a long fun street to live on.

I am from a place where the village has a lot of businesses and people.
A place where during Christmas we have a tree lighting in the village.
The village has good restaurants to eat at.
It also has a lot of good people to meet.

I am from Ireland.
Ireland is a place with many shades of green grass growing on the mountain sides.
It is a place with lambs crossing the roads.
Ireland is a place with beautiful castles.

In the future I would like to be a doctor.
I want a dog and a bird in the future.
I would like a nice home with lots of friends in the future.
Mary Coughlin, Grade 5
St Brendan Elementary School, MA

I Am a Book

I am never alone.
People read me over and over again.
All the characters always want to jump out at me.
If someone in my book gets in trouble or is mischievous, I get in trouble.
I get frustrated when people put stickers on me.
When people laugh, it always blows out my eardrum.
I have been everywhere you can think of.
It's so hard holding my characters in when people read me.
My biggest fear is sharp things, writing tools, but most of all, dogs.
Hope Schreier, Grade 5
Old Saybrook Middle School, CT

My Favorite Season

My favorite season is fall.
It's the most colorful season of all

The leaves are yellow orange and red
You can imagine it in your head

In the morning the frost covers the ground
When I step on the frost, it makes a weird sound

Sometimes it's warm, sometimes it's cold
For me fall never gets old

Austin Siebenhaar, Grade 6
Graham Middle School, VA

My Life as a Worker Bee

I'm a big bewildering bee,
I've got compound eyes so I can see.

My stinger is scary although it is small,
And it can really hurt, just ask that boy named Paul!

I live in a small, sticky hive,
Where many others live and strive to survive

My stinger also defends the hive,
So other bees can hatch and come alive.

I also have two other things,
An antenna and two wide wings.

I like to explore anywhere at all,
Be careful I could even be in the mall!

I've finished telling you about me,
I hope you've liked my story!

Jessica Twardus, Grade 6
Immaculate Heart of Mary School, DE

Sports

I like sports.
Football and basketball
They are fun
There is also racquetball

I like sports
Tackling and whacking
Shooting, running, and passing
Throwing and sacking

I like sports
Helmets and touchdowns
Sweating and energy
A lot of first downs

Nick Meding, Grade 5
C Hunter Ritchie Elementary School, VA

An Amazing, Alphabetic Alliteration

A lex's **A** mazing
B rother, **B** en
C ould **C** ount
D ata and **D** etails
E very **E** vening.

F or **F** ive **G** reat, **G** lorious
H ours, **H** e'd
I dentify **I** tems to **J** uxtapose **J** ust to
K eep "**K** ounting."

L ads **L** earn early that
M ost **M** oms **N** ever **N** eed
O ur **O** verseeing because
P arents **P** erform **Q** uite **Q** uietly,
and **R** ather **R** eliably.

S o **S** urely, **T** he **T** allying brother, Ben,
U ndoubtedly **U** nderstands the
V ery **V** aluable and **W** ell-known **W** isdom:

"**Y** eah, **Y** ou can count on Mom!"

Brian Cooper, Grade 5
Pemberton Elementary School, VA

Halloween

It was so spooky this night.
Everyone was acting weird.
They screamed and fainted when I walked by.
Then one kid survived and said nice mask.
The only problem was I wasn't wearing one.

Jasper Lee, Grade 5
North Star Elementary School, DE

Ripples in a Pond

Ripples in a pond are wonderful things.
Like little waves in an ocean,
But just one little thing.

Circles in the water, about an inch apart.
But when it reaches the sand,
We are left apart.

But when a person throws a rock, they appear!

Sometimes they collide,
When the rain flies down from the sky,
They make little ripples everywhere,
Then here's the sigh.
After circles in the water about an inch apart,
Collide they say "Goodbye."

And when winter comes, they are covered by ice.
Until spring we don't see them.

Christopher A. Myers, Grade 5
St Joseph's Catholic School, MD

Your Eyes Will Deceive You

This castle is no ordinary one.
It sucks out all imaginable fun.
It may look pretty out in that shining sun,
but it's really a haven for criminals on the run.
It's a perfect plot, it looks so innocent with those ruby red vines.
All of the criminals come out when the clock chimes.
It used to be used for good out in those rolling plains,
but oh how it's used for evil, here they come down the lanes.
It's made of grey stone and beautiful craftsmanship.
In those dark corridors, you'll hear a big rip!
You will see something as bright as the sun that will catch your eye and you'll be tempted.
It will allure you into a wardrobe by a divine red ruby, to retrieve it everyone has attempted.
There have been many tragedies inside and about.
Many people have come in and never come out.
I'm telling the truth, don't let your bright, sharp eyes deceive you.
With the green grass and blue skies, your eyes will trick you, is what they'll do.
I'm giving you a tip, because I'm one of those people,
who has never come out, and is stuck in a steeple.

Shannon Duffy, Grade 5
Infant Jesus School, NH

Chesapeake Bay

I'm sitting.
In the tidewaters on a dock on Chesapeake Bay. Under my feet there are little cat fish playing tag. I can hear the big fat frogs croaking off in the woods next to the dock. The shining sun is blazing down at me. The coolness of the sparkling bay tickles the tips of my feet. A mile behind me is my uncle cooking hotdogs and hamburgers. As I walk back to my house I feel the sun on my back saying goodbye.

Grace Douthit, Grade 4
Jamestown Elementary School, VA

Self Portrait

A social girl surrounded by a bunch of friends
sitting on the ground as happy as could be
When she gets home, you can tell love is in the air
'cause the smell of warm cookies while Mom bakes,
Dad is practicing archery in the backyard

"I love my daughter to death" Mom says,
"Though sometimes I get annoyed when she runs around the house blabbering at the speed of light"
Her dad talks about her all the time "She is always so happy,
but every Monday when I leave for guard, her eyes fill with tears," he tells his closet friends

"My sister always annoys me," I hear him say aloud
"When I'm not around she hides my stuff and when I'm playing my game on the couch, she rambles on and on"
Coach Merolla tells her all the time she's perfect for the squad,
"You're outgoing and enthusiasm is what every cheerleader needs," she says right before a game

"What a great friend she is. She's always got our back,
her kind and friendly personality makes her lots of fun," her closest friends explain
She and her dogs have a special sense, she knows she's their favorite
"Her personality is great and she has much time for fun with us"

Now you can see the many sides of me
The talkative, outgoing girl with an awesome family and many good friends.

Becca Reeves, Grade 6
Middlebrook School, CT

Ice Cream (Banana Split)

Yummy, soft, mushy, banana on the sides,
Chocolate ice cream as dark as a chocolate chip,

Sticky, gooey, smooth hot fudge,
Strawberry ice cream with real strawberries in it

On top of the strawberry ice cream is crunchy, munchy
walnuts and vanilla ice cream white as snow,

With piled whip cream as soft as a kitten's fur
And a big ruby red cherry on top.

Andrea Pincus, Grade 5
Long Meadow Elementary School, CT

Stars and Stripes

Red, white, and blue are
Fifty stars and thirteen stripes
Waving with the wind.

Shea Rowell, Grade 5
C Hunter Ritchie Elementary School, VA

Love and Hate

Hate is like someone leaving you behind
In a dark forest with no one to be with,

Leaving you with no light to guide you
To a place where you can be loved.

Love is like floating in midair
On a cloud in the sky,

Surrounded in happiness
And friends.

Hate is like someone slapping you across the face
You feel the burning pain outside,
But your broken heart kills even more.

Love is like someone giving you a kiss
Opening the door to your heart.

Hate is like dying, and even more painful.
Love is like heaven.

Gabby DiMaio, Grade 6
St Paul School, CT

Me, Myself, and I

My hair is like waves in a cold blue ocean.
My eyes are stars twinkling at night.
My heart is full of excitement like when you wake up
on Christmas morning opening presents.
My life is chaotic like when you're getting ready for
school on Monday morning.
I live in a mall and eat all the clothes I don't like.

Lexi Albrecht, Grade 6
Tolland Middle School, CT

My Small Black Kitty

I have a small black kitty
His coat is shiny and he's very pretty
He loves to pounce and bounce and play
He thinks he's a hunter searching for prey

One day he'll be bigger and stronger and faster
Chasing small mice as if he were their master
For now he's my little black kitty
He makes me laugh because he's ever so witty

Emily O'Hara, Grade 4
Litchfield Intermediate School, CT

Inspired by "Island of the Blue Dolphins"

Red is the color I fear
The sails of the men who struck my dear
The eyes of the devil fish swimming near
The blood on the deadly spear
Red is the color I fear

Black is the color I admire
The cave that helped me when I set fire
The beautiful otter skin attire
The magnificent necklace that I desire
Black is the color I admire

Blue is the color I love
The calm skies above
The soothing seas peaceful as a dove
The island that I am of
Blue is the color I love

Green is the color I see
The leaves on the old tree
The eyes of the dog beside me
The robes of not the white men unknown to thee
Green is the color I see

Miela Mayer, Grade 6
Foote School, CT

Fall

Yesterday fall came in,
That means the leaves will change,
Hunting seasons will begin.
The weather will change,
We may even get snow,
That means Halloween is coming,
People will buy pumpkins,
And people will carve pumpkins,
You will hear some people knocking on doors,
For some Halloween treats,
With some costumes on!
And some Halloween parties,
They are cool and fun!

Cody Shifflett, Grade 5
Linville-Edom Elementary School, VA

Winter Wonderland

Playing in the snow,
Building a snowman.
Having snowball fights,
Oh, it's such a blast.

Sharing gifts and presents,
Also Christmas cards.
Having fun at Christmas
Oh, what fun they are!!

Spending time as family,
Having so much fun.
Surely Christmas is time
To thank
God for what He's done.

Adam Muraca, Grade 6
St Mary of Czestochowa School, CT

Sun

The Sun praises the world below in joy.
It lights darkness
and makes me feel happy when I'm sad.
The Sun is my friend.

Jennah Schlude, Grade 4
Center School, CT

Walrus

I saw a fat walrus
looking down at me.
He looked really gloomy
because his cage wasn't roomy.
He wore a top hat and a pink shoe.
Surprisingly, his wife wore one too.
His name was Fred.
He sat on his bed.
Then Fred said,
"I know you're not allowed to,"
"But pretty, pretty, please,"
"Can you let me free?"
"There's a whole world outside to see."

Sarah Pappa, Grade 6
Beacon Middle School, DE

Snow

Snow comes in softly
Like that of a cat
It flies through
The sky
By twisting and
Leaping high
It plays in the sky
On fluffy white clouds
And then disappears
Without a sound

Nancy Michaud, Grade 6
St Rose School, CT

The Valuable Vacation

Come take a valuable vacation
So we can have fun, and run in the sun,
We'll play tag and say oh yeah
We'll be so warm we'll have to take our sweatshirts off.
We'll smell my mom's waffles and after that you'll taste them too.
So won't you sail away with me and take a valuable vacation
Because if you don't come it won't be valuable at all.

Christian Sorensen, Grade 4
Cranston-Johnston Catholic Regional School, RI

My Imaginary Garden

I have an imaginary garden
Each plant in my garden likes to do different things, like celebrate or sing
I add soil to my garden every day
My imaginary garden is growing

Molly Helmer, Grade 5
Wakefield Forest Elementary School, VA

Rainforest Rap

The rainforest is a special kind of place.
Where monkeys always swing and toucans always race!
The snakes eat the insects and there it always rains.
Don't worry the tigers aren't trained.
Don't worry the tigers aren't trained.
Don't worry!
But we want to save the rainforest and the animals that are there.
Because if you think about it the fagervik kids were willing to care.
Yeah! Yeah! Yeah!
They used their imagination to see what they could find
And to save the animals climbing on the vines.
You can help too all you need to do is pay a donation
To the founders of the Children's Rainforest Foundation.

Lexi Duncan, Grade 5
Pasadena Elementary School, MD

A Lost Friend*

There is an ominous feeling in the air
Where have you gone I ask myself
I need…you
I stop, as a quick air runs by my face
Then I got a flash back of all the memories I have had with you
I would die if I can't go back
I look around and I see that you were right there the whole time
Looking over my shoulder with a smile upon your face
Although no one can see him
Although he is gone you look at his clothes
But nobody knows why
Does it matter what they think of me
"No" someone whispers in my ear
A quick tear runs down my face
It is a feeling I can't replace
Although you can't see me my love is still there
I love you Elizabeth.

Haley Zigas, Grade 6
St Paul School, CT
*Dedicated to my grandmother and her husband Burt

Skiing

Skiing is so fun
It's very easy to have fun in the icy mountain sun
Going down the mountain
Turn after
Turn after turn
It takes a while to learn
Skiing is so fun
Beautiful scenery is all around you
Freshly groomed trails are so new
All the trails have different logos
Test yourself and try the moguls
There are diamonds, squares,
And circles, take your pick.
The ice is something very slick
Watch out for snowmobiles when they beep
Go over advanced jumps and leap!
It's so cold your lips will turn blue
The mountain at night will enchant you
Skiing is so fun.

Michael Papazian, Grade 5
Lincoln Central Elementary School, RI

Cape Cod

I go to Cape Cod every year,
I have lots of fun where the ocean is near.

The sun shines so bright,
When it sets it is such a pretty sight.

There are many things to do there,
One year at Cape Cod we went to a fair.

With aunts, uncles, and cousins too,
With seafood and beaches with much more to do.

Playing in the ocean with all my sisters,
But sometimes my water shoes give me blisters.

Crabbing and fishing are fun on the rocks,
Once I fell in the water with my socks.

Cape Cod is one of my favorite places to go,
As a family we live and grow.

Kaitlin Parenteau, Grade 6
St Patrick School, MA

Block Island

It is a beautiful place,
with long sandy beaches,
full of colorful shells yet to be discovered,
waves the height of trees pound against the rocky shore,
hills over look the crystal blue water,
Block Island.

Thomas McDonald, Grade 4
Dr Charles E Murphy Elementary School, CT

Halloween, Christmas or Thanksgiving?

I like Christmas
Mom and Dad don't
They like Thanksgiving

My birthday is on Christmas
So I get more gifts then everybody.

Sometimes my mom designs things.
Like Halloween costumes.
So I go trick or treating.
Then I eat my candy!

After that I open my gifts.
I got a Wii and a new doll.
Holidays are great!

Alexia Allen, Grade 4
Valley View Elementary School, MD

Flags

Flags
Red and blue
Swaying, hanging, and pledge
Look at the flag
Symbol

Darren Bindloss, Grade 4
Dr Charles E Murphy Elementary School, CT

My Cat Jester

My cat Jester sometimes he is funny
And sometimes he acts like a bunny.
His color is gray
And he likes the time of day.
He is soft
And sometimes he coughs
But I still love him
But he does not like it when the lights are dim.

Hilary Soto, Grade 4
Marsh Grammar School, MA

Dance, a Sport I Love

Dance is awesome, dance is fun
Dance is what I'll always love
Leaps, jumps, and turns
That is what you'll learn

Classes every week
Soon you'll feel like you've climbed a peak
Practicing anywhere, everywhere, every day
Till the end of May

Dance recitals at the end
Invite your family and friends
Dance, dance till you're done
Now they'll clap for everyone

Alysia Leung, Grade 6
Graham Middle School, VA

Briana

B riana is my name.
R espectful to others.
I like the snow.
A n angel.
N ice and smart.
A nimals are my favorite

Briana Castro, Grade 4
St Augustine Cathedral School, CT

The Sun

Sun
Hot, bright
Burning, shining, tanning
Burns my skin
Star

Katherine Sasu-Twumasi, Grade 6
Floyd T Binns Middle School, VA

The Fashion ABC's

A pply **B** eautiful **C** osmetics
D uney and Bourke **E** dith Head
F ashion Designers
G isele Bundchen **H** eidi Klum
I man **J** anice Dickinson
K imora Lee Simons
L ip gloss
M ary Janes
N ail polish
O rdon, Julie
P rada
Q uant, Mary
R ebecca Stamos
S andals
T wiggy
U ggs
V ersace
W ardrobe
X -it
Y anuk
Z engara

Gabrielle Camilli, Grade 6
Wakefield Forest Elementary School, VA

Unforgettable Memory

Silently waiting in the stand,
As the large buck approaches.
Wandering around
not knowing what is going on,
the large deer comes closer.
As I wait for the kill,
the deer wanders off.
I've missed my chance,
but I'm sure I will get another.

Todd Keen, Grade 6
Beacon Middle School, DE

Cats, Cats, Cats

Soft cats
Fluffy cats
Big, small, medium cats
Nice, gentle, mean cats
Those are just a few.
Smart cats
Dumb cats
Playful, lazy, hunter cats
Brown, white, black cats
Calico cats too!
Striped cats
House cats
And don't forget fat cats.
Last of all
Best of all
I like caring cats!

Lauren Susi, Grade 6
Juliet W Long School, CT

Best Friends

Kailee and I are such best friends
We will stay together 'til the end
We have lots of fun playing together,
Even in stormy weather
First we act like we are cooks
Then we read entertaining books
Kailee and I are best friends forever
And we will always stay together.

Vanessa Cuevas, Grade 4
JF Kennedy School, CT

Christmas Night

My mom tucks me under my covers,
And turns off the light.
I hear Christmas bells jingling,
Throughout the night.
There's a thump on the roof,
Whoever could it be?
I say to myself "Let's go and see."

I tip toe down the stairs,
And say "Who's there?"
I see red and white,
At the bottom of the stair.
I tap the stranger on the back.
He says "Who's that?"

"I'm Jimmy McDee!"
I ask him who is he?
He replies "I'm Santa Claus!
Ho, Ho, Here have this bear,
And off to bed you go."
He leaves without a sound and
Off into the distance he goes.

Emily McCarthy, Grade 6
St Joseph School-Fullerton, MD

I Have Eaten the Dodo Bird*

I have eaten
The dodo bird
That was
Lying on your lawn

And which
You were probably
Saving
For the apocalypse

Forgive me
It was furry
So meaty
And so feathery

Tom McAuliffe, Grade 5
Clover Street School, CT
*Inspired by William Carlos Williams

Chocolate

Chocolate
Very tasty
Many different kinds
It is very sweet
Yum

Daniel Shupe, Grade 5
McCleary Elementary School, VA

I Am Air

I am breezy, I keep moving
Windy
Atmosphere all around like me
Breathe you can catch up
Oxygen keeps me going
Everywhere I've been
Crisp
I am a tornado, wild
Temperature
Sky
I am air

Ryan Rossum, Grade 5
Wakefield Forest Elementary School, VA

Snow

On a snow day I like to play.
Home from school I like to stay.
I love the snow it is all white.
My sister wants to do a snowball fight.
Outside my house I always say.
I wish the world can have this day.
I love when snow covers the ground.
It's clean and beautiful all around.
As you see I love the snow.
In the sky I see a special glow.

Christina Decola, Grade 4
JF Kennedy School, CT

Winter

Watching the snowflakes.
Glittering so beautiful!
I want to go play!

Caroline Beard, Grade 5
C Hunter Ritchie Elementary School, VA

Being Around the Ocean

The ocean has bubbles of white,
Just seeing it is a wonderful sight!
I see all the grains of sand,
When I hold it, it falls from my hand.
See the whales blow water from their spouts,
It looks like they're mad and want to shout!
Breathing in the fresh, salty air,
Treating this calm place with all my care.
But now I see the sun set low,
It is telling me I have to go.

Lian Atlas, Grade 5
E Ethel Little Elementary School, MA

Midnight

Black and white cat.
Very fat. Eats too much.
Large, yellowish-green eyes with usually wide pupils.
Looks like a badger when he walks.
White paws and a star shape on his head.
Tail as black as a moonless night.
Puffy fur on his face.
Small head.
Two large, white splotches on his stomach.
Fast when he is after something.
High pitched meow.
Happy most of the time.
Only lets ME pet him.
Not too smart.
Attacks unusual objects.
Comes into the kitchen when he hears the icemaker start.
Knows how to knock.
Likes going in my bedroom.
Watches outside from the window.
Likes lying on the kitchen floor.

Truly, my cat.

Ken Lippo, Grade 5
Highland Park School, CT

Fall

Leaves flutter and float
Down
  Down
    Down
And fall to the hardening earth below
All day long they look at the pale blue sky wishing
That they could once again fly

Anna Lee Riccio, Grade 5
Osborn Hill Elementary School, CT

Sunset

At night I take a walk,
I stop in my tracks,
And see the beautiful sunset,
Red, orange, purple, pink, yellow, and blue.
As I watch, the colors remind me of cotton candy,
I watch 'til the beautiful sunset slowly fades away,
Then I feel peaceful, and slowly walk home.

Hannah Fisher, Grade 5
Pollard Elementary School, NH

Crickets

In the peaceful lonely night
a cricket chirps you slowly to sleep.
In the quick morning you hear
a tiny green insect singing you a beautiful song.
During the daytime
the cricket you heard
is usually sleeping under a rock
in the meadow eating on plant material.
You hear no more until you go to lie down again.
You see it start to get dark again
so then you start to listen very closely
and you hear your song replayed.
It comes back again to sing you to sleep
and let you sleep very restfully.

Sierra Wesmiller, Grade 4
Pleasant Valley Elementary School, MD

Escaping My Family

People, there are people everywhere growing up in a big family.
Sometimes I need a space a place to call my own.
A place where I can breath, think, reflect
kind of like putting myself in a time-out.

Space is small and dark
kind of like a mother's womb.
The walls are close
it's my own secret escape.

Some days its fragrance reminds me
of a spring day or fresh laundry
Other days the fragrance can be
foul as my old Etnies.

I am removed from the chaos
yet I am able to hear comforting sounds
knowing that I am part of something as special as FAMILY.

People joke about "coming out of the closet"
well, I haven't always had my own room
but I have always been able to find a closet
so, when I want to escape siblings
I take cover beneath my wardrobe.

Karie Kovacs, Grade 6
Floyd T Binns Middle School, VA

Dog

I dreamed
I was a dog
On an obstacle course
Going through a waterway
Quickly.
Tyler Fleming, Grade 5
Cooper Elementary School, VA

Mountain Life

In the mountain rain falls
Colder than the snow
In the mountain I saw
The wonderful show
Logan J. Shurina, Grade 6
Floyd T Binns Middle School, VA

Midnight Dreams

You catch a star upon a string
And you hear the angels sing
You see the deep dark moonlit sky
And the lonely dimmed stars cry

Across the sky, you see a shooting star
That crosses the Earth and passes us far
Cloudy images fill your mind
And all your thoughts are intertwined

The dew on the grass seems to glitter
And the silence outside is so bitter
The midnight sky is my lover
Protector of us all, the Earth's cover
Amanda Misak, Grade 6
Graham Middle School, VA

The Beautiful Rainbow

I shine in the sunlight.
I curve in the sky.
I fade after the storm.
I am the beautiful rainbow.
Matthew Berthiaume, Grade 4
Greylock School, MA

Freedom

Wonderful it is
To be free of
Chains that bind you to the wall
So tightly that your hands are numb
So your life, but someone else's
Giving you a
Pure evil
Nightmare
Freedom is a
Fragile beautiful bird giving kindness
And fairness
Daniel Pyle, Grade 6
Juliet W Long School, CT

Petals of a Rose

As I watch the red-orange sun sink below the rolling hills
I think about life
How beautiful it is to be alive
To have a loving family
I honor those who lost their lives fighting for my country
I honor those who have lost their loved ones
But still have the strength to carry on without them
We bow in respect for our soldiers
Who risk their lives for our safety
As the red-orange sun sunk behind the rolling hills
A tear fell from my face onto a petal of a rose that lies at a grave...
Melissa Billing, Grade 6
Juliet W Long School, CT

Beautiful Vermont

The sky is painted blue with just a touch of smeared clouds.
Mountains are like a gray layer of rock with a sheet of forest green.
The fields are like strands of a boy's hair after their summer cut.
Trees like slender swords shoot up from the soil.
Noises, the loon's morning song to the midnight traffic.
Vermont's beasts, the moose, the doe, the loon-Vermont's flying wonder.
When Vermont's lakes twinkle to when they are frozen solid like precious stone.
To when white flakes float down from Vermont's crisp sky.
To when sun's rays beam down on a summer's daybreak.
However you look at Vermont, it will always be magnificent.
Dominique Rispoli, Grade 5
Pike Creek Christian School, DE

Song of Myself

I sing of...
Snickers bars and cotton candy,
Daisies blooming in the warm summer air.
Pizza, Popsicles and peppers dipped in ranch,
The cool sheets against my legs when I climb into bed.
Swimming in our pool, sledding down our hill,
The twinkling stars in the sky.

A life that is alive within...
Juicy cherry tomatoes, squirting in my mouth,
The wind in my hair as I swing.
A smooth hot chocolate after a cold winter's day,
My brother scoring his first goal in hockey.
The smell of the ocean in Maine every summer,
Getting good grades and seeing my mother.
Jumping in piles of leaves in the fall.

A life with sounds that live within...
My dogs clicking nails on the shiny wood floor,
Robins singing their songs in spring.
Mom frying bacon in the morning for breakfast,
The clapping of friends and family when I score a goal in soccer.

All, yes, all living sounds within my song.

Alyssa Barrett, Grade 6
Main Street Middle School, VT

Butterfly

Little butterfly
Floating in the warm crisp air
Sits on leaves and waits

Brian DeShields, Grade 4
Dr Charles E Murphy Elementary School, CT

Squirrelly, Squirrelly

Squirrelly, squirrelly in the tree
Why do you sit and stare at me?
All day you sit outside your hut
And look at me while eating a nut.

Squirrelly, squirrelly in the tree
You must be happy as can be.
We give walnuts for you to munch
But you bury them, not eat them for lunch.

Squirrelly, squirrelly in the tree
Will you come down and play with me?
You sit atop that tree all day
Never coming down to play.

Squirrelly, squirrelly in the tree
Aren't you tired of staring at me?
I do the same thing each day through
Do you have nothing better to do?

Squirrelly, squirrelly in the tree
Must you sit and stare at me?

Carrie Lambert, Grade 6
Belfast-Elk Garden Elementary School, VA

Woodward

I always liked summer the best,
but I know you remember
our first week of Woodward.
It was a dream, I thought.
It had everything from
a vert ramp
to a mini ramp
a canteen
to a cafeteria.
We stayed up
like owls at night
drinking soda and Red Bull.
The last day
you realized you wanted to go down
the twenty seven foot roll in.
You went down wobbling
on the board I had loaned to you
You came up and slammed your shoulder.
"I did it," you said.
I knew I wanted to go back next year.

Neil Hailey, Grade 5
Old Bridge Elementary School, VA

Spring

S un and rain
P ansies and leaves
R ings and weddings
I nspire and picnic
N ice and fun
G ood and laughing

Angela Marie Sharp, Grade 5
Rosemont Forest Elementary School, VA

Lice

I am a lousy louse. I live on your head.
The very sight of me, you will dread.

You people think that lice are not nice
But that is silly, we are smaller than rice!

If you use one of your friend's combs,
You might end up with lice on your dome.

When you try to get rid of me,
Let me tell you, it won't be easy!

When I am gone, you'll be so glad,
As for me, I will be very sad.

Luisa Crawford, Grade 6
Immaculate Heart of Mary School, DE

Sunrises in the Morning

The sun rises slowly in the sky.
The sound of dogs barking and waking people up.
I am excited.
What will the sunrise bring us?
The world is in harmony.

Lacy Bortz, Grade 5
John J Flynn Elementary School, VT

This Feeling

Every day I see you.
You make my heart flutter.
I can't stop thinking about you for one moment.
I melt like a puddle.
Sitting there with no idea what is going on.
Pictures of you rush through my mind like a slideshow.
You are the one.
Why don't you notice me?
Why can't you at least say Hi?
You are the only person I think about.
I can't describe this feeling for you.
I get it every day I see you.
I have never had it before.
What does it mean?
Does anyone notice?
Can you see it in a person?
This feeling is Love.

Elizabeth Mullin, Grade 6
St Joseph School-Fullerton, MD

Life's Game!

He stumbles,
He falls,
He yelps in vain,
It is the game he is playing,
He is playing in pain,
Our whole life is like this,
With the ups and downs,
But what can we do,
As we tumble to the ground,
Life is hard, I know,
I am going through it too,
But if you hold your head up high,
You can only imagine what you can do,
Believe in yourself,
And trust in your friends,
Because if they're really there for you,
They will be with you until the end!
Alexandra Michelle Femc, Grade 6
St Paul School, CT

Basketball

B est sport to play
A ctivity for me
S kills are needed
K eep on trying
E xciting to watch
T ournaments with others
B rilliant
A lways fun for me
L osing isn't always bad
L earning about the sport
Rebecca Day, Grade 6
Graham Middle School, VA

Matthew

I have a new cousin Matthew.
He moves his arms and legs a lot.
He stretches in his sleep.
He doesn't cry that often.
He doesn't like his carrier.
He doesn't like the buckle to the carrier.
He starts to cry then he stops.
And gets all calm and quiet.
He's very cute.
And very small.
He's my wonderful cousin
Matthew.
Tony Gentile, Grade 5
Pollard Elementary School, NH

The Oak Tree

An old oak stands tall
Above the oak ducks fly high
Owls live in it
Devan Clegg, Grade 4
Brookside Elementary School, MA

Sun

I dreamed
I was the sun
In space
Shining so the Earth can see
Brightly.
Iyana Carter, Grade 5
Cooper Elementary School, VA

Nature's Singers

When I wake up
in the morning
I love to hear
the birds singing.
It is a very sweet
and soothing sound.
Sometimes,
I go outside
and throw scraps of bread
on the ground
for the birds to eat.
They linger around the bread scraps
and eat a little bit.
Then they take off
gracefully
into the sky.
Mishu Barua, Grade 6
Kenmore Middle School, VA

Ballooning

Feeling the breeze
As you float o'er the land.
The lovely tingling sensation you get
As you soar through the air.

The sweeping swooping feeling
In your stomach as you
Look down on to the slowly
Departing ground

The excitement you feel as the
Smaller ground unfolds
You can see places you
Never saw before

The people like ants
The steeples like pins
You can see all the hustle
And bustle of city life

Wonderful it is
Yet a sickening sight
To be floating in the air
For that is what ballooning is like
Aidan Gorman, Grade 6
Chase Collegiate School, CT

Paw by Paw

Paw by paw
the dog leaps,
drooling drooling
the dog sleeps.
Paw by paw
my dog soars
Sitting sitting
by two doors.
Paw by paw
he goes to bed
slowly
bringing down his head
Patrick Carberry, Grade 5
Zervas Elementary School, MA

Dance the Tango

Let me dance the tango
With the liars and the
People who don't have value,

Let me dance the tango
With the people who forgot
Their own names,

Let me dance the tango
With the people who
Play dirty games,

Let me dance the tango
With the skeleton who
Sits in the dark side of the cemetery,

Let me dance the tango
With the mother who
Ruined my childhood,

Let me dance the tango
With my dad so I can
Forget my sadness
Forever.
Ben Haideri, Grade 6
Lyndon Elementary School, MA

Autumn Leaves

Changing colors, red, orange and gold;
Surrounded by the autumn's brisk cold.
Floating down from nearby trees;
Colorful piles up to my knees.
A gust of wind suddenly blows;
Into a cyclone the leaves will grow.
Spooky sounds rustling about;
On a dark cold night they all come out.
Dancing in the bright full moon;
Autumn leaves will disappear soon…
Taylor Koretsky, Grade 5
Oak Lawn School, RI

I Used to Be

I used to be a swimmer
But now I am a basketball player

I used to be a wimp
But now my brother taught me different

I used to be a little girl
Now I have grown up

I used to be a girl that plays with dolls
Now I play with a basketball

I used to be a girl that whined about everything
But now all I say is, "Tough luck!"

I used to go to Longfellow School
But now I am at St. Brigid School

I used to be a little girl that rode in a stroller
But now all of that has changed

Stephanie McKew, Grade 6
St Brigid School, ME

Paradise Island

Come sail away with me
Where the palm trees sway
In their very own way.
The crashing water looks like
It was blown by a fan.
The sand is as soft and smooth as a kitten's fur
As it cures your aching feet.
Where a little bird's song goes in harmony.
In the air there is a taste of
Pumpkin and berry pie.
The warm sunbeams are perfect
Like a little puppy in your lap.
So will you come sail away with me?

Emily Tovar, Grade 4
Cranston-Johnston Catholic Regional School, RI

Christmas Eve

It's Christmas Eve
You can't wait.
Tomorrow is the day
To celebrate
Tomorrow is Christmas
Hip hip hooray!
So come!
Let's have some fun today
Go outside or stay inside
Just have fun
Be bright!
And now guess what?
It's time to say goodnight.

Kristina Stelmashova, Grade 5
Litwin Elementary School, MA

Melissa

M odel to everyone
E xtraordinary in every way.
L oving me every day
I nspires me to do different things
S he is the one to talk to.
S oftball is her thing.
A great sister to have.

Shawna McCann, Grade 5
C Hunter Ritchie Elementary School, VA

Gus

Ecstatic!
I splash in the refreshing pool.
It glistens in the mid-morning sun.

The water is cool dew
on the early morning grass.
I celebrate my 10th year.
I cautiously unwrap a box
revealing…

Little beady eyes, like a pair of shiny marbles,
a firm nose, black as night,
and four stubby paws.
Pink and tan ears rest at the top of his head.
The fur around his eyes is a mischievous mask.
His walnut face is cleverly disguised.
Looks as though he might have just robbed a bank.
Scratching, screeching, talking, chattering,
is all I hear.

Not just a stuffed animal
a family member.
GUS

Rachael Brown, Grade 6
Mystic Middle School, CT

Leaf

Crisp and wrinkled
Like an ancient document
Preserved through time,
While riding on the wind.

Connor Sager, Grade 5
West Woods Upper Elementary School, CT

Jessica

J elly goes with peanut butter on my sandwich.
E ntertainers are exciting to watch.
S ending letters are fun for me.
S andy beaches are fun to make castles with.
I ce cream is a great treat in summertime.
C andy is my favorite part of Halloween night.
A fter school I ride home on the bus with my friend.

Jessica L. Armstrong, Grade 4
Dr Charles E Murphy Elementary School, CT

The White Gull

Above my head,
a white gull flies,
soaring through the sky.
Its wings spread out,
its head up high,
he looks so bold and triumphant.
I wish I could go fly with him,
let all my worries float away,
the breeze against my face.
Alas, I cannot grant my wish,
so here I sit and dream,
as the white gull flies away.

Isabella Husu, Grade 5
Davenport Ridge School, CT

What My Curse Would Do

If I could put a curse on you
you would cry in just a few

May your bed fill with honey
and you cry to your mommy

May your dog eat your shorts
may you fall in the dirt

May you have a cold shower
and not have a towel

But I would not do this
because I'm not a jerk

Aidan Kennedy, Grade 6
Village School, MA

Just Like That

Joyfully Happy
Tingly tummy
Dazed
A whole other world
Bam
Broken Voice
Broken Spirit
Broken Heart

Kia Rae B. Hanron, Grade 6
Main Street Middle School, VT

Christmas

Santa is here
To give all of us cheer
Presents and cards
Under the tree
Snow is fallen on Christmas Eve
Morning has arrived
And guess what
Christmas is finally here

Rocio Trevizo, Grade 6
Melwood Elementary School, MD

Having the Chicken Pox

Having the chicken pox isn't cool at all.
You'd probably want to be outside having yourself a ball.
You will get itchy all over and when you think it can't get any worse
you'll want to itch until they burst.
Every time you look at them you'll think "Man this hurts."
But when your mom comes with the lotion
you'll say "Is the some magic potion?"
When you have the oven mitts on your own two hands
you'll try to itch through until they become strands.
The oatmeal baths feel squishy and steady
I think I'm getting itchy already.

Jack Bacon, Grade 5
Lincoln Central Elementary School, RI

Love That Dad*

Love that Dad,
like a star loves to twinkle.
I said I love that Dad,
like an angel loves to shine bright.
Love to play in the daytime.
Love to call him, "What's up Dad!"
He thinks he's the president, smiles as bright as the sun.
I said he thinks he's the president, and smiles as bright as the sun.
And when he's sad, he smiles some more.

Alex Simon, Grade 5
Clover Street School, CT
*Inspired by Walter Dean Myers

Swimming

I love to jump into the sea,
or pool, or pond it makes no difference to me.

I love the water swishing around
just like a dishwasher that makes no sound.

Through my fingers, through my toes, through my hair. Oh my!!!
I love the way my body feels as water rushes by.

On a very hot day I like it best.
Especially in the ocean with a great big life vest.

That concludes my poem. All of it.
Now…if you will excuse me I want to go outside and swim a bit!

Trey Butrym, Grade 5
Davenport Ridge School, CT

Guitars

G uitars are something I like to play.
U nder the six strings there are pick-ups which make the guitar's sound.
I t makes a beautiful sound when strummed.
T o me, guitar playing is cool.
A nd I look up to many guitarists.
R unning your hands down the fret board will make the pitch higher or lower.
S ix strings going down the guitar strum them and hear them play.

Jacob Britton, Grade 6
Graham Middle School, VA

Turkey Day

T oday is the day for food, fun, family, and festivities
U nited is my family, thankful for everything
R ejoice we shall, for we have each other
K iwi is the item my grandma said she would bring
E veryone bows their head, to give thanks for everything
Y es, we have corn, mashed potatoes, and green beans

D umb is what I am, for I forgot the turkey
A nd yet, I will not forget the taste of the delicious corn
Y ams are the item my Aunt Fern was supposed to bring

Dakota Miller, Grade 6
Graham Middle School, VA

My Chocolate Dream

My chocolate
Labrador retriever
will make you a true believer

His love is true
as the sky above is blue

His eyes are dreamy
his breath is steamy

He is lovable
And huggable

His name is
Bubby bear.

Katlyn Hoke, Grade 5
Friendship Valley Elementary School, MD

I Am

I am a boy who likes sports a lot.
I wonder if I'll be in baseball.
I hear the bat crack and the player catch
the baseball in the outfield and is caught.
I see the bat hit the ball in the air.
I want to play in the major leagues in college.
I am a boy who likes sports a lot.

I pretend that I am in the major league baseball.
I feel the ball hit my glove as it soars through the air.
I touch the hard, wooden bats.
I worry about the pitcher hitting me in the batter's box.
I am a boy who likes sports a lot.

I understand that I can play in majors.
I say that I'll play majors.
I dream that I'll make a team.
I try to make any team.
I hope I make my favorite team New York Yankees
I am a boy who likes sports a lot.

Richard Ledoux, Grade 5
Blackrock School, RI

Flying Cars

Flying cars in the future and in our car we're just driving.
But when everyone flies there is flight congestion above.
The year is 1 B.C. — rent a dinosaur to ride on!

Peter Rommel, Grade 4
Wapping Elementary School, CT

Come Sail Away with Me to a Lighthouse

I see a bright light peaking out behind the clouds.
I hear crashing waves hit the rocks like thunder.
I smell fresh green trees blooming,
Their pink buds smile, I feel water splashing
Like rain drops above.
I taste salt water in my mouth
I can't believe without your scene
So beautiful and peaceful at night
The lighthouse shines in bright light
So when boats come in
The stars shining their pretty light
The waterfall with its crystal ice cube waves
Feel so beautiful
So why not dip your feet in today
I can't wait to go in
I put on my PJs
And go to bed for now
I dream and dream and dream when will I go again?
Come sail away with me to a lighthouse.

Jenna Costantino, Grade 4
Cranston-Johnston Catholic Regional School, RI

Season's Portrait

Drops trickle down twigs
Melting snow floods the dead lawn
Roses sprout towards the sky
Birds chirp from tree tops
Emerald flakes of grass pop up the sun shines the world

Landscapes devoured
Swimming through cold fresh water
Dry plants withering
Drinking lemonade
Families on vacation shorts and short sleeves out

Yellow orange red falling leaves crunch when stepped
Leaves float to reach ground
Colorful forests
Cool fresh air blows by us
Temperatures change

White barren landscapes
Hot chocolate warms the room
White trees surround us
Snuggled families
Snowballs away back and forth
The silent wind blows

Jenna Lee, Grade 6
Middlebrook School, CT

The Tiger at the Zoo

The tiger at the zoo sways his tail when he is happy.
He rubs his soft, silky fur in the dirt, and then he is all messy.
When he is angry sometimes he will attack the metal bars around his cage with his razor-sharp claws,
At night, you can see his yellow gleaming eyes watching your every move.
Once in a while, he will attack his rubber ball and bite it with his scary ferocious teeth.
Then, he starts chasing the ball. "Crash," he collides with his brother.
I really admire that tiger at the zoo!

Christian Thompson, Grade 5
Long Meadow Elementary School, CT

The Quietness of Nature

I hear a soft roar of a jet passing overhead, produced by its two engines.
The leaves rustle gently in the breeze.
I can smell a wood fire, burning away.
The green grass, covered with a blanket of brown, fallen leaves.
Every now and again, a Wheaton College student will walk by on the path.
The musty smell lingers close to the ground, waiting to be blown away by the powerful, yet innocent wind.
The occasional bird flies overhead; though most have flown south, some still remain.
The soft sway of the four swings, made for those who attend Pinecroft.
Leaves still falling, covering the ground.
Winter is approaching fast, but not so fast that someone can't jump in a leaf pile, one…last…time.

Colin Noel, Grade 5
The Pinecroft School, MA

I Am From

I am from decorated evergreens and red sleighs with gold bells
I am from white fluffy snow; orange red leaves that feel and the dense green forest where the animals dwell.
I am from the dazzling blue ocean that befriends the whistling wind and jokes with the glowing moon.
I am from chocolate pudding and creamy mint ice cream that I eat with a silver spoon.
I am from Christmas Eve when we open three special presents and joyful Easter after solemn Lent.
I am from my choice of birthday dinners, clothes that are new and sitting together at Church in the same pew.
I am from shiny black and white soccer balls, kitty cat collars and listening to birds' tender calls.
I am from pictures of relative and friends.
I am from a bond with books that never ends.
I am from family trips, listening to music and playing games.
I am from Monica and Priya, both Indian names.
I am from exploring the woods and building forts.
I am from jeans, tee-shirts and sweaters with hoods.
I am from "I love you's" and "Whoop-dee-do's."
I am from "Peace, dude" and "Amen" too.

Priya Swyden, Grade 5
Jack Jackter Intermediate School, CT

Race Cars

RACE CARS ARE AS FAST AS A SPEEDING BULLET and when they crash they smack a wall or go in the grass, tumble down the track! When I was at Talladega nights it was the 500th lap when a crash happened it was only two cars left and they crashed the two cars had rolled, flipped and stopped.

Travis Shumaker, Grade 6
E Russell Hicks School, MD

A Fall Hike

As I walk through a red orange and yellow forest of leaves I hear a crunch crinkle as I slowly walk through many many leaves. Some are falling like fireworks. Some trees are bare some are still green as I hear crunch crunch crinkle crunch snap I sit on a rock thinking about the colorful forest around me.

Jacob Ayers, Grade 6
Ashford School, CT

Forest

Oh, only if trees could talk
They'd tell those lumber-jackers to stop!
Stop slicing and chopping and cutting them down
Oh, only if they could hear the animals
How furious they are about losing their homes
The squirrels and the owls
They'd be so very mad
Oh, only if they could talk!

Nicholas Phillips, Grade 5
E Ethel Little Elementary School, MA

Water Scavenger Beetle

I was walking by a small pond
And saw a bug with hairs the color of blond.

I looked at it very closely
And wondered what it could be.

It had legs as thin as a needle
It must be a water scavenger beetle!

Across the pond, I saw him swim
To the other side, and climb a tree limb.

From the tree limb, he flew out of sight,
When I looked up, I was blinded by the light.

Matthew McQueston, Grade 6
Immaculate Heart of Mary School, DE

The Four Seasons

As I rake the leaves making gigantic mountains
More leaves spin and fall
Apple picking starts
Orchards of delicious fruits
Pears and pumpkins too

Lights shine in windows
Beautiful evergreen trees decorated well
Snow covers the grass
A warm blanket in the cold
Preserving for spring

Flower start sprouting
Bright bursts of green and yellow
It is colorful
Eleven candles
Whoosh! Are all out in one breath
Earth Day, my birthday

A heat wave blows through, to remind you of summer
You don't need it much
Skiing on the lake
Cool water engulfs my feet
I fall quickly down

Molly Hoch, Grade 6
Middlebrook School, CT

Sydney

Sydney
Kind, generous, caring
Wishes to marry and die happily
Dreams of flying on a magic carpet
Wants to raise money for charity
Who wonders who will be elected next president
Who fears swimming
Who likes to be active with other children
Who believes you can do anything if you put your mind to it.
Who loves to baby-sit my neighbors
Who plans to have two children and to live happily with a family
I wish for all this to be true.

Sydney Pence, Grade 5
C Hunter Ritchie Elementary School, VA

Colors I See

White as a snowy day
Black as the midnight sky
Blue as the flowing river bend
Orange as the fire that lights my heart
Red as a morning rose
Green as nature's flowering trees
And yellow as a heavenly light
But will I ever see these again?

Veronica Rodway, Grade 5
C Hunter Ritchie Elementary School, VA

October

October leaves are falling
So colorful they are
Winter is coming
Take out the shovels
Rake the leaves
Go trick or treating
Bats, goblins, ghost
Scary creatures of the night
The winter comes have to shovel the snow
Then it's back to spring yeah, yippy, hurray

Noah Moreau, Grade 6
St Patrick School, MA

Spring

Flowers and birds and squirrels are here.
That means springtime must be near.

In like a lion, out like a lamb.
March marches by, it's April now.

April showers bring May flowers,
Then May flowers bring June lawnmowers.

That brings a sad thing,
The end of spring.

Eva Putnam, Grade 5
Southbrook Academy, MA

Fall

Crunching like the chipmunks
In the air
Howling like the big oak tree
With the leaves blowing through,
The dark blue sky,
Whistling through the air
The big orange sun
Ripping through the clouds
It is time for autumn
And the leaves are turning colors.

Joey Pariseau, Grade 5
Pollard Elementary School, NH

The Navy

The Navy is there
To protect the water for us,
They sail their ships
And they never make a fuss.

The sailors wear uniforms
Which are all white,
Sometimes they have to
Use weapons to fight.

The Navy risks their lives
They must be strong,
They go out to sea
And they stay VERY long.

Collin Sykes, Grade 5
Pemberton Elementary School, VA

Christmas

C hrist is born
H oliday time
R ed Santa suit
I s in December
S anta comes
T iny elves make gifts
M istletoe
A great holiday
S tockings full of candy

Daniel Cole, Grade 5
Pemberton Elementary School, VA

For The…

For the mind that cannot speak
But for the mind that has intelligence.
Always, the words may come
That are unspoken.
For the world that cannot see
What is changing,
But for the people that are changing it.
For the things that are changing
We are to blame.

Brittany McAllister, Grade 6
Kate Collins Middle School, VA

Season Change

During this time the leaves are no longer green but, different
    shades of red, yellow, orange, and brown.
During this time, people change
    Their skin is no longer tan and golden, but only light shades
    of white and black.
During this time clothes change
    We pack away our shorts and tanks, and replace them with
    jackets and scarves.
During this time, weather changes
    What once were warm sunny days are now ones with cool crisp air.
It is fall.

Megan Salerno, Grade 6
St John the Evangelist School, CT

Christmas Excitement

Jingle Bells down the road. A pony trotting with a cart behind her.
White snow sprinkles my hair. Reindeer feed scattered on the ground.
Milk and cookies are put out, gingerbread and chocolate chip.
A delicious lasagna for dinner. I cannot fall asleep.
Eight, nine, ten, almost eleven o'clock, slowly, softly I finally fall asleep.
Morning comes. Look up! It's only five thirty.
I lie in bed and wait. I get up when six o'clock strikes on the wall clock.
A gray day outside. A blanket of white snow lies on the ground.
We fly down the hall. Glistening gifts wait to be opened.
A fire is lit in the fireplace. Breakfast of pancakes and hot chocolate.
I enjoy my gifts. My favorite traditions!

Paige Williams, Grade 5
Shaftsbury Elementary School, VT

Fall

Whistling wind blowing through the trees knocking the leaves down
Bright sunny day
Wind chasing the leaves around like a tornado through the great tall grass
Sending a warning that winter is coming
Leaves move from one spot to another
People stepping on the crunchy leaves
The wind catches the leaves and scrapes them on
the wet, cold ground
Making people happy
Jumping into rustling piles and piles of leaves

Paul Palasits, Grade 4
John J Flynn Elementary School, VT

Sunset

The Earth dims and all becomes quiet
Everyone glances and becomes inspired
The Earth's essence is spectacular
You begin to feel as if nothing can go wrong
The colors change in the horizon and the Earth gets to the point of gold
You'd think it were a painting the colors ever so brilliant
Then the stars awaken and the sky becomes dark
You begin to release and head home for a good night's sleep
Until next time sunset

Amy Quinonez, Grade 6
Floyd T Binns Middle School, VA

Eagle

Eagle how long do you fly? Searching for food in the sky.
With hungry chicks in the nest. Feeding them you'll need a rest.

Eagle where is your nest? In the trees would be the best.
It is very hard to fly. But you do it without a try.

Eagle who is your friend? The ku ku bird or maybe a wren?
Maybe you don't have time to play. If you don't teach your chicks how to neigh.

Eagle what do you eat? A nice fresh treat or some berries ready to eat?
Berries would be great! A fish treat you might have already ate.

Eagle do you live in the zoo? They would probably cage you up with other eagles too.
That wouldn't be nice. They would probably just feed you rice.

Eagle now that my poem is done, I'll see you. I've got to run.
Bye bye eagle. You're so great. I wish I could stay but I have to leave at eight.

Evelyn Needham, Grade 5
Hinesburg Community School, VT

New York

Bright lights encounter Market Street, hot dogs sizzle under a red and white umbrella, buildings touch the sky and sway in the breeze.

New York!
Nothing to do in New York!
Oh no!
Visit Broadway and see if you can imitate an act when you get home.
Walk into a shop and count how many post cards there are.
Take a subway into Coney Island and taste every single flavor of ice cream until you get sick.
Hop into a taxi and watch all the rats climb on a trash can. You can count the stinky rodents!
Visit New York where upbeat Broadway, cluttered shops, busy amusement parks and stinky rodents is what it's all about!

Kailey Rhone, Grade 6
St John Regional Catholic School, MD

Night Before Thanksgiving

'Twas the night before Thanksgiving
I was talking to a horse.
He said they should eat me, not the turkey of course.
The stuffing was cooking and the oven so hot.
When you wake up tomorrow, you will be drinking tea from a pot.
It was 40 degrees colder than cold, but the horses were warm, so I've been told.
The cows were going out, the horses are coming in.
I am predicting that VT will win.
I went in the kitchen and they were mixing batter,
When I walked outside, my teeth started to chatter.
I ran inside to get my coat, then I looked up on the mountain and there stood my goat.
I got my shoes and scarf and ran up the hill.
The hill was so high, it made me feel ill.
The sun was rising, the feast was ready as I came inside so stiff and steady.
When I was inside, I stared at the turkey.
I was so happy I did a hurkey.
We ate and we ate until we were 20 pounds more.
So we went to the store and tried to find more.

Colby Hill and Nick Moore, Grade 5
Graham Intermediate School, VA

Ach-ooo!

There once was a girl at the zoo.
Who suddenly went "Ach-oooo!"
The giraffe said "Ick!
I'm going to pick
a new home away from you!"

Lizzie Michael, Grade 5
John J Flynn Elementary School, VT

9-11

9-11, sent many people
To heaven
Several callous men
Just had to steer a plane
And yes, it was
For no one's gain
They are no heroes
To anyone
Their suicide mission
Made NYC a prison
Yes we shall remember
Those Twin Towers
For those troubled hours
Gave us many strong powers
No one cowers
Right now this is 2007
That was and is 9-11

Marla Gordon, Grade 6
Pikesville Middle School, MD

The Trophy

A gleaming trophy,
bright as a sun,
shines at me as I awake.
I roll out of bed
and glance at my
marvelous prize.

It was time
for the hot shot
competition.
My turn came.
I nailed all my shots
like a meteor
going through a giant hoop.
I won.
I was so proud.

This trophy
is my gleaming light
that brings the shining sun
out of me.
It is a treasure
I will always keep with me.

Hunt Welch, Grade 6
Mystic Middle School, CT

Going Off to Florida

I'm going off to Florida
I think it should be fun,
I'm going up in a plane
So I may see the sun

Such fun I'll have in Disneyland
But I really will miss you,
I'll bring you back a piece of paper
Signed by Winnie the Pooh

I'm going to a fine hotel
With a towel rack,
But it won't be as fun
As when I'm coming back.

Kevin Hilli, Grade 6
Charlton Middle School, MA

Parents

I dreamed
I was a parent
In a house
Teaching kids how to read and write
Faithfully.

Janelle Washington, Grade 5
Cooper Elementary School, VA

Moody 2's

The Moody twins are different
And that you could not tell.
Because every freckle,
On their faces are the same.
But if you saw the inside,
This is not a bet,
But you'd then know
The differences they surely
Never would show.
They call themselves the Moody 2's
Because that's what they want to say.
But I will always know them as
Emily and Miranda Moody,
And that's the only way!

Olivia Meehan, Grade 5
St John Neumann Academy, VA

A Winter's Night

The quiet reflection
On the
Sparking white snow
Feet splashing
On the damp ground
What will happen tomorrow?
I'm tired
It's peaceful
A winter's night

Drew DeMaggio, Grade 5
John J Flynn Elementary School, VT

Autumn Days Are Here at Last

Autumn is here
Time to close your pool
And get back to school
Leaves are changing colors everywhere
Kids dressing in costumes, what a scare!
Witches, ghosts, goblins too
All here to scare you.

Julia Farquharson, Grade 4
Alma E Pagels Elementary School, CT

A Pig and His Owner Lance

There once was a pig from France
He really loved to dance.
His owner was so dumb
He broke each thumb.
The owner's name was Lance.

Dancing was so simple to the pig
His favorite dance was the Irish jig
Lance, his owner, was too weird
He tripped over his long, long beard
And he fell over a twig.

Erin Clarke, Grade 5
Clover Hill Elementary School, VA

Candles

C andles are a gift of light,
A tiny sun, a bit of star.
N o other dancer in the sky.
D ances with such sheer delight,
L ittle souls warm and glowing
E ach a glimpse of what we are
S hining innocent and pure.

Jason Krajnak, Grade 4
Riverfield School, CT

My Dog Nell

I love my dog Nell,
She is so cuddly and sweet.
When I'm not feeling well,
She curls up at my feet.
Nell loves to chase a ball,
And she's learning to play catch.
She usually comes when we call,
And soon she'll learn to fetch.
Nell runs with a dog all day,
Darcy is her name.
When Darcy goes away,
Nell's just not the same.
Now it's time for bed,
And she leaves her active state.
Then she lays down her head,
In her quiet, cozy, crate.

Gregory Zoda, Grade 6
Infant Jesus School, NH

Stairs

Stairs are like a passage way
To the heavens they give us
The key to the clouds
As we rise they go down
But we need them
For the key to the clouds
We need them
For the key to
The heavens.

Jackson Hamburg, Grade 4
Riverfield School, CT

Blessing to the Orphans

All locked up in a crammed house.
May you find a family that will take care of you.
May you never be left on that train to nowhere.
May you never make it to the last and final stop; the street.
May you find a parent, or two.
May you receive a worth-opening present for Christmas.
May you wear a brand new outfit.
May you not be starved through the day and night.
This is the Blessing to the Orphans.

Monica Thorne, Grade 6
Village School, MA

Silver

S hining in the mine
I t is the color of riches
L ikely in a mine
V ery hard to find
E verlasting amount of riches
R ight behind gold

Jordan Rijke, Grade 5
C Hunter Ritchie Elementary School, VA

Ode to a Winters View

Standing on the mountain's peak
Taking in the view is like taking a giant leap
Falling through the clouds
The white puffy mounds

Looking at the valley below
The snow sparkling so

Towns lights shine bright
Through the day and night

Trees that were once green and lean,
Are now white with light

Then you float back up
Just like the fall you breathe it in
Embrace the beauty and you're on top of it all

Caroline McKenna, Grade 6
Juliet W Long School, CT

Space

In space I was in a race with my friend Ace.
I needed to pick up the pace.
I like a place where it is black with white stars,
That connect like a lace.
This is my home this beautiful place.
Where things can disappear without a trace

Victor Nwaulu, Grade 5
Melwood Elementary School, MD

My Favorite Horse Maverick

I mount, I fix the stirrups
I give him a kick and he goes
When he stops I pat his shoulder
While saying in hushed tones, "Good boy Maverick"
He replies by moving forward into a fast trot
And then a canter around the ring
I loose a stirrup then another
Then I fall off
He turns around and comes to me
Turning around is the way I know he loves me
I take off his bridle and saddle and we walk together to the barn
As I walk I think about how nice he is
And how bad he could possibly be
That is the other way I know he loves me
I turn to give him a hug and then I hear something
I hear something I wish I had never heard
I heard "It is time to wake up honey"
Suddenly my dream became a blur
As I wake up

Eva Branson, Grade 6
Grace Episcopal Day School, MD

Origami

O ne type of Japanese art
R eally fun when you get used to it
I t's challenging if you make it challenging
G ood folds, makes the thing you're making look cool
A wesome in several ways
M akes you think about how to do certain folds
I t has cool things you can make
    Did you guess what it is? It's ORIGAMI

Dexter Kirk, Grade 6
Graham Middle School, VA

Seasons

Leaves lightly land as gracefully
As the morning mist.
Fall feels frosty, like a harsh snowy winter.
Spring comes, with cool clean air.
Days come as clear as water.
Summer comes and it gets as hot as a pepper,
And also warm and hazy.
Then it starts all over again
Like a circle that never ends.

Olivia Lafferty, Grade 6
Wakefield Forest Elementary School, VA

Drawing

I love to draw,
I do it every day,
Pictures on the wall,
Instead of going out to play.

Kaitlyn Jenkins, Grade 6
Floyd T Binns Middle School, VA

Signs of Autumn

I could taste the sweet pumpkin pie
I can smell smoke from each chimney
I feel the wind against my cheek
I hear the hooting owls in the night
Halloween comes soon
What a fright!

Rosemary Sanchez, Grade 4
Alma E Pagels Elementary School, CT

Up to Bat

When I get up to bat
under my helmet I am wearing my hat.

It is just my thing
that when I swing
I see the ball hit the bat and hear a cling

I wait for my pitch down the middle
When I see it I try not to fiddle.

I see the bat smash the ball
In the air I hope it doesn't fall
in left field it hits the wall.

I hit the ball nice and strong
I know it is right not wrong
the ball is going to travel long.

Neiman Levenson, Grade 5
Pemberton Elementary School, VA

Hurricane Lands

I begin at the ocean,
Where I gain force and blasts.
Gaining power I spin to the lands,
I gyrate to land,
And I shine my eye.
A fine day is it, children?
I have deceived you!
My body grows,
I collide into things,
And I harm people.
After hours and hours,
I start to relapse.
Retreating to the ocean,
It will be soon,
Before I come again.

Allen Cheng, Grade 5
Four Seasons Elementary School, MD

Gymnastics

Gymnastics is fun
I like the wind blowing in my face
Yet I'm inside and technically I'm not running
How does this happen?
GYMNASTICS
It's like magic, a weird kind of magic
It feels good when you accomplish something new
It gives you a new feeling
A new sensation of wind
For instance,
Back tuck you go back wind whirling around the radiance of your body
Your legs tucked in,
Layout, your body straight
You are going against the wind, yet you are not
It pushes your straight body back or forward
Like a piece of paper whirling in the November wind,
Branny you are straight, like a layout, yet at the last millisecond
You turn your body, my personal favorite, on trampoline, front layout
You just keep your body straight and let the air do the rest
My favorite on floor, back tuck. You carry your hands back and tuck
Once again the wind does the rest

Isaiah Marshall, Grade 6
Grace Episcopal Day School, MD

Wolf

Wolf, Wolf I here you howl, Or sometimes there is your scary growl.
All the animals fear your name, they all wish they could be the same.

Where did you get those yellow eyes? That look so hungrily to the skies.
You use them to find your prey, for you must eat sometime every day.

How can you take down big game? Every kill you make goes under your name.
You have those fierce claws, they give many animals pause.

Why do you hunt in a pack? Do you do it so you can have some slack?
Or are you just afraid to be alone. Even though you sit on the throne.

How do you run so fast? There is no animal that can outlast.
And why are you such a sneak? How you wait and never make a squeak.

Wolf, Wolf, I hear you howl. Or sometimes there is your scary growl.
All the animals here your name, they all wish they could be the same.

Jonathan Buzzell, Grade 5
Hinesburg Community School, VT

Blue

Blue is everywhere.
On birds, berries, and even the sky.
It makes the day colorful.
Then the sun sets.
Blue turns to black.
There is no color.
Then, as the sun rises, the black turns to red and yellow hills of color.
But gradually even that fades, and soon the blue is back.

Jeffrey Wood, Grade 5
North Star Elementary School, DE

Thunder

I am trembling,
tremendous
booming.

I scare people away.
Sometimes I make
boisterous noises
that sounds like I'm crashing into cars
and houses.

I am very frightful sometimes.
I make people
pass out and when that happens I get mad at myself.

I am very dark when I make my colossal noises and sounds
like I'm angry.
Thunder

Dalton Stewart, Grade 4
Pleasant Valley Elementary School, MD

The Birds Fly

Geese glide gracefully through the sky
Under the moonlight shed by the snow white moon
The birds are like shining gold
Behind them little baby birds follow
Like birds tied to silver strings

Caitlin Barbieri, Grade 5
Wakefield Forest Elementary School, VA

Soccer

S occer is great and fun
O n the sidelines people are watching and cheering
C oncentrate on the ball to make moves
C ut off the angle so the other team doesn't score
E njoy the game, even if we lose
R ejoice if we win the game!

Kylee Windyka, Grade 5
St Patrick School, MA

The Sun Shall Rise Again

In a dark corner I sat
wondering when I will get out,
out of this terrible state
for my body did not agree
that I was ready to go out
but my mind decided to not be sick
no more doctors
no more hospitals
I have had enough
for I am truly the healing one,
and I am the one and only that can heal me.
So I will step out of my dark, sad, miserable
corner and back to being me
for in my path, the sun shall rise again.

Lena Stone, Grade 5
Millis Middle School, MA

Lying Leon the Lion

Laughing at limericks out loud
I'm the KING and I don't use bait

I shield all of you
I break up all bungles

I'm the KING and I don't use bait
I'm the KING and this is my fate

"Time for supper, and
STOP
Giving little children illusions about you."

Caty Galligan, Grade 6
St Brigid School, ME

Setting Sky

The warm heavy sun sets over the condos
Happy feelings come over me
Soft colorful rays go through the clouds
The sounds around me are only the chirps of the crickets
What will the morning bring?
Colors Galore!

Jessica Boylan, Grade 5
John J Flynn Elementary School, VT

Fall

The leaves are changing colors,
The birds are flying south.
People are outside raking,
Squirrels are putting acorns in their mouth.

Colds are going all around,
People are getting sick.
Please don't give me one of them,
That will give you a kick.

People are putting their decorations out,
They'll give you a big fright.
The nights are getting darker,
The moon is getting bright.

Rachel Kenney, Grade 5
St Patrick School, MA

Ballerinas

Ballerinas are quite a treat.
When they go up on their feet.
They go around here and there.
They go around everywhere.

Some people call them twinkle toes.
I'd like to see their shows.
They work all night they work all day.
I hope there is no delay.

Rachel Waltz, Grade 5
Rosemont Forest Elementary School, VA

The Cool Ocean

The cool ocean breeze
Water rolling in and out
Making crashing sounds
Creates a calming effect
Giving us water to drink

Brandon Fox, Grade 5
Highland Park School, CT

Montpelier

Montpelier is beautiful
The capitol's dome gleams
Living here is wonderful
The woods have small streams.

Oliver Sherman, Grade 6
Main Street Middle School, VT

Living Life to the Fullest

Run, jump, glide, ski
Be who you want to be
Live life to the fullest
Never give up
No one can stop me from
Being me
I'm living life to the fullest
Hopeful and dignified
I'm living life to the fullest
And that's what I'll ever do.

Stephanie Carter, Grade 6
Melwood Elementary School, MD

Crocodile

Crocodile, crocodile,
Why do you wait upon the Nile?
Your mouth agape into the sun,
Swallowing light from the Nile.

James Johnson, Grade 4
Jamestown Elementary School, VA

Fall Is Around

Fresh air is around
Bats hiding in hollow trees
Brown leaves are falling
Fall is around.

Anthony Garrett, Grade 5
Pollard Elementary School, NH

Leaves

Jumping kids
Gloomy weather
Breezy
Crunchy leaves
Screaming kids
Excited for leaves to fall
Will leaves fall forever?

Admir Ugarak, Grade 4
John J Flynn Elementary School, VT

I Have Eaten the Chicken*

I have eaten the chicken
out of my sister's room

which you were
probably saving
for when you woke up

Forgive me
I was so hungry
I saw it in your room
I just had to eat it

Kayla Reid, Grade 5
Clover Street School, CT
*Inspired by William Carlos Williams

Sunset

The sunset creeps
through the evening sky,
whispers a song
to go to sleep.
Colors fill the air.
It takes over the responsibility
of coloring the black night.
A black cloth sweeps it away
after time.
Just wait 'til tomorrow.

Franny Bernstein, Grade 5
Zervas Elementary School, MA

Halloween

Halloween is that time of year,
That fills us with thoughts of fear.

Children running all about,
Listen to them holler and shout.

Witches, goblins, and vampires too,
Roam the town to scare you.

After trick or treating is done,
There is candy for everyone.

Kelsey Prive, Grade 5
St Patrick School, MA

Me

I love gymnastics
And dance too.
I love to play around,
Hop, skip, and have fun all day,
And not do any work!
I love pets, and animals.
I love having lots of things to do!
And that's me!

Monica Stemski, Grade 5
St Joseph School-Fullerton, MD

Broken Hearts

B adly hurt
R ugged edges
O ver dramatic
K ept secret
E vil
N ever forgiving

H eadaches
E motional
A poison inside
R azor sharp
T imid
S everely ruined

Molly Winstead, Grade 6
Floyd T Binns Middle School, VA

Acorn

I am an acorn
All the squirrels want me bad
Because they eat me

Taylor Champlin, Grade 4
St Brigid School, ME

U.S. Army

Pledge to the U.S. Army
Raise our American flag
Keep it safe and bag that
The U.S. Army keeps us safe

From if it's the stars above
Or clouds in the sky of day
They fight for our freedom
And they fight for us to live

They give up their lives
They give up everything they loved
Everything they cherish
To keep us safe

Blade Jones, Grade 5
Pasadena Elementary School, MD

Fire

Flicker, flicker,
Dancing, prancing,
Twisting, turning,
Barely glancing,
Burning to the very touch,
Doesn't care for water much.
Colors twisting in the core,
Lovely to watch, impossible to store.
Not a thing, just simply power,
Burning throughout every hour.
Something I truly admire,
Is that beautiful force of fire.

Christine Aucoin, Grade 6
Thomas Blake Middle School, MA

Smelly Socks

Smelly, icky, dirty, rotten
what can we do with spoiled cotton.
Smelly socks on everybody
all we can do is smell real muddy.
After we ran fourteen miles
my socks smelled like two garbage piles.
Quick, quick the washing machine
thirty minutes later my socks were clean.
I couldn't believe it right before my own eyes
my socks were clean.
What a pleasant surprise!

Kristen DeCiantis, Grade 5
Buckley School, CT

Winter

Temperatures drop down to below Celsius
The cold has arrived

Streams no longer run long covered over by ice
They're liquid no more

Streets are now covered with sheets of slippery ice
None can stay upright

Snowflakes beginning their frenzied dancing descent
To the wide white world

Whipping winds swirl now snatching hats and biting toes
Then they are long gone

Sheets of hail plummet
Setting the whole town awry as they hurry down

Gray clouds start to clear
Snowfall begins to lessen the storm is clearing

All is now silent
Soft white blankets of fresh snow cover the landscapes

Kathleen Smith, Grade 6
Middlebrook School, CT

A Fantastic Vacation

Maybe I should take a vacation to India
to see the magnificent Taj Mahal,
Or a trip to Paris
to look at the beautiful Eiffel Tower,
Or a getaway to California
to see the wonderful Golden Gate Bridge,
Or a trip to Africa
to see the amazing and longest Nile River,
Or a vacation to Australia
to see the colorful coral reef underneath the ocean,
Or I'll just stay home and relax.

Rima Viradia, Grade 6
Irving School, CT

I Am a Dobsonfly

Hello, I am a scary dobsonfly,
After two or three days as an adult, I die.

But I live as a larva for two or three years,
And if I bite you, you might be filled with tears.

Sometimes I am very active at night,
And I am often attracted to very bright light.

When I am a larva, I might be used as fishing bait,
And larger game fish could seal my fate.

Sometimes I reach all the way up to 5 inches!
And when I do, you should be afraid of my pinches.

Brian Canfield, Grade 6
Immaculate Heart of Mary School, DE

My Hometown

I live in a place named Adam's Village,
It's a great place to live.
My friends, memories, and everything else,
Live somewhere in this town.
Born here and raised I am proud to say,
This is my home and I will always stay.

Elders chatting outside the corner stone.
Kids roaming around,
Adults running from store to store.
This is what I see every day,
In my hometown!

Ashley Penella, Grade 6
St Brendan Elementary School, MA

The Turtle of the Sea

As the turtle flows gracefully down to the floor,
a school of fish swim by.
The hard brown design on the turtle's smooth shell
help it soar in the ocean very swift.
As it searches for food, it flies steadfast,
straight and unremitting.
Then it disappears to the surface
to lay on the sand and lay eggs.
She buries them deep, then departs.
She goes back to the ocean and swims
steadfast and straight.
And plans to come back for her young.
Then she goes deep to the North Atlantic Current
and swims gracefully
D
O
W
N
To the ocean floor and hopes
that her young are safe.

Paul Rochford, Grade 4
Pleasant Valley Elementary School, MD

New Hampshire

New Hampshire is stunning,
New Hampshire's top one,
Enjoy it, or destroy it,
It is our only one.
White, icy snow is
A true winter wonderland,
While reds, yellows, browns, and greens,
Make up a fall fantasy land.
Scorching hot sand,
On warm summer beaches,
Cannot compare to what
The spring season teaches.
New Hampshire is stunning,
New Hampshire's top one,
Enjoy it, or destroy it,
It is our only one.

Shivani Shrestha, Grade 6
Infant Jesus School, NH

My Sleep

Hearing the prickling sound
of rain on the roof.
Dreaming about my future or
having nightmares about aliens.
My electric blanket keeps me
warm as a hot summer day.
My favorite pillow fluffy as a rabbit
touches my head before I go to bed.

Timothy Cate, Grade 5
Highland Park School, CT

Inside a Horse

Inside a horse
is a spirit that is wild
dying and bursting to break free
it wants to run and play
Inside a horse
is a spirit that is wild

Morgan Hamilton-Butts, Grade 6
St Brigid School, ME

Stew

I'm making a stew
a stew made of you
with a pinch of your love
and a dash of your kindness
a sprinkle of your beauty to create flavor
Now this stew is not to eat
It's just to show
that you're sweet
and so I'm here
with a spoon in my hand
and making a stew
a stew made of YOU!

Diana Smith, Grade 5
Osborn Hill Elementary School, CT

Trenches

T renches were where the men would hide —
R ounds of bullets came for them.
E verything the men needed to protect them was in that trench.
N ever-the-less, the cannon balls hit the men inside —
C annons hit the men inside —
H elp! The wounded men would cry in despair!
E arth and air began to fall.
S un goes down upon the trench, bloody; broken is all we share.

Joshua Criss, Grade 6
Blueberry Hill School, VT

The Happy Helmsman

In a boat while it floats, lightly rock and
Heavy squall,
In a gale,
Spearing whales
He's at the helm day or night
Always in that constant fight,
With the wind and weather helm,
And every time you think he's lost he raises right back up to course.
With a grin on his face he's surely having fun.
Even when the day is done the smile's never gone.

Douglas Schweid, Grade 6
Mystic Middle School, CT

The Ostrich

The ostrich is the largest living bird,
Ostrich is an odd spelled word.
The ostrich weighs about 345 pounds,
They eat lizards, but only if they can be found.
They help their digestion by eating lots and lots of sand and gravel,
Ostriches can go 40 mph, that's how fast they can travel.
They have gloves, shoes, and bags made from their skin,
But their neck and legs are extremely thin.
The ostrich does not bury his head in sand,
The ostrich has wings, not one five-fingered hand.

Gregory Landry, Grade 5
E Ethel Little Elementary School, MA

Winter Wonderland

Build a snowman, sleigh wherever you can
in this beautiful winter wonderland.
The sparkle of its terrain from the snow.
These gray clouds are…well, I think you know!
With forests of candy canes of all flavors you see
and miles of decorated Christmas trees.
Snowflakes falling through the night, with designs I can't explain
Making Frosty the snowman with giant snowballs, you can't really complain!
Now the day is over and it's time to go to bed.
I think I'll have some milk and cookies and then rest my head.
Looking out my window, I see all of the snow.
More adventures tomorrow in my winter wonderland?
Boy, I hope so!

Jessica Martin, Grade 6
St Joseph School-Fullerton, MD

Mountains

The ripples make the blue river look like it's moving
The red boat floats in the wavy river.
Lime green pine trees shedding pine needles.
White clouds floating through the windy air.
The grass flutters in the wind.

Nicholas L'Abbe-McNulty, Grade 5
Pollard Elementary School, NH

Colors I Like

Yellow is the sun shining.
Orange is a pumpkin waiting to be picked
Green is the leaves on the trees
Gray is the sky during a storm
Brown is the bark of a tree
Black is the sky during the night.
White are the clouds in the sky
What colors do you like?

Matthew Sprague, Grade 5
C Hunter Ritchie Elementary School, VA

I'm a Water Strider

Hi I'm Willy the wet water strider
When I'm on the water, I wish it was wider

Sometimes I even live on the ocean
But it's scary hearing all the people's commotion

I eat dragonflies and also worms
I try to catch them while they squirm

I have two antennae on top of my head
I live in the water so I have no cozy bed

Newts, birds, and fish are the ones who eat me
Like a human eats apples out of an apple tree.

Matt Shackleford, Grade 6
Immaculate Heart of Mary School, DE

Water, Water, Water

Pool water
Fish tank water
Salty, stinging, ocean water
Green, mossy, pond water
Those are just a few.
Cold water
Old water
Disgusting, yellow, toilet water
Purified, plastic, bottled water
Lake water too!
Sewer water
Tap water
And don't forget backwashed water.
Last of all, best of all
I like clean water!

Jack Desormier, Grade 6
Juliet W Long School, CT

Spring, Summer, Fall, Winter

The flowers have bloomed
They sway with the gentle wind
They are everywhere
The rain trickles down
As I look out the window it's a rainy day

Hot sun shining down
Proves to me that summer's here
During the warm day
Dolphins in oceans
Daisies swaying in motion during the hot time

Brown leaves falling down that make noises when I walk
Are vibrant colors
The leaves are changing
The air is cooling down now
Halloween's coming

The cold air stings me
The icy air bites my toes as I ski down hills
Christmas is coming
New Years will be soon after
The year is near end

Natalie Danielski, Grade 6
Middlebrook School, CT

A Day as a Chef

In my kitchen, my cooks were fighting
On how much paprika to put in the stew.
The stew was supposed to be enlightening.
Then I shouted, "Just add a few!"

They added the wrong ingredient!
"A rat! A rat!" shouted a cook.
"Kill it! Kill it! You're obedient."
"Over there look! LOOK!"

I scurried over there,
With a broom in my hand.
It went into someone's hair!
It's the hair of a guy in a rock band!

Then he yelled "Dude!"
"Where's my food?"

Patrick McGee, Grade 6
Charlton Middle School, MA

My Silly Puppy

My puppy's name is Binx.
He likes to play outside all day long.
He loves to chew his toys all day long.
He likes to bark at night
And keep me up half the night.

Miranda Pinet, Grade 4
Marsh Grammar School, MA

An Even Pace

I find myself at the start of my journey to the great summit.
I am eager to start it, though criticism showers me like a thick acid rain.
But still I keep an even pace of one step at a time.
I find myself out of the rain and into the forest.
I am not safe, and I am filled with fear.
I know this is still the beginning of my journey.
So still I keep an even pace of one step at a time.
I find myself out of the forest and into the desert.
The sun dominates every living thing with its blazing heat.
I grit my teeth, knowing the hardest part is here.
And I still keep an even pace of one step at a time.
I find myself out of the desert and into the snow.
I can see the mountain before me, and I am filled with unending cold.
This is another of the hardest parts.
Even now I keep an even pace of one step at a time.
I find myself out of the snow and onto the rock.
On the mountain I know that at any moment I could fall and have to start again.
I know my goal will be achieved when still I keep an even pace of one step at a time.
I find myself finally off of the rock and onto the summit.
My journey completed, I am eager and happy, forgiving those who criticized me in the beginning.
I finally made it to the summit because I kept an even pace of one step at a time…

Jonathan Medley, Grade 5
Pemberton Elementary School, VA

My Life

I am from a place with bright lights from a TV,
A place where video games are waiting to be played, a place where a springy, comfy bed lies.
I am from home — laughter and joy in the air with smiles on people's faces.
I am from a neighborhood where silence is common
An area where I feel very serenely, some people walk by, not to say "Hello" or "Hi"
We stay inside, but not every day, because sometimes my sister Hailey and I ride our bikes or go out to play.
I am from a city not far from Fenway Park. Also in the city, there are a lot of churches nearby.
The city is sometimes noisy and active like Boston. Also fancy and new cars dash by!
The state I live in is different by its size. I know it is the 44th largest state,
It is also in the Northeast region and the state has four seasons!
I am from a country that has rights,
Some of my country's famous landmarks are the Empire State Building, Hollywood, and NASA.
I love this country because without its devices, crops, electronics, etc. we wouldn't be here right now.
I really care for the people of America because if I didn't, people would think I am a bad person.
But I am a great, generous, reliable person.
I am from a very stern type of people; but they are industrious. They also are very poor people.
I am from a Caribbean place called Belize, which has many keys and seas!
The place is so warm and so fine that you would hatch an egg from outside!
I am from a home with three kids named Avril, Ciara, and Nick.
A home that is a mansion being enchanted with moments. A home where I have company.
I want my future to be the best part of my life.

Cherese Shaw, Grade 5
St Brendan Elementary School, MA

Taaj Explained in Great Detail

My personality is a fun newborn kitten smelling catnip and running like it's on fire. My ideas are like a big deck of cards being shuffled randomly with no order of thought. My hair is like a wave in Hawaii slowly rocking up and down. My ears are clogged so I can't follow directions just like a bad criminal is never willing to follow the law. I live in a world full of people running the New York marathon and eating Cinnamon Toast Crunch for breakfast.

Taaj Cheema, Grade 6
Tolland Middle School, CT

Daddy

Thank you for taking me to all my practices
And teaching me how to work

And thank you for grounding me
And showing me I was a jerk

Thank you for helping me with my homework
Although it's not fun

But I thank you for that now
Because I'm not dumb

And thank you for tucking me in so tight
I'll thank you for that every given night

And thank you for caring
And teaching me right

And I'll promise to thank you
For loving me with all your might

Madison Miller, Grade 5
Belfast-Elk Garden Elementary School, VA

The Fox

There once was a fox
Who lived in a box
The box was red
And so was his bed
Including his fuzzy socks

He hated his smock
Because it was not red
"I want a red smock," he said
So he got a red marker and colored his locks
Now he does not look like a fox

Megan Herceg, Grade 5
Clover Hill Elementary School, VA

Birthday

Wake up, rise and shine
It's time, your time!
Have a ball
With the most special friends of all!
Cut the cake
You just can't wait!
Eat loads and loads
Don't worry 'bout the plate!
Everyone knows that when that special song begins,
Family and friends will surely join in!
And remember whether you're young or old
Birthdays, always a precious celebration to behold!
So Enjoy It!!!
Happy Birthday

Kelci Crounse, Grade 6
Tyrrell Middle School, CT

Halloween

Creepy haunted houses
Filled with cobwebs and spiders.
I wish it wasn't so spooky,
With all those creaking doors.
As if I was in a world with goblins and ghosts
And no one there except me.
Trick-or-treating is fun,
With all of those bags of candy
Everybody is dressed up in costumes —
The world is full of this on October 31st.
I want to run and hide,
However there is no place to go.
Is this a dream? No it is Halloween.

Walker Helms, Grade 5
St John Neumann Academy, VA

Colors

Orange is the color of pumpkin pie.
White is the color of that cloud in the sky.

Yellow is so merry!
Red is the color of cherry.

Green is the color of a Christmas tree.
Purple is the color of a present I see.

Blue is the color that is right for me.

Ashley Lynn, Grade 5
C Hunter Ritchie Elementary School, VA

Pie

I see the cherry filling slowly cooking.
I hear the soft, tan crust snapping and crackling.
I take the pie out and smell the sweet aroma filling the air.
I can taste all the love Mom put in it!

Lexie Brown, Grade 6
Juliet W Long School, CT

Merry Christmas

M ary gave birth to Jesus on this day
E ager children open their presents
R eindeers guide Santa's sleigh through the night
R udolph takes the lead
Y ule tide carols are sung

C hrist was born in Bethlehem
H am is part of the holiday feast
R ibbons are used to decorate the packages
I cicles hang from the rooftops
S tocking are hung by the chimney
T he three kings brought Gold, Frankincense, and Myrrh
M ass is held on Christmas Eve by candle light
A ngels spread good tidings that the Savior was born
S anta Claus is coming to town

James Roman, Grade 6
St Joseph School-Fullerton, MD

Nature

The freezing wind blows
The clouds come and go by me
To shine this clear day

Christopher Collins Grant-Winsborrow, Grade 6
Juliet W Long School, CT

The Zoo

There was an old man who supposed,
That the door to the zoo was closed.
He got into the zoo
While passing right through
The gate house where the guard dozed.

Devon Sharafanowich, Grade 4
JF Kennedy School, CT

The Fierce Guard Dog

I fiercely bark to protect my owner.
I pounce like a tiger on the intruder.
I run as fast as lightning.
I am the mean protecting dog.

Kayla Vivori, Grade 4
Greylock School, MA

I Wonder…

I wonder what would happen
if I stole myself away
I wonder how much I'd pay myself
to come back and to stay

I wonder if I'll ever be cool
or if I'll ever be smart
I wonder how that could ever be
'cause I'm off to a bad start

I wonder when the alarm will go off
or when the lights will turn on
I wonder if I'll ever be caught
trespassing on my lawn

I wonder why I'm talking to you
why are you even here.
I wonder why you're scaring me
is it because your face spreads fear?

Flynn Aldrich, Grade 6
Main Street Middle School, VT

My Dog Is My Best Friend

My dog is my best friend,
she's with me till the end.
She's number one,
and likes to play in the sun.
She's with me till the end,
my dog is my best friend.

Erica Maheu, Grade 6
Ashford School, CT

A Great Day!

The weather is perfect and the sun is shining
The flowers are blooming and the birds are singing;
I can smell the burgers, fries, and the peanuts from the concession stand
What a great day for baseball!

They players all dressed in their uniforms
with their glove, bats and balls,
The announcer always adds life to the game;
especially when the player hits a home run.

The reliever warms up in the bull pen while the team is in the outfield
the game is always exciting when the players try to steal
the catcher makes the winning play
and the scoreboard shows it all
What a great day for baseball!

Tanner Martin, Grade 5
Pemberton Elementary School, VA

Hurricane

I had seen it on TV
I had tried to leave but couldn't get away
So I hid in the stadium waiting for the storm to pass
Outside, the winds howled like wolves
Soon, rain lightly fell like leaves on a fall day
Sunshine changed to dark clouds franticly dancing around

The storm got stronger and stronger
And I wondered, would I live any longer?
Thunder clapped like cymbals in the sky
Rain now poured down to the ground
Lightning streaked across the sky like wild horses
Then suddenly, the sky became clear
Light winds swirled 'round me like a blender
And sunshine streamed out of the sky, its warmth calming me
But this didn't last long, for all chaos broke out again
The storm strengthened again
Ripping down trees from its roots and buildings from the ground
I waited and waited until finally, the storm passed
The storm had left ruins in its path

I looked back at the remains of my home
I mourned and mourned, but I am just glad I'm still here today

David Tang, Grade 6
Wakefield Forest Elementary School, VA

The Fish

I wish, I wish, I wish I were a fish
Swimming on the ocean floor
Searching for where I've been before
Among the seaweed and the snails the water slowly goes and flows
In the ocean or the sea
This is where I long to be
Among the fish
I'm a fish

Faith Rider, Grade 6
Main Street Middle School, VT

October

October is when the leaves
Fall from the trees like crisp apples.

October is when kids go out to trick-or-treat
On a dark gloomy night.

October is when birds migrate south
Like a retreating army.

October is when houses have sweet,
Wonderful smells like pumpkin and
Pecan pie cooking in the oven.

October is when energetic squirrels are
Busy collecting nuts and fruits for
Their long sleep like a dormant volcano.

The days are colder and shorter,
That is when October is in the air.

Marco Amleto, Grade 6
St Mary of Czestochowa School, CT

Beach

Splash!
A rough sea wave hits.
Seagulls fly by
Quawk, quawk!
They go.
Then there was silence
Slowly the gates open,
Footsteps.
Slowly people walk through the gates.

Ryan J. Williams, Grade 4
Dr Charles E Murphy Elementary School, CT

Christmas Day

He is coming down the chimney.
But you can't hear anything.
Because he is as quiet as a mouse.
So when you wake up on Christmas morning,
look under the tree to see if what you wished for is there.
All you see is what you deserve.
There it is — a gift that you would die for.
And it says, "From St. Nick."

Paul Paquette, Grade 5
Litwin Elementary School, MA

Sea Storm

See the mist go swirling 'round
See the foam go up and down
See the grey sky
And see the bubbling clouds
Way up high
Where the birds fly

Olivia Thomas, Grade 4
George Hersey Robertson Intermediate School, CT

I Am a Shark

I am a shark that swims around.
I do not live upon dry ground.

I am looking and looking, then spot my prey.
For this lunch I need not a plate nor tray.

"Child, stop looking at me like that!"
The prey then asks a friend; "Does this suit make me look fat?"

How dare she! I am not a child!
A shark! A shark that lives in the wild!

I swim up and give the victim a pinch.
She then screams a scream that makes me flinch.

She then looks at me as harsh as night.
She gives me a stare that gives me some fright.

No longer am I a shark that swims around.
But a roadrunner who runs from coyotes on ground.

Brieona Rosa, Grade 6
Covenant Life School, MD

Gilmore Camps

Where wildlife roams and where friendships are made,
Where secrets are kept and memories have stayed,
Where lobsters and hot dogs have found a home,
Where friends can never truly be left alone,
Where the beach is warm and the water cold,
Where friends come back both new and old,
Where dreams fly high in cabins of wood,
Where I always realize *this is all good!*

Olivia Jones, Grade 6
Juliet W Long School, CT

Insects

We are insects with mandibles
Please don't say we are cannibals

We love to eat your crumbs and stuff
Our mandibles are pretty tough.

If you receive a pinch from us
Do not go running in a fuss

"Give me all your food" I say
"Or our colony will make you pay"

We have been around since the dinosaurs
We'll escape underneath your doors

You might try to guess, but I bet you can't
I have to tell you, I'm an ant!

Hunter Hedinger, Grade 6
Immaculate Heart of Mary School, DE

Fright Night

On Halloween night
No mummy, zombie, or ghost
It is the Fright Night!
Timothy Coffman, Grade 5
St Joseph School-Fullerton, MD

Dogs

Dogs, dogs, dogs
Fat dogs
Skinny dogs
Nice, curly, lovable dogs
Fast, athletic, mean dogs
Those are just a few.
Rat dogs
Small dogs
Kind, stupid, smart dogs
Red, white, black dogs
Police dogs too
Firedogs
Weird dogs
And don't forget cuddly dogs.
Last of all
Best of all
I like my dogs!
Quinton Swan, Grade 6
Juliet W Long School, CT

Spring Becomes a Wonderful Dream

It's winter and I am cold
I have a splinter
And it's old
I go into my house
Sitting by the warm fireplace
It makes you daydream
About spring
And how your eyes shine
When you
Look at the sun
You feel like…
You just open a new world
Armoni Davis, Grade 5
Perrywood Elementary School, MD

Halloween

Dark, heavy costumes
mummies escaping from
moss covered tombs,
kids trick-or-treating
and lots of candy eating.
Strolling through streets
house after house,
it's the opposite of silent
and quiet as a mouse
Gabby Fantasia, Grade 5
Southbrook Academy, MA

Kitty Kacy

As I pet her soft, cozy fur,
I notice that she has gray as a winter sky
color of fur.
Kacy also has claws,
short as a super small nail.
With eyes as blue as a sunny sky,
she can nibble like a dog on my finger.
When I visit her again,
I hope I can bring her home with me.
Jenell Mershon, Grade 5
Long Meadow Elementary School, CT

Fall Wonders

Wind is whispering in my ear,
Howling for everyone to hear.
Leaves are falling, then drifting away,
Swirling around the kids that play.
Stars are twinkling on this frosty night,
Shimmering as I turn out the light.
Tiffany Zukas, Grade 5
Pollard Elementary School, NH

My Mom

Her once young face
is getting old
growing lines
and wrinkles
But her
soft, brown eyes are
still bright
that twinkles
I feel alone
when she's not
at my side like an
invisible man
But I feel cared for
when she's at my side
I met her right after
I was born
from her
large, balloon-like tummy
It was the happiest moment
of her life when
I was born
Kyuwon Park, Grade 5
Zervas Elementary School, MA

What School Means to Me

School is fun, it is great
So many classes you can take
History will take you into the past
You can also have fun learning math
School is fun with your friends
Until the school year comes to an end.
Stefano Guerriero, Grade 6
St John the Evangelist School, CT

On the Road

My family rented one R.V.
to go on the road.
I felt so blue
because I left my dog
at home.
We arrived to our house
I kissed my dog
and I regained strength.
Marlon Vasquez, Grade 6
Kenmore Middle School, VA

Chess

How about a game of chess,
To see who can be the best?

I'll move my pawn,
That's like a fawn.

I moved my rook,
Your knight it took.

Now I can castle,
Without a hassle.

I've moved my queen,
To be very keen.

It is too late,
Let's call checkmate.
Patrick Asselin, Grade 6
St Francis Xavier School, VT

Flowers

Out, Out
Out I go
Blooming, blooming all around.
Orange, yellow, purple of course,
White, blue, and red, why not?
Pick me once, pick me twice,
put me in a vase, all right!
Jessica Miller, Grade 4
Center School, CT

The Pueblo

There was a civilization
Group that was
Having a ceremony
By a pueblo.
At the ceremony
The civilization
Group was planning
A way to hunt.
Nancy Esparza, Grade 6
Kenmore Middle School, VA

Love That Girl

Love that girl
Like a cat loves to purr
I said I love that girl,
Like a cat loves to purr.
Love to see her in the night.
Love to call her, "cutie."
She walks gracefully like her mother
Pretty like a sunset
I said she walks gracefully like her mother,
And she's pretty like a sunset.
Smiles when she's doing gymnastics,
When she's with her friends, she smiles again.

Jevaughn K. Campbell, Grade 5
Clover Street School, CT

Me, Myself, and I

My heart is a dam holding
    in friendship and good memories
but; letting out sad memories.
    My mind is a pool of overflowing
thoughts and
    imagination and new ideas.
My eyes are indefinite pools of
    laughter plunging into my head forever
and never stopping.
    My mind is a bottle of sparkling cider
exploding and uncontained with a hint of sparkle.

Britt Mooney, Grade 6
Tolland Middle School, CT

Nature's Wonder

I look at the forest I look at the fallen tree
And I listen to them.
The grass is prickly, the leaves crumble and rumble about,
I feel the wind soar.

I look at the twigs. It looks like a bush without leaves,
What could it ever be?
I picture it a home for an animal with legs,
A soft place to sleep.

I go through the forest, I walk toward the calm river,
How wonderful it feels.
It feels good on my feet, feeling the water on my toes,
rushing water as the wind

I felt a little sleepy, so I slept out in the open sun.
What a wonderful day
What an awesome day, wandering around the forest.
I have to leave now.

I will come again to enjoy the beautiful place
I will live here forever.

Kaylen Harrington, Grade 5
Fairfax Collegiate School, VA

The Real Me

When I look at me.
Here is what I see.

I see a happy smiling face.
Then, I see a frown in the same place.

I see skies of blue on a happy day.
Then, I see skies of gray.

I see the best person in the world.
Then, I see the worst girl.

First, I see a "girl who serves."
Then, I see someone who gets on everyone's nerves.

First I see Christian Collins, me.
Then, I see no one I want to be.

But when it's all said and done,
I see sometimes, I'm number one.

Christian L. Collins, Grade 6
Homeschool Plus, VA

Acting on Broadway

For one month I have studied the script,
I know all the steps,
I know every song,
Tonight is the night I get up and shine,
I'll go up on stage and do nothing wrong.

The noise of the audience is barely muffled by the curtain,
It sounds as if all of New York is watching me,
The lights dim and they all get quiet,
They are all waiting and ready to see,
Me act.

I hear my mom call my name,
I wake up from that dream,
That silly dream,
The one that will never come true.

Later, I come across two paths,
To follow my dream and win the spotlight,
Or to help the world and make things go right,
I took the second path leading my dream to fate.

Dorothy Hastings, Grade 6
Grace Episcopal Day School, MD

Friends

Friends can be the sky in your life
Friends can be the brother or sister in your family
Friends can be the closest to you
So you should keep your friends together
Friends keep you going…

Michael Shamberger, Grade 5
Clover Street School, CT

Thank You God

Leaves drop to the ground.
Dying maple leaves are sad.
Thank you God for fall.

Kaylee Fuentes, Grade 4
St Augustine Cathedral School, CT

My Australian Friend

Kangaroos hop around
They go flying up and down
When I'm with them I don't frown
I like kangaroos.

Kangaroos have long tails
If they balance it won't fail
When I watch them I won't wail
I like kangaroos.

Kangaroos have a pouch
Their babies use it as a couch
If I see them I won't grouch
I like kangaroos.

Janelle Orndorff, Grade 4
Covenant Life School, MD

All Caged Up

Sitting on concrete stairs thinking,
About where my family could be.
I sit here alone wondering,
Why can't someone be with me?
Every day I lay here dreaming,
Of what it would be like to be free.
There's a big world waiting,
Is there a place in it for me?

Nicole Falzarano, Grade 6
East Shore Middle School, CT

Nighttime Gaze

Staring out my bedroom windowsill,
Feeling the cool breeze rush past me.
Looking into the starless sky,
The firefly's light lit the night.

Victoria Huynh, Grade 6
Wakefield Forest Elementary School, VA

Christmas

C hildren
H ugs
R inging of bells
I ce
S inging
T ravel
M oms and Dads
A gold necklace
S now

Cody Whitt, Grade 6
Monelison Middle School, VA

I Am a Football Star

I am a rough boy who likes football
I wonder if I'm going to catch this
I hear the crowd gasping and yelling at me
to catch the 40-yard flying fast football
I see the ball being kicked by the strong kicker
I want to recover a fumble by the other team's big players.

I am a rough boy who likes football
I pretend I'm in the NFL blocking players everywhere
I feel the leathery touch of the ball on my soft, tan, squishy fingertips.
I touch the other team's players
I worry if I'm going to be a star on the team.

I am a rough boy who likes football
I understand how to run the big plays
I say I will win this
I dream to be on a football team in college
I try to be the best
I hope to play football in college and in the NFL
I am a rough boy who likes football.

Joseph Foley, Grade 5
Blackrock School, RI

Christmas

Christmas is a joyful time of year.
Santa and his reindeer fill the thoughts of many.
Friends and family exchange gifts and cheer.
Because our lives are filled with plenty we forget what we should hold most dear.
Christmas is not a celebration of our bounty.
It is the celebration of the birth of someone near —
Jesus!
Christmas is a joyful time of year.

Joshua Bazzoli, Grade 4
North Star Elementary School, DE

The Dragon

Dragon, Dragon, is it true hiding deep in the dew
That you could breathe puffs of fire or is that a story of a liar

Where'd you get such enormous wings and all of those beautiful rings
Where'd you get such magnificent scales and such a long elegant tail

How did you get such a triumphant roar that could bring a single man to war
How'd you get such bright white teeth and hundreds of golden sword sheaths

And all of the kings knights could not stand up to you in a fight
How'd you get such powerful claws that sit connected to your striking paws

How'd you get such amazing eyes that hide all your terrible lies
How'd you get to be king of all hiding beneath a roaring waterfall

Dragon, Dragon, I know it's true hiding deep in the dew
That you could breath puffs of fire and I know it's not a story of a liar

Olivia Matthews, Grade 6
Hinesburg Community School, VT

Colors of the World

Red is the color of powder.
Gray is a tall towering tower.

Black is the color of the dark.
Green is the grass in the park.

Yellow is the color of the bright sun.
Brown is a freshly baked hot bun.

Claire Downey, Grade 5
C Hunter Ritchie Elementary School, VA

The Wonderful Time — Winter

Happy
Sledding will be fun
Wonderful snowmen
When will the winter end?
Snowpants and mittens
Plunking, crackling, dripping and slurping
Winter is here!

Garrett Harriman, Grade 4
John J Flynn Elementary School, VT

Rainy School Day

Rain pours gray all over the sky
Faces hide warm like bears in their hoods
Children huddle together under an umbrella
Beside the bus stop sidewalk, small icy cold streams form

Sara Prince, Grade 6
Wakefield Forest Elementary School, VA

Think, What a Simple Dream!

A simple dream, doesn't seem,
As good enough for you,
    Well it is the good, and it could,
Happen to be true.
    I have something better than it all,
Just a simple dream.

Things aren't always how they seem,
So think and love a simple dream.
    Kids think that they are cool, or even very neat,
With things that shine, or things that ring or beep.
    I have something better than it all,
Just a simple dream.

Dreams can go on forever,
So think of one now,
    Absolutely anything!
This I will allow.

You may think everything can start from what it will seem.
Good grades, ballet steps and soccer goals,
    Everything starts with a simple dream.
Just a simple dream.

Mia T. Tuccillo, Grade 4
Canton Intermediate School, CT

I Am a Girl Who Loves Horses

I am a young girl who loves horses
I wonder if I'll ever horseback ride
I hear the horse's hooves hit the ground
and hear the crowd cheering on supporting their daughters.
I see the tallest horse standing in front of me
I want to be a professional horseback rider when I grow older
I am a young girl who loves horses

I pretend I am a rodeo national champion rider
I feel the air in my hair when I ride my brown spotted pony
I touch and brush him daily
I worry about falling off my horse and seriously injuring myself
I am a young girl who loves horses.

I understand how to make the horses walk
I say I love riding horses
I dream to work with horses forever
I try to do better every day
I hope I will get a brown pony to play with
I am a young girl who loves horses

Nicole Fochler, Grade 5
Blackrock School, RI

The Mark of Winter

The season of snow
Ice is covering the road
The powerful winds whip across the once
green landscape
It's almost as if it were a dream
The silence is unbearable
A winter to remember
Has come upon us

Alex Furbank, Grade 5
Wakefield Forest Elementary School, VA

Deeper into the Forest

I'm walking thru the bushes,
That my mom said not to pass.
I'm ducking under the low trees,
Where my dad would pick the raspberries.
As I approach the tall trees at the forest edge,
I see a figure in the distance,
It sees me, and rushes toward me.
I see that it's just a friendly wild cat,
Purring happily at my feet.
I see why it is always muggy in the air.
The water from the spring is in the air.
Deeper into the forest,
I see an area with no trees.
There I see the spring.
And a field with beautiful, rare flowers.
I return to my house with my memories,
And the wild cat

Cristin Lalumiere, Grade 5
Hinesburg Community School, VT

Spring

S is for the plants that are sprouting
P is for playing in the sun
R is for riding bikes
I is for increasing temperatures
N is for not having to stay indoors
G is for great weather

Nicholas Estey, Grade 5
St Patrick School, MA

Pride, Power, Pinstripes

Yankees
Powerful, strong, great,
Heavy-hitting, catching, throwing
They are 26 time world champs!
Bronx Bombers

Matt Van Volkenburg, Grade 6
Juliet W Long School, CT

Saber-Toothed Tigers

Saber teeth like Stakes
Slashing the Skin of a giant Sloth

Pounding short faced Pandas
With their Pointed claws

Tar pits Trapping them
They try to escape
Treading then dying

Biting Bison
Being Brave
Bouncing after mammoths
Bears charge
But the Beastly tiger
Takes it down
Winning itself a meal.

Richie Bellucci, Grade 4
Riverfield School, CT

Fall

Fall is finally here,
We all shout and cheer.

We can't wait for Halloween,
When people in scary costumes are seen.

It's time to take out our warm clothes,
The difference in weather really shows.

The leaves are colorful and also, bright,
They are truly a beautiful sight.

Playing in leaves is lots of fun,
I'll stay outside 'till the day is done.

Jason Kulig, Grade 6
St Patrick School, MA

The Hat

There once was a cat named Pat
Who loved wearing his hat.
He fell asleep at night.
He liked being right.
He found out he was smart as a rat.

Kenan Elkaz, Grade 5
John J Flynn Elementary School, VT

Squirrels Are…Adorable!

Squirley Squirley
tail so curly,
come on down and
don't you worry.
up and down that
tree you scurry,
round and round
up and down.

Ahh!
you scared me,
jump off that big oak
like a tsunami.
    Thump!
like a wave in the ocean
can't control,
so stiff, so scared
like an English officer
on patrol!

Roda Ibrahim, Grade 5
Marley Elementary School, MD

An Ode to Flowers

Oh, how I love flowers,
Their scented sweet aroma,
Glazed petal tips,
And wonderful colors of the rainbow,
As honey bees fly by,
They glisten in the sun,
Blooming and blooming,
Until their petals grow wide,
Roses, daisies, and tulips too,
Cover the garden,
As I plant them all day,
See the raindrops on their tips,
In a summer's rainy day,
But, in the winter they fade away,
They curl up, but do not worry,
Their colors will come back,
In a warm summer's day,
The flowers will come back to
Enjoy another day,
Oh, how I love flowers

Megan Grahne, Grade 6
Beacon Middle School, DE

Baseball

I like baseball.
I play in spring, summer, and fall.
Steal, pitch, and hit,
Catch balls in my mitt.

I play with my friends.
Some games don't end.
I hit homeruns
I have a lot of fun.

I want to be a star
Play baseball every day,
I would travel far,
Baseball is what I'd play.

Joshua Hughes, Grade 4
Memorial School, NH

Teacher

Teacher Teacher
Teacher is also our preacher
she is a true and trusted friend
Who helps us learn.
She is great to have
When mom's not there.
I thank You God
For You have made the teacher
She is smart and kind.

Adrien Thokalath, Grade 5
Good Shepherd Catholic School, RI

Bird

There once was a bird that flew
and had a cold and said "ACHOO"
he sneezed on a Yankee
instead of a hankie
and the Yankee got it too.

Curtis Fleming, Grade 5
John J Flynn Elementary School, VT

A Blank Piece of Paper

I like to draw, I love to sing,
But writing is my favorite thing.
There is one problem
I won't ever forget;
I've no clue what I'm writing…
At least not yet.
It bothers me so,
I want to write so bad.
With a stub of eraser,
A pencil and a pad.
But look here before you,
On this extra-special pad…
A fully-written poem,
Not so good, but not half bad.

Lyric Spencer, Grade 6
Broadview Middle School, CT

Sunset

The beautiful sun sparkles on the water.
I can hear the cheerful waves crashing on the shore.
I am excited to see the sinking sun.
The pink sky fills me with happiness.
Why must it end?

Gary Pasquale, Grade 5
John J Flynn Elementary School, VT

Messy Room

My room is messy
It's kind of dressy
There's clothes on the floor
There's shoes at my door
Everywhere I go
I always hit my toe
My room is messy I can't even walk
But all I do is talk, talk, talk
So one day my mom said clean your room
But all I did was get the broom
Then one day I got out of bed
And when I got up I hit my head
Then my mom herd a big bang
She went into my room
I was quiet as a mouse
She told me once again to clean my room
But I didn't really need the broom
My mom came to take a look
She was surprised how long it took

Alicia Lightner, Grade 6
E Russell Hicks School, MD

Silent Speaker

Silent speakers whisper in the wind
Give you shade on a hot summer's day.
Silent speakers grow fast but yet so slow
You climb up them to reach great heights.
Silent speakers give life to all
Silent speakers provide beauty for this world.
Many people do not care about silent speakers
For they are nothing but plants to them.

Clair Huffine, Grade 4
Mary Walter Elementary School, VA

The Hunter

Just because I am a hunter
    I still love to shop
    I like to wear makeup
    I wear skirts
Just because I am a hunter
    I still love cheerleading
    Does not mean I am a tom boy
    Does not mean I am gross
Just because I am a hunter — please let me be a girl.

Brittany Boggs, Grade 6
St Rose School, CT

Call of the Forest

Oh, what is that melodious sound,
Drifting closer and closer on the warm summer breeze.
Maybe it is the trees softly swaying,
Or a horse happily neighing.
The sounds of a forest
With its frogs and the birds.
Croaking and chirping in harmony.
You might see a fish, with its glistening tail;
Splashing in a clear little stream.
Moonlight dancing on its delicate scales,
Watch them gleam, gleam and gleam.
Look at the sunset, through the trees,
See the warm oranges, pinks, reds and greens.
Matched with a magnificent chorus, it becomes a concert
So listen carefully on a warm summer night,
To hear the voices of animals,
Let the call of the forest lure you deep into another world.
Into the world of …
Nature

Agnes Cheng, Grade 4
Jamestown Elementary School, VA

Rushing

I rush against the rocks and am pulled back every time.
I'll always come back no matter how much I try.
All day, kids splash around and with me.
As the sun sets, I'm lonesome but golden.
What am I?

The Ocean

Caterina Wu, Grade 5
Four Seasons Elementary School, MD

I Am

I am a boy who loves to skate.
I wonder if I can go pro.
I hear the sound of the skateboard
crashing on the ground and the sound of my helmet.
I see everything so fast it's blurry.
I want to be a pro and be successful with my life.
I am a boy who loves to skate.

I pretend I am in a big skate competition.
I feel the wind in my hair when I go fast down the street.
I touch the skateboard when jumping.
I worry that I might fall and hurt myself very badly.
I am a boy who loves to skate.

I understand that skating is a difficult sport.
I say I can do this.
I dream that I can go pro.
I try to skate every day.
I hope that I will be successful in ways never imagined.
I am a boy who loves to skate.

Justin McGinnis, Grade 5
Blackrock School, RI

Life Is Good

It was Spring
and no one could deny it.
The bees were very busy,
flying from one flower to the next.
The mass of honey
was slowly increasing.
The flowers were blossoming beautifully.
Everything was at hearts content.

Ajha Eidi, Grade 6
Kenmore Middle School, VA

My Cat Airy

My cat Airy is as fat as a
Whale
He is as lazy as a
Sloth
He is as loving as a
Dog
He hunts like a jaguar
Stalking its prey
He's as orange as
The sun
And as white as
The moon
His eyes are as
Proud
As the roaring
Lion within
He is proud to
Play with his
Powerful brother
He is my cat
Airy

Marley Crooks, Grade 6
Juliet W Long School, CT

Alone

Alone on the couch,
Thinking of the times
Of being together with you
Waiting for the moment
You arrive at the front door
Saying, "Hi Allison! I missed you!"
Never wanting you to leave my arms
From the warm feeling of love
But sometimes
You will have to
Alone again
On the couch
Thankful for everything
Your love, your kindness,
And especially you.
Love your sister,
Allison

Allison Dewey, Grade 6
Greenwich Country Day School, CT

I Am

I am a good baseball player.
I wonder if I will be a pro.
I hear the crowd cheering for my team
    and my team is cheering for me when I am batting.
I see people running the bases and hitting the ball.
I am a good baseball player.
I pretend I hit my first home run.
I feel happy to hit my first home run and I felt great.
I touch the smooth, round ball.
I worry about not getting to the ball in time.
I am a good baseball player.
I understand that winning is not important.
I say "Good game!" to my teammates.
I dream of becoming a professional baseball player.
I try to do my best.
I hope to become a professional baseball player when I grow up.
I am a good baseball player.

Matthew Monti, Grade 5
Blackrock School, RI

The Strangest Day

I felt kind of sleepy. But there was a lot of heat so it was scorching hot.
I was in a shady area. Most of all that bothered me was the mosquito.
The mosquito was annoying me so much that I killed it.

Max Manivong, Grade 6
Kenmore Middle School, VA

A Sight of Glory

ARIZONA'S a one of kind place
GRAND is a simple explanation of the canyon
CANYONs of glory as far the eyes can see
IS one of the most stunning national parks
A painting of maroon and burnt orange folds lining the sun-kissed desert
MAGNIFICENT ruins paint the cracks of the canyon deserted by the ancient Apaches
SIGHTs of insurmountable beauty surround you
TO witness this beauty of nature is jaw-dropping
BEHOLD the supreme of all the national parks, the one, and only, Grand Canyon

Claire Carnevale, Grade 6
Beacon Middle School, DE

Rainy Day

Plip, plop, rain, spotting the driveway with droplets of cool water.
Children splashing in the driveway, getting soaked to the skin.
At the bus stop, kids and parents wait for the bus on the wet, gloomy day.
Holding their faces up to the rain, they get a good feeling inside them.

McKenna Deal, Grade 6
Wakefield Forest Elementary School, VA

Birthdays

A birthday is very important to people in the U.S.A.
Most people have fun on their birthdays.
Birthdays include: restaurants, malls, parties, cakes, ice cream, and presents.
What is your favorite thing to do?
By the way when IS your birthday?

Mkayla Broadie, Grade 5
Valley View Elementary School, MD

I Am

I am strong and brave
I wonder if I'm going to the NBA
I hear breathing
I see injured people
I want to live long
I am strong and brave

I pretend I am the best basketball player
I feel that I can fly
I touch the hand of God
I worry when I hear bad things on the news
I cry when Mike died
I am strong and brave

I understand stories and books
I say good things
I dream of the game winning shot
I try to be good
I hope to have many friends
I am strong and brave

Isaiah Webb, Grade 5
Clover Street School, CT

Homecoming Right Before Christmas

Homecoming
Right before Christmas
To America
From Romania
The airport
So many people
My sister and I
Astonished, scared, excited, overwhelmed

Homecoming
Five years past
Christmas Eve
Uncle Dan reads "The Grinch"
We sing "We Wish You a Merry Christmas"
Over the phone to Nana and Papa
Cousins, Secret Santa
Family

Adriana Putney, Grade 6
Milford Middle School, NH

Crunch!

As I glide through brightly colored leaves,
the cool breeze whizzes by you,
Sending leaves to fall like snow
leaves scattered everywhere,
like clothes on my bedroom floor
A whiff of my grandmother's pumpkin pie settles in my nose,
tempting me to have a bite
Rich sticky sap oozes into your mouth,
sending you a surprise of a bland and sticky sensation.

Isabelle Albin, Grade 6
Canton Intermediate School, CT

My Brother

This is my brother.
My brother is so cute.
He likes music.
His favorite is the flute.

This is my brother.
He likes to play games.
He loves Mancala
Don't worry, he won't call you names.

This is my brother.
he has a lot of hair.
It's hard to comb through
If you pull it…Beware!

Jasmine Webster, Grade 5
C Hunter Ritchie Elementary School, VA

For the Fun of Love

As soon as the sun sets in the west,
we will go out dressed our best.
For a moonlit walk, in which we shan't talk,
for the fun of love.
We'll go to the school all happy and cool,
for the fun of love.
We'll go to the play and stay all day
for the fun of love.
I will buy you a ring covered in bling
for the fun of love.
We'll buy a pet and take it to the vet
for the fun of love.
I love you and you love me let's go and get married
for the fun of love.

Tiffany Anderson, Grade 5
Jordan Small School, ME

My Life as a Walkingstick

I'm a walkingstick serenely swaying in the breeze
Eating the leaves of walnut, oak, and cherry trees

I can reproduce, I don't need a mate
Isn't that cool? I think that's really great!

When I drop my eggs to the ground
They hatch into little nymphs, small and round

If my leg should suffer damage or separation
I am lucky; I can use partial regeneration

It's an unusual ability I know
That's why I can get up and go

Now I know I may look harmless
But beware! Don't be too careless!

Alison Hopkins, Grade 6
Immaculate Heart of Mary School, DE

Winter

Winter
Cold and hollow
Leaves falling, trees bellowing, wind screaming
Empty trees, birds flying south, crystals on your tongue, and paw prints engraved in the snow
Snow, fluttering, dancing snowflakes
A white winter land and a winter storm brewing
Snow

John deAndrade, Grade 6
Juliet W Long School, CT

Ode to Nature

Oh! Nature you give everything shelter! From your trees to your grass you got our backs when you give us shelter. Yet we will kill you with ills and litter. You wish we would be good to you, by stopping the use of cars and stop cutting down trees and using them for making houses. We destroy you doing many things and causing things like acid rain and pollution that's how we kill you in so many ways.

Kenneth McCoy, Grade 6
Juliet W Long School, CT

Christmas

Christmas is a very beautiful holiday
Every Christmas you go outside and play in the clear white snow
Every Christmas kids are happy because they get presents
Sometimes on Christmas you invite all your family and cousins and have a big feast
You and your family might have a special dinner with good food
When you play in the snow you might pile up the snow and jump in it or you can make a snowman
At Christmas you go outside and you have snowball fights
And now you're so cold so you go inside and drink a nice warm hot chocolate
Then it gets dark and you're ready to go to sleep
When you go to sleep someone very special will come SANTA CLAUS

Kristina Biblekaj, Grade 6
Irving School, CT

Conservation

Blue birds fly through the endless sky and chipmunks scamper on the ground, but why should we
so smart and free destroy the wonderful world.
We have no right to fight the laws of nature,
The laws that keep us here.
It is not good that we should pollute Mother Earth's sacred skin.
We are harming the plants and the animals,
But mostly we're harming ourselves.
Many will perish from our sins and from the ashes will rise better beings,
Beings that will care that the Earth is dying,
But it will be too late for we have killed the Earth and ourselves.
It will be so dry and desolate just like the moon a lifeless planet in space.
So please take a moment to stop and think about what you can do to stop killing the Earth and
start helping.

Aja Procita, Grade 6
The Well School, NH

America, Today

Today's America is not the America we knew long ago, the LOYAL America, the America of LIBERTY and JUSTICE. If only that America lived in today's America of crime, war and evil. Where did that America go? What happened to the good America of LOYALTY, LIBERTY and JUSTICE? I thought I knew what it took to be a GOOD American, to be a good citizen…but there is more. Everyone does something that makes them a bad American. EVERYONE…

Nicholas Laughman, Grade 6
Everett Meredith Middle School, DE

My Dogs

These are my dogs, Lucy and Ellie
They are very cute and small.
They get excited.
They never will be tall.

These are my dogs, Lucy and Ellie
They like to sleep all day.
They are very nice.
Then at night they like to play.

These are my dogs, Lucy and Ellie.
They love the sun.
They won't ever get mad.
And they re so much fun.

Jessica Mikulas, Grade 5
C Hunter Ritchie Elementary School, VA

Scorpion Flies

See us scorpion flies, scorpion flies
We really will amaze your eyes

We patiently wait on the underside of a leaf
Because soon our prey will surely feel grief

We will use our big long chewing snout
To eat those bugs like humans eat trout

When we were little we lived in the ground
We will eventually eat dead bugs that we easily found

Although we are scorpion flies don't be frightened by our tail
Because it is as harmless as a wandering snail
Chris DiSabatino, Grade 6
Immaculate Heart of Mary School, DE

Red Sox Nation

The Red Sox are my favorite team
when they hit a homerun I always scream.

This year they are in the world series,
when they win they will make me delirious.

When the Rockies get beat,
I will be jumping off my seat.

I hope Big Pappi hits a homerun,
then I know Colorado is done.

Go Sox, Go Sox,
win, win win.

I know like in 2004,
you can do it again.

Shannon Denault, Grade 5
St Patrick School, MA

Snow

Those fluffy little flakes
dancing down to Mother Earth
blanketing themselves on the freezing ground
looking like stars in the midnight sky
when they sparkle on the snow covered ground
it's beautiful when the snow lightly plummets down
from the white sky and discovers a spot for it to lay
on the cold brisk ground

Tommy Casper, Grade 5
Amherst Middle School, NH

The Magical Silk Scarf

The Silk Scarf was blue,
As blue as the sky,
It changed with the sunset,
Pink was it one day,
A girl picked it up,
And found it was magical,
She ran to her father
And told him it was so,
The father took it from the girl,
And the girl started to cry,
Her father sold it on eBay,
And in return got a pillowcase,
Now folks our lesson in this is,
Not to sell something unless,
You know what you will receive in return.
Julia Duval, Grade 6
Juliet W Long School, CT

What an Adventure

A local dog sniffs a thread on the floor.
To the foolish minds of humans it's simple.
But to that dog it's a world of adventures.
Liam Brandel, Grade 5
Zervas Elementary School, MA

Gracefully

I am moving forward,
Gracefully,
I am living in a paradise,
Gracefully,
I am watching bubbles as they pass by,
Gracefully,
I smile as if I'm at the top of the world,
Gracefully,
I do not have enough time to see everything
But I shall be back soon,
As gracefully as before
It is all, special in its own ways,
Beautiful
And,
Finished
Gracefully.

Abbi Sparks, Grade 6
Graham Middle School, VA

Soccer

Time to play soccer,
Soccer is fun,
We play on the grass,
And under the sun.

The ref blows his whistle,
And the game officially starts,
And now a striker is coming,
He's racing down the line.

The defender harasses the striker,
Now both are tangled like vines,
The striker breaks free,
And now he's the only one,
To take the shot and score.

And now he shoots, and then he scores,
So now we have won.

Winston Jiang, Grade 5
Lincoln Central Elementary School, RI

Fall Time

Summer's gone and fall is here,
that's my favorite time of year.
Leaves are changing in the trees,
Falling, blowing in in the breeze.
Pumpkins lying all around,
Scarecrows planted in the ground.
Apple butter in the pot,
Man! I love that stuff a lot!
Raking leaves in a pile,
Just to play a little while.
Air is cool and oh, so sweet,
Say good bye to summer's heat!

Sarah Jo Wampler, Grade 5
Linville-Edom Elementary School, VA

Fall Flavors

Fall daisies blooming
Leaves changing colors
Falling to the ground
I feel the wind against my face
I smell spice cookies baking in the oven
I love the flavor of pumpkin pie
What a great time of year!

Erica Maggiore, Grade 4
Alma E Pagels Elementary School, CT

Slide

I dreamed
I was a slide
On a playground
Having fun with children playing on me
Happily.

Chanaire White, Grade 5
Cooper Elementary School, VA

Dare to Be Different

I walk down a path nearly paved with roses
looking at each creative masterpiece, hurry before the garden closes
I turn the corner to unveil a beautiful sight
all the pink roses seem in place and all right
but then something catches my eye
I spot what I really want to buy
I pick it up and put the lovely white daisy in my basket
I treat it as if it were a jewel going into a jewel casket
even though it is a daisy it is the prettiest thing of all
This is a rose garden if I correctly recall
then why is this daisy growing here too?
Everything now is very askew
This might be tragic
why it must be Mother Nature working her magic.

Heather Mikles, Grade 5
North Star Elementary School, DE

My Life Changed This Morning/I Need a Saturday Morning

My life changed this morning
The soothing morning
Feeling so relaxed
So warm — inside my heart
I hope my mom doesn't wake me up
Wake up Ryan!
Angry
Need more sleep like a bear in hibernation
Icky, mad, depressed
Need more sleep
I need a Saturday morning!

Ryan Tran, Grade 5
John J Flynn Elementary School, VT

Love…

Love the soft voice of the wind whistling solemnly.
Love the dancing, multicolored leaves gently fluttering to the ground.

Love the crashing of brook water splashing against the innocent moss covered rocks.
Love the peace when sitting upon a high ledge watching the sunset melt.

Love the screaming and hollering of that joyful kid, me.
Love the tears sprouting from my eyes and dripping to the ground.

Love the taste of the crisp autumn air and the awesome apple pie.
Love the thoughts and wonders about what will happen next?

Love the sticky, slippery ice that freezes over rocks and logs.
Love the silence, the peace and the joy of snow.

Love the feelings of dreaded sorrow and magnificent laughter.
Love the soft blanket of moss that gives frost a home.

Love the passion given to you as a gift.
Start to love…

Gabriella Roncone, Grade 5
Jack Jackter Intermediate School, CT

Christmas Day

On Christmas Day I wish for snow.
On Christmas Day I wish for gifts.
I wish for Santa Claus.
I wish for love and compassion.
I wish for a big tree.
I wish for lots of family.
I wish for peace on earth.
I wish for a perfect Christmas.
I wish this to be the best Christmas ever for my sister and my
Wonderful mom and dad.

Chris Healy, Grade 6
Juliet W Long School, CT

A Magical Time

Snow falling and fires burning
Chestnuts roasting
Hot chocolate brewing
Gliding on ice
Sledding down steep hills
Presents under trees
Snow burning on my skin
Feeling the coldness of winter
No school for two more weeks
Decorating gingerbread houses
Chopping down a Christmas tree
Decorating the house and the tree
Wreaths hanging from door to door
Trees decorated with twinkling lights outside
Gingerbread cookies baking
Giving and receiving presents
Santa Claus on his way
Gathering around as one family

Caroline Miao, Grade 6
Greenwich Country Day School, CT

Breathtaking Rainbow

Colors so magnificent
So unique and bright
Could hardly breathe
Overwhelming me with its creative patterns.
Lights up the dark sky
4 times the size of my house
Way up in the sky, touching the white puffy clouds
Right above me, I could hardly stand it

Emily Reed, Grade 6
Beacon Middle School, DE

Leave Me Alone

Sunset is coming,
I keep working.
My hands are getting tired from raking.
It seems the distance of leaves never end
Children are playing.
I keep working.

Achbold Tseveensuren, Grade 6
Kenmore Middle School, VA

Orange and Black

Halloween is the scariest time of the year.
This day is the day that ghosts and goblins appear.
Children run around in costumes.
In here, out there.
Kids ask for candy saying
"Trick or treat!"
Or "Happy Halloween!"

Crystal Dong, Grade 5
St Joseph School-Fullerton, MD

I Am the Mighty Dragonfly

I do not even think to bite,
Although I might give you a fright.

My nickname is the devil's darning needle,
Please don't mistake me for a beetle.

A pond is where I make my home,
Although as an adult I like to roam.

I look like the colors green or blue,
Even though it is not really true.

My color comes from the reflections of the sun,
I migrate from pond to pond and it is very fun.

Giles Bradford, Grade 6
Immaculate Heart of Mary School, DE

A Small Filly

We soared over the bush of lilies
I heard a soft little neigh
As I searched I saw a small filly
When we got closer I saw it stray

When we run we feel so free
We let the wind blow thru our hair
We fly across a fallen pile of trees
Out of the corner of my eye, I see a mare

My horse saw the mare
He started galloping while watching her
As you can see he did not want her seeing him stare
she ran away you could only see a blur

We started listening to hooves pounding on the ground
When we heard no more we started hearing calls
Turning to hear them better we follow the sound
Until we come across really big stalls

Once we finished we galloped away feeling the wind in our hair
After we had been galloping for a while
Our hair had made a different shape, like a flare
As we pushed it down, it was dark. We went home with a smile.

Elizabeth Strickland, Grade 6
Blue Ridge Middle School, VA

Ice Skating

The cool breeze hits my face
As I glide across the ice
I zoom by people
For a moment, it feels as if I am flying
Then the excitement stops
I start up again
And I get back to flying
I love ice skating

Langley Parker, Grade 6
Grace Episcopal Day School, MD

When All Is Dark

When all is dark
I lay in bed,
Waiting to embark
On the journey ahead.

I think of the days to come.
Will there be many,
Or only some?

Then I dream,
Of anything it might seem.
To soothe my restless mind.
To help me find,

A way to spread my wings
And fly.
Out in to the dark, quiet,
Open sky.

Niamh McAdam, Grade 6
Miles River Middle School, MA

This Is Just to Say*

This is just to say
I drank the juice
That was in the
Fridge

Which
You were
Probably
Saving for
Dinner

Forgive me
It was
Delicious
So pure
And so
Juicy.

Damarkus Williams, Grade 5
Clover Street School, CT
*Inspired by William Carlos Williams

Numbers

When
Your
Number is
Called
It's time
When you
Answer it's
Time to go
You can't
Say call
Someone else
It's your time not mine

Chryshele Henderson, Grade 5
Keene Elementary School, DE

Halloween

Having candy
At night
Loving trick or treating
Like having fun
Oh what a fright
We play games
Eating candy
Eeee, a ghost in the woods
Nice night

Megan Cotellese, Grade 4
St John Neumann Academy, VA

Puppies

There were seven puppies
Gnawing on a bone
The first one fell asleep
And rolled into a stone.
The second one got into a fight
The third one left to eat puppy chow
The fourth one got a big bite
The fifth one got bored and left
The sixth one rolled over
The seventh one got called
By his master, Dover.

Gradeigh Purcell, Grade 5
Highland Park School, CT

Santa Claus

S weet
A wesome
N ice
T alented
A mazing

C ool
L ots of fun
A ll the family is together
U nder the tree
S uper Duper!

Nicholas Maggio, Grade 5
St Joseph School-Fullerton, MD

My Favorite Season

Summer could be my favorite
Warm freedom to play
And big ice cream sundaes

Winter could be my favorite
White blankets on the ground
Christmas cheer all around

Fall could be my favorite
Halloween trick or treats
Caramel ones taste sweet

Spring could be my favorite
Warm rain greens the Earth
Flowers grow bring rebirth

Which season is the best,
Better than all the rest?

All are great, are first rate
The year must stay complete
I love the changes
No rearranges

Bridget Alessi, Grade 5
Lincoln Central Elementary School, RI

Bubbly

Bubbly is a feeling I get
when I see all my friends and family
I get that feeling because
they are important to me
I love them and they love me
and when we see each other we feel
Bubbly

Caitlin Agneta, Grade 5
Pollard Elementary School, NH

A Man Named Dave

There once was a man named Dave
He dreamed to live in a cave
He said to himself
I can't because I'm an elf
He really needed to shave

Tyler Robert Short, Grade 5
John J Flynn Elementary School, VT

Caterpillar

I dreamed
I was a caterpillar
In a tree
Eating a leaf
Loudly.

Sierra Crippen, Grade 5
Cooper Elementary School, VA

Rock Star

Happy days to you rock star
I hope your instrument is great
I hope you play with soul and rhythm
And play with excitement and get good rates
So jam with all your buddies
Enter the talent show
I'll be there with the tape recorder
In the very first row
I hope this gift is musical
Just like it was to me
Start that band you have always dreamed of
Be the rock star you were meant to be.

Kyle Griffin, Grade 6
Charlton Middle School, MA

Fireflies

A dancing little firefly
caught the corner of my eye.
Although it was small and meek,
I could hear the words it would surely speak.
It would feast on a drop of dew.
Like a poor child would a stew.
Crisp new wings meant at night,
the fireflies would turn on their lights.
And dance
to nature's song.

Stephanie Satterlee, Grade 5
Fairfax Collegiate School, VA

The Path Next to the River

I am walking in the wilderness on a path and I see
an eagle swooping down from a tree branch.
It lands right beside a river.
It turns side-to-side looking for prey.
Then I turn away for a second and when I turn back
the eagle is flying miles away from me.

Drew Treger, Grade 6
Wakefield Forest Elementary School, VA

A Cry of a Girl

She sheds a tear.
It drops into a puddle vibrating
She stares like a
Werewolf walking
and staring at its prey,
while her uncle, in the rusted casket,
her puddle and her self pride is being lowered.
She wonders why this is occurring.
Where will he go?
She thinks, "Am I the only one frowning?"

Is there someone far away smiling?
Hatred fills the air.

Janell Tyson, Grade 6
Tomlinson Middle School, CT

Cicada Killer

I am a cicada killer living on a forest edge,
Some of my family lives under a city park hedge.
If you are a cicada, I will certainly harm you,
But if you are another animal, I might sting you too.
I will take a paralyzed cicada back to the nest,
But I have to get more cicadas so I still cannot take a rest.
All my children live in a cocoon,
But they will not be coming out any time soon.
My house is east of the Rocky Mountains, near the Poconos,
And this is where my story comes to a close.

Sean Deely, Grade 6
Immaculate Heart of Mary School, DE

The Friend Blues

Oh, how I sing the blues.
It comes to me every night.
Oh, how I sing the blues.
It sometimes leads to a fight.
Some of my friends are cruel.
My dreams are not very bright!

Oh, how I sing the blues.
I can't go to sleep.
Oh, how I hate the blues.
I end up counting every 56 sheep
Some of my friends don't like me!
I wish I could have friends that I could keep.

Oh, the friend blues
They make me very sad.
Oh, how I disgust the blues
They make me very mad.
Are my friends angry at me?
I wish I was glad!

Kaitlyn Ridenour, Grade 4
Boonsboro Elementary School, MD

The Big Tree Adventure

One day I thought I'll climb a tree
On the way up I saw a bee
When I annoyed him he stung me.
I was so shocked that I fell out of the tree.
On my way to my house my brother said, "Dee"
Look at your knee!
Then to the house went we
Thank goodness Ma didn't see!

Amber Curry, Grade 5
Mary Walter Elementary School, VA

Jacob

My baby brother Jacob is cute,
but he can be vicious at times.
He cries when I leave,
it's hard for my Aunt Gail to calm him down.

Chelsea Fortune, Grade 4
JF Kennedy School, CT

Alone

The pond sparkles invitingly,
everything about it silent and perfect.
A dragonfly skims
over the surface,
its gauze like wings whirring madly.
Faces flit across my mind,
remembering, regretting.

Ruby Grace, Grade 6
Kenmore Middle School, VA

Friday

Friday is great
Please don't be late
This is why our teachers faint:
in art the walls are painted neon yellow,
in the gym we say "this is our gym"
every Friday that's what we do
but this Friday I have the flu.

Ryan Mercier, Grade 4
Brookside Elementary School, MA

Fire Dragon

I was playing in
The mountain mist
There was little
Sunshine
I looked up at
The sky
What I say
Defies knowledge
A dragon
A real fire dragon
The dragon was majestic
In the small sunshine
It looked like
A gem
One with vibrant colors of
Fire

Melea Huon-Dumentat, Grade 6
Kenmore Middle School, VA

Berries

Berries on a tree
Blue sky, green leaves in the sun
Red leaves a 'rustling

Emma Clark, Grade 4
St Brigid School, ME

Muffin/Pet

Muffin
Small, beautiful
Running, chasing, eating
Lick your face happy
Pet

Nikolas DeVincenzi, Grade 4
Brookside Elementary School, MA

The Beauty of Nature

I feel the wind blowing on my face
The birds chirp their sweet morning songs and
A white mist made of water fills the air
The leaves fly through the sky like green birds leaving behind their family and friends
The cloudless sky sparkles like a beautiful blue ocean stretched above us
The sunlight flits through the sky and enters the garden
The dappled sunlight dances on the trees, shining like gold
The fresh smell of the day floats in the air and
The dew shines like diamonds frosted on the trees and bushes
The flowers bloom everywhere, little sprouts of color standing alone
In this beautiful and enchanting green world of mine.

Pooja Chandrashekar, Grade 5
Fairfax Collegiate School, VA

Outside

Outside is beautiful.
The flowers are blooming in the garden.
Then the leaves softly fall to the cold ground.
The snow glitters in the sun as it quietly lays on the earths ground.
Then the heat comes and water rushes down the beautiful babbling brooks.
The cycle then starts all over again, again, and again forever, forever and ever.
Outside is keeping the earth the beautiful planet it is.
Outside is beautiful.

Brooke Noel, Grade 6
Ashford School, CT

The World as I See It

In November, the old pumpkins sit by the door, their grins drooping, skin shriveling.
The birds are out, like children, squabbling over seeds.
The days are shortening, almost as if the world is coming to an end.

Russell Allen, Grade 5
Whately Elementary School, MA

I Am

I am a person who loves playing baseball.
I wonder if we'll win the championship.
I hear the crack of the bat hitting the ball
and the crowd cheering my name, "Tyler!"
I see myself round the bases for a huge home run.
I want to get a walk off home run to win the game.
I am a person who loves playing baseball.

I pretend bases are loaded and I'm Big Papi.
I feel the energy from the fans and I feed off of their energy.
I touch bag one of four.
I worry about their replacement pitcher and getting through the ninth.
I am a person who loves playing baseball.

I understand that sportsmanship is just as important.
I say, "Balls in, coming down!"
I dream of becoming a professional player.
I try to get a home run.
I hope I play in Fenway Park with all my idols.
I am a person who loves playing baseball.

Tyler Boudreau, Grade 5
Blackrock School, RI

Girl with a Hoop

Pretty little girl wearing a bluish-green lace and silk dress
With a morning glory sash,
Peach colored pale skin with golden brown hair
And button blue ribbons
Hazel eyes,
Deep red colored lips,
She wears navy blue shoes with bluish-green socks,
She holds an oval shaped hoop that's made of bamboo
The hoop is a shade of gold,
The garden is peach and gold with a hint of magenta and indigo
And robin's egg blue with salmon pink and maroon
With a splash of violet and apricot.
The flowers are daisies and posies with some dandelions
And tulips and roses
With a couple of marigolds, morning glory's,
Sunflowers,
and lovely dahlias.

Caitlin Briggs, Grade 4
Boonsboro Elementary School, MD

Birthdays

Birthdays are the day of your birth
The day your little toes touch the earth
It only comes once a year
Maybe one day you'll get bike gear!
There's mom and dad and grandparents too
They're all coming just to see you!
Friends and family gather all around
There's no way you could have a frown

Emma Salerno, Grade 5
Davenport Ridge School, CT

I Am

I am a tough boy who plays football.
I wonder who will win the game.
I hear my pads smashing into the team's players and
my mom screaming out my name loudly.
I see me tackle the kids right to the ground.
I want to make the best tackle in the whole entire game.
I am a tough boy who plays football.

I pretend I am a huge NFL football player.
I feel extremely tough when I swing my body to
make a really big tackle.
I touch the ground, I'm ready.
I worry if I don't win the game or make tackles.
I am a tough boy who plays football.

I understand how to play the football game.
I say I love to play.
I dream I'd be an NFL player.
I try to win the game.
I hope I could win all the games and the championship.
I am a tough boy who plays football.

Noah Volatile, Grade 5
Blackrock School, RI

True Friends

T rusting each other with everything
R eal with each other
U nique in their own special way
E ncouraging to each other in every situation

F ight sometimes
R eally know each other
I nto a lot of the same things
E ntertain each other with the weirdest things
N o matter what you know they are there
D on't get envious but are happy for each other instead
S trong when with each other

Sarah Grace Moxley, Grade 6
Graham Middle School, VA

Basketball

My heart,
On a treadmill.

My hands,
grabbing orange sphere.

Grab, go, grab, go
I thought,
moving around
like berserk monkeys grabbing one banana.

Sophia Carrano, Grade 4
Riverfield School, CT

Colors

Colors will make your day,
Make you smile with its own special way.
Colors are the sun rays of all the beautiful days,
It's like the fragrance of sweet honey,
Like the feel of a tropical breeze.

Without colors everything would be plain.
And we would be insane.
It's like a zebra without its stripes.
A piece of candy without its taste,
A book without its cover,
So now I think you know what I mean.

Colors are like friends,
They bring color into your life.
Colors laugh with you,
Colors cry with you.
Colors do everything with you.
That's all I want to say…

Colors are immortal,
More precious than gold,
Without colors I don't know what we all would do.

Niti Patel, Grade 5
St Brendan Elementary School, MA

What I Hate About You
Dancing around.
Singing loud.
All in my head.
Please go to bed.
Can't take it anymore.
You're such a bore.
Go away.
I'm not playing today.
"Goodbye little sister."
I say that in a good way!
Krista Nayden, Grade 4
Weston Intermediate School, CT

My Mom
My mom works a lot.
She gets to places on the dot.

She cooks and bakes
You'd love the things she makes!

She helps me with my homework
And she does all the tough work.

I love my mom.
She does not yell.
She is very calm.
Olivia Kaiss, Grade 5
St Joseph School-Fullerton, MD

Ravens
Flying through the skies
of forests and trees

Swooping down
to eat what they see

Stealing smaller birds nests
when the time is right

Blending in
with the pitch black night.
Noisy large
two-feet-long birds

Bright red eyes,
helping to see their prey
Making it hard
to run away

Largest songbird
to ever exist
Singing the traditional
"Kaw Kaw"
"Kaw Kaw"
Dominic Smith-DiLeo, Grade 4
Pleasant Valley Elementary School, MD

Itchy
I went to see my family
And get some needed rest
My cousins had two kitties,
And Itchy was the best.

I watched him fight his sister,
I pet him every day,
I snuck away to see him,
I never went away.

When I had to leave him,
I was really sad,
I wanted him to come with me
Oh, that would make me glad!

I looked at many pictures,
I dreamed of him each night,
I drew him 'til my pencil broke
I missed how he would fight!

But then I got an email
That was a cause for mourning,
Itchy had been run over
And buried Monday morning.
Rachel Thornton, Grade 6
Thomas Blake Middle School, MA

The Freedom Flag
Oh flag so bright.
Of blue and white and red so strong.
It dangles high with great pride.
that is why we sing a song.
Jeffrey Pride, Grade 5
Good Shepherd Catholic School, RI

An Ode to Friends
Friendship is special,
Fragile
Something you can't touch.
If they have your back,
You care for them very much.
They make you laugh
They make you cry.
To protect their feelings,
You might tell a lie.
Friendship is bigger than the sky,
Unremovable like a knotted tie.
A friendship could be as simple as a line,
Or as complicated as an unsolved crime.
Friends may move along with time,
But never fear
They have not left you behind.
Mercedes Madsen, Grade 6
Juliet W Long School, CT

Harvest
Fall leaves on the ground
Colorful red, orange too
They are also crisp
Noah Warmuth, Grade 4
Brookside Elementary School, MA

One Window Is All I Need
One window is all I need
To see what my life will hold for me
To see everything around me
To love you the way you loved me
To be adventurous
To change the world
To make a difference
Lena Harris, Grade 6
St Rose School, CT

Canines
Dogs, dogs, dogs
Loyal dogs
Brave dogs
Happy, sad, fast dogs
Mean, fat, skinny dogs
Those are just a few.
Scared dogs
Slow dogs
Playful, bad, good dogs
Aggressive, protective, sleepy dogs
Energetic dogs too!
Furry dogs
Furless dogs
And don't forget lovable dogs.
Last of all
Best of all
I like my dogs!
Tyler Smith, Grade 6
Juliet W Long School, CT

Football
Hut 1, hut 2, hike!
Football flying through the air
Who will catch it now?

Ball dancing on hands
If Randy catches the ball
It will be a score!

They fly through the air
Randy has caught the football
The crowd goes crazy!

The fans jumped up
Randy is touchdown dancing
I adore this game!
Trent Duffy, Grade 5
Old Saybrook Middle School, CT

The View from the Lamp

Lamp:
Ugh! That annoying, reading,
Night-owl kid.
Using my light
Till all hours of the night.

Even when her parents yell,
"Turn it off and go to sleep!"
On light rabbit-feet, she tiptoes down the stairs,
Very discreet, to check if her parents are awake

If they are not, it's back upstairs
To become entranced in another story
Keeping me up
I wish that girl would forget how to read

Isabel Zayas, Grade 6
Middlebrook School, CT

The Race for Hope

The race for hope,
A race to help find a cure,
A cure for brain tumors.

Dorothy and I together,
Run to save lives,
People like Drew Neally.

Each person runs,
Three more miles of hope,
We all are much closer.

Donations are helpful,
Donate even if you're not in the race,
These donations support kids and families.

I run the whole way,
I only stop for water,
If I slow down I will feel dizzy.

I cross the finish line,
And have a smile on my face,
I know I have helped save a life.

Clare K. Specht, Grade 6
Grace Episcopal Day School, MD

Don't Just Reach for the Stars!

Your parents always tell you do your best
Right? Don't they always tell you reach for the stars!
They don't know you can go higher!

Instead reach for the moon! Even if you miss the moon
You will land on the stars. So the next time your parents say
Reach for the stars remember to reach for the moon!

Ashley Rodriguez, Grade 6
Western Middle School, CT

Oddie

O utrageous
D orky
D im-witted
I ce cream lover
E asily excited

Jackie Doores, Grade 5
C Hunter Ritchie Elementary School, VA

Ode to Pie

Oh Pie,
How your gooey
Inner filling
Makes me feel
All warm inside,
No matter if you are
Apple, Blueberry,
Cherry, Strawberry or Éclair,
Your sugary sweet sensation
Is like taking a bite
Out of happiness

Oh Pie,
How I love you for dessert
With a spoonful
Of whipped cream on top.
You are perfect
On an autumn eve
When the breeze is cool
And every forkful
Gives my mouth
A warmth only you can give it

Catherine Bogdan, Grade 5
Friendship Valley Elementary School, MD

I'm Me

Everyone sees me through different eyes

Annie, as a best friend
sees me as a basketball player, hurling the ball into the net

From Abby, another best friend,
I'm loud, always ready to meet someone new
outgoing, encouraging

I'm a helpful daughter to Mom and Dad
most of the time eager to help out

From Chester I'm calm
and the only one who gives him attention

But Lily, my other dog
Sees me very hyper throwing the tennis ball for her

I'm a different person to everyone but still, I'm me.

Emily Alonso, Grade 6
Middlebrook School, CT

Fall Features
Chipmunks scurrying
Red leaves falling to the ground
Sky peeking through trees
Corinne Hennessey, Grade 5
Pollard Elementary School, NH

The Cow
Upon the farm,
I see a cow,
Grazing in the flowing grass,
By the rivers edge,
He will stay for hours and hours,
Eating and sleeping in the autumn sun.
Carly Berkebile, Grade 6
Floyd T Binns Middle School, VA

Trees
Big green monster waving in the breeze.
All its hair swaying with ease.
I hope it won't try to get me.
But I bet it won't hurt a flea.
Sara Mitnik, Grade 4
Litchfield Intermediate School, CT

Christmas Night
As you fall asleep
you count some sheep.

As you hear some feet
you hide under your sheet.

You hear something coming down
now you don't have a frown.

When you peer
somebody is coming near.
Corinna King, Grade 4
Brookside Elementary School, MA

Untitled
Tropical
Sunny, warm
Swimming, tanning, hula dancing
Beach, Caribbean, iceberg, winter
Freezing, biting, frosting
Cold, snowy
Arctic
Lee Hayes, Grade 5
Wakefield Forest Elementary School, VA

Leaves
Red colorful leaves
Fall from the beautiful trees
And they fall softly.
Shaquille Epps, Grade 4
St Augustine Cathedral School, CT

Writer's Block
I told my friend,
"I have writer's block."

He said,
"What is writer's block?"

I told him,
"If your imagination was your home territory,
writer's block would prevent you from getting there.

If you had to be in the sun to think of ideas,
then writer's block is a giant oak tree cast you in shadow.

When you try to get out of the shadow, the tree will move
to make sure you stay in the shadow,
until you can cut down the tree without a chain saw.

If you had to be in the White House to think of ideas,
writer's block takes the form of bodyguards that want to keep out every intruder."

And my friend said,
"Then it sounds like you've escaped your writer's block."
Patrick Dunbar, Grade 6
St Brigid School, ME

Why Oh Why Said the Elephant
"Why oh why?" said the elephant,
"Must I be o o so large? Why
oh why" said the elephant "Must my name
be Marge? Why oh why must I
be so pink? Why oh why cannot
I shrink? Why can't I be
checkered or polka
dotted? With patterns
exotic and colorfully
spotted? Why oh why
must my nose be so big?
Why can't it be stubby
and squashed like a pig?
Why oh why must my ears
be so bulky? Why can't I
be cheery, and not always
so sulky? Why can't I
have horns like the ones
on a ram? Heck, I like
me just how I am!"
Lucy Jermyn, Grade 6
Main Street Middle School, VT

Cats
Cats are fluffy, soft cuddly, and nice sometimes, lovable, and funny.
I have two cats, one is a girl and one is a boy.
Watch for my girl or she will follow you.
Chelsie Perzan, Grade 4
Wapping Elementary School, CT

My Dog

My dog is so cool.
He is so silly.
He is cute and cuddly.
I wish his name was Billy.

My dog is so cool.
He likes to dig in dirt.
He likes to play with girl puppies.
He loves to flirt.

My dog is so cool.
He is brown and white.
He loves to cuddle,
But he might bite.

Lindsay Dodson, Grade 5
C Hunter Ritchie Elementary School, VA

My Life

I am from my bedroom,
Yellow walls with hardwood floor,
Laptop plugged in to play with,
Soft bed for sleeping on at night.

I am from home.
Watching TV on a leather couch,
Playing the Wii happily,
Peaceful quiet street with children playing.
Leaves falling covering the backyard.

I am from Dorchester.
Kids walking or riding the bus to school.
Cold chilly weather,
Cars going to the highway, filling gas in cars.

I am from Vietnam.
Vietnamese people raising animals,
Sandy roads with noisy motorcycles zooming, beautiful beaches,
People working in a poor country to raise a family.

I will be a teacher.
Teaching brilliant kids,
Living in a regular house,
And having a bright future.

Michelle Nguyen, Grade 5
St Brendan Elementary School, MA

Summer

Summertime, summertime, a time to relax.
When bees have fun.
They sting, you lunge.
Almost like a tiny band or orchestra.
They make sound, like tiny music.
Profound tiny creatures pollinate flowers.
Why you pass hours gazing at flowers.

Jesse Stewart, Grade 5
Perrywood Elementary School, MD

I Am a Softball Player

I am a young girl who loves softball
I wonder if I'll make the cut
I hear the crack of the bat smacking the ball,
    and the hustling when it nears
I see the sweat dripping like tears off the team.
I want to see myself on a major league team someday
I am a young girl who loves softball

I pretend that I'm playing in the major leagues
I feel when I'm on the pitcher's mound I'm on top of the world
I touch the hard, smooth leather
I worry I will pitch a home run and lose the game
I am a young girl who loves softball

I understand that winning isn't everything teamwork is
I say no team no game
I dream to pitch a no hitter
I try to be my best
I hope to travel the world playing softball someday soon
I am a girl who loves softball

Brittni Capozzi, Grade 5
Blackrock School, RI

In the Distance

I gazed out the window
To see in the distance
A showering of breathtaking sparks.
I felt the power of the crowd near my house.
It was the most beautiful thing
I ever laid eyes on.

Sky Bechtold, Grade 6
Kenmore Middle School, VA

Dreaming Big in the Middle School

I have a lot of dreams in the past
But I want a really good one to come to me fast
I want the one that shows me getting a job
Like the one where I'm choosing my career

I really want to make good grades for the rest of my years
So when I go to college I'll have a lot of knowledge
My future job is to become a doctor
So I'll have to work really hard to get this profession

I'm going to follow my dreams
And try to follow all these dreams
This life that I imagine I know to get there it'll be difficult
So I'll have to have confidence in myself

I just hope I be the best I can be
And not let anybody stop me
I'm going to get ready and go
Start living my dreams and get on with the show

Rehan Razzaq, Grade 6
Graham Middle School, VA

Summer

Why? Why? Why does summer have to end? I used to love to watch the waves move when I am at the beach, people burying me in the sand, the seagulls flying in the air. I use to love throwing a Frisbee in the air, catching a ball in a game, and playing with my friends. I used to love riding my bike, feeling the air hit my face. Oh, how it felt so good. Seeing all the friendly faces as I passed by. But one thing that I will never forget is the chilly water that was so fun to play in. The only reason I could think of summer ending is because next year there will be another one.

Richard Quiles, Grade 6
Irving School, CT

Just Me

My brother thinks I'm really annoying,
but sometimes I'm O.K.

"She's full of excitement and brightens my day,"
my grandfather says.

"I love to watch her running down the soccer field
and giggling with her friends," says my mom with a smile.

My dad thinks I'm joyful, caring, and smart.
He loves it when we do things together on the weekend.

Maisy, my rabbit, loves it when I pet her and give her treats.
She hates it when I try to brush the knots out of her soft, thick fur.

Goldie, my cat, says "I love sleeping on her big pink bed where she gives me tummy rubs,
but I like it best when she feeds me!"

My soccer ball dreads the moment when I approach for the big kick.
He knows he's in for a rough ride down the field.

My cute little cousin, Teddy, knows that I love him the most
and that he should run when I come in for a giant hug.

Athletic, energetic, smiley and caring...
It's just me!

Liza Lindgren, Grade 6
Middlebrook School, CT

The 4 Seasons of the Year

Winter, spring, summer, and fall joy will come with them all.
First comes winter with hailstones crashing to the ground there's also snow, sleet, and ice all season around.
Next there's spring with different color leaves with bright sunny skies and a warm weathered breeze.
Then there's summer as hot as the sun with kids going to the beach having lots of fun.
Lastly there's fall with thunder booming all over the sky making cold breezes that keep whooshing on by.
All 4 seasons will end here but they will come back next year.

Thomas Mohr, Grade 6
E Russell Hicks School, MD

Wave Obituary

A dazzling wall of water dances against the blood red sunset
Foam is strewn from its robust form as it rolls gracefully onward
A crest of white stands out on its bubbling, frothing surface, growing and strengthening
At last it breaks, and a shower of droplets like shimmering diamonds explode into the indigo sky
A swell forms far off in the horizon

Madeline Cowan, Grade 6
Brunswick Jr High School, ME

Fearless of Life

My life protects its secrets and thoughts
The protection of friends I'm unable to measure
Life holds all the things I am yet to be taught
All of this is like a dragon's treasure

It's fearless of what challenges life holds
It will never let down challenges since there are many.
It analyzes whatever it's told
I'm like a dragon against an army

The shelter of my life is warm
My shelter can be anywhere
A dragon will be friendly and lay down its arm
As long as you know the words to bear

My life is as mysterious as a dragon's life
It stays quiet if not threatened
It is humble when it has lost to a knife
It keeps its secrets when beckoned

A dragon's life is wide open
My life has choices I need to make
The chosen choices I store in my den
I hold my life like the coils of a snake

Anna O'Connor, Grade 6
Blue Ridge Middle School, VA

Come Sail Away

Come sail away to a relaxing place
Where you see fish bubbling and grumblin'
Where the coral is pink
It will make you blink you see
The bubble moves toward the light
Pop goes the bubble
You see the sparkling water glisten in the sunlight
Listen to the seagulls sing in the wind
The sand looks like cocoa
With little pebbles that look like little marshmallows
Flipping back and forth when the fish go by
Come sail away to a relaxing place
You will have fun with me

Haley Pimental, Grade 4
Cranston-Johnston Catholic Regional School, RI

The Doggy Paddle

Emerges swiftly
The dog
Don't laugh — in its clown suit for Halloween,
His cuteness is telling me he's saying trick-or-treat,
Why not love him?
With his puppy power pout.
Well this dog is powerful
only Conner shall trick-or-treat with me.

Janayjha Gray, Grade 5
Clover Street School, CT

Pets!

There's big pets and small pets
Skinny pets and fat pets
Fuzzy pets and bald pets
Hyper pets and hungry pets
Silly pets and smart pets
Bossy pets and sweet pets
No matter how fat or bossy I love them all.

Kendra Short, Grade 6
Graham Middle School, VA

Winter

I see white on the ground
I hear a very joyful sound.
I smell what the eye can't see
I taste what is right in front of me.
I feel excitement here and there,
Winter is finally here!

Justice Thomas, Grade 5
Abbs Valley Boissevain Elementary School, VA

Self Portrait

Room full of blue and green decorations everywhere
Vera Bradley around the room
Basketball and Yankee posters on the walls
Pictures of big, fluffy dogs on the tables
Pictures of her boogie boarding
A bed that looks like heaven

Books full of suspense with eye catching covers
And well-known authors on her shelf
Yankee things everywhere
Basketball accessories on each table

CD's lying around, boom boxes here and there
Lyrics to songs on chairs
Laughing with friends, coming up with crazy ideas
Goofing around like a maniac

Acting hilarious, very energetic, jumping all over the place
Likes to sleep in late
Lounging and doodling are fun for her
Listening to music is relaxing to her
Decorating, reading, acting crazy, hilarious
But can be quiet…sometimes.

Kylie Cafiero, Grade 6
Middlebrook School, CT

Autumn

A sea of exquisite leaves above and below
U nique colors everywhere you go
T ime to spend some time outdoors
U nder your feet the dry leaves crunch
M any lovely sights to see
N ature's most beautiful season

Kate Greenberg, Grade 5
Davenport Ridge School, CT

Beatless Heart

Flying in the sky above.
Speechless
without love
Looking down so carelessly
Sinking, sinking, sunk
Leaving the sky as I flunk
I may be bad
Sad, mad,
All these emotions are making me crack
I'm definitely packed,
as I back
Nothing to do,
Nothing to say,
Today wasn't like any other day
I will never forget it,
Always
Speechless, breathless,
My heart is beatless.

Jordan Emily Richard, Grade 5
Toy Town Elementary School, MA

Dawn

Rays pierce the hazy mist
Sunshine floods the dim sky
Dewdrops sparkle proudly in the valley
The silent world slowly stirs awake

Dianne Lee, Grade 4
John Ward Elementary School, MA

Poems

I do not like poems.
I do not like them at all.
they give me a headache,
Especially in fall.
I hate writing poems!
I don't know what to write!
I just sit at my desk thinking
All day and night.
Hey, is this a poem?
Oh, can it be true?
I'm writing a poem!
I no longer feel blue!
I no longer think poems
Are so full of sorrow.
Hey, maybe
I'll write a poem tomorrow!

Taryn Nugent, Grade 6
St Joseph School-Fullerton, MD

The Queen

The fairy queen is beautiful
She is quite smart
The fairy queen is dutiful
Her people love her to the heart

Charlotte A. Lewis, Grade 6
Floyd T Binns Middle School, VA

A True Friend

What is a true friend?
A true friend knows what you are saying without a word spoken.
They do you favors without you asking.
A true friend tastes your homemade dinners, knowing you aren't the best chef.
A true friend laughs at your jokes when they're not funny.
A true friend keeps your secrets without slipping a word.
A true friend knows exactly what to say when you are hurt.
They know you better than anyone.
A true friend catches you when you fall.

Robin Owens, Grade 5
Pemberton Elementary School, VA

Autumn Season

A corns falling from the trees
U nharvested crops dying
T ree's leafs turning colors
U n-fallen branches will fall
M ice get ready for hibernation
N ewly grown apples ready to be picked

S ummer is now over and school begins
E veryone preparing for winter
A utumn is here and winter will follow
S now will come after the leaves fall
O ctober is the time of autumn and everyone's favorite Halloween
N ovember is coming when autumn will end

Ryan Gasparini, Grade 6
St Patrick School, MA

A Dreamer Within

Not many people are just down to earth
Not many people are dreaming all of the time,

Hannah doesn't have any connections to earth when she is daydreaming,
— Mom

Her mind soars with flocks of wild thoughts,
— Dad

She could stay up in her room for hours with one simple dream,
— Olivia

BANG

A slammed door awakens her from her
Chamber of imagination,

Her daily life is like any other's,
But her imagination can run free like a wild mustang,
Every thought is like a little wave in the ocean of dreams,

And those are the thoughts of the
Dreams that brought Hannah to find
A dreamer within.

Hannah Borden, Grade 6
Middlebrook School, CT

A Seasonal Argument

Which season is the best? I wish I never asked,
If this mouth stayed shut there'd never be, this argumental task,

Said Spring: So wonderful am I,
More beautiful then all the rest,
With flora and fauna abroad,
Surely that makes me the best,
Said Fall: What are you, a fool?
I am Autumn and I'm Fall,
I have two names and you do not,
I am better than you all!

Said Summer: I beg to differ Fall,
But that cannot be true,
I bring warmth to everyone,
So I am better than you!
Said Winter: Nonsense! Listen up!
You all just bring plain rain,
I bring all the happy snow,
It's me that should be vain!

And so the seasons argued long, each sang its own vain song,
Though each one had made a point, everyone was wrong.
Daniel Grotz, Grade 6
Floyd T Binns Middle School, VA

Peace

Peace
like a graceful dove
flying in the morning breeze.
Peace
like the shining stars
dancing in the moonlight.
Peace
feels like the world
belongs together
in one big loving family.
Suzanne Woller, Grade 6
Lenox Memorial Middle and High School, MA

Feelings of the Week!

On Sunday I sit in my bed thinking:
If school will excite me tomorrow because…
On Monday I feel sleepy,
On Tuesday I feel energized,
On Wednesday I feel bored,
On Thursday I feel weird,
Finally it's Friday and I can go home.
To play with my friends
I've missed for so long.
On Saturday I wake up and go to my grandparent's house.
On Sunday I do the same thing
Over, and over, and over, and over,
and over, and over, and over again!
Julie Strawderman, Grade 5
Linville-Edom Elementary School, VA

The Rainforest

Out in the mist a forest rises,
Full of adventure and filled with surprises.
Parrots screeching,
Monkeys are reaching for branches high up above.
Eagles soaring,
Cougars are roaring on a cool day.

In the forest rain starts pouring,
In the trees a sloth starts snoring.
Frogs come out, they chirp and shout, softly in the terrain.

In the night,
Anteaters come out sight, slurping the ants away.
Squirrels gliding through the air,
Man, they are everywhere!

These are our friends from the forest floor,
But believe me, there are much more.
Valerie Gayevskaya, Grade 6
Pikesville Middle School, MD

Spring

In spring weather flowers bloom,
Everything's beautiful and quiet.
When rain pitter patters on the ground,
I hear crickets and frogs at night.
There are many other things that I hear and see,
But most of all I hear and see a lovely family.
Natalie Dest, Grade 4
Litchfield Intermediate School, CT

A Gift in Spring

As I step on the pale, as snow, sandy shore.
The sun is setting. Unleashing,
bright rainbows, soaring space high.
Turquoise water, swaying back and forth,
like a wondrous dance in the breeze.
I stand tranquil.
My feet placed in the cool sand.
Stem stillness, I'm planted.
I wait and watch, for the perfect gifts from the sea
to sputter out from the
twinkling water below.
Florida's beach silenced.
Waves picking up pace.
Soon a shimmer comes into view.
Two, no, three ridged bumps
pop out of the ocean and leave ripples behind.
I stare into my palm at the objects from the deep.
Three lightly speckled tan shells dripping wet.
Drops slip through my fingers.
A whirlpool of joy
ending this magical March day.
Rebecca Brand, Grade 6
Mystic Middle School, CT

Water

The cool refreshing water
that turns into ice when it's cold
and when it melts, the sweet sound of
drip,
drip,
drip.
The big, wavy, blue water
flowing in the pool,
the sea,
the ocean.
The cool single tear drop
of water running
down a
human's
face.
The cloud evaporating into a rain drop
falling
upon the world.
The snow, falling
to the ground to melt into water
to help plants GROW.

Zachary Zimmerman, Grade 4
Pleasant Valley Elementary School, MD

The Fox

I look out my bedroom window.
Through the mist
a shadowy figure appears.
Its tail twitches and its ears perk up.
It is a fox
with silent paws padding swiftly
over the damp moss.
Those stealthy paws bring him weaving
through trees and across my lawn.
All of a sudden
the dawn grays and just as suddenly
as it appeared
the fox vanishes.

Bryan Curtin, Grade 6
Kenmore Middle School, VA

A Boy from Spain

There once was a boy from Spain,
Who came to America without a name.
He got in his pajamas,
And petted his two llamas
And the next day, they were taken away.
He cried for a while,
But began to smile
Because he got very hungry
So he munched on something chunky
And didn't feel like a child anymore.

Gabby Legas, Grade 5
Clover Hill Elementary School, VA

Lavender

Lavender looks like waving flowers
In the breeze.
Lavender smells like
The ocean air in the sunlight.
Lavender tastes like
Frosting sitting on a chocolate cake.
Lavender feels like
A soft satin dress.
Lavender sounds like
A dainty violin.
Lavender is a beautiful color!

Madison Harlow, Grade 4
Boonsboro Elementary School, MD

Naruto

N inja
A crobatic
R ough
U zamacki
T ough
Awes **O** me

Mark Padilla, Grade 5
St Joseph School-Fullerton, MD

Waves

Rushing to get in
Elegantly retreating
Shining in the sun

Colors of all blues
Combining with the sunset
I stare so blankly

Michael Martin, Grade 6
Beacon Middle School, DE

Big Papi and the World Series

Big Papi up at bat,
Ball one, ball two,
Smack…going, going, going, gone!
Red Sox win the World Series!
Everyone screams for joy!

Rebecca Fisher, Grade 4
Brookside Elementary School, MA

Pillow

Pillow you are
soft sweet cream,
you make me have
the happiest dreams.

Soft and fluffy,
a cuddly puppy,
you help me fall
asleep.

Rachel Samuels, Grade 5
Zervas Elementary School, MA

Birds of All Creation

Birds are joyful.
Colorful and more.
Respect all of the birds.
For they respect you.
Birds are God's creation!

Sam Haley, Grade 5
St Mary's School, MA

The Fox

The fox sniffs
The sweetest maple tree
And now growls
While he prowls
Towards a chicken
Who makes him start
Licking his chops
The chicken pauses
Then clucks
Tries to flutter
But a second too late
The fox eats his fill
Then sniffs the air
The farmer will come
And suspicion will rise
The fox flees
Snow falling lightly
On his muzzle

Kristen Sarasin, Grade 5
Pollard Elementary School, NH

Christmas Time

C hrist is born.
H appy is everyone.
R eady for Santa to come.
I love getting together again.
S oon it will be Christmas day.
T onight is another snowy night.
M erry Christmas!
A day of fun is coming.
S anta is here!

T omorrow I wake.
I 'm ready for presents.
M om makes cookies.
E veryone is happy.

Ashley Chase, Grade 6
St Mary of Czestochowa School, CT

Peaceful Tree

Growing many years
Reaching up high to the sky
Letting its leaves thrive

Zachary Knight, Grade 6
Juliet W Long School, CT

Eagle

E nergetically flying in the wind
A n eagle's nest is called an aerie
G racefully flapping its wings
L oving its eggs so nicely
E nergy bolt with sharp talons

Jesse Jones, Grade 4
Dr Charles E Murphy Elementary School, CT

Spring in NH

I walked into the garden,
Littered with beautiful flowers,
Like tulips and roses with magnificent colors.

It was the day,
Of the beginning of spring,
When all birds wanted to sing.

The air was full,
Of chirps and tweets and
Caws and cackles sounding so sweet.

But there was a sweet little song,
That rang out above all,
After a bird saw a pink flower fall.

It felt like the greatest time in NH,
The whole aura of spring,
The best that NH would ever bring.

Ananya Jha, Grade 6
Infant Jesus School, NH

Fall Foliage

Massive bronze trees stand broad and strong.
Gold, pumpkin, and cherry colored leaves flutter to the ground.
Patches of emerald grass stand small, but straight,
like flimsy silk blowing in a cool fall breeze.
In the sapphire sky, the sun smiles brightly.
Fluffy, silver clouds glide across the sky in the crisp air.
Fall Foliage!

Hayley Barriere, Grade 5
Shaftsbury Elementary School, VT

Flowers Had Their Last Hours

Flowers had their last hours,
They seem to be nowhere in sight,
Flowers had their last hours,
To gardener and flower lovers this is a fright,
Flowers had their last hours,
Their very last hours of light,
Flowers had their last hours,
Also their very last night,
Flowers had their very last hours,
They seem to be nowhere in sight.

Tori Schaufler, Grade 6
Juliet W Long School, CT

The Flag

The flag is serious, it makes me cry in vain.
I really can't stop staring there.
I have to be aware, suddenly another star appears,
The world is getting bigger.
And you, are making it change.

William Tripp McGarrie, Grade 4
Riverfield School, CT

Seasons

Crimson leaves drift down
Wind rustling the leaves like a hidden creature

Pure snow sprinkles down
The new immaculate world lies there motionless

Blooming flowers peek from buds
With a fragrant scent, a sweet aroma

Beaming sun rays weave through tree branches
Creating a dancing shadow

Vermilion streaks a glowing sky
Bleeding into the vibrant red leaves

Barren trees now clothed with snow
Bow down to the swirling powder

A once silent world now aroused
Brimming with life as nature's song revives

Sunshine pours onto the Earth
As rare fresh breezes taunt the sweltering day

Jill Detrick-Yee, Grade 6
Middlebrook School, CT

Puppies

Running and pouncing.
Playing outside in the bath.
Running pouncing fun.

Brook L. Ivory, Grade 4
Dr Charles E Murphy Elementary School, CT

Witches Attack

The witches are stealing candy double time.
With their broomsticks causing a chime.

The witches are making humans into their slaves.
We are being taken over, so are the caves.

There is a castle in which they all live.
They mostly sell bad candy which they make and give.

Then there's living Frankenstein.
His parents call him scary stein.

Tyler Jezak, Grade 4
Brookside Elementary School, MA

Sparkling Day

Children playing
Children calling
Freezing cold windy day
Sparkling neighborhood
First snowfall
I am excited!
Dark gray gloomy clouds
Trees shaking
What's the weather?
Playing hard all day
I am tired
Warm hot chocolate
That's good
Time for bed
Good night

Emina Kezo, Grade 4
John J Flynn Elementary School, VT

Preparing for Thanksgiving

Pumpkins rot and are thrown away
Turkeys meet their delicious day
Potatoes are cut
Stuffing is cooked
The bell rings and traffic is created
Holiday math problems are taken home
The second holiday in the season is here
And it's time for some fun

Thomas Byrne, Grade 5
North Mianus School, CT

Penguins

Penguins can swim,
Penguins can play,
Penguins can go outside during the day
They swim in the ocean,
They slip on the ice,
Whatever they do,
I know they are nice,
Penguins

Kierra Harper, Grade 5
Pollard Elementary School, NH

Blue

Blue is bright
Blue is calm
Blue is water
Blue is the sky
Blue tastes like blueberries
Blue smells like fresh fallen rain
Blue sounds like the ocean waves
Blue feels like a blanket falling over me
Blue looks like the beautiful blue flowers
Blue makes me happy and calm
Blue is wonderful

Hanna Bareihs, Grade 6
Wakefield Forest Elementary School, VA

I Am

I am a boy who likes baseball
I wonder if I'll be in MLB
I hear the umpire call strikes on all my
good pitches I have thrown to the sly catcher
I see the catcher go in position to catch the ball
I want to be in the Major League to play with Boston.
I am a boy who likes baseball

I pretend that I am the best player in majors
I feel the taped handle of the big huge, long, fat bat I'm swinging
I touch the hard metal bat
I worry that I am going to be seriously injured
I am a boy who likes baseball

I understand all the position rules of baseball
I say when the ball goes
I dream to be the best pitcher
I try to play my best
I hope to play baseball for the rest of my life
I am a boy who likes baseball

Gregory Tougas, Grade 5
Blackrock School, RI

Feathered Blessing

A blessing that God has sent me,
A piece of happiness that is always there.
Cheerful and joyous is she that perches on my shoulder.
A companion, a dear friend that is always there.
Her song is sweet music to my ears,
And is a love-filled song.
I know she was sent from the heavens above to give me cheer and company.
I will thank the Lord every day of my life for sending me the wonderful blessing.

Haley Eiler, Grade 6
Home School, VA

The Amazing Castle

The amazing castle has many things in it.
Knights, jesters, and magicians…pretty impressive, I have to admit.

The castle is tall, gray, and very, very wide.
The owner must have a lot of pride.

A huge river flows around the massive thing.
It's as wide as an airplane wing.

In the castle lives a beautiful queen and a brave king.
Once in awhile you can hear the princess sing.

People visit from all parts of the land.
To see inside all that is grand.

Just imagine this castle in a fairy tale,
And let you imagination set sail.

Jacob Burbank, Grade 5
Infant Jesus School, NH

Cheetahs

Hunting, hunting,
Short head, slender legs,
Hunting, hunting,
Short rounded ears, striped tail,
Supple, muscular back, narrow dog like paws,
Hunting, hunting,
Sharp claws skin their prey,
Hunting

Gabriela Cruz, Grade 5
Long Meadow Elementary School, CT

Dinner Time

When it came time for dinner
The Lins were not prepared
They sat down at the table
And the food at which they stared

The celery was stringy
And green as the grass
The table was tired
With all that food to grasp

Everything was serene
But then it got old
Everyone had to cope
With every
Slurp, slurp, slurp of the Lin family, so bold

The Lins were ecstatic
At how much everyone ate
For they had very little
On their very own plate

Alexia Fornaro, Grade 6
St Brigid School, ME

Winter

It's snowing and blowing and freezing
the air. Hailing and storming,
I'm glad I'm not there. In the air, on the ground,
It doesn't matter, it's everywhere,
ground so white
sky so gray.
I can't wait until it's another day.

Bret Stokes, Grade 4
Mitchell Elementary School, CT

Fresh Air

The sky is as blue as the Bahama water.
The Bahama water is as smooth as ice cream
The ice cream is as tasteful as pizza.
The pizza is smaller to me than it is to my friends
My friends are as nice as my dog
My dog is as soft as the air blowing on me
As I dive through the big blue SKY.

Peter Kotula, Grade 6
Main Street Middle School, VT

Fwoosh

Fwoosh!
The only thing
I heard as I tumbled down into the glassy black water.
I sliced through the speeding rapids like a knife.
I struggled, my lungs burning like fire, gasping for air.
The rapids held me under
as though they were made of iron.
A strong hand wrapped around my ankle
like someone tugging a rope.
I was pulled in, a fish on a hook.
The slippery side of the ocean blue raft
was so slick I felt as if I was coasting
over a fish's stomach.
As I flopped onto the bouncy blue seat,
I felt the last of the blizzard cold water
slip off my body.
The concert fans screaming filled my ears.
Relief flooded through my body
as I finally realized it was all over.
I was safe!

Alex Orf, Grade 6
Mystic Middle School, CT

Ladybugs

I am a lovely ladybug, beautiful and red,
The cutest feature about me is my little black head.

I can live in a garden, meadow, or farm, which is fine,
But I would like some more space that is all mine.

I sleep in the hay which is not warm and cozy.
Come to think of it, the animals are quite nosey.

For my dinner I eat aphids all day,
Boy! I wish they were cooked by Rachael Ray.

As you can see, no other bug has more,
I was even elected state bug in 1974.

Rachel Grant, Grade 6
Immaculate Heart of Mary School, DE

What School Means to Me

Science, English, Math and Reading
When will the bell ever ring?

The teacher just goes on and on and on
I just wanna be gone, gone, gone!

All I do is doodle in my notebook
"Teacher, Teacher, please don't look!"

Don't you worry, school's not always this bad
So if you must go to school don't be sad

Karina Wohlhieter, Grade 6
St. John the Evangelist School, CT

Waterfalls

Waterfalls are natural
and very beautiful to see
they come down hard
then to mist
blue then white
what a sight

Emily Sargent, Grade 4
Brookside Elementary School, MA

Sports

S uper fun
P erfect
O verhand throw
R unning
T errific
S pecial to play

Connor Freeburger, Grade 5
St Joseph School-Fullerton, MD

My Bird Is Special

R ainbow is my bird
A very cute face
I n a cage
N ot too big
B ites but not hard
O pens your eyes to life
W hen we play he chirps

Rainbow is right for me!
Elizabeth Lelonek, Grade 6
St Joseph School-Fullerton, MD

The Red Marked Heart

The king is scattered, beaten, hit,
And all his rights are banished.
All his wounds are dark and pit,
And blood as pure as ice.
Although wasted upon a hill,
The master was not raged.
Because he knew with all his will,
We would all be saved.
Beaten and thrown
Down on the cross,
My sire will only moan.
He sees the ropes get tossed across,
And still strives to groan.
The hammer goes down,
And thunder cracks.
The hammer goes down,
And lightning shines.
The tears of all stream smoothly down,
And pure darkness is filled inside.
Faces of children stained with frown,
Destiny calls on them to decide.
Mike Ogego, Grade 6
Hoover Middle School, MD

Colorful Leaves

Red, yellow, orange
Leaves blowing in the cool air
Colorful red leaves
Pamela Smith, Grade 5
Pollard Elementary School, NH

Tiger

Tiger
Orange, black
Running, swimming, hunting
Jungle, food, enemies, mean
Prowling, jumping, climbing
Fast, scarce
Scrawny
Stephen Turner, Grade 6
Juliet W Long School, CT

Books

It holds the world,
or nothing at all,
thick or thin,
short or tall,
it tells a story,
without speaking a word,
it has a voice,
that cannot be heard,
everyone knows,
what this object is,
hers cannot close,
without opening his,
with every page you guess,
what will happen now,
you are surprised nonetheless,
with who, what, when, why, how,
guides, poetry, instructions, news,
fantasy, nonfiction, mystery, how-to,
anything that you can use,
written by me, read by you.
Rachel Nolan, Grade 6
Irving School, CT

On the Field

Racing with speed
Tossing the black and white ball
Shooting to make goals
Wind zooms, it flies
It swirls around you
Crowds cheer, they clap
Glory blasts from afar
Friends come
You shake with the other team
Rejoice in victory
Katherine Tiffany, Grade 5
Shaftsbury Elementary School, VT

Prince of the Creek

One day the small boy
went down to the creek to play.
He ran and ran
through the trees
to get to "the log."
The log was his favorite place
to be in the creek,
just sitting there
watching the water flow by.
He would stride across the log
balancing as he walked,
there he declared
himself prince of the creek.
Jacob Payne, Grade 6
Kenmore Middle School, VA

St. Brigid School

In Saint Brigid School
The teachers can be very cruel
The work they pass out is a pain
Like the devil beating God in a game

The work is never done
We always get a ton
It's not a lot of fun
But don't lose faith, I know!
It's imperative to help me grow
Into a smart young man,
I know!
Nick Russo, Grade 6
St Brigid School, ME

Soul

Thy soul is thy heart
Thy soul is thy name
Thy soul is thy freedom
Thy soul is thy shame
Thy soul is thy love
Thy soul is thy mind
Thy soul is thy truth
I shall never find
Junelle Lynch, Grade 6
Brunswick Middle School, MD

Halloween

H appy night
A ll the candy you can get
L ots of costumes
L ots of goodies
O ctober
W hat a lot of fun
E xciting
E xtra scary
N ight of frights
Samantha Donatelli, Grade 5
St Joseph School-Fullerton, MD

The Violin

The violin is soothing
It helps to relax your mind
You express your feeling in a peaceful way
Classical music helps invigorate your soul
When all the anger balls up inside of you
It allows you to meditate and
It gives you the grace to become relax and free

The violin is soothing to the mind, spirit, and body
If you listen to it on the radio
It's like you're floating on a cloud
You're dancing in the sky or relaxing by the ocean
It makes the birds sing
And the sea calm down
It brings you to a place of serenity
I love the violin

Brittani Campbell, Grade 6
Grace Episcopal Day School, MD

Where I Can Be Me

The only place I could be me is in…
The meadows of Holland

The sky so blue
Not a cloud in the sky

The noonday yellow sun is shining
The sun seems to smile at me

Tulips, roses, daisies, and wildflowers
Creating a rainbow as far as the eye can see

Birds flying overhead bring the scene to life
The swift breeze makes the gray-brick windmills turn

All the colors together create
My mosaic

I wish I can stay here forever!

Joseph Tramontozzi, Grade 5
E Ethel Little Elementary School, MA

Halloween

Halloween is…
— hissing vampires ready to suck your blood
— screaming terror haunts the night
— glowing full moons have a creepy effect
— running kids hide from ghosts
— buying all sorts of candy
— frightening werewolf howls, makes kids jump
— scaring adults surprise the kids
— haunting skeletons making clicking sounds on the street.
      That's what it's all about!

Shane Harris, Grade 4
St Augustine Cathedral School, CT

Mirror

You ask me these questions but know it's true,
There's nothing else better than you being you.
I look in the mirror and finally see
A person staring back at me.

She has gorgeous eyes and a wonderful smile.
I had wished that she would stay a while.
My mom came upstairs and guess what she saw?
That girl and I on the same call.

I'm not as pretty as those other girls.
I wish I had all the curls.
Everyone says I look like a geek,
But my family says I look chic.

I looked back in the mirror and do you know what I found?
I found a girl that was me and there was no sound.
Now I know not to listen to what others say,
Because I am beautiful in my own way.

Heather Pickerall, Grade 6
E Russell Hicks School, MD

The Music Maker

She sings to her child
While the moon is light,
She hums to her child
While the moon is bright.

He listens to his mother
While high in the sky is the moon,
To listen to his mother forever
Would be his wish if he were granted a boon.

And while he listens
To the music that's played
That is as nice as cool white snow
On a hot summer's day.

His mother, the music maker,
Sinks down below the trees,
Until the rising sun is gone,
She's ready to make tomorrow's breeze.

Anya Conti, Grade 6
Thomas Blake Middle School, MA

Soccer

Soccer is like the sound of thunder,
But it is only the crowd.
It feels like your cleats are on fire
It's like you're running the speed of lightning
When you punt the ball, it looks like it goes around the world
When you kick the ball,
It feels like you're kicking the earth
Truly soccer is AWESOME!

Leif Heaney, Grade 4
Boonsboro Elementary School, MD

Earth Song

Plant some
Green trees
Love the blue water
Shine like a yellow sun
Live like you dream
Sing that song
Fly to this moon
Emilia Onthank, Grade 5
Mission Hill School, MA

Mist

I am a mist
The ghost of the morning
Breaker of dawn
I blind everything in my path
There is no true form of me
Enemy of the clouds
My body slithers through towns
I cannot be destroyed
My tomb lies within the wind
Shuo Jin, Grade 6
Beacon Middle School, DE

Sights

Seeing what everyone else can see,
I'm thinking, thinking, I believe,
Flying across the sky up high,
Sight of a dragon! A butterfly!
The horse is running, far away,
Wants the future, a change of days,
Saw a snake coiled high,
A toad eating up a pesky fly.
An ant is walking, strong and tough,
Walking on the ground — too rough!
Keeps on going, to his hill,
Feeds his family, as a good ant will.
Orchid Woodrow, Grade 5
North Star Elementary School, DE

Roller Coaster

R eady to board the coaster
O ver the big hills and turns
L ooping around and upside down
L ooking down at the people below
E verybody screaming out loud
R iding through the twists and turns

C arrying many passengers
O ver the sturdy metal track
A mazing views along the way
S earching for my friends below
T errified but having fun
E very turn must have an end
R iding it over and over again
Jane Heithoff, Grade 5
Pemberton Elementary School, VA

Multicolored Parade

Children screeching, their feet thudding against the ground.
Cymbals clanging, costumes rustling.
Music blaring from the marching bands' instruments.

The bold, crisp costumes fill every part of the audience with glee!!!
Black and blue, mystery of the marching band.
Bright, dazzling effects keep the crowd from silence.
Multicolored costumes flying around corners, through alleys.
Just look at the wispy, shiny, bold colors of the costumes.

I can almost smell the excitement in the air!
The fragrance is so clean, so fresh,
But then again so greasy with the smell of French fries!
Popcorn is popping over top the machine!!!
Do I smell sweet candy apples?

This sight is so amazing!
Icy, earthy, flaming, brown, white and red.
Bright as sunlight, and dark as midnight.
Glowing costumes like candles, flickering in the moonlight,
Shining like the stars!
Swirling colors of the sea, twirling around in the streets!!
The time has come, My Friend, to say good-bye to the multicolored parade!!!
Abbie Jones, Grade 4
Boonsboro Elementary School, MD

Shadows

The shadows of the trees dance as the wind blows
Their branches and sticks fall gently to the ground
If only the people walking by would notice
The sun hides behind the mountains causing the shadows to disappear
Afternoon has faded to night

Townsend Brown, Grade 6
Wakefield Forest Elementary School, VA

Red

If I could feel *red*, it would be of soft leather or friendship;
Sometimes the stripes of freedom.

If I could hear *red*, it would be of a not-so-friendly battle;
Or karate warriors sharpening their skills.
Maybe someone or something important;
Sometimes even romance.

If I could smell *red*, it would have the aroma of freshly baked bread;
Or of sweet, sweet smelling roses.
Sometimes the spools of thread women are weaving.

If I could taste *red*, it would be seven cockroaches in my mouth all at once;
Or burning flames stinging my mouth nonstop.

When I see *red*, I'm looking at the first color of the rainbow:
One of God's flowers.
One of God's promises.

Viviana Marshall, Grade 4
North Star Elementary School, DE

Silent Man

Lights reflect off a cart with cans piled into it.
The night is quiet except for the soft wheeling of the cart.
The Silent Man wearing a crumpled scarf and ruffled clothing
With an unshaven beard, whimpers in the moonlight.

A car stops at a red light as the Silent man walks toward it.
He desperately asks the man in baby language for money,
Cupping his hands toward the driver's eyes.
But the man doesn't understand as he drives away.

Then the Silent Man walks away, whimpering in the moonlight.

Benjamin Crosby, Grade 4
Riverfield School, CT

Palm Tree Island

Come sail away to where the bright sun shines over the horizon.
Where you can free yourself.
And where fish explore the ocean floor.
A rainbow land of beautiful color.
Where salty waves hit the shore.
Come sail away to my dream land.

Madison Waterman, Grade 4
Cranston-Johnston Catholic Regional School, RI

Hip Hop

Into the radio
Sounds come out
You
Know
What
I'm
Talking
About
And the rhythm
Rap
Beats
Oh so
Rhyme
With
50 Cent
Young Joc
T.I.
They also shine
Hip is in the hop
Hip Hop

Ryan Troxell, Grade 5
Friendship Valley Elementary School, MD

Wall to Wall

The day the Twin Towers fell,
I fell and turned really pale.
I started to cry,
As I went by.
As I heard the church bell.

Tyler Belcher, Grade 6
Belfast-Elk Garden Elementary School, VA

center stage

the moon creeps onto the stage of the sky.
the stars clap at his performance.
a little girl stands at her window,
staring in amazement at the show
that the night has put on

it is morning now.
the night is over.
the little girl is still awed by the moon,
but the night exits the stage.
it's the sun's turn to go on stage now.
too bad it has stage fright.

Cashen Conroy, Grade 6
Wayland Middle School, MA

The Thing

I sense some thing,
   that I cannot see.
     I sense some thing,
      that is not well.

Are you that thing,
   I cannot see.
     Are you that thing,
      that is not well.

I feel so tense,
   at night.
     I feel so tense,
      in the morn.

Are you the thing that,
   makes me tense at night.
     Are you the thing that,
      makes me tense in the morn.

If you can,
   stay away.
     But if you can't
      that's ok.

Emily Chamberlain, Grade 5
Rosemont Forest Elementary School, VA

Wrestlemania

Watching wrestling is fun and exciting too
When you see all those crazy stunts
The wrestlers can do
There is Triple H, with the Pedigree
That slick move will drop you to your knee.
There is Rey Mystereo and the 619
They give their opponents a pain in their spleen.
Even though it's make-believe, when I watch it on TV
It makes a believer out of me.

Christopher Washington, Grade 4
Mary Walter Elementary School, VA

The World Around Me

A field of poppies lay beyond me,
A field of orange and red speckles,
Beyond the poppies are the mountains where a river runs clear and crystal.
The mountain holds sacred trees and plants.
Past the mountain sits the ocean where creatures swim and play.
The ruffles in the jade blue sea behold tiny secrets.
Then the palm tree swings nearby.
Each particle of sand tiny and wonderful.
Farther still is the desert where snakes and horses roam,
Each tiny small and delicate drop of dew or rain is savored in the moment.
The thick tan sand sweeps over you like a blanket of nothingness, and when you awake it seems to dissolve.
The jungle is far away where leopards lurk and kill.
Every shade of green you can imagine.
And what is closest, and always will be, is your soul
Your red hot soul, burning like fire, burning like wisdom, like strength and like inner beauty.
You know who you are
Keep your head held high,
Wherever you go the world around you will follow.
How will it follow?

Reilly Mahoney Loynd, Grade 5
Fayston Elementary School, VT

The First Sign of Hope

As I walk down the cold chilling road,
I see the sadness that comes from the depressed souls.
It is the last day of winter.
There was no sight of hope for a single snowflake to fall to the ground this boring season.

I sat down and joined the sad depressed souls on the sidewalk.
As my burning flame of hope and joy turns in to a dull, dreaded, dying candle.
I ask my mother,
…Is snow…
Depression,
Sadness,
Coldness,
Or tears
That I am feeling right now?

She answers me with a smiling "no" and says it is that beautiful thing behind you.
I don't see anything but,
A single, graceful, and hopeful drop of white ice falling delicately from the darkened sky.
I look at her, and tell her that it was the first sign of hope in this dreadful town.
She just smiles at me as more signs of hope fall and turn depressed souls in to cheerful friends.

Angelica Pancho, Grade 5
Rosemont Forest Elementary School, VA

West Virginia

West Virginia is green and brown.
In the winter it is all about white grass.
It sounds like the rustle of the leaves on the bushes when the deer go running from the shot of a gun.
It tastes like Fritz's cranberry cookies and Ruthie's fruit salads.
It smells like marshmallows roasting on a bright glowing fire.
And it looks like big mountains on which lay a huge forest separated only by winding roads and twisting paths.
It makes you stop and think, "When is my next vacation?"

Mara Sherline, Grade 5
McDonogh School, MD

My Day as the Sun

When I wake in the light, gray mist of the morning.
I have a difficult time getting up and ready today.
During the beautiful daytime,
I love to skip and soar across my favorite blue blanket,
Like a caged dove set free in the sky, flying high,
And in the cool, crisp evening,
When my brother, Moon, comes up to play,
I say, "Good night, see you another day."

Jessica Boesch, Grade 5
Four Seasons Elementary School, MD

Gum, Gum the Third

Uh oh!
Gum, gum got stuck, stuck in a girl's hair, hair
and it stuck, stuck like muck, muck.
The girl tried to tear, tear the gum, gum
out of her dumb, dumb hair, hair.
The girl was as mad as a grizzly bear
because she couldn't get the gum, gum
out of her dumb, dumb hair, hair.

Matt De Rienzo and Jack Tomas, Grade 4
Long Meadow Elementary School, CT

Your Worst Enemy

I am a spotted cucumber beetle all green and yellow,
I could be your meanest little fellow.

I eat cucumbers and all your other crops,
I eat all your hard work and, make you drop.

From under the plants I can pop out and say, "Boo!"
You will scream because I scare you.

I am only one-fourth of an inch, but I am mean,
I might look cute but I am gross and green.

I have polka dots, six on each wing,
In your garden or on your farm I will add some bling.

Amy O'Neill, Grade 6
Immaculate Heart of Mary School, DE

Close Your Eyes

The best things in life are unseen
that's why you close your eyes at the scene
Like when you wish or when you dream
or cry of joy and want to scream
Like when couples hold hands
or when they make plans
or when they fall in love
or wish on a star above
What happens most
is their eyes are closed
So close your eyes… and dream

Kayla Humel, Grade 6
Bellamy Middle School, MA

Friendship

Friendship is a feeling between you and me,
Friendship is laughing and crying with somebody.
Friendship is not always being in a good mood,
But friendship is knowing we are being understood.
Here's what I'll tell you now,
Friendship is a miracle you have found.

Katarzyna Fladro, Grade 5
Good Shepherd Catholic School, RI

Leaf

L ovely leaves are fun to watch.
E xtravagant colored leaves fall from the trees.
A utumn is when leaves float in the air.
F abulous colors everywhere.

Joshua Valmond, Grade 4
St Gregory Elementary School, MA

Butterfly

Oh, butterfly, butterfly
You are so beautiful.
Oh, butterfly, butterfly,
I love to touch your beautiful wings
As they glide through the soft wind.

Oh, butterfly, if you can't see
You are so beautiful to me!
I love it when your gentle wing
Lands on the May flowers.
But butterfly, butterfly,
Fly somewhere warm to avoid the harsh winter flakes.

Sarah Melanson, Grade 4
Portsmouth Christian Academy, NH

Dreamer

I am artistic and kind
I wonder what's going to happen in the future
I hear birds singing in my ear
I see unicorns in the sky
I want a million dogs
I am artistic and kind

I pretend to be a bird in the sky
I feel rabbits nibbling on my hand
I touch the sky when nothing is there
I worry about my sister when she walks home alone
I cry when there is nothing to cry about
I am artistic and kind

I understand what people think
I say I will always come back
I dream of a better day
I try to succeed in everything
I hope for you to heal
I am artistic and kind

Hannah Ketrinchek, Grade 5
Clover Street School, CT

Trick-or-Treating

I hear weird noises of the wind
I see darkness all around
I feel the wind blowing as I walk
I smell candy on Halloween
I taste the good candy

Dominic DeRuosi, Grade 4
Brookside Elementary School, MA

Time for Halloween

Boys and girls everywhere
Now it's time for a really good scare!
Trick or treat.
Don't be mean!
Now, it's time for
HALLOWEEN!
WHHHHHHHEEEEEEEEEEEE!!

Allison Sevidal, Grade 5
St Joseph School-Fullerton, MD

Microorganism

Ah-Ha! A microorganism I see.
Now I'm filled with glee!
They're little living things you know.
I guess they're really stealing the show!

Maximo Catala, Grade 4
Wapping Elementary School, CT

The Girl from Woonsocket

There once was a girl from Woonsocket,
Who had her hand in her pocket,
She had a big dream,
And then she did scream,
That she had a shark in her locket.

Thomas Marcet, Grade 5
Good Shepherd Catholic School, RI

Snow Everywhere

The snow flows,
As it goes,
Everywhere around,
The town's ground.

Edgar Gaeta, Grade 6
Floyd T Binns Middle School, VA

Pizza Nightmare

People will eat it
And chew it
And rip it apart
Crunch it
And smash it in their mouths
Until suddenly it stops
And everything goes black.
And that is the nightmare of pizza.

Freddy Bashara, Grade 6
Main Street Middle School, VT

I Am

I am an aggressive and courageous soccer player
I wonder if I'll ever be a professional
I hear the roaring crowd and my coaches
cheering for me when I kick the winning goal
I see the goalie hoping she can block my shot
I want to score the winning shot in the Coventry Soccer Championship
I am an aggressive and courageous soccer player

I pretend I'm playing in the World Cup
I feel proud when I score a goal because I'm helping my team win
I touch the soccer ball's patches
I worry I won't be able to play if I'm hurt
I am an aggressive and courageous soccer player

I understand that I need to play fair
I say "yes" when I score
I dream that I'm playing with Mia Hamm
I try to score a goal
I hope that I become a professional and play for Italy
I am an aggressive and courageous soccer player

Natalia Angelone, Grade 5
Blackrock School, RI

The Perfect Sunset

On the perfect night.
With the sun so bright.
I feel warm with the sun beaming on my body.
The brilliant eye blue water now orange-red, cooling me down

I see the beautiful, swift water coming upon the rich, dark orange sand.
Then again going back to where it belongs.
Also, the orange sunset up in the sky.
The water is reflecting the sunset.
I hear the seagulls squawking, as if in a fight.

The waves I hear are making a pattern, coming in, and again going out.
I'm able to smell the salty water in my nose.
I taste the salt water in my mouth.
All together, it makes a beautiful sight.
Worth more than a million dollars.

Julia McIlmail, Grade 4
Cranston-Johnston Catholic Regional School, RI

Traveling Leaves

In autumn leaves fall down
They go all the way down to the ground
Where they lounge around
They blow by bounds and cover the ground
It makes me frown when they blow out of town
They come in colors such as yellow, red, orange, green and brown
You try to rake them and take them
You make them into mounds but they go all over town
The traveling leaves

Emily Bak, Grade 5
Lincoln Central Elementary School, RI

Winter

Darkness and frost cover the land,
All is lost in an icy sand,
Bitter winds chill the lakes, and slowly they turn to ice.
Crystal teardrops fall from the sky,
Turning to snow as they float by,
Floating, flying,
winds are sighing,
All on this winter night.

Amanda Laidler, Grade 6
Vincent J Gallagher Middle School, RI

A Day at Sea

I glow like the stars in space.
I shine like a rainbow in sun and rain.
I drift with a floating cloud.
I am the amusing changing horizon.

I leap like a huge spring.
I leap like a professional swimmer.
I flip like a person on a trampoline.
I am the playful, glorious fish.

I glide like a plane in the sky.
I soar like a colorful hang glider.
I dive like a speeding bullet to get a fish for dinner.
I am the flying, colorful bird.

I sway like leaves in the wind.
I flow like a boat in the sea.
I change like the western Massachusetts weather.
I am the colorful, reflecting water.

Emily Andreatta, Grade 4
Greylock School, MA

Busy Like a Bee

My life is like a bee
Because I have so much to do
Bees are busy just like me
Making honey and collecting too

Bees have a spoiled queen
I have a bossy mom
We treat her like a royal teen
Do what she says or she'll blow up like a bomb

My life is busy because
I have homework, sports
Chores and more, following the laws
Siblings, practice on the court

I like my life busy because it's cool
Not too much free time but,
Too bad bees don't have school
For they may fall into a rut

Amanda Hutchison, Grade 6
Blue Ridge Middle School, VA

My Cat K-Zin

Soft, furry, and orangey brown,

His beautiful coat shines as he takes a nap in the warmth
of the sun.

His eyes glow like two full moons on a dark
midnight sky.

He is always there for me when I'm feeling depressed.

"Click clack, click clack," his paws say as he walks on
the hard wood floors.

He loves to be petted.
But watch out, he will bite after only one warning!

I love you K-Zin.

Colleen O'Sullivan, Grade 5
Long Meadow Elementary School, CT

I Am

I am a tap dancer and animal lover.
I wonder what the world will be like in many years.
I hear the beat of the drums.
I see the flag waving in the wind.
I want my brother to love me once again.
I am a tap dancer and animal lover.

I feel the waves roll and crash on me.
I touch his heart but pull away.
I worry I won't make it to college.
I cry when I think…death.
I am a dancer and animal lover.

I understand why my parents got divorced.
I say we should have a longer recess at school.
I dream I fly with Peter Pan to Never Never Land.
I try to *always* do my homework on time.
I hope to never stay back a grade.
I am a dancer and animal lover.

Emily Hodsdon, Grade 6
Amherst Middle School, NH

Summer Rain

Summer weeks, summer weeks, tough hard heat
So hard you can't beat
To thrive a storm
BOOM! BANG!
Finally hear banging in my ear
Thunder as loud as a lion's roar, rain is coming
It's going to poor
Pop on my roof
The fall is here

Kayla Rumage, Grade 6
E Russell Hicks School, MD

Fish

Fish, fish, fish
Scaly fish
Shark fish
Rainbow, yellow, green fish
Ugly, bug-eyed, striped fish
Those are just a few.
Fat fish
Slippery fish
Freshwater, slow, fast fish
Ocean, skinny, scary fish
Perch fish too!
Bass fish
Trout fish
And don't forget pet fish.
Last of all
Best of all
I like gold fish!
Zach Higgins, Grade 6
Juliet W Long School, CT

Winter

Winter is chilly
But always silly
Under the tree
There's presents for thee
Outside we play in snow
Oh look I saw a doe!
Inside we sit by the fire
While my mom gets me what I desire
Kylie Murray, Grade 4
Brookside Elementary School, MA

Ode to the Jonas Brothers

Hair so black and sleek,
Skin as soft as snow,
Voices heard across the world,
Band of brothers 3.

Family so loving and caring,
Supporting them all way,
Giving people a laugh,
Giving children hope and glee.

Hearts broken many times,
Disappointed in many ways,
Tragedies appearing from nowhere,
But still as cute as can be.

The Jonas brothers,
Lives filled with happiness,
Hearts filled with love,
My heroes for me and only me.
Salina Michelle George, Grade 6
Beacon Middle School, DE

The Sky Above

The sky above is
the one we see
every single day.
We look up above
and smile because
we don't know
what to say.

The sky above is the
one we love for the
rain, hail, and snow.
The sky above is
the one we love
because it makes
the world glow.

The sky above is
the one we see
every single day.
We look up above
and smile because
we never know
what to say.
Tatyana Geneste, Grade 5
Davenport Ridge School, CT

Friends

Friends are nice to have.
They can be helpful and glad.
They can be useful.
Jamie Teramani, Grade 5
St Joseph School-Fullerton, MD

A Blessing to All

As the smoke blows,
Through the sky,
The sky turns gray,
Will the totem poles
stand high?
My tribe is blessing
The dark gray sky.
Moussa Dia, Grade 6
Kenmore Middle School, VA

Monkarand (A New World)

Everything that walks,
Everything that talks,
Everything that moves,
Everything that grooves.

It's all on Monkarand
All throughout the land,
Through the skies and seas
Are all the creatures and bees.
Samantha Sebert, Grade 5
Marley Elementary School, MD

Snow

White fluffy balls
bouncing on trampolines
make me feel happy
and make me feel free.
Galina Gruder, Grade 5
The Pinecroft School, MA

Life Is So Sweet

I love my life it is so sweet and cool.
I spend my life on video games.
Like other kids being a kid is so fun
You can't imagine being a kid.
But the only thing is that being a kid
Does not mean you can rent a car
Like a grown up can.
It means just be a young person.
I am a kid and I have my own room.
That's why life is sweet for a kid.
Yassin Elhilo, Grade 6
Kenmore Middle School, VA

Free to Be Me

How can I be free?
To be anyone I want to be
and choose my own path
to fly solo

When can I be free?
To see everything there is to see
and follow my own dreams
to be myself

Finally I can be free!
Not to follow your rules and commands
now I can truly take a stand
to be free
Catharine Windsor Dawson, Grade 6
Beacon Middle School, DE

Lacrosse

Racing down the field,
my lacrosse stick I wield.
An opponent tries to check me,
I knock him down and break free.
With strength I cradle the ball,
one by one more enemies fall.
And now with just the goalie to beat,
I hope for an amazing feat.
Heart beating, feet throbbing,
but I show no signs of stopping.
I aim, I shoot, I score.
Goal!
Matthew Charno, Grade 4
North Star Elementary School, DE

Cutie Pie

I wake up, still half asleep.
I view the biggest surprise in the world.
Right there in front of me,
a big fur ball snuggling up to the side of my leg.
Its yellow-lime lizard eyes meet mine.
Meow! It's Cutie Pie.
Her meow is smooth as glass.
She walks up to me from the bottom of the bed.
My hand rests on her soft as silk head.
Slowly I move it down to her fuzzy back,
further down to her soft curious snake-like tail
and start all over again as she circles the bed.
Cutie is a scrapbook
sometimes fun but also sad to look through.
I see my heart. I can't remember when I didn't have her.
She peacefully lays down by my side.
Her eyes start to close. So do mine.
My hand drifts away from her back.
Again,
I'm off to another land.
The land of dreams.

Sydney Banks, Grade 6
Mystic Middle School, CT

Music

Music, flowing and free.
Words put together, words making rhythm,
Sounding beautiful,
Crisp and clear.
The voice of birds,
The rush of a river,
The whisper of a cool wind on a summer day,
All are music in every way.
The tap of a pen on the desk in the den,
The cry of the little girl two doors down,
Or the tap on a beautiful queen's crown.
Listen, hard and well, you'll hear the true music of the world.

Isabelle Ballesteros, Grade 5
Rosemont Forest Elementary School, VA

Soaring Through the Sky

As I fly so high into the sky,
and coming down so fast, going up into the sky so fast,
and gently coming down, gently going up, and fast going down,
it feels so good wind blowing in my face,
almost falling off I try again,
trying so hard to reach my goal,
going up so fast, coming down so fast,
gently going up, and gently coming down,
as I stop to rest,
I know that I am done, out of strength,
I cannot go up, or come down anymore,
I knew I have reached my goal.

Justin Wines, Grade 6
Monelison Middle School, VA

Listening to Classical Music

Soft notes start off with the song,
Suspense rising right along.
It's coming to a crescendo now!
Longer notes on violins,
Basses are going deeper in.
Cellos are strumming right along.
Violas give the tune a slight spin,
Every instrument is at its peak
Playing with its heart —
Not one note is slightly weak.
Beauty is found in all of the parts.
The ups and downs,
Sudden soft notes or tremendous booms!
The amount of feeling swimming around,
The unique story being told dramatically with the sound.
Whatever it is,
It's music to me,
And all of it fits perfectly into harmony.

Anna Seo, Grade 6
Wakefield Forest Elementary School, VA

Pumpkin

Round and plump
Orange and hard
Scary and funny
Bright and spooky
Still, but real
Scares you in windows
Fun to make come alive
SQUASH
Pile of goo
Orange and bumpy
Plain and dull
Unfriendly and squashed
Unreal and dripping all over
Won't glow in the dark
Makes you crack up
No soul,
What can I say it's the life of MY pumpkin!

Meghan Curran, Grade 5
Osborn Hill Elementary School, CT

Football

Charging at my man
The ball falling into hands
Busting a big run.

Mark Malchiodi, Grade 4
Dr Charles E Murphy Elementary School, CT

Kitty

It is so cute.
Some of them have collars.
If it meows, leave it alone
Cutie

Sara Dunbar, Grade 4
Dr Charles E Murphy Elementary School, CT

I Wonder Why

I looked up at the sky,
watching the clouds go by.
I wonder why,
I wonder why the sky is blue?

Why the grass is green.
I wonder why,
I wonder why there is war,
the sick and poor.

They should have more.
I wish I could help
all the people in the world.
I wonder why?

Lindsey Pusyka, Grade 6
St Rocco School, RI

The Mystery Cave

One dark night
My dad and I
Were in a cave.
We decided to sit down for a rest.
We started to hear
The echo of someone's foot steps.
It was getting louder
and louder
Until it sounded
like it was around
the corner.
Then it stopped.
It was very mysterious.

Douglas Rohr, Grade 6
Kenmore Middle School, VA

Nkenge

Funny as a clown
Sweet as a strawberry
Sleepy as a bear
Smarter then all moms put together
Loves to read and make up songs
Loves to dance and play
She's the best little sister ever
And that's Nkenge

Nikongo BaNikongo, Grade 5
Perrywood Elementary School, MD

Praise in a Nutshel*

May you still have fun,
May you find the sidewalk's end,
May you meet Runny Babbit,
My you finally fall up,
May you live on forever, Shel Silverstien.
P.S. Don't drain your brain!

Matthew Felsenthal, Grade 6
Village School, MA
**Dedicated to Alan "Shel" Silverstien*

My Life

I am from a place with a lazy dog
That is sleeping next to a big leathery couch
Who gets woken up by fighting over the remote when people say ouch.
I am from a place full of fun and laughter.
I am from a place with so many mini hockey tournaments
Followed in the summer by very aggressive wiffle ball tournaments
That has to move every five minutes from speeding cars.
Who beep, yell, and scream.
I am from a place that is good in some parts and bad in others.
I am from a place with so many traffic jams that it drives me crazy
It makes so many happy people become angry.
I am from a place with many happy people that
Go to big and wide parks with all sorts of dogs.
I am from a place that you may think the language is funny,
But to some they think it's nice, I hope you may have guessed
It's Ireland and it comes with the sweet smell of the farmland,
With the many counties to see I hope we never leave.
I will be a professional NHL goalie
Who plays for the greatest team
I will take the number thirty
Then take my team to the Stanley Cup.

Ryan Sweeney, Grade 5
St Brendan Elementary School, MA

The Afterlife

Through the skies and down the streams
Crashing into clouds and bathing in warm rays of sunlight
The sun a great ball of energy in the far distance
Shining with fiery power
Out of heaven I fly with the soul of the eagle
With a falcon chirping with joy as air passes through its glorious feathers
And a hawk dancing in the air to my left
The birds a pair of jetting rockets in the sky
They chirp and screech
Amongst themselves in argument
Deafening my ears
Yet they are the brave and strong birds of prey
The most loyal and giving friends I have ever had
The adventure with me in an everlasting journey
Flying through great adventures and helping God
We are the souls of three great symbols
And we journey together
They are the greatest friends and
My faithful companions in what I call
The cloudy and heavenly
Afterlife

Justin Ku, Grade 6
Hoover Middle School, MD

Homework

I love homework; I think it's so much fun.
I've done something that no one has done.
I really don't get bad grades on homework.
It's actually fun to throw away your homework when it's all done.

Madeleine Hayes, Grade 4
Wapping Elementary School, CT

Leaf

L ovely levitating leaves go into the air.
E verywhere I go I see one leaf.
A pril is when they become amazingly green.
F all is when they are fabulously falling bright colors.

Brendan Lenane, Grade 4
St Gregory Elementary School, MA

Graceful Darkness

The sun sets over a blue red sky.
Darkness falls with a starry sky.
A nighttime draft stirs the trees,
as a cricket sings its nighttime song.
The big city and countryside
rustling has stopped.
As the birds crawl next to each other,
the squirrel opens one eye at the sound
of a falling leaf.
And as the old man,
who was watching this all,
closes his eyes,
his last thought: "What a Graceful Darkness."

Rob Lewis, Grade 6
Kenmore Middle School, VA

Wasps

My wings are made of membrane,
And when I broke them I was in a lot of pain

Wasps can fly and wasps can sting,
And wasps work hard for farmers in the spring

We can be friendly and we can be kind,
We are always trendy and one of a kind

We wasps are classy so we never gloat or showboat,
That's for cicadas and other tacky oafs

Yes it is true we are supreme,
And because you cannot top us it makes you want to scream!

Gray Flanagan, Grade 6
Immaculate Heart of Mary School, DE

Never Trusting Friend

Time to time we talk again
Soon you're feeling like my friend
You know my secrets, and you say you will never again
turn your back on me, a friend.
Then I slip up
I let you in
You get upset, yet again
You block me out
I don't exist
Sooner or later you are back again
You are my never trusting friend.

Emma Shawcross, Grade 5
Maybeury Elementary School, VA

Praying Mantis

Hello there, I am a praying mantis either green or brown,
You can look everywhere because I might be in town.

I lay my eggs in a frothy mass,
Sometimes even in the green, green grass.

After mating I may eat the male,
So if he ever sees me he may want to sail.

If you ever see me in the light,
You may want to be careful because I can bite.

For many hours in the day,
I hide in places and wait patiently for my prey.

I am so, so sorry that I have to go,
But if you ever look down you might find me near your toe.

Kate Davis, Grade 6
Immaculate Heart of Mary School, DE

The Jump

"Now line up and do jetés girls"
my ballet teacher ordered.
Lining up with my friend, I start.
'Run, run, jump, run, run, jump'
I order myself.
Leaping up in the air
I feel like a bird with wings soaring in the air
my legs split perfectly and place my
arms as graceful as a swan's neck.
Landing loudly, I repeat the
process with the equal amount of
effort.
"Very nice Claire" commented my
teacher.
"Other side now, 5, 6, 7, 8"
Ballet has been everything for me
and I would never trade it for anything.
I live, breath, and eat ballet every single
day of my life now for five
wonderful years.

Claire Lewis, Grade 6
Kenmore Middle School, VA

Trick-or-Treat

I heard doorbells and tape recorders
scary screams
I see different costumes and haunted houses
lights turning off and on
I feel fog from a fog machine and leaves falling
I taste candy I got Trick or treating and a soda
I smell candles burning in the
jack-o'-lanterns and candy melting

Nick Lacagnina, Grade 4
Brookside Elementary School, MA

Winter to Summer

Winter
Snowy days
Snowball fights
Hot chocolate
Cars not starting
Water pipes freezing
School delays
Snowboarding season

Thawing snow and ice

Pool opening
Skateboard season
Summer break
Beach vacations
Sandal weather
Sizzling sidewalks
Bring out the short sleeves
Summer!
Zack West, Grade 6
Wakefield Forest Elementary School, VA

Smilies

Big smilies
Small smilies
Nice, happy, moving smilies
Mean, evil, sad smilies
Those are just a few.
Bad smilies
Good smilies
Yellow, pink, purple smilies
Crying, sleeping, baby smilies
Nerd smilies too!
Smart smilies
Sick smilies
And don't forget loving smilies.
Last of all
Best of all
I like my smilies!
Stormie Fortner, Grade 6
Juliet W Long School, CT

Snowfall

Chilly nights bring
Cold breezes and
Warm fires to winter
I'm thinking are angels here?
Are angels here?
Lighting up the sparkling snow
Streetlights glow
Barking dogs
Footsteps in the snow
I feel warm inside
So very warm inside
Lena Burns, Grade 4
John J Flynn Elementary School, VT

My Sister

My sister knows how to dance.
One day she'll be a star.
When my sister dances
She dances with sparks.
When I grow up
I want to be a dancer.
Bruna Soria-Galvarro, Grade 6
Kenmore Middle School, VA

When You Smell a Flower

When you smell a flower
It will bring joy to your life.
When you smell a flower
It's like a daydream
That will last forever.
When your mom smells that flower
That smell will come
From your daughter's heart.
Jennifer LePrevost, Grade 5
St Mary's School, MA

Mommy

She has that special hand,
To wipe away my tears
She has special touch
To take away my fears
She has that special heart
To know I tried my best
She has that special eye
To know when I need rest
She gives that special trust to me
So I know she'll never let me fall
I know she'll always love me
All and all
Caroline Kelley, Grade 6
Graham Middle School, VA

Snowflakes

Sparkle shimmer
Dazzle glimmer
Beautifully white
Cold and bright
Like an angel flying through the night
Soaring through the trees
Like buzzing bees
Soaring aloft
Landing ever so soft
Coming from the sky
Soaring about and awry
Like a raindrop
Falling into the perfect backdrop
On a brisk and frigid winters' day
Olivia O'Connor, Grade 6
St Rocco School, RI

My Brother

My brother likes to tease me
He likes to make me cry
He likes to beat and pound on me
I can't imagine why.
He teases me about my looks
My ears, my eyes, my face
I don't know what to say to him
To put him in his place.

My brother likes to play with me
He likes to make me smile
When it's time to teach me sports
He goes the extra mile.
He compliments me on my hockey
My baseball and all the rest
When it comes to being a brother
He definitely is the best.

My brother went to college this year
He is so far away
I have to say I miss him more
With every passing day.
Jeffrey Kurzman, Grade 5
Davenport Ridge School, CT

Fall

Fall is coming ever so fast,
I just can't wait; it will be a blast.
The wind is blowing
And the leaves are flying,
But none of the kids are ever sighing.
Let's fly a kite
Or throw a ball,
Rake some leaves,
Then jump in and say, "Whee!"
If you really want some more,
Just wait three seasons.
Why? For all those reasons!
Katie Lee, Grade 5
Windermere School, CT

Snowy Skies

Snowy skies
So sparkly, so soft,
Falling from the sky,
As if they were butterflies.

I stare at this satin sight.
Sunlight shining bright,
Summer left behind.
Snowflakes sticking on the window sill.

Jewels of snow falling from the sky.
Oh snowy skies.
Misbah Muzaffer, Grade 6
Graham Middle School, VA

Poetry

What can you put in a simile?
Oh, you could use a shoe and a tree!

Personification, personification
Ooh, oh, what a temptation
It makes you just want to say,
The clock belched every second of the day

Metaphor, a simile without like or as,
It's a pizza without the spazz

Alliteration you know you have to say…
The Aslan Alligator has come to save the day!

Repetition, repetition what is that?
Oh, I just said one! How cool is that?

The end rhyme is a good hobby
I used it in the poem
Starting with the word tree

Onomatopoeia, words that mean the sounds they provide
Buzz! Buzz! A bee passed by my side…onomatopoeia
Woosh! Bye!

Aslan Bakri, Grade 5
Wakefield Forest Elementary School, VA

The Joy of December

Think of Christmas trees, menorah candles too,
the joy of December thinks of you.

If you're sad or feeling blue
just think of the joy December brings to you.

Snowflakes falling here and there;
the joy of family they hold each other near.

The laughing, the dancing, the singing too,
so be happy by a fire when family's with you.

Lexi Bardos, Grade 5
Old Saybrook Middle School, CT

5th Grade

5th grade the best in the school,
the oldest, the smartest,
we're the coolest of the cool.
The little kids look up as we pass in the halls,
but we don't notice them 'cause they're too small,
too bad this glory only lasts for a year
'cause next year we'll be full of fear,
the youngest, the smallest,
we're the lamest of the lame,
so this is the last year to enjoy the fame!

Tamar Bulka, Grade 5
Zervas Elementary School, MA

Me

My hair is the color of dark chocolate
And as long as a garden snake
My skin is the color of a palm trees trunk
That gleams in the summer sun
My legs are like a clown on stilts
That has very long strides
My eyes are the color of mud
But shine and sparkle in the sun
My smile is as big as the ocean
Which makes you feel very good
I like to be as free as a gazelle

Delana Sobhani, Grade 6
Fairfax Collegiate School, VA

Friends

F aithful and present when you need them most
R espectful to you and to others
I maginative and intelligent
E ncouraging you to keep striving for goals
N ever unfair or unkind by intent
D etermined to do nice things for you
S omeone honest and trustworthy

Shane Cyrus, Grade 6
Graham Middle School, VA

I Am

I am a humorous friend and a lover of football and basketball,
I wonder if the stars of the dark space actually dance,
I hear the rushing wind in a brutal hurricane storm,
I see Papa Smurf laying on the soft green grass in the sunlight,
I want there to be peace throughout the world,
I am a humorous friend and a lover of football and basketball.

I pretend I am the greatest sports player ever,
I feel the cold winter wind rush against my back,
I touch the steaming hot sand of the sandy beach,
I worry I won't score the touchdown,
I cry for my family,
I am a humorous friend and a lover of football and basketball.

I understand why we fight wars,
I say I'm good enough to play pro football,
I dream to be recognized of doing something amazing,
I try to do things the way they should be done,
I hope the Iraq war will soon end,
I am a humorous friend and a lover of football and basketball.

Matt Nelson, Grade 6
Amherst Middle School, NH

Fall

F athers going to work with hot cocoa.
A pple cider steaming hot can burn your mouth.
L eaves falling orange and red from every tree.
L eaf piles I like jumping in.

Katharine Woodmansee, Grade 4
Dr Charles E Murphy Elementary School, CT

Baseball Is the Best

Baseball is my favorite sport.
I like to play it all year round.
Winter, spring, summer, fall,
Are the times I play ball.

When the pitcher pitches,
I swing the bat.
I hit the ball very far,
Maybe I'll be an All-Star.

I play by the rules.
I always try to do my best,
And hope my team beats all the rest.

I love baseball,
There is no doubt.
One, two, three strikes
YOU'RE OUT!

Daniel Robushi, Grade 5
Davenport Ridge School, CT

War

War an endless fight
Like hurting people and killing
Like hurricanes ripping through towns

Like endless explosions
And it keeps going on and on and
Never stops.

Kyle Lesko, Grade 4
Riverfield School, CT

The Holidays

Winter is the best
Christmas is coming tonight
We make a snowman.

Yesterday it snowed.
It was very cold outside.
We did not have school.

Julianna Jandreau, Grade 4
Brookside Elementary School, MA

A Camera

I flash with a button.
I take pictures.
I hold them.
One day, I give them back.
I see good times and bad times.
I go to places all over the world.
I feel glad when I am used.
I get more power when I'm charged.
I am steady and perfect when I'm held.
My pictures always turn out fantastic.

Garritt Rehberg, Grade 5
Old Saybrook Middle School, CT

Halloween

Today is Halloween and it's the spookiest night of all.
Mask, costume, gloves and belts, it's also held in fall.
Children hoping to get a lot of candy.
This night will be simply fine and dandy.

Little children will be taken for a fright.
Walking around late at night, scared to be out of mommy's sight.
Goodnight from Halloween. I hope it made you scream.

Andre Davis, Grade 6
Melwood Elementary School, MD

Hidden Secrets

Shhh…listen to the secrets around you.
Don't you hear them? Listen closer.
Zone out the obvious around you.
The wind is whispering secrets.
The sunshine carries unknown stories, yet to be discovered.
The stars are twinkling shared sparkles of insight.
Secrets of nature, in front of out faces, rarely noticed, deeply seen, or heard.
So listen closely, look around, they're always there.
We just don't know it.
Secrets. Hidden in full view.

Kelsey Carvalko, Grade 6
Irving School, CT

Overflow

Drip, drop as the droplets of rain fall down like it's raining cats and dogs.
The pond is overflowing as the water rises.
The frogs hurry and leap to the trees.
Circles are forming in the pond.

Cynthia Wang, Grade 5
Wakefield Forest Elementary School, VA

Christmas Day

We set out the milk and cookies and went to bed.
But not because we wanted to our mother and father said.
As we laid down our head, we were simply just too excited about the Christmas ahead.
As we shut our eyes, we doze into a sleep, until our morning surprise.
As they awake they give themselves a shake.
Then they get up to wake up their parents to go downstairs.
As they open their presents their parents joyfully glare,
while the children are just smiling getting their share.

Anna Durst, Grade 6
Beacon Middle School, DE

Drop of Dew

A droplet of dew falls upon a leaf.
It keeps falling until it reaches a clear pond of peace.
The frogs welcome the drop of dew as they sing their song of summer.
When the song is done,
the silence of the frogs circles the beautiful pond.
And the drop of dew has mysteriously disappeared,
Into the magical wonder of water.

Francesca Falvo, Grade 5
Wakefield Forest Elementary School, VA

Dogs

I really, really like my dog
Good thing she looks nothing like my hog
She is very sweet
But I couldn't say that for her feet

Brianna Via, Grade 5
McCleary Elementary School, VA

Dream Catcher

I will hang onto your dreams
So you shall
Not lose them
Give up on your dreams and

You give up on your soul
I
Will catch your dreams and give them back
So you don't feel without a purpose
Your dreams are everything

I am the Dream Catcher

David Czako, Grade 6
Canton Intermediate School, CT

Flag

I climb up a pole that is 50 feet high.
I am not afraid of heights.
At my house, for advertisement,
I climb a pole and wave to people.
I am as strong as our flag that owns all 50 states.

Alexandra J. Pink, Grade 5
Old Saybrook Middle School, CT

Look at Your Snowman!

Look at your snowman!
You built him all day,
And watched him all night.
In bed you lay,
Wishing him life.
All of a sudden,
What do you know!
You think you see movement.
He's starting to go!
You get up real fast,
Pull on your coat and boots
You head for the door,
But you hear some weird hoots.
Is your Snowman worth the risk?
Or should you build a new one tomorrow?
But then you remember,
Dad's special coat you borrowed!
You run at full speed,
But can you catch up?
Then you realize,
It's just that kid, Billy Nup.

Savannah Bedard, Grade 6
Juliet W Long School, CT

Heat Bugs

It was a blazing hot Wednesday.
When I opened the door,
I decided to take a stroll outside.
I started walking down the street.
When I realized I was melting from the heat.
But the mosquitoes were worse.
They were eating me alive!
I needed shade!
I ran back down the street to my cousins' house.
I sat down on the sofa.
And I started to get sleepy.
I went upstairs and went to bed at 1:04 p.m.

Sabah Geme, Grade 6
Kenmore Middle School, VA

German Shepherds

A German Shepherd is quite a good pet,
But you better cross your fingers when you go to the vet.

Shepherds have a twenty percent chance of getting hip disease,
And if you're allergic, you certainly will sneeze.

They sure are playful I can say,
Even on their worst of day.

Here is a good thing you should know,
German Shepherds love the winter snow.

German Shepherds are great dogs, that's all I can say.
I would suggest them for a real fun pet any day.

Justin Kerhulas, Grade 5
E Ethel Little Elementary School, MA

The Midnight Sky

Stars are twinkling bright,
The sky is black and blue all through the night,
Everything is dark and still,
Animals roam silently over the hills.

The neighborhood is sleepy,
Sometimes the darkness of the night is creepy,
The moon is a big lit circle in the sky,
It's so peaceful, time just flies by.

Like quiet figures lurking,
Shadows keep jerking,
Even the littlest bit of light,
Can be seen very bright.

After hours and hours pass away,
The night is just turning to day,
A morning mist starts to fall,
We know by the rooster's call.

Amita Sastry, Grade 4
Mathewson School, CT

Maryland

A wonderful place to live in.
B ay is perfect place to catch a crabs.
C ome to crab shops and enjoy your days.
D elicious foods for you in many restaurants.
E xtremely welcomed.
F air weathers.
G reat government and police so you are safe.
H ighly recommended to live in.
I ncredible movie theatre you could watch.
J obs are greatly waiting for you.
K ind people live in here.
L ush, green grasses and trees.
M ore place for family vacations like six flags.

N ow is your chance.
O f course air is clean and not polluted.
P erfect for your free time.
Q uiet, peaceful public libraries you could go.
R eally great aquariums you could go and watch.
S parking bay water you could enjoy watching.
T his state I say is best of all.
U nforgettable good memories in Maryland.
V isit Maryland today.
W hy say no to come?
X -rays are always available for you.
Y ou wish you wants to be there?
Z ap and you will be in beautiful Maryland.

YoonSun Jee, Grade 6
Old Mill Middle North School, MD

About Me

My eyes are like an ocean on a sunny day with seagulls circling and making a black dot on the ocean. My heart is happiness that I pump through me. My brain is like a fountain of information with thoughts. My bones are the support of all my family and friends. I live in a house that is like we were separated for a year and found each other. I eat a healthy variety of food like a foe.

Amanda Talbot, Grade 6
Tolland Middle School, CT

Feelings

How do you feel today?

Anger
Anger can be a lion on fire prowling around in your heart, running from side to side

Happiness
Happiness can be a rainbow going from one ear to the other, growing every second of the day

Sadness
Sadness can be a downpour that floods your heart full, drowning every thing in its path

Humor
Humor can be somebody tickling your tongue

Hurt
Hurt can be like someone talking about you behind your back

Guilt
Guilt can be a friend hitting your heart constantly

Right
Right like helping someone who really needs it.

Nicki Brown, Grade 6
Tomlinson Middle School, CT

My Cousin's Cry

One day when I heard my cousin's best friend died I was furious and I thought he would be so sad and terrified. Things like that don't come up every day. I thought it must be so hard to withstand the pressure of one of the worst things that can ever happen. I know if my friend died I wouldn't be able to hear about him without a tear running down my face. He lost his bro, his buddy, his friend.

Kenyon Day, Grade 6
Everett Meredith Middle School, DE

Lightning

The zig zaggy lightning makes me smile
so bright to see a different change.
The swervey lightning is so colorful
It's even hotter than the sun.
Sometimes when it's very powerful
some people get really lazy.
The flashing lightning
makes my eyes hurt very badly
People say lightning gathers up
electric from your television.
Lightning comes with loud rumbling thunder
and dark puffy clouds.
It strikes big bolts of lightning
over the mountains.
So if you see lightning go in your house
and don't look out your window.
I bet lightning and thunder will come again.

Emily Rhinaman, Grade 4
Pleasant Valley Elementary School, MD

I Am a Guitar Player

I am a boy who loves guitars
I wonder if I'll be a star
I hear the loud noise from the amp
as I strum the strings and try to play
I see the crowd waving their arms in the air
I want a four-necked guitar when I am 15 years old
I am a boy who loves guitars

I pretend I'm playing in a rock band
I feel the vibration of the amp as I am playing the guitar loudly
I touch the strings while playing
I worry that I will mess up and ruin the show
I am a boy who loves guitars

I understand that I might not be famous
I say one, two, three, four
I dream I will be a star
I try to play very well
I hope that my band is the hit of the show
I am a boy who loves guitars

Brett Catlow, Grade 5
Blackrock School, RI

I am a Pencil

People use me and my tip breaks.
I get shorter when I go in the sharpener.
My eraser gets worn out and I have to get an eraser cap,
but then it looks like I'm wearing a colored hat.
I get lost on the ground and people pick me up off the ground.
People put me on a desk or put me in the garbage can.
Some people even put me on their ear.

Thanousay Sourignamath, Grade 5
Old Saybrook Middle School, CT

Summer's Gone

Summer's gone and I'm out of the pool
But I don't mind, going back to school

I have arithmetic, science, and art
Then when I go home, time for homework to start

Making a rhyme is like a test
But I will try my very best!

Isabella Casale, Grade 6
St Brigid School, ME

School Is So Uncool

School is so uncool.
We have to follow every rule.
The good part is gym.
But they work you 'til you're slim.
Each class is 45 minutes long.
We get in trouble if you do something wrong.
All thought school is extremely boring.
I'll try to keep myself from snoring.

David Patrick, Grade 4
JF Kennedy School, CT

Naomi

N ice to other people
A thletic and smart
O wn horse farm in future
M ight read every night
I ce cream

Naomi Clark, Grade 4
Dr Charles E Murphy Elementary School, CT

In the Barn

I was in the barn on a hot summer day
I went to lie down on the soft fuzzy hay.
Inside the rink the horses will run
They're happy and free and have lots of fun.
The sun is setting so I put the horses in the stall
I guess I had a good day after all.

Juliette Braccio, Grade 4
JF Kennedy School, CT

Heat

There was a tiger named Heat.
He liked to eat meat.
One of his favorites was Antelope.
He also likes Cantaloupe.
He hates it at the zoo when there is sleet.

One day there was sleet everywhere.
It got balled up in his hair.
He didn't like it one bit.
He wished it would quit.
The people ran when they saw him snarl and stare.

Shane Borden, Grade 5
Clover Hill Elementary School, VA

Supplies

Binder, filling up with papers
Textbooks, ready to study
Snack, waiting to be eaten
Books, set to read
Homework, many problems
Bookmark, get writing
Pencils, sharp like a knife
Glue stick, sticking to my backpack
Lunch box, full of goodies
Will Lightfoot, Grade 5
Wakefield Forest Elementary School, VA

It's Cold Outside

It is time for Fall
Jump in the leaves it is fun
The leaves are falling.

The air is windy
It is getting very cold
Let's go inside now.

It is cold outside,
That means it's time for winter
It is so pretty.
Allison Streeter, Grade 4
Brookside Elementary School, MA

Going into Winter Days

Breezy when falling leaves come down
Relaxing, blazing sunsets
Gray, upsetting days
Rustling delicate leaves
When will winter come?
Full of joy
When snow starts to fall
Keana Moreau, Grade 4
John J Flynn Elementary School, VT

Love Gymnastics

Winning Gold medals
Olympics, you can go to
Medal are rewards.
Emily Meyerl, Grade 5
St Joseph School-Fullerton, MD

I Wish

I wish it wasn't so cold
I wish it would snow
I wish people wouldn't litter
I wish the leaves covered up my yard
I wish the air would be fresher
I wish the birds would come back
I wish the leaves would not blow all over
I wish it would just snow!
Joseph Tilton, Grade 6
Juliet W Long School, CT

A Mother's Love

A Mother's Love
Is something that never ends
Is not a matter of who or when
A Mother's Love
Is always there, from the womb through the rocking chair
Even when she's gone, she never leaves you alone
It's something warm and fuzzy
On a cold winter night
It's something you usually take for granted
Since it fell so high
A Mother's Love
Is something that can't be brought
Is something you're sure to use always
A Mother's Love
Is like opportunity knocking at your door
It's the best, worse, the brightest, the dreamiest and everything within.
In between, it's something that makes a little girl feel like a princess
A mother's gift is her love, it's the best ever given
A gift that's been granted from high in heaven
God gave us the best gift above
God truly blessed children when he made mothers.
Tayla Coates, Grade 6
Melwood Elementary School, MD

Days Off

Days off are very happy.
Weekends are the best.
The weeks off are awesome like scoring a touchdown.
Staying in your jammies all day and watching TV, reading a book.
I can picture the days off that we sometimes have.
When school is out, that is when I want to play.
I like riding my bike.
The END of school, that is the BEST part!
Kevin Herrick, Grade 5
Highland Park School, CT

Blue

Blue is the waves crashing on the golden yellow beach
It's the sky getting darker and darker

It is the sweet taste of a blue lollipop slowly dissipating in your mouth
The taste of a freshly twirled cotton candy from the fair

The smell of the salty blue sea
The smell of a ripe blueberry in the middle of spring

It's the feeling of swimming in the reefs of Aruba
The feeling of a tear slowly dripping down your face
Blue is the wonderful feeling of the sky falling down on the Earth

It's the sound of the waves lapping on the beach
The sound of the saxophone blues
Blue is the American flag surrounding the stars that represent our country
Blue…it's a wonderful color
Chayce Horton, Grade 6
Amherst Middle School, NH

The Haunted Forest

In the wind, blackened trees swayed
There were somber shadows in the shade.
An owl hooted.
Its yellow eyes stared me down
He turned my smile into a frown.
A strong gust blew and sent chills down my spine
I just wish the sun would shine.
"Ouch" my foot just banged on a stone
Wait, there are words, R.I.P. JOHN BLACKHONE.
This place is so creepy,
It gives me the heebie-jeebies.
The full moon filled the sky
It was time for all the light to say good-bye.
A moan, a screech,
It reminded me of my minister when he began to preach.
As quickly as I could,
I galloped through the wood
Good riddance forever,
Next time I get dared I'm going to say never!

Joshua Gillen, Grade 5
Lincoln Central Elementary School, RI

Green Machine

I'm a katydid, and I'm green,
Even though I'm green, I'm not mean.

I can blend into my surroundings,
Because I have green, leaf-like wings.

I'm an omnivore just like you,
And, yes, I know that you are too!

I like to sing my mating call,
Especially as it gets closer to fall.

You can see that I can jump well,
Because I have big thighs to help me propel.

I am a very interesting bug,
So you may want to give me a hug!

Brian Neubauer, Grade 6
Immaculate Heart of Mary School, DE

Basketball

B e smart, don't give up!
A n emergency might come up, and that's fine
S chool is more important, stay in school
K eep practicing, you will get better
E nergy is what you need to get up and play
T eam work is needed in this game
B ring family to watch you play
A lways think about your team
L ook around to see if anybody is open for a pass
L eader of the team is watched by all.

Eddie Cabrera, Grade 5
Litwin Elementary School, MA

William the Wonderful Wasp

I am a wasp that is yellow and black.
You better watch out I have a stinger in my back.

Bees and ants are like my brothers.
We are so close that we watch out for each other.

I can live all over the U.S.
I also live in a very big nest.

My nests can be either in a tree or the ground.
My nests can be oval or they can be round.

Unlike a bee, I can sting over and over again.
Just ask my poor little friend named Ben.

Patrick Spillan, Grade 6
Immaculate Heart of Mary School, DE

Fall Is Coming

Fall is coming,
Oh, fall is coming,
Fall is my favorite season,
With all these beautiful leaves hanging!

Fall is coming,
Oh, fall is coming,
How wonderful it is to jump
into the leaves,
With your dear, dear siblings!

Fall is coming,
Oh, fall is coming,
All those squirrels going up and down the tree,
Just looking at them makes me feel so free!

Emily Zhou, Grade 5
Linville-Edom Elementary School, VA

Prayer for Family

They are so close
I will not let them go.
But when they do
My heart will snap and crumble
For all I will have is memories,
Memories that sleep inside my head at night.

Caroline Vannah, Grade 6
Village School, MA

Love

LOVE smells like just-baked cookies
LOVE tastes like a Slurpee on a hot day,
LOVE looks like a lake of melted chocolate.
LOVE sounds like doves in spring time.
LOVE feels like a warm bath with bubbles.

Vivian Gray, Grade 4
Fairfax Collegiate School, VA

Thanksgiving

let's have some turkey
I hope it's not jerky
pass the ham
please sam
thank God for this feast
now we'll all eat like beasts

Allison Zerofski, Grade 4
Brookside Elementary School, MA

Tree

Big, tall
Moves when windy
Calm, relaxing, serenity, peaceful
Plant

Logan Kerns, Grade 5
Boonsboro Elementary School, MD

Basketball

We are the G-Men,
The mighty G-Men.
When we come to play,
The fans scream "HOORAY!"

See us pass, dribble and shoot.
The fans think it's a hoot,
Because we blow the teams out,
They are all in a drought.

We are the G-Men, playing for Graham.
We are proud, we are a team,
Just come watch us shine,
Your court or mine?

Chase Illig, Grade 6
Graham Middle School, VA

Frightful Journey

I'm on a frightful journey,
Not knowing when it will end.
May be scary,
May be fun,
May be…frightful.
While I'm on this frightful journey,
I'm learning as I go.
This journey teaches all kinds of things
How to live,
What to do
Everything you need to know
On this frightful journey.
Now that my journey is over
I see how scary and frightening it was.
With memories to last a lifetime,
I'm done with my frightful journey.

Elizabeth Sparks, Grade 6
Beacon Middle School, DE

Football

The roaring of the crowd weakened,
The football thundered through the air
Like a bird.
The receivers shot down
The giant rectangle, the field
Faster than speeding bullets
Look! One of them is wide open!
He caught it! Go! Go! Go!
Smack!
He was hit hard!
But he scored.

Colin Mannix, Grade 4
Boonsboro Elementary School, MD

A Bee

Music to my ears
What do I hear everywhere?
I think it's a bee

Emily Silver, Grade 4
St Brigid School, ME

Just to Say*

I have eaten
the steak
that was in the refrigerator

which you
were probably saving
for dinner

forgive me
but it was so delicious
and sweet
so good.
Forgive me!

Amarilyz Candelaria, Grade 5
Clover Street School, CT
*Inspired by William Carlos Williams

Spiders at Dawn

Dawn brings many things.
Spiders are one of them.
They march across the dew-stained grass
Leaving their lacey homes far behind.

Sandra Webb, Grade 5
Wakefield Forest Elementary School, VA

The Clouds

The clouds remind me of cotton candy,
So light, delicious, fluffy and dandy.
Beautifully crafted to look so delicious,
But I'm suspicious.
It looks so delicious,
But ick — it's wet and full of water.

Anna Kilpatric, Grade 5
Boonsboro Elementary School, MD

Childhood

Red velvet cupcakes,
to silky smooth skin.
A warm bath,
to a dreary sleep.
An unharmful sleep,
to candy land.
It's your childhood,
"Live while you're alive."

Ashley Davidson, Grade 5
Zervas Elementary School, MA

Feelings Within

I feel so cold inside
But deep down I can pull through
I'm so weak and dull
I want a hug
I dropped to the ground
But I am too sad to get up
I burst with rage
Why does it have to be this way?

Malik Yarde, Grade 6
Vernon Center Middle School, CT

The Wind

As the wind blows
The sheets on the clothesline
Wave like the sails on a ship
You can almost imagine
A glorious ship
Sailing through the water

Gaby Teran, Grade 6
Kenmore Middle School, VA

Snowball

white
fluffy
bright
a perfect snowball
as if created by gods
sparkling in the sunlight
dancing in the moonlight
wonderful in every way
so dazzlingly beautiful
like magic
I have never seen anything more pure
than this one, perfect snowball
my masterpiece
I will give it as a gift
I think
from all of the heavens blue
from me
to you.

Colby C. Goodrich, Grade 6
The Well School, NH

Sports

Sports can be really fun
Especially when you have to run
I like soccer and basketball too
Even sometimes I don't have a clue what to do
I dribble and shoot
And I hope it will go in the hoop
I shoot and scream
And root for my team
And hopefully we will win
I love both the sports that I play
And maybe I will be a professional one day

Morgan Whisman, Grade 6
Graham Middle School, VA

World Trade Center

The World Trade Center was like a big cloud covering a harbor
Then on September 11th that big cloud got struck down
The two buildings plunged to the ground
Killing thousands of people

Then I think about the people that died
I know nothing can make up for all the people
That died on that day

That moment changed every bit of my life
I will never forget that tragic day

Luke Vitale, Grade 4
Riverfield School, CT

The Ocean Blue

Corals and seashells line the ocean floor
Oh, what a wonderful ocean world
Dolphins in dozens and swordfish in packs,
What a sight it would be to tour the ocean blue
Fish swimming and sharks gripping
Turtles make an effort to keep on swimming
Seaweed waving and clamshells sunbathing
I dream of this wonderful world

Marissa Mancini, Grade 5
Lincoln Central Elementary School, RI

Green Back*

The slippery green back
Emerges swiftly and gracefully
The alligator
Don't laugh — in the royal lime green clothes
His razor sharp teeth and thick tail
Why not love him?
With his huge roar and his slippery green back.
Well, this slippery green back is beautiful and strong
Only alligators shall hang out with me

Nyeemah Hightower, Grade 5
Clover Street School, CT
*Inspired by Marianne Moore

I Miss You

When I cry myself to sleep
You're the one I think of
Every day I cry and weep
Because you're the one I knew and loved
You lit the darkest nights
And helped me through my darkest hours
You brought courage to toughest fights
It's just like you had magical powers
You were a family member and a friend
And you loved me like I loved you
You stood by my side until the end
Without your presence I don't know what to do
So I sadly said good-bye
And I forced myself to know
We all sat and wondered why
You suddenly had to go
Now there's only one place that you'll always be
That's in my loving heart
Up away or next to me
You'll still be there as you were from the start

Halle Fridman, Grade 6
Pikesville Middle School, MD

I Am

I am a boy who loves playing baseball.
I wonder if I'll ever play professionally
I hear the umpire calling strikes and outs,
    the bat cracking when I hit the ball.
I see the ball flying out of the ball park.
I want to play on the Red Sox and hit 50 homers.
I am a boy who loves playing baseball.

I pretend I'm the best player on the team.
I feel so happy when I hit the winning homer
    and my team cheers.
I touch the rough, wooden bat.
I worry I will get hurt and not get to play.
I am a boy who loves playing baseball.

I understand why baseball is not very easy.
I say baseball is awesome.
I dream to hit 500 homers
I hope that I stop every grounder hit to me
I am a boy who loves playing baseball.

Michael Pitt, Grade 5
Blackrock School, RI

The Joy of Christmas

On Christmas Eve I stay asleep
Dreaming I see sheep
When I wake up
I see presents
And I say in my mind
Thank you Santa for this wonderful Christmas

Noah P. Sykes, Grade 5
Rosemont Forest Elementary School, VA

Stories of the River

I see shadows lurking
around the riverbank.
They are waiting,
waiting for the river
to tell a story.
The river has
many stories and secrets,
and the shadows
are waiting to hear them.
The river is very old and slow,
but soon it will tell the shadows
a history.

Eikra Shithil, Grade 6
Kenmore Middle School, VA

Puppies

Cute, small little pets
Playful little animals
That love you so much.
Rachel Contreras, Grade 5
St Joseph School-Fullerton, MD

Camping

Out in the woods
Bushes and trees
Animals all around
Even bees.

Out at the river
Fishing for trout
As I like to say
It is good to be out.

In the cozy tent
Sitting on a pillow
Telling ghost stories
And roasting marshmallows.

Camping is enjoyable
And very fun
Playing outside
In the bright hot sun.
Bradley Hicks, Grade 6
Graham Middle School, VA

Baseball

B est game ever
A wesome
S core
E rror
B all
A merican
L eagues
L eaders
Tyrone Murray, Grade 5
St Joseph School-Fullerton, MD

The Pencil

I'm a pencil made of wood.
I come in all different colors and sizes.

It hurts when they have to break my tip.
They have to grind me down into the dreaded pencil sharpener.

When they write with me it hurts as if you were scraping your leg on cement.
They put a metal shackle on my head.

Then people stuff lead into my body.
Their sweaty hand is on me all day long.

Some people even bite me, ouch that hurts!
As if you were bitten by a dog.

I'll work hard.
Please use me wisely.

Ryan McDougall, Grade 5
Cunningham School, MA

Chairs

You can find a chair just about everywhere.
Yet no one seems to care
    about these beautiful chairs.
On the fabric ones you'll find rips and tears.
On the plastic ones you'll find lots of spots.
You can also find some polka-dots.

Some chairs are gentle and kind,
    and don't very much mind
    that you sit on them.
Some chairs say that squishing you make by sitting on them, mayhem.

Sometimes they're fluffy and soft,
    other kinds are so small they make you feel so squished that you're in a tiny loft.
When you sit it's usually a lovely surprise
    and makes sparkles appear in your eyes.

Chairs are all around, anywhere you look,
    you can also find them in a decorating book.
They are just about everywhere
    and that's because you sit on a chair.

Megan Reilly, Grade 6
Infant Jesus School, NH

My Dog Fred

My dog's name is Fred which rhymes with bed.
Whenever you want him, that's where he'll be so it's said.
He's not a great watch dog, he'll greet you with tons of licks.
And Fred's not very talented, he knows very little tricks.
But his tongue's slurppy and wet, and shoots out of his mouth like a jet.
Fred's paws have huge claws and make a beat when he runs through the heat.
Once my dog Fred is fed, he's exhausted and goes straight to bed.

Elliot Sirchio, Grade 5
Davenport Ridge School, CT

My Culture
I am from the flag waving proudly in front of my school.
I am from the ball in a soccer game that gets shot in the back of the net.
I am from the game of Sorry on the coffee table relaxing after a nice dinner and having some family time.
I am from the green of Saint Patrick floating on the Irish Flag.
I am from the cross in the church looking over you every Sunday.
I am from the woods with whistling birds upon you dancing in the air.
I am from the picture that hangs upon my family's living room every day of my life.
I am from the stew in your favorite bowl that you had at Christmas time.
I am from the sound of your "Good Night"
I am from my family carving a pumpkin on Halloween.

Patrick Egan, Grade 5
Jack Jackter Intermediate School, CT

Snow
Let it snow, and cover the earth with an enormous white blanket. The feeling of my face turning red, and my body turning numb is always a sign of fall turning to winter. The sight of trees turning white, and snow falling from the sky is when I know winter is here. Snowmen, snow angels, snowballs and igloos. Snowboarding, skiing, sledding and more. So many activities to do in the snow, too bad winter is coming so slow!

Emily Freedland, Grade 6
Village School, MA

Dreams
Dreams are beautiful. You dream of great things. If you don't like it, change it. Dreams come from the heart. When you dream you might be sad. When you dream you might be happy. That is what dreams are made of. One day you might dream this. The next day you might dream of that. Some days you might not dream at all. There could be different types of dreams. You can also dream with cartoons or real people. Dreams are beautiful. This is what dreams are made of.

Zuri Lopez, Grade 6
Irving School, CT

Touchdown
I feel like my bones just fell out of their sockets.
The polka-dotted pig skin is a bullet rocketing down,

down
down
down
down
down…

I get into a sturdy position ready to catch the pig skin.
The cheerleaders screaming like crazy!
T.H.O.M.A.S.

My eyes open wider than the Empire State Building.
My jaw dropped as fast as a pitch by Lyell Malone.

It hits my hands with
a powering pop like popping popcorn
My hands throb as if they were being stung by a million baby bumblebees.

Touchdown!
Spike it!
Win!

Thomas St. Rock, Grade 6
Mystic Middle School, CT

Field of Golden Sun

Field of golden sun calls to me.
I walk instinctively;
So natural,
Just like breathing.
The gold so pure;
My heart beating fast.
The prickliness of the grass,
As I walk so hypnotic.
My mind belongs to the field.
Field of Golden Sun.

Heather Dumond, Grade 5
Owls Head Central School, ME

Lamborgini

L eader in
A utomobile
M akes Gallardi's
B eats other cars
O ther cars are slow
R acing vehicles
G allardi
I s fast
N eeds vroom
I nto 5 gears

Andrew Ukadike, Grade 5
St Joseph School-Fullerton, MD

Jeremy

Jeremy
Nice, animal lover, learner
Brother of Jason
Lover of family, bamboo shrimp, rice
Who feels happy, joy, confused
Who needs water, food, shelter
Who gives joy, ideas, a helping hand
Who would like to become a vet,
An architect, or an animal discoverer
Resident of Stratham
Johnson

Jeremy Johnson, Grade 4
Portsmouth Christian Academy, NH

Christmas

Christmas time
Christmas is a time for sharing.
It's also a time for love and caring.

Christ boy
In a manger where he lay.
Christ was born on Christmas day.

Save us all
Just a baby it seemed to Him.
You'd never know He'd save us from sin.

Catherine Walbrecher, Grade 6
St Joseph School-Fullerton, MD

Pumpkin Farm

Tall and fat
Round and small
Pumpkin farms have them all!
Pick them fresh.
Pick them old.
Pumpkin farms will get them sold.
Paint them mean,
Or paint them sweet.
Pumpkin farms are such a treat!

Kelly Majerowicz, Grade 5
St Joseph School-Fullerton, MD

A Miracle

There once was a frog named Fred,
He ate a blue piece of bread,
His body started to shake,
His brain felt like it was fake,
He thought he was going to die,
But instead he started to fly!
So remember if you ever see a flying frog
It might be Fred, not a dog.

Rebekah Hebert, Grade 4
Wapping Elementary School, CT

Lilies

Lilies
In grass and ponds
With beautiful meadows
To pink to yellow to green
The sweet flowery smell of flowers
Like ponds with beautiful waves
Lilies

Alyssa Mantzouranis, Grade 4
Four Seasons Elementary School, MD

The Wind

The wind is blowing softly
Through my hair,
It calls me there,
There in the air,
Up in the clear blue sky,
I glide and I fly.

The sun is high in the sky,
But, alas! I cannot stay,
I have to go to land today!

Away,
Oh! So far away
From the sky,
Where I fly,
In my world of dreams!

Caroline Kempfer, Grade 5
Linville-Edom Elementary School, VA

Babies

Babies are so messy
You will need a lot of help

But when it comes to diapers
You can count me out

They complain about their bib
And spit out all their food

But that is not as bad
As when they cough up day old goo

They will never sleep
Either day or night

But when they are in a good mood
They are rather nice

Rosie Sparrow, Grade 5
Mary P Hinsdale Elementary School, CT

Winter

Grass cut by farmers just in time
Crispness of the wind
Honking geese flying overhead
Warm and toasty beneath my coat
Cold frost upon my lips
Winter is finally here

Stephen Walsh, Grade 6
St Rose School, CT

The Lottery

If I won the lottery
I would buy my mom some pottery.
I would buy myself a bike,
In any color I like.
I would love to buy a big pig,
That could sing and dance a jig.
I would drive a nice car,
And drive it very far.
Buying a truck for my dad
Would make him very glad.
I would buy my teacher a book,
That would teach her how to cook!
I would buy a new tent,
Before all my money was spent!

Jesse Pierce, Grade 5
Linville-Edom Elementary School, VA

War

In sorrow times sacrifices must be made
Humans die for what they think is right
Blood and flesh splatter to the ground
Souls rise to the clouds
At the end all that's left is the sadness

Ethan Peters, Grade 6
Bethlehem Elementary School, NH

Connor

Connor
Athletic, smart, swimmer
Wishes to play soccer.
Dreams of being famous
Wants to be a famous swimmer
Who wonders who will be the next president.
Who fears poisonous animals.
Who likes the Bears and Eagles
Who believes in God
Who loves soccer and football
Who plans to rule the universe
Who wants to meet the whole Bears' team

Nick Cornwell, Grade 5
C Hunter Ritchie Elementary School, VA

My Life Is Like a Tulip

Morning I wake up and get ready for the day.
My tulips spread themselves out.
I am the tulip who opens today,
In the evening I close and I dream and pout

In the morning I bloom into a tall flower,
Each day I get more fulfilling.
Of course I don't grow to be a tower!
But please fetch plenty of water to keep my filling.

But spring comes and spring goes.
I call to it each morn.
Now summer comes and no water flows,
I find my petals are torn.

Spring never answered for two more seasons.
Each day I feel I am going to die,
It is hard to stay alive for all these weird reasons.
I lay down and sleep and say goodbye world, goodbye!

Brooke Bergman, Grade 6
Blue Ridge Middle School, VA

Soldier

U.S. soldier
Healthy, kind
Helping, fighting, thinking
Sad leaving their families
Marine

Kevin R. Doherty, Grade 4
Dr Charles E Murphy Elementary School, CT

Winter

W inter is a wonderful time of the year.
I love to play in the snow!
N oel, Noel a wonderful song.
T oday the snow is tumbling down.
E ager to put on my boots and my coat to play outside.
R acing with our sleds.

Calvin J. Mackey, Grade 5
Rosemont Forest Elementary School, VA

The Race

Off they go!
Their tremendous parkas flying.
Look at the twirling snow.
So fast!
It looks like those dogs could touch the sky.
The dog's booties stay on tight
    all through the frigid winter night.
In the morn, the booties might be torn,
    but that's just the race.
The race when the dogs and their mushers must pace.

Robert Adams-Michaud, Grade 5
Highland Park School, CT

After School

When I got home from school,
I ran right in the pool.
I went inside to watch TV,
And then we had some tea.
Then I turned it off and went to get a snack,
But I tripped and got a scratch.
I went to get a Band-Aid,
But instead I had some lemonade.
It's about time to sleep,
But first I read about sheep.

Henry Heilshorn, Grade 4
Mitchell Elementary School, CT

Leaves

In the heart of the woods
I see colorful shapes of autumn leaves

I touch the prickly ones that stay green all year
With the morning dew all over them
My hands get all wet

The high-pitched sound of crackling leaves
Beneath my feet like the crunching sound of chips

Caitlin Blanche, Grade 4
Four Seasons Elementary School, MD

School

School is not my favorite thing
I'd rather hear the bell go ding

Every first Friday I go to church
Although I want to perch in a birch

My buddy is not here with me
But I'll get him here just wait and see

I'd rather be home and watch my show
But I'm stuck here now, learning to know

Rodney Miller, Grade 6
St John the Evangelist School, CT

The Sparkling Snow

Snow falls to the ground
And makes it sparkle
Like a treasure chest
Filled with crystals.
The snow blankets the ground
Like my soft, warm quilt
Covers me.

Elizabeth Criss, Grade 5
Blueberry Hill School, VT

Perfection

There is no such thing as perfection
In the world these days
It's impossible in work
It's impossible in play

There is no such thing as perfection
As you know by now
There might be a way to find it
But no one knows how

There is no such thing as perfection
As I said before
You might have seen it once or twice
But it walks right out the door

There is no such thing as perfection
This is the last time I say
But there are ways to get close
Each and every day

Just try your hardest and your best
You just might succeed
Not in perfection
But getting in the lead

Michael Lally, Grade 6
Reed Intermediate School, CT

Summer Is Gone

Swimming, jumping, splashing
All the waves were crashing.

I wish we had more time for fun,
Unfortunately, we've lost all our sun.

Goodbye bathing suits and beach towels,
Now it's time for boring vowels.

Melissa Hill, Grade 5
Highland Park School, CT

Peanut

He was a nice dog.
But he had to say good-bye.
He is in our hearts.

David Young, Grade 5
St Joseph School-Fullerton, MD

The Sound of My Life

The sound of my life sounds like an angel singing
The sound of my life sounds like my life
The sound of my life is what makes you wonder
The sound of my life makes you think of me
The sound of my life sounds like wedding bells
And that sound after you drink a drink of cooled water on a summery day
The sound of my life sounds like a dream that thinks about me
The sound of my life, the first dollar bill you spent on candy
The sound of my life sounds like me on my dad's shoulder
watching the giraffes go by
The sound of my life is me loving you

Jordan Phelps, Grade 5
Clover Street School, CT

My Life Is Like A…

My life is like an ocean I can hear the waves splash and splish
I feel a smooth motion I hope I won't wake up from my wish

As my mind rests, I suddenly feel calm
I yawn while I make my nest then I lay my head in my palm

When I smell the waves, they smell a little fresh,
For my mind is like a maze oh thank God! There is no mess

As I'm smelling the breeze I am getting a reaction
I think I have to sneeze suddenly there is an attraction

The ocean looks so bright I could silently sleep
I hope I will remember tonight when I sleep I am in a hole that is deep

Everything I look at is like looking at a baby so beautiful and gorgeous
Maybe, just maybe I can be glorious

Amber Grey, Grade 6
Blue Ridge Middle School, VA

Nature as a Dream

As I look through my window,
I see the autumn leaves floating to the ground like a
piece of paper.
I hear the wind blowing through the trees,
talking to them.
I feel my face pressing against the window frame,
straining to see the little birds flying from tree to tree,
and hope, that in the future, humans will continue to appreciate nature.

Sydney Michalak, Grade 6
The Well School, NH

Snow

Snow is as white as a wolf's tail.
They are as cold as an ice cube.
They melt in your hand just like water drips on your hand.
When you jump in snow it is just like when you jump in a pool.
Snow comes down to the ground just like rain comes down.
Snow can be fast like a cheetah and as slow as a snail.

Owen Bartolotta, Grade 4
Long Meadow Elementary School, CT

Cheese

There once was a funny mouse
Who lived in a human's giant house.
There was a fridge with lots of cheese
He begged his parents saying please, please, please, please.

He snuck out at night
And the cat gave him a fright.
So instead he went to the store
To get some more.

At the store there wasn't a fare amount of food
That made him in a very bad mood.
He has enough now
Because from a farmer he bought a cow.

He makes his own
When he is all alone.

Kiera Kennedy, Grade 4
Infant Jesus School, NH

My Cat

I love my cat.
Her fur is as soft as cotton.
Her purr is as loud as thunder.
Her warmth warms me on a snowy day.
My favorite animal to sit with.

Jerry Kadinger, Grade 4
Dr Charles E Murphy Elementary School, CT

The Crusader

On the hill he stood,
Flag and sword at hand,
Under his thick leather boots,
Was dirt of crimson.

Hour after hour he stood,
Waiting for the Turks,
Under his armor his heart thudded,
Too long he had only smelled blood.

Along came the Turks,
Scimitars at hand,
They galloped over the crimson land.
They shouted their war call and came the reply.

So the crusader raised his weapon,
And soon did the Turks,
The crusader then bane them,
Cleaned his sword and stood,

He then fell down and died,
Too long he had only smelled blood.

Joseph Finnian Martin, Grade 5
St John Neumann Academy, VA

The Special Flower

It is raining
And I am inside
Watching the rain fall down outside
Then I see this sparkling rain drop
Fall onto a seed
It suddenly blooms into a flower
Everyone can see
The flower is red and shiny
It doesn't look like a regular kind of flower to me
Suddenly the rain stops
And the sun comes out
Now I can call my friends
And we can play outside again

Michelle Runge, Grade 6
Ashford School, CT

Earth

A world of life with a light blue sky.
A light blue sky with soft white clouds.
Soft white clouds falling gracefully
To the cold hard ground.
The cold hard ground dark brown being
Shaped by the smooth clear river.
The smooth clear river rushing to the ocean.
The roaring ocean filled with large and small.
These are some of the wonders life has to give.

Josh Wilcox, Grade 6
Main Street Middle School, VT

The Amazing Castle

Magical and mystical, a castle in a cloud,
Beautiful and tall, the golden top standing proud.
People gather along the edge, which is jagged and snowy white.
Living in this pretty castle would be a great delight.

Walls of yellow, brick, and blue,
It is an amazing world I never knew.
Clues within the castle will certainly convince,
That somewhere inside this castle lays a princess or a prince.

Forests form borders around this lovely domain,
As for the person living here, over nations they may reign.
Secrets will remain inside this castle true.
From the top of this castle is a fantastic bird's eye view.

Many things are inside this lovely castle place,
Every single detail will fill your soul with grace.
As the night falls down, my smile becomes a frown,
And the queen will don her royal nightgown.

Now the day is done and I can't see this sight.
I guess I'll have to wait until the coming morning light.
I can't wait until tomorrow, when this castle will shine,
Oh how I wish this palace was mine!

Katie Brink, Grade 5
Infant Jesus School, NH

Home

B ig, blue, briny body of water, beautiful beige beach beckons
E veryone enjoying expending energy, endless excavations emerge from the sand
A wesome, arching waves attack all around, another and another and another and another
C awing seagulls circle continuously, clams, crabs, and crustaceans cluster in crevices
H eavenly heat hails from the sun, hearts heavy, we head from this "Home"

Timothy Jerome, Grade 6
St Brigid School, ME

Fall

It's all about fall!! Costumes scarecrows, Halloween, Thanksgiving, pumpkins, and pies, full moons in the sky. It never ends until it all begins! Leaves that are orange some that are brown some that are red like a princess crown. Piles of leaves cold on with jeans. Hay rides and pumpkins raking with pride. Pumpkins full of candy!! Farms full of pigs. Thanksgiving is coming so put on your black or brown hats. Make a play rowboat until I get back. Going to school to see all your friends. Make straw hats and paper leaves. Watch the leaves change before your eyes. Fall.

RaeAnn Brainard, Grade 5
Keene Elementary School, DE

What the World Means to Morgan

I will change the world someday after I go to college.
I will change the world someday by spreading all my knowledge.
I will help by showing big companies that healthy people and a clean environment are more important than money.
These businesses should not use toxic plastics, lead paints, and more.
People should check products carefully before taking them home from the store.
I want to be an environmental health officer when I grow up and graduate from college.
To help people realize that there is one life, one Earth, one world. This is something everyone should acknowledge!

Morgan Brokaw, Grade 6
Wintergreen Interdistrict Magnet School, CT

Dr. Seuss Story

I'm having such a bad day today because I forgot about my friend named Dr. Seuss.
His birthday is today! How will he celebrate? Should I get him a yertle or turtle?
A wocket to put in his pocket? One fish, two fish, red fish, blue fish?
Perhaps Dr. Seuss might want a fox in his socks. Maybe a weller, peller, or an oobleck?
I don't know what to do. I just might get him Thing 1 and Thing 2 and a trip to Solla Sollew.

Samantha Taylor, Grade 5
Keene Elementary School, DE

Owls

Owls
Soaring high in the sky, fluttering wings all around the tree tops

Owls
They come out at night to seek their prey, and their wings are soundless, like an empty house.

Owls
Shiny sharp beaks that are lined with scratches from bones and coated in dried rat blood

Owls
Flashing sharp claws that sometimes hold unlucky mice or other victims

Owls
To me they are the most exquisite birds to ever soar the huge night sky

Owls

Erik Ouellette, Grade 5
Jack Jackter Intermediate School, CT

Nantucket Shore

Flowing moving
Fizzy fizz fizz.
Sand castles
As high as the sky.
Mr. and Mrs. Crab love it there!
Waves higher than 10 feet!
Getting washed up on the beach
By getting boiled by the waves.
Sand in your ears, sand in your hair
Mind boggling fun just can't get enough!
Sand in your bathing suit
Having the time of your life
By just being you!
Digging, digging in the sand.
Long walks on the beach
Soaring across the ocean on a boogie board.
Swimming like a seal.
Hermit crabs running for their lives
Trying not to get caught
Sand crabs wriggle like worms
What a day at the Nantucket Shore!!

Grace Hoffman, Grade 5
Osborn Hill Elementary School, CT

On Halloween

I hear scary screams in children's dreams
I see witches in the sky flying high
I feel whiskers in the wind and bones on my chin.
I smell freshness in the air and the scent of fear.
I taste sweets in all the places and smiley faces.

Nicholas Lawrence, Grade 4
Brookside Elementary School, MA

A Bird

The piercing tip sprouts up.
A black bowl, an impenetrable fortress
stands guard protecting
it's innocent bird perched at the bottom.
I identify…
the green head like an obese olive
still waiting in the shallow martini.
Its eyes,
the plunging daggers, digging at my soul.
the turquoise lines
like a waterfall never resting.
The feathers carved
like a tree budding for the first time.
Death defying darkness, a never breaking beak,
bulging beady eyes complete the beast.
Mary Poppins
hands grasping looking, listening.
She leaps up.
The umbrella catches as she
slowly sways down.

Paige McLoughlin, Grade 6
Mystic Middle School, CT

The Bald Eagle

On a cold November day,
I saw an eagle flying my way.
Not just a regular one you see,
It looked like a bald eagle to me.
Ah ha! I was right,
I found out that same night.
I will always treasure my first sighting ever,
Of that beautiful bird,
The American Bald Eagle.

Mary Kendall Pennington, Grade 5
Pemberton Elementary School, VA

Halloween

Owls and cats
Goblins and ghouls
Haunting around
Looking for children to spook.

Monsters and witches
Getting ready to seek and scare
And following children everywhere.

Ghosts and bats
Flying around in the wind
Spooky creatures hiding around the bend.

Mummies and vampires
Ready to walk the night
And see little trick-or-treaters dancing
Oh, what a sight.

This is the end of Halloween night
Oh, what we have seen
But before it's time to go to bed
I think I just might write
About this evening's delight.

Victoria Williamson, Grade 6
St Patrick School, MA

Mountain High

Climbing a mountain so high in the sky,
Don't look down for it is too high
One step after the other
It's so high don't you bother,
Take the next step to the top,
Don't you look down and don't you stop,
Close your eyes you're almost there
You can climb anything anywhere
Take those steps I know you can get to the top
You did it you made it to the top
Now here is your pillow rest your head
I hope you like your new bunk bed

Jennifer Holstein, Grade 6
Hoover Middle School, MD

Deer in the Forest

A deer gallops
through the forest,
where crimson leaves
laden all the trees
and the sodden ground.
The exhilarated deer
runs wildly
through the muggy woods
to greet his family.
Though as mysterious
as the rest of the forest is,
it all acts as one family,
not as an uncountable many.

Lauren Karpinski, Grade 6
Kenmore Middle School, VA

A Swimmer's Quest

Fast or slow
Four strokes to go
Butterfly
Backstroke
Tired yet? You bet!
Breaststroke
Last turn
Arms burn
Freestyle
Done! How fun!
Fast or slow
Way to go

Peyton Hall, Grade 5
Pemberton Elementary School, VA

Friends

You see them here, you see them there
Having fun laughing up a storm.
They're at the mall
At the park
And at the store,
You see them whisper,
You hear them giggle.
Friends are with you till the end.
That is why they are called friends.
They stick together
And always know what to say.

Melissa Ruel, Grade 6
St Mary of Czestochowa School, CT

Summer

Wind whispering in my face
Feelings like the
Baitfish bubbling on the water
Beautiful sunset
Sun glaring off the water
When will it end?

Kyle Kerrigan, Grade 4
John J Flynn Elementary School, VT

My Life

I am from a clean room with lots of sunlight
A cozy bed with a dog sleeping on it
People always in it on the computer
A snake in the corner that hisses his slivery tongue
I am from home

I am from a loud community with a park next door
Fire station with fire trucks whirling down my street
I feel safe because there are lots of cops on my street
There are cars flying down my street and everybody complains
I am from Dorchester

I am from a cheerful country
With people drinking and watching soccer
Parties all the time
I am from Germany

When I grow up I want to be a baseball pitcher throwing strikes
I want to be a soccer player and score a bunch of goals
I want to be a sports broadcaster and travel to talk about sports
I want to be a track runner and fly by people
If I'm any one of those then I'll be happy because I'll be what I want to be

Randy Pollis, Grade 6
St Brendan Elementary School, MA

It's a Bird, It's a Plane, No It's Me!

My hair is like a field of grain on my head during harvest time.
My eyes are like two little islands in the middle of an ocean.
My bones are like miniature steel beams holding up a structure.
My heart is like one big pump letting goodness flow through me.
I live in a football helmet eating the offense away in a game
while trying to succeed.

Chris Berner, Grade 6
Tolland Middle School, CT

Birds

The most important thing about a bird is that they eat spiders.
Most of them can fly high in the sky,
They have one pair of delicate wings,
They sing beautiful yet sometimes annoying songs every morning.
And they feed their young worms and insects.
They make warm and soft nests to lay their eggs in,
They fly south for the winter because they hate the cold,
And can be any color that you can imagine.
Lastly, they sometimes stand on electrical wires,
But the most important thing is that they eat spiders!

Kylie Frink, Grade 5
Jack Jackter Intermediate School, CT

Ireland

The people of Ireland don't have to be afraid of snakes anymore.
There are no snakes in Ireland because Saint Patrick scared them away.
Instead of snakes jumping out and scaring you, little leprechauns do!

Jadzea Tully, Grade 4
Wapping Elementary School, CT

Butter Lost

It was a cold winter day
I was sitting inside
When I heard my horse, Butter, nay.
I thought something was wrong,
So I went outside to check.
When I saw he was missing!
I panicked!
I hung up some signs, and there were a lot of sighs…
He didn't come back for a week.
So I invited some friends over to play hide and seek
Paula was behind a tree,
Mark hid in the playground, and I hid in my garage.
I felt something warm and fuzzy.
I wasn't sure what it was.
I turned on the light…
It was my horse, Butter!

Merina Novak, Grade 5
St Joseph School-Fullerton, MD

A Blissful Winter Experience

P is penguin plump and round
P is a polar bear rolling on the ground
P is a play land filled with white
P is a peaceful snowflake blowing out of sight
P is a present on Christmas Day
P is all the possibilities of life

Alison Schaejbe, Grade 5
Pollard Elementary School, NH

Hockey

Hockey is fun.
You hear the crowd cheering.
You get all wound up.
You are on the ice, in the center.
You glide down the ice.
You are about to shoot.
The whistle blows.
Now you are mad.
You feel sweat rolling rolling down your face.
You shoot.
You score.
This is my life — hockey!!!!

Caitlin Fortin, Grade 4
Highgate Elementary School, VT

Dream Morning

I woke up at a sunrise morning and
Walked outside barefooted. When I went I stepped on
Beautiful green grass and it felt sharp. I was getting the
Paper for my folks because they like reading it in the morning.
Once I got it I looked at the words about the football game.
Then I went inside because the green grass hurt my feet.

Steven Penarrieta, Grade 6
Kenmore Middle School, VA

My Grandmother

She's sugar and spice, and all things nice,
Always ready to give me a good advice.
She is kind and smart, and very deep.
This special love I'll always keep.

So much good she is willing to do,
No other grandma would ever do.
She is loving, caring and very sweet,
She always keeps my places neat.

I love her very much, indeed,
On this all children have agreed.
She is the best in the whole world.
For this I bet, it is my word!

Yo Elena Tkebuchava, Grade 4
Memorial-Spaulding Elementary School, MA

Tennis

Tennis is awesome
My dad and I coach tennis.
Tennis is my life.

Connery Ryon, Grade 5
C Hunter Ritchie Elementary School, VA

Holy

God's creations
What an honor it is to be in His presence
It's a shame that people are taking advantage of Your birthday

Amen

Chelsea Colvin, Grade 6
Floyd T Binns Middle School, VA

I Can Almost Do It by Myself

I can almost do it by myself
Just help me get to the highest shelf
You don't need to tell me how to reach
You just need to lift me up
Not give me a speech
I'm growing up from small to tall
It is just time, it is going to happen
Like from winter to fall
I need inspiration
I don't need a talk or another negotiation
I do want to learn but from my mistakes
You can give me suggestions
But let me find my way
You do not need to give me directions
You have to find a way to let me go
I can shine myself
I will glow
So when you help me up to the shelf
Remember
I can almost do it by myself

Annie Lion-Lee, Grade 6
Juliet W Long School, CT

The Beautiful Sea
Look in the sea.
What do you see?
I see all of God's wonder
I see beautiful seashells
All shapes and sizes
I see fish swimming
Fast and slow
I see coral reefs of all colors
You swim out farther
And you see more and more
You see sharks,
Plants
Reptiles
And even mammals
So jump into the sea
And explore it all!
R. Jacob Brunell, Grade 5
St Mary's School, MA

I Used to Be a Light
I used to be a light
I shined extremely bright
That night I was shamed
Our house was up in flames

Finally the firemen came
I was the one to blame
The fireman started to shout
Later the fire was out
At court I was guilty they claimed.
Rebecca Moncayo, Grade 5
Clover Hill Elementary School, VA

I am a Book
People read me.
I make them laugh.
They take me on trips.
I've even been on buses.
They put me on shelves at home
Hands hold me lightly.
I have many colors inside of my covers.
I feel happy when people read me.
When I close, my heart just stops.
Daniel Torres, Grade 5
Old Saybrook Middle School, CT

Music
Music
Nice, relaxing
Playing, rocking, yodeling
Peaceful on a sofa
M'usica
Will Hudak, Grade 5
Pemberton Elementary School, VA

Blooming Flowers
Smelling the flowers
Blue Sky
I wonder why flowers smell so good?
I hear stomp stomp stomp
In the flowers
Flowers are important to me
They are part of my world.
Krystal Limoge, Grade 4
John J Flynn Elementary School, VT

Snowflakes in the Sky
Snowflakes, snowflakes in the sky
Watch them dissolve as they fly,
Snowflakes, snowflakes in the sky
Hopefully they won't go Bye-Bye!
Sarah Daniels, Grade 5
Windham Center School, NH

I Have Eaten…*
I have eaten
a piece of chocolate cake
on top of a plate.

which you
were probably going to eat
for dessert.

Forgive me
it was so chocolaty
and sweet.

Akbar Maliki, Grade 5
Clover Street School, CT
*Inspired by William Carlos Williams

Winter
The jingle of bells
The sound of laughter
The hum of carolers
The shriek of sledders
The crunch of snow

The glistening icicles
The tall snowmen
The piles of snow
The sparkling Christmas tree
The graying sky

The freezing snow
The nipping chill in the air
The numbness in my nose
The heat of the fire
The burning taste of cocoa

This is why winter is my favorite
Abigail Nolan, Grade 6
St Mary of Czestochowa School, CT

The Fly That Never Died
There once was a guy with a pie
Who then tried to beat up a fly
And what was the matter
It ended in splatter
And sadly, the fly never died.
Eldin Korajkic, Grade 5
John J Flynn Elementary School, VT

My Bad Day
Today in school,
My pants fell down!
The teacher called me,
The new class clown!

Then at snack,
I ate the class pet,
I was sent to the office,
Just like that!

So, then at lunch,
I spilled my punch!
So, now they say,
My shirt ate my lunch!

Then, at recess,
We were playing tag,
Then a big kid,
Hung me with the flags!

Then, on my way home,
I lost control!
My day was bad,
Now I'm mad!
Mychell Brewington, Grade 5
Perrywood Elementary School, MD

Cheese
Makes nachos
They're really delicious
They are at Wendys
Good
Austin Matthews, Grade 5
McCleary Elementary School, VA

An Ode to Dragons
Oh, how I love dragons
They breathe fire and eat meat
Mythical creatures
Really really neat.
Oh, how I wish I had one to keep
At least
Until it wants to eat!
Joe Astuti, Grade 6
Juliet W Long School, CT

Dawn

I wake up to the crack of dawn
And look out to the graceful morning sky
Trying to forget all the terrible flaws in my life, but failing
My one chance at perfection is over

Annika Hackfeld, Grade 5
Wakefield Forest Elementary School, VA

Hurray for the Sun!

I'll write a story just today
Because it's too cold to go out and play
I would play with my ball, jump rope, and jacks
But I don't want to slip flat on my back
My mom said to relax and stay inside
But I just stomped my feet and started to cry
My mom couldn't take it she said, "That's enough!"
And she made me a sandwich with my jelly called Juff
The sandwich made me happy
I'll say that is true
But the fact that I can't go outside makes me blue
Then my little sister came running downstairs
With her collection of Teddy Bears
She smiled at me
Then jumped up with glee
And said the sun is out
Oh golly gee!
I spun around
And did a cheer
Hurray for the sun, the sun is here!

Bianca Volpicelli, Grade 5
Good Shepherd Catholic School, RI

Lizards

L iving in deserts
I nside rocks and wood.
Z ebras fear their mutated Godzilla
A aron sees them and cries
R eading lizard books is interesting
D orks don't usually like them
S ometimes they are spikey

Zech Taylor, Grade 5
C Hunter Ritchie Elementary School, VA

Far Away Father

"Put your seatbelt on," I screeched to my father!
He told me it's okay don't worry.
My father was a master
when it came to driving on the road, he loves to drive.
Until one horrible accident we got in.
The car was flipping,
my heart was rapidly beating I could feel it popping out.
Then the worse thing happened to my father and
the car was full of flames,
he had died because he didn't have his seatbelt on.
This memory ruled me forever.

Alberto Polo-Herrera, Grade 6
Kenmore Middle School, VA

Winter

The whipping of the snow,
It stung and felt like needles,
Crunching beneath my feet.
Glinting snow in front of me,
Animal tracks are the mysteries,
Of the beautiful countryside.
Smells of trees and fresh sap,
All around the cold winter forest.
Carving of ice skates,
Sounding like metal scraping against metal.
Maple sensations of syrup on snow,
Soothes and warms my cold insides.

Morgan Brown, Grade 6
Bethlehem Elementary School, NH

Rain

When life is driving you insane,
You should sit outside and watch the rain.
On a cold and wet and dreary day,
Listen to what the rain has to say.
It speaks to you as it batters and pours,
Of other people's hurts and sores.
And sorrow is not the only thing
Of which the dripping rain sings.
It sings of beauty, near and far.
It sings of creeks where otters are.
They splash and play in the great black storm,
Oasis of happiness in a desert of forlorn.

Nat Dunn, Grade 6
The Well School, NH

Santa Claus

A cold winter's night asleep in my bed
When I heard a little jingly noise just above my head
Startled me a little excited me a lot
Now I know it's not just mere thoughts
Santa Claus was on the roof
Along with the tip-tap of each reindeer hoof.
With his big bag of toys
For every good child to enjoy
Down the chimney in his fluffy red clothes
And twitched his little red nose
As he picked up the cookie he just had chose
He got to work without a sigh
With a big bright twinkle in his eye
He caught a glimpse of me and got back to work
But still I could see that friendly little smirk
He finished his job as quickly as he could
Just as I know he should
He was back up the chimney in the blink of an eye
On his sleigh and in the sky
finally I ran out the door and yelled goodbye

Britainy McDowell, Grade 6
Warwick River Christian School, VA

At the Pound*

Small, dark, cold, and dirty cages,
little food, water, and no treats,
no attention, no dogs dare to bark.
We are hopeless.

Trevor DeMilt, Grade 5
Osborn Hill Elementary School, CT
*In the voice of a dog.

The Colorful Days of Fall

Frosted leaves and grass
Leaves are swirling all around
Naked trees are cold

Blake Rooney, Grade 5
Pollard Elementary School, NH

Morning and Night

Hope sings in the morning sunlight,
Snow dances across the night,
Rain tiptoes at twilight,
Wind whistles at evening,
Morning and Night

Loves skips in early morning,
Sadness fills the night with sorrow,
Imagination lights evening sky,
Anger lights the sun each morning,
Morning and Night

Catherine Hawfield, Grade 4
Boonsboro Elementary School, MD

Time

Time is passing by,
We're growing
We're changing,
Time is flying by,
We're learning,
We're taking
Time into our own hands,
And manipulating,
It until,
It's over

Bryanna Faith Miller, Grade 6
Beacon Middle School, DE

Fall Has Begun

Leaves
Falling, shaking, floating
Twirling, dying, scattered too
As they are falling
They change from
Green to red and other colors too
Animals
Hibernating and whining from the cold
Fall has begun

John-Lucas Z. Varney, Grade 5
Pollard Elementary School, NH

Life and Death

Is it better to live a life of pain
Or pass on to a life free of agony, grief or strife?
Would it be better to trade your life for a tranquil existence
beyond soil, planets and time, where age is no more and
you don't have to wait — to worry that one day your solid
being will be no more?
Where you gain the lost but lose the present.
Where people will all join one day, a place where there is no war.
Or is it better to live your own life and learn all you can
before your time has come?
To enjoy what you can, and live life on this lush planet
to its full extent?
Maybe pain strengthens the soul if you use it wisely.
What I'm asking is, do you choose life or death?

Sebastian Taylor, Grade 5
The Burnham Elementary School, CT

Kindness

Can you imagine what the world would be like if everyone was kind?
Opening doors, helping each other, and keeping others' feelings in mind.

The fighting would stop, the crimes would all end, and people would mend their ways,
True happiness, peace, love, and joy for all the rest of our days.

Remember to do unto others, as you want them to do unto you,
This rule is so important and it'll always see you through.

So I challenge each and everyone, to try to start being kind,
Saying please, thank you, and pardon me, and always keeping others in mind.

Cristina Montemorano, Grade 4
Mary Walter Elementary School, VA

Song of My Life

I sing of
     Ben & Jerry's ice cream on a hot summer day,
     Rainy days on the couch with caramel popcorn,
     Sledding down my favorite sledding hill and
     Then coming inside and drinking hot cocoa while it warms me.
     All a part of my life.
A life with sounds that live within
     Alive with surrounding smells of cinnamon rolls,
     always rushing down the stairs.
     Alive with the thick taste of my milkshake.
     Alive with the chilling metal of my watch,
     ticking, ticking, ticking away.
     Alive with the feel of my pencil gliding across the paper,
     making a masterpiece.
A life with sounds that live within
     How I love the sound of my iPod allowing
     My ears to dance to the music.
     And the breathtaking sights of the mountainous
     Ice cream in the bowl at Friendly's.
All, yes, all living sounds
     within my song.

Madeleine Squier-Paine, Grade 6
Main Street Middle School, VT

My Sour, Green Blueberry

I found a small green blueberry
in the blueberry box
I picked out from the grocery store.

It was not a perfect blueberry,
or even close to perfect.
It was tiny, about half the size of my pinky fingernail.

It was so small sitting in the box
amongst all of the other regular blueberries.

I pop the blueberry into my mouth.
It is sour, very sour.
My mouth puckers.

I swallow the blueberry.
Now it is gone,
my sour, green blueberry.

All the is left of the blueberry
that I just ate
are happy memories.

Rachael Sandri, Grade 6
Grace Episcopal Day School, MD

My Beautiful Angel

You are my beautiful angel and I love you so much.
You love me too.
You are faster than all the cheetahs,
Brighter than all the stars, stronger than all the seas.

You are my beautiful angel that loves me.
You are always around me
Because that is your favorite place to be.
Cayla Bajus, Grade 5
Four Seasons Elementary School, MD

Flea

Hey look at me I am a flea.
Aren't I the ugliest thing you ever will see?

I live in your clothing and even your hair.
When you find me ooooo what a scare!

Please do not go looking for a fight
Or you are the one I will bite.

I might be only the size of a spec,
But believe me I can make you a wreck!

You do not want to see me leap.
I don't know why but it gives some people the creeps?!?!?!
Kacey Cornely, Grade 6
Immaculate Heart of Mary School, DE

If I Could See the Future

If I could see the future
Imagine how blissful my life would be
I'd see the grade on my math test
And know I did my best
If I saw something not pleasing to the eye
I'd shoo it away like a fly
Now I think that
Seeing the future wouldn't really be fun
For what I see in the future
I doubt could be undone
If I saw my little bug die
I won't be able to change it
No matter how hard I try
Now I've learned my lesson
For now I see
The future is supposed to be a secret
For just you and me

Erin Monahan, Grade 6
Grace Episcopal Day School, MD

American Pride

Thank you for all you've done
We know you give so much
They say it's an Army of one
But we know that isn't such
With your brothers and sisters at your side
You do your job with American Pride

Robby Nelson, Grade 5
Pemberton Elementary School, VA

Shadow

As I walk I see something following me.
Is it a dog? Is it a cat? I don't know.
I look back again. It's gone!
And then it clicks.
It was my shadow!
Then I skip home without any fear inside.

Hannah Bockus, Grade 4
Highgate Elementary School, VT

Coming to America

When I was four
I took a trip.
To a place I did not know.
This place was America.
My mom and I were all alone.
We didn't' speak the American language.
Now I am nine,
I speak English,
I go to school.
When I am all grown up I will travel back
To my native country.
I miss my friends and relatives.
But life is still good here.

Rebeca Rivas, Grade 5
Valley View Elementary School, MD

Child in the Wild

She climbs and creeps,
like a snake slithering
across long leafy limbs.
A lion gracefully
pouncing on a mouse
rips through the
jungle with her
sharp long nails.
Swings tree to tree, with the monkeys,
enjoying every part of the way.
When the rain comes pouring,
she hides in the hollow
trunks and talks to the
nearby chipmunks.
When she creeps on the torn leaves
you know you're being followed
by the child in the wild.
Where the trees run out and
the rolling plains come into view
she runs with the herds
into the setting sun.
Najiye Honça, Grade 5
Zervas Elementary School, MA

The Sky's Message

The rain is heaven's tears
rolling down the sky.
The sunset is the night light
burning before bed.
In the night you will see stars
so bright as if your wildest dreams.
The sun is like the smile
reflecting on Earth.
When the snow comes,
they are angel's visits from above.
The sky's message will be changing.
All year 'round.
Candace Ho, Grade 5
University of Hartford Magnet, CT

Fruit Family

My brother is a banana,
He's nice when you look inside.
My daddy is a pear.
Calm even on the outside.
Mother, a pomegranate
With a fiery stubbornness.
My doggy is a coconut
With her confused craziness.
My baby brother is an apple
Wise, and funny, and sweet.
And I am some unknown thing
That everyone has yet to meet.
Nell Sather, Grade 6
Main Street Middle School, VT

Bad Cold

Feeling:
Bad.
Having the unexpected cold
Waking up.
Coughing like a maniac.
Nose stuffed and yucky.
Feeling like it now.
Matthew Reich, Grade 4
Riverfield School, CT

Blue Jay

I spy a Blue Jay,
Flying around the bushes,
Eating the cherries.
Justin Vanover, Grade 6
Ashford School, CT

An Ode to Math

Oh! How I love math,
math is great to do
all of its numbers
I can't wait to learn.
There are different types of math
that happens around the world,
when people do math
I want to learn all math.
Math can be taught to
anybody to learn all the numbers
from adding to multiplying
and from subtracting to dividing.
There is some geometry in math
equations that help me learn
all of this math, and all this math
comes from our school.
Timothy Miles, Grade 6
Juliet W Long School, CT

What School Means to Me

School is so much more
Than an institute of learning
It's a place for fun,
A place of upbringing

It may seem annoying
For quite a while
But remember,
Intelligence is always in style

Got to go!
Have to study for a test
To be in such a great school
I am blessed.
Luis Da Silva, Grade 6
St John the Evangelist School, CT

Thunder

The thunder BOOM cannot be seen
So quick and keen,
Sounds like bowling
Rolling, rolling.

The rain and lightning come with it
Comes like a kit,
Thrashing and crackling
All night singing.

Thunder so thunderous and loud
Comes from the cloud,
Comes out the sun
Thunder, all done.
Jaycie MacArthur, Grade 5
Princeton Elementary School, ME

Zeke

Your ears are velvet
You're as black as the night sky
Come play fetch with me!
Katie McCann, Grade 6
Wakefield Forest Elementary School, VA

Ricochet and Gilligan

Rachel loves Ricochet
He's a very handsome horsey
Cute as pie
Oh Ricochet
Canters slowly
Eats a lot of grass
Tries his hardest
The best horse around
Elephants are a little bigger than him

Gives his best work
I love Gilligan
Pretty horsey
Loves Jessica
He's a good horse
Good and sweet
A pleasure to ride
Nothing bad about him
Rachel Pratt, Grade 6
Juliet W Long School, CT

The Sea

Salty air clogs my throat.
The waves come in and out.
Schools of fish scatter.
Sand moves between my toes.
The sea is blue and green.
The sea.
Ariyanna Pounds, Grade 4
Riverfield School, CT

My Socks

These are my socks.
They stink and they smell
They are moldy and green
Just like an old jail cell

These are my socks
There is a hole near my heel.
They are dirty and brown
You wouldn't want to smell them
    During a three course meal

These are my socks
In comparison they make a hobo
    Smell like perfume
They are all mine, all stinky and fine
They will bring us to our doom

Evan McNeal, Grade 5
C Hunter Ritchie Elementary School, VA

Writing a Poem

Sitting, waiting, thinking
I sigh while finding a topic
It's quiet, thoughts run through my head
The light bulb flicks on, I pick up my pencil
And start writing
Emotions and ideas spill onto the paper
I finish and reread my work
I nod my head, fix some words
And then I'm finished, *finally*!

Ally Mastrota, Grade 6
Wakefield Forest Elementary School, VA

I Am

I am a boy who enjoys playing baseball.
I wonder if I'll win the game.
I hear the bat smack the ball out of the park
and the crowd cheering for me.
I see the white ball fly across the brown baseball diamond.
I want to go to the All-Stars and win a trophy.
I am a boy who enjoys playing baseball.

I pretend that I'm diving for a rolling grounder.
I feel scared before the game.
Our team might lose the game today.
I touch my brown autographed glove.
I wonder if our team will win today and tomorrow's game.
I am a boy who enjoys playing baseball.

I understand that I'm playing to have fun.
I say one... two... three... TIGERS!!!
I dream to win a gigantic trophy.
I try to win tough games
I hope I will be an awesome champ at baseball.
I am a boy who enjoys playing baseball.

Christian Sorensen, Grade 5
Blackrock School, RI

What Is Blue?

Blue is the time to loosen up
Blue is sluggish as a salamander
Blue is special as a shiny sapphire
Blue is my favorite color
It's the color of the calm sea
The time to relax in a cooling pool
Blue is a bluebird singing in the tree tops
Blue is sweet as a blueberry
I see the wonderful blue sky
As the babbling brook goes by
Blue is the taste of savory bubble gum
Blue is cold as dry ice
Splash, smash in the Bering Sea

Patrick Dubois, Grade 6
Spring Hill Elementary School, VA

Mice on a Mission

When mice desert their house it is very dark
when they're running they don't make one mark.

It was two in the morning
and it was pouring.

When they go out they look for food that they adore
they find all kinds that they're in the mood for.

The food was bait
so they got caught in a crate.

So when they got caught
they fought.

The mice got so terrified
they died.

Megan Ward, Grade 4
Infant Jesus School, NH

The Coolest Bug of All

I am a cicada killer cool and black,
I wear an orange sweater and a nice pink hat.

I fly around cool as can be,
No other insect is better than me.

There once was a contest called "Most Cicadas Stung,"
After I got there, the fat lady sung.

The cicadas I catch I give to my young,
And when I lay my eggs, my life span is nearly done.

I hope you've enjoyed this story of me,
Now my life has ended, and I must let my soul free.

Ryan Williams, Grade 6
Immaculate Heart of Mary School, DE

Flag

It's big like a teacher
So blue like the sky
So red like the flower
So white like the snow
It has a lot of stars up
In the sky
It has a sharp pant like a sharks teeth
It has a stick like a witch.

Megan Hamel, Grade 4
Marsh Grammar School, MA

Chicken Nuggets

Chicken Nuggets
Hot, soft, brown
Dip them in Ketchup
Eat them with my hand
Together with Daddy, Mom, and Emily
Yummy, mmm, yummy

Brandon McCormack, Grade 4
Marsh Grammar School, MA

Books

Books, books, books
Small books
Large books
Funny, mad, sad books
Short, long, ignoring books
Those are just a few
Blue books
Red books
Mystical, yellow, happy books
Orange, fiction, scary books
Good books too!
Bad books
And don't forget the fast books.
Last of all
Best of all
I like action books!

Davin Santagata, Grade 6
Juliet W Long School, CT

Forest

Forest
As still as a statue
Like nothing is there
Look harder
And there is life
Ants marching
Birds flying
And snakes slithering

It is amazing
How they all work together
To form a forest

Kevin Jones, Grade 5
E Ethel Little Elementary School, MA

Timeless

On a hot summer's day I went out to play
The stream's water is flowing the colorful flowers are growing
    Everything is timeless

It goes all the way to fall when most trees grow tall
That's when you wear a jacket fall is when you don't hear a racket
    Everything is timeless

Now it's the wintertime hot chocolate costs a dime
It's getting so cold seems the days are growing old
    Everything is timeless

It's spring now and again the sun shines like heaven
It's so shiny and bright you need glasses to block that light
    Everything is timeless

It's summer, and on a hot summer's day I go out to play
The stream's water is flowing the colorful flowers are growing
    Everything is timeless

Atang Agwe, Grade 5
St Joseph's Catholic School, MD

On the Staircase

I sat at the beginning of the staircase,
I sat listening to the jumbled up voices
of the visitors my parents invited.
They talked about how nice the house was,
about their day at work and my parents were touring the guests.
My mom focused more on her boss.
For one long hour I listened sneakily until
I fell asleep to the tick-tock of the clock.

Narankhuu Ganbaatar, Grade 6
Kenmore Middle School, VA

Teach Us!

Dawn, teach the raindrops to be glistening magenta.
Moon, show the dawn to sparkle at night
Raindrops, guide the moon to falling drops of blue.
Fire, dance to the sky, let there be light
Sky, tell stories to the young and faint stars.
Stars, at last, let the sparkling blue, purple, pink, red
And all the other colors too … the shiny, bright Northern Lights
Northern Lights: What can I do?
You can shine the brightest in all Alaska
Oh!

Mackenzie Peperak, Grade 4
Boonsboro Elementary School, MD

Christmas

Christmas is when you can spend a lot of time with family.
Christmas is a day when you can open up presents from special family members.
Christmas is a time when you can sing with family.

Roneeyah Napper, Grade 5
Keene Elementary School, DE

Grind, Grind, Grind

Grind, Grind, Grind
My friends will come and go as they please,
But I enjoy all their visits
Simply because they're my only friends in this imperfect world.

Grind, Grind, Grind
When I am full of shavings
A very annoying massive blob
Comes to empty me, and then I get filled up again.

Grind, Grind, Grind
When that blob is foolish,
And sticks a stick of colored wax in me,
I get very angry, so I skin it into a small pile of nothing.

Grind, Grind, Grind
I am used every day, but I don't mind.
I am proud to be me
Because I am very good to everyone.

Grind, Grind, Smash!
I'm seeing my life go by,
I'm falling in slow motion
Straight to the tiled floor, so Good Bye.

Julianna Chen, Grade 5
Cunningham School, MA

The Diamond in the Sky

The angel brought the girl up to the sky
and gave her a diamond necklace.
Then the girl came back down to her house.
Her alarm clock woke her up.
The sparkling diamond was around her neck.
Was she dreaming?

Cara Maisel, Grade 6
Kenmore Middle School, VA

Night Time Beach

The small stars lay over the beach twinkling,
the salty wave's water splashing and sprinkling.

The freezing waves wash upon the sand,
it feels like you're in a magical land.

The big moon so full and bright,
sets the reflection, the ocean's light.

The gallant waves love to laugh,
stars dip in the water for their nighttime bath.

Sadly the moon and stars slowly descend,
the nighttime beach has come to an end.

Amy Addington, Grade 6
Milford Middle School, NH

Love That Dog*

Love that dog.
Like a dog that loves to play with me.
I said I love that dog.
Like a dog that loves to play with me.
Love to feed, drink, and train in the big, blue, house.
Love to call her: "HEY BABY DOG!!"
She sometimes drools like she's any other dog.
Whines like a lonely puppy.
I said she sometimes drools like she's any other dog.
And whines like a lonely puppy.
Whines when she's hungry and wants to eat human food.
When she is hungry and wants human food, she whines again.

Octavia Samone Hall, Grade 5
Clover Street School, CT
Inspired by Walter Dean Myers

Thanks Daddy

I want to fill my daddy's shoes,
The man who wears the Navy Blues.

He works on an enormous boat,
across the International waters the crew, they float.

Fighting for our freedom and rights,
So we all can sleep safely at night.

Sacrificing each and every day,
So we can live in a more peaceful way.

Bringing presents from different countries and places,
Waiting to see the joyous look on our loving faces.

Coming back from his long journey away,
I wonder this time how long he'll be able to stay.

Kiliegh Longeway, Grade 5
Rosemont Forest Elementary School, VA

Damion

Damion likes to be called a clown.
He is very funny.
He makes everyone laugh.
Every weekend I can come home
And tell my friend and my cousin
About him and what he did that was funny this week.

Maria VanGeystelen, Grade 4
Portsmouth Christian Academy, NH

Sports

S occer is one of my favorites.
P assion is something you need.
O thers are teammates that encourage and help you.
R unning is what you do.
T eamwork at its best means success.
S tamina is what you must have.

Lindsay Berg, Grade 6
St Joseph School-Fullerton, MD

The Old Book Store

I went to an old book store; it had dust all around,
I could tell that for a while there hadn't been a sound
I saw a mouse scatter on the shelf; if you ask me I was scared by myself
I saw a book with a dragon on top; the scary picture made me hop
Still, I read the back and was surprised to see; that this dragon book was of interest to me

I started to read right away; it was a very good book I read all day
It started to rain I had to go home; I was out on the streets I was all alone
But I kept going back I wouldn't stop; until I finished that book with the dragon on top

I was finally done I was kind of sad; but I found a good reason to be glad
I would go to that bookstore and I would soon find; another good book another kind

I finally found a good book and it was really good; so every day in that bookstore I stood

For the rest of my days I read and read; I read books until I was dead
But don't be sad it is okay; I'm in heaven still to this day

Hannah Schmidt, Grade 6
St Stephen's Classical Christian School, MD

Who Am I

I am sensitive and stretch my mind and heart as a tree stretches its branches,
I wonder why a cloud of loathing hovers above us, creating war and tearing families apart,
I hear the wind rustle the autumn leaves as I lay on my back in the grass,
I see snowcapped evergreens and meandering rivers while standing at the peak of a mountain,
I want to know why in a world of beauty and simplicity, hideous wrongs still exist,
I am sensitive and stretch my mind and heart as a tree stretches its branches.

I pretend to know everything, even though I know that's not true,
I feel overwhelmed with felicity when I see my hard work pay off,
I touch the inspiration of a novel, for they say a picture is worth a thousand words,
I worry about the day when my times of being an innocent child turn into times of dedication and work,
I cry when I see others who are heart sore, when I see others shed tears,
I am sensitive and stretch my mind and heart as a tree stretches its branches.

I understand that everyone is a unique piece of art, and even more so, a masterpiece,
I say you can't judge a book by its cover, for underneath the cover, there is a story,
I dream of the day passion replaces hatred, when peace replaces war,
I try to be the best that I can, not only in school, but more importantly, as a person,
I hope that people see me for who I am, for who I want to be seen as, not for who I'm not,
I am sensitive and stretch my mind and heart as a tree stretches its branches.

Abbie Jameson, Grade 6
Saxe Middle School, CT

Song of Myself

I sing of my loving and caring parents, my annoying sisters, my cute, sweet dog, my loyal, nice friends, I sing of my best friend
Raychel who is beyond explanation, and my other Ferry Beach friends. All a part of my life.
A life that is alive within. Alive with the sweet taste of the rare Raspberry pie, and the taste of the apple pie frequently on the
table, the soothing warmth of our home when I walk through the door in the winter, and the cool air in the house in the summer
Alive with the comfort of my mother and father's warm hugs, and the feeling of safeness when my mom tucks me into bed.
A life with sounds that live within the chirp of birds in our backyard, the bubble of the hot-tub water, the tappity-tap-tap of my
sister's computer, and the warmth of my mother's voice saying "Good-Night."
All, yes, all living sounds within my song.

Lily Russo-Savage, Grade 6
Main Street Middle School, VT

Who Am I?

I'm floating gently on the breeze.
My scales will help me fly with ease.

Although many people enjoy seeing me,
Some of us look like a leaf or a tree.

When I was a larva, I was ugly and green,
But now, I'm the prettiest bug to be seen!

I emerged form my chrysalis just yesterday,
And, as soon as my wings dried, flew up and away.

I quickly fly south as winter draws near.
For soon, it will be much too cold for me here!

I alight on a flower, uncoil my tongue,
And after a drink, leave as quick as I'd come.

What a graceful and beautiful insect am I;
For I am a high-flying butterfly!

Maddie Rizzo, Grade 6
Immaculate Heart of Mary School, DE

Thunder

T hunder is big and jumpy
H e is black and brown all over.
U will love him like me.
N o one loves him like my family and I.
D o you like him so far?
E veryone thinks he is bad but I don't.
R uining is what he does but I love him so much.

Avery Santiago, Grade 4
Marsh Grammar School, MA

Leaf

L ots of pretty colorful leaves.
E ach one on a special tree.
A ll of them are very excited about autumn.
F all is a fantastic season
  so come on jump and enjoy the fun.

Janaya Dailey, Grade 4
St Gregory Elementary School, MA

How Is This Funny?

There's thunder, there's lightning,
It's all very exciting,
It's raining, it's pouring,
That big tornado's roaring,
The windows rattling, the people all running,
I'm just thinking it's all very funny,
The roofs blow off, the cows are flying,
Those little kids are really crying,
The hail comes down, right on the ground,
And that old man's just sleeping sound.

Devin Plourde, Grade 6
Ashford School, CT

My Trip to Niagara Falls

My trip to Niagara Falls was crazy,
Everyone was up and outgoing, never lazy!
From my hotel room I could see the pretty falls,
Light up with colors, it was better than going to the mall.

A ride on the Maid of the Mist,
Was at the top of everyone's list.
Visiting the Butterfly Conservatory,
Was like stepping into a colorful laboratory.

The Imax movie on daredevils,
Showcased heroes and rebels.
Who tested the power,
Of the water tower.

Some survived the act,
Others never came back.
The ferris wheel to the top,
Had a beautiful view when we stopped.

And nothing could beat,
The 38th floor of the Embassy suites!
This trip was a blast,
Our family was one at last!

Amy Doyle, Grade 6
St Patrick School, MA

My Nature Walk

As the leaves blow by my face
I see the wind pick up
Rushing through my hair
And shivers down my back

The sun is trying to heat me up
The sun is in my eyes
I feel the rough grass beneath me
Because of winter I know it dries

On a walk so cold but a sight so beautiful
I can't believe my senses
I also hear branches chip and break as
Animals move to shelter and food

The tree branches hang so low
Brushing the top of my hat so soft
As I breathe the fresh air
I know nature is my home…

I hear the wind as quiet voices
Not cold whooshing sounds
As I huddle close to my friends for warmth
The wind comes to a stop

Emily Marquardt, Grade 6
Juliet W Long School, CT

Sandy

I got a new hamster,
her name is Sandy,
She looks like a big puff
of cotton candy

She likes to run
on her wheel real fast,
I wonder how long
she is going to last

She likes to snuggle
with me at night,
I do not want to take her
out of my sight

I am really happy I got her
I love her so much,
She is very friendly
and soft to touch

Brooke Haley, Grade 6
St Joseph School-Fullerton, MD

Santa

Santa's on the way
Down the chimney he will come
Wearing his red suit

Melanie Engle, Grade 6
St Joseph School-Fullerton, MD

Mother Nature: Night and Day

With golden hair,
and gentle lips,
she whispers the wind.
Nature is her name.

With silent steps
over fallen leaves,
padding like a cat,
Nature is her name.

With wind-swept tears,
and burning reign,
why, she can bring a storm.

She carries the sun
in the palm of her hand
and shields it from every raindrop.

She stops the rain,
and throws it up,
dancing around and around,
for she shields the precious sun,
after she gets things done,
and that is why it is dark.

Maria Rector, Grade 6
St John Regional Catholic School, MD

Soof

Mama said soof and no one knew exactly what it meant,
Heidi went out to see what it meant and found it was just a name,
when she came back to the house that day she would never hear it the same.
One broken part in mama's machine and
one kiss good-bye was the last.

Grace Collins, Grade 4
Lincoln Street Elementary School, NH

L.R.

Love is a treasure,
Love is here for us all,
Love is here for a reason

Love is like romance,
Romance is like love

Love includes flowers, chocolates, hearts, surprises, and dinners,
Not just fast food, but fancy

L.R. stands for love and romance,
Just like E.R. stands for *Emergency Room*

Love is here for a few quick reasons,
Like for amazing and adventurous movies and to learn something
about someone you like

Everyone has to like love or else you will have no future,
Or just not a good one

Love is compassion,
Love goes through wild adventures,
Love is what we call extraordinary!

Kaylie Melanson, Grade 5
Rosemont Forest Elementary School, VA

Summer Is Here

Today is the last day of school,
And everybody is going crazy.
Everyone is exited about summer.
We all have been waiting for this time to come.
I am counting down the last seconds.
Then finally the bell rings and everyone jumps out of their seats.
Then I just think to myself I'm going to miss this school.

Oxzana Ayala, Grade 6
Kenmore Middle School, VA

Snow Day

All of the adventurers are playing in the streets,
The snugglers drinking cocoa by the fire,
All of the late sleepers are still huddled in their sheets,
The artists making snowmen to admire.
Now, if you asked me what I'd do,
I don't know what I'd say,
But who you are or how you play won't matter on this fine snow day.

Brittany Averill, Grade 6
Thomas Blake Middle School, MA

It's All About Me

My hair is like a river flowing down a healthy green hill
My eyes are like a crystal clear pond with little fish zooming by
My thoughts are like a leaf pile building over time
My friendships are strong like a gate with a building inside
that never shuts, always letting people in
I live in the world eating all negative things

Becca Eathorne, Grade 6
Tolland Middle School, CT

The Snowy Day

Gray clouds
Rain falling
Turning into snowflakes
Falling all over
Waking up in the morning
Watching the snow fall
My mom takes pictures of me in the snow
All on a cold snowy day

Zachary Oestrike, Grade 4
John J Flynn Elementary School, VT

Crickets!

Hi, I'm a cricket and am active at night
So sit down and listen to your delight.

I have a song that is as rare as can be.
I have my own song but the female can't hear me.

I eat insects, seeds, fruits, vegetables and even cloth.
For sure, I certainly don't eat the sloth!

I have ears on my legs and wings on my back
I can't fly, but I'm a regular jumping jack!

I can be found in deep, dark places
A forest, a rock, a burrow and other spaces.

Moira McCarron, Grade 6
Immaculate Heart of Mary School, DE.

Thanksgiving

T urkey is nasty
H oliday is very special to my family
A lot of chocolate pudding pie
N ever been sad on Thanksgiving
K ind of like sweet potatoes
S tuffing is really good
G ravy on my potatoes
I love to eat cranberry sauce
V arious amounts of pies
I get stomach aches from eating so much
N ever want to eat a lot of cranberry sauce again
G iving thanks to my family and friends

Yasmeen Smola, Grade 5
Litwin Elementary School, MA

Great Grandma

I lie in bed twisting and turning
With a tear dropping down my cheek
Like a raindrop tumbling down in the night
But I think of her
Watching me
I know she's there

But when I wake up nightmares
She's not
Nightmares I'll forget her
But how

Is it possible?
It hasn't been in 5 years

I cry of the feeling I might
Of the feeling I might forget

When I was pushing her in the wheel chair
Only my eyes would show

And when it was winter
When we were done sledding
We'd visit her

Things like this
I couldn't just couldn't forget

Carrie Amicucci, Grade 4
Riverfield School, CT

Thanksgiving Feast

Corn and mashed potatoes go together
Turkeys have really pretty feathers
Turkeys and stuffing goes down my tummy
Pilgrims think that's really yummy
In the Autumn leaves fall
My cousins and I love them all

Amanda Huoth, Grade 4
Brookside Elementary School, MA

Pumpkin Patch

One autumn I grew a pumpkin patch
They were ripe and huge and plump and fat
But then the next day, I found it all gone!
Where did it all go? Something must be wrong!
I looked and searched around for clues
Hoping to find out who did it soon
And after a while I found animal tracks
That led to the one who ate pumpkins for snacks
Near the end of the tracks I saw a cute bunny
That sounds quite odd and peculiarly funny
I decided to leave and headed towards my right
And spotted the creature eating a pumpkin…
What an appetite!

Tina Li, Grade 5
E Ethel Little Elementary School, MA

Where Am I?
The soft sand on my feet,
A few seagulls I do meet,
The shells on the shore sparkle,
The rocks as black as charcoal,
The breeze on my skin makes me cold,
This beautiful place will never get old,
The waves crashing crash, crash, crash,
It sounds like a big monster mash,
The people wandering around the shore,
It's a great place to go explore,
Play a game of volleyball,
And watch the crabs as they crawl,
On a sunny day get a great tan,
Can you guess where I am?
Brooke Benedict, Grade 6
Warren Community School, ME

Great Afternoon
Eager
Sirens blare
A happy kid
Light sparkling and bright
What time will the sun go down?
I am proud
My afternoon begins.
Hannah Cheever, Grade 5
John J Flynn Elementary School, VT

Fun at the Field
It's fun to play but you get very dirty
After the game you do not look pretty
You get dirt on your face.
When you pass first base.
Your helmet is like a shield.
It may fall off as you run the field.
When you get a double.
The other team's in trouble.
If I'm safe when I slide.
I get lots of pride.
Nicholas Catandella, Grade 4
JF Kennedy School, CT

Bird Watching
I glance at the sky.
I see a silhouette
of a hawk chasing after his prey.
I see movement
as the hawk changes direction.
I see the feathers
flowing in the sky.
Then I look at the fire.
I see sparks rising into the sky.
Yanglei Cato, Grade 6
Kenmore Middle School, VA

Soccer
I walk on the field.
I hear the crowd screaming, and ready,
Ready for a good day of soccer.

The ball is in play.
The game is tied.
30 seconds left.
I don't know what to do.

I get the ball.
Defenders in front.
I go pass them.
SHOOT, SCORE, we WIN!
Chelsey Minton, Grade 6
Graham Middle School, VA

What's This?
What is this feeling
The girl I see
It's my heart she is stealing
The way I feel for thee
She sits in the sunlight
I think of her from day to day
I dream of her in the moonlight
Oh — my she is looking my way
Trevor Sullivan, Grade 4
Brookside Elementary School, MA

Soft Easy Wind
The soft easy wind fluttered in my face.
I stood there relaxed and calm.
I know it will be there forever.
I know there is something I need to do.
But the soft easy wind keeps me here.
So I will lay here forever.
Conor Bolduc, Grade 4
The Pinecroft School, MA

Diving
Scuba diving really could be,
An absolute catastrophe.
For just think of sharks,
Behind every rock they lurk.
And all those fish,
Usually they end up on your dish.
And I am sure,
That to crabs,
My toes would be a lure.
Puffer fish I know would be,
Very, very, very, very, VERY, scary.
Diving might be fun to *HIM*,
But the thing is…
I can't swim.
Dan Harrington, Grade 5
The Well School, NH

Fall
Summer gets blown away
By autumn's breezes.
There trees seem to be on fire.
As I walk, my feet crunch on a rainbow
The only green is covered in frost
Fall turns into winter.
Skylar Brenton, Grade 4
Memorial School, NH

Soccer
Soccer is a lot of fun.
I celebrate every time we've won.

All my friends are on my team.
None of my teammates are ever mean.
Matt Azzaro, Grade 6
St Joseph School-Fullerton, MD

Jawbreakers
Jawbreakers
Very hard
Sweet and tasty
Breaks most all teeth
Ouch!
Joseph Joyce, Grade 5
McCleary Elementary School, VA

My Backpack
My backpack is,
Folders, with new papers
New ideas, full of excitement
Colors, bursting out
Four pockets, holding your features
Binder, papers through the year
Notebook, of written paragraphs
Lunch box, full of great foods
Old stuff, memories
Wheels, that travel
Books, great adventures
WFES spirit, that lives in me.
Stephen Workman, Grade 5
Wakefield Forest Elementary School, VA

Wampanoag
I want to meet the wampanoag
I wonder if they liked eggnog
I bet they were very weird
I think some of them have a beard
The wampanoag are very cool
I bet they didn't have a pool
The wampanoag all died some day
I wish they were alive today.
Jacob Fascione, Grade 4
Brookside Elementary School, MA

Diamonds

Diamonds come from the core of the Earth,
Which is mostly coal.
Hot coal, carbon, and hot lava make a diamond.
Kings usually have tons of diamond.

Eric Bat-Erdene, Grade 6
Kenmore Middle School, VA

F

"A+" is what I always hear
From the people next to me.
But when I look on my test,
I see an "F," oh gee!
My teacher says, "Work harder."
My friend says, "Try not to lose."
I would do both of those things,
If I had a head to use!

Katie Tyner, Grade 5
West Woods Upper Elementary School, CT

Rainbow

I am gleaming,
And full of radiant colors.
Some people say they find riches near me,
But I haven't seen any yet.
I only come,
When there is a shower and some sunshine.
But when the sun goes to sleep,
I slowly fade away,
And go into a peaceful rest.

Hannah Lloyd, Grade 5
Four Seasons Elementary School, MD

Our Place, Our Memories, Our Town

The sunset, the beach
The families, the friends
This is Little Compton
The laughter and the courage
The bluff and the stone house
This is Little Compton
Wilber's woods and Warren's Point Beach Club
The corn on the cob and Walker's
This is Little Compton
Our rocks and the small campfires
The fish and the bees
This is Little Compton
Tubing and boat rides
Seaweed and swimming
This is Little Compton
Common's Breakfast and Wilber's General Store
Red flag and green flag
This is little Compton
Sakonnet Golf Club and the Brown Cow's
The lighthouse and the Yacht Club
This is Little Compton

Cameron Carpenter, Grade 6
Greenwich Country Day School, CT

Oreo

I had a cat named Oreo
She died a couple months ago
And this is how it
Happened

She was sitting on our couch
As quiet as a mouse
Then she started coughing,
And wheezing
She was having trouble breathing
She was suffering
I wish I could do something
I started crying
And suddenly
Everything
Was quiet
And
She Was Gone
Forever

Collin Hopkins, Grade 5
Friendship Valley Elementary School, MD

Come Sail Away with Me to Cape Cod

Come sail away with me to Cape Cod.
I feel all the rocks at my back cool like a pool.
I hear the turquoise water call my name.
The bristling trees make me want to whistle.
I hear the crickets from the forest behind me.
They rhyme like someone who keeps clicking a stapler.
If you like to fish…
Then grab a rod and come to Cape Cod.
It was so peaceful so very peaceful
I fell to sleep
Without a peep.

Christian Martinelli, Grade 4
Cranston-Johnston Catholic Regional School, RI

Halloween

I hear creatures screeching and footsteps
getting closer and closer to me.

I see skeletons dashing from road to road
and darkness falling from the sky.

I feel the skeleton's bony hands on my shoulders
and now chills running down my spine.

I taste the candy corn and hot cocoa
as it gets cooler and cooler every night.

I smell the smell of candy and the smell of Halloween.
That must mean Halloween is here.

Olivia Jean, Grade 4
Brookside Elementary School, MA

6 Definitions of Nadia

Subtle,
but singular

A moth to light —
she to friendship

A fountain
of jealousy

Limber
in life

A performer
on an empty page

Interesting
and inscrutable

Nadia
Julia Cornell, Grade 6
St Brigid School, ME

Never Forgotten

I will never forget how he went
Ice skating with me,
He taught me how to skate

I will never forget
Playing baseball with him,
He taught me how to play

He teaches me right from wrong.
I will never forget that
I look up to my dad,
When he swims,
That is why I swim my hardest every day

Now nine,
Now reflecting,
I love my dad,
He loves me.
Regan Steed, Grade 4
Riverfield School, CT

Halloween

H aunted
A ll kids are in costumes
L ots of candy
L ots of kids coming out to have fun
O utside ghosts wait to haunt you
W itches and goblins come out
E ating candy
E ternal fun
N ever ending
Lauren Jenkins, Grade 5
St Joseph School-Fullerton, MD

Feelings

Fun, the joy and laughter that is shared.
Stubborn, the stain that just won't come out.
Comfort, knowing that there is that hug that just feels good.
Nervous, those butterflies that flutter around in your belly.
Relieved, when that 1,000 lb. weight has been pulled off your shoulders.
Weird, the puzzle piece that doesn't fit in.
Bright, the beginning of a new day.
Wild, an untamed lion roaming in the jungle.
Freedom, the eagle soaring into its own world.
Paradise, your dream place you've always wanted to go to.
Where do your feelings take you?
Julie Connor, Grade 6
Main Street Middle School, VT

I Am

I am a young athlete who plays baseball.
I wonder if I'll make the all-stars.
I hear the ball hit the bat when I swing my hardest, the crowd roaring loudly.
I see a player throwing the ball to home plate.
I want to make it to the MLB someday for the Yankees.
I am a young athlete who plays baseball.

I pretend I am smacking the ball into right field.
I feel my sweat hand in my glove hoping to catch a pop fly.
I touch my blue water bottle.
I worry if my team is going to lose the baseball game tonight.
I am a young athlete who plays baseball.

I understand if my team makes a mistake.
I say good game to myself.
I dream that I'll meet the Yankees.
I try my best every game.
I hope that I'll be the best player in the league.
I am a young athlete who plays baseball.
Domenic Tamborelli, Grade 5
Blackrock School, RI

Just Because

Just because I'm nervous
Don't make fun of me when I'm not looking
Don't criticize me for doing something wrong
Still ask me if I'm all right

Just because I'm nervous
It doesn't mean I will break down if something bad happens
It doesn't give you the right to tease me about it
It doesn't stop me from being good at something if I get it wrong the first time

Just because I'm nervous
You can still talk to me and stop ignoring me
Can't wait to have more friends
Just because I'm nervous — please stop making fun of me for it
Meghan Marini, Grade 6
St Rose School, CT

Who Is That Girl

Who is she that girl
laughing with her friends
having fun talking and walking
her friends tell jokes while she laughs
and they all enjoy the day

who is she that girl
reading quietly at home
engrossed in her favorite novels
sitting in her chair
once her door closes the world outside is quiet
still to her

who is she that girl
running playing soccer
sprinting passing shooting scoring
she is a team player
trying with all her might
eager to play her hardest

who is she that girl
that girl is *me*.

Mary Beth Greer, Grade 6
Middlebrook School, CT

A Day in the Tropics

The Tropic, blazing, sun shimmers and glistens on the water.
The blanket of blue stretches across the horizon.
The sand is scorching hot like pavement.
The salty aroma of the water draws me in.
I float above the water and stay in tranquility listening to
the seagulls fight for food.
The water uplifts and energizes my spirit. It embraces me.
The man that is selling coconuts gives a coconut to my sister.
I hear giggles and laughs from kids playing tag on the shore.
The sun is just about to set.
The sky fills with blue, pink, orange and yellow.
I get out of the water and play in the sand with hopes that
a breeze will soon seep through the humidity and heat.
The waves crash and wash away the remains of footprints.

Brenna Oricoli, Grade 6
Tomlinson Middle School, CT

The Karate Boy

The karate boy did a kick
that chopped the big red brick.
His instructor entered him in a contest,
but when he lost, he started to protest.
His mom was really sad,
because he was so mad.
But after eating a big bowl of ice cream,
he fell asleep and had a peaceful dream.

Olivia Gould, Grade 5
Good Shepherd Catholic School, RI

Calm Water

Calm water waiting helplessly.
Dark clouds take control of

```
R           Y    W
O           P    A
U           P    T
G           O    E
H     H          R
            C
```

Fast slim boats sail noiselessly by
Toward the horizon.
The sand bank nearing.
The boats swerve of course
to avoid getting bottomed out.
White puffy clouds hang overhead.
The boats glide toward the horizon.

Manny Harden, Grade 6
Canton Intermediate School, CT

Life

Life is full of hardships,
Cruel and terrible hardships,
Hardships with no faith,
Hardships we all face.
Life is full of happiness,
Beautiful and wonderful happiness,
Happiness with hope and love,
Happiness we all have.
Life is full of sadness,
Horrible and terrible sadness,
Sadness with no smiles,
Sadness haunts the earth.
Life is full of love,
Wondrous yet horrible love,
Love with kisses and hugs,
Love that can break our hearts,
Love is with us everywhere.
Life is many things,
Can be horrible, sad, and good,
Yet all the things in life,
Give us an adventure.

Morgan Shauger, Grade 5
Rosemont Forest Elementary School, VA

Curse

If I could put a curse on you,
I would have a laugh or two.
May your face fill with boils and zits.
May you have smelly pits.
May you trip and scrape your knee.
May your kite get stuck in a tree.
May you be kissed by a toad.
May your football be popped on the road.
May all these things happen to you,
one by one or two by two.

Will Tentindo, Grade 6
Village School, MA

Mono

Sleep, sleep, sleep
Do not leap!
It affects your spleen you know,
It is called Mono.
Your head hurts and your muscles ache.
This is something you cannot fake.
It makes you feel very weary,
But when you are better, you feel cheery.
Caroline Cottrell, Grade 4
Mary Walter Elementary School, VA

A Special Kind of Animal

Roaming around
Wild
Feeding off grasslands
Protecting each other from danger

Running in herds
Like a flood of different colors
Strong, mighty, loyal animal

The Wild Mustang
Mary-Kate Harper, Grade 4
Wapping Elementary School, CT

Army of White

A special group
Serving the empire
Loyal as always
First in last standing
Showing no emotion
Wearing armor of white
Their ghostly faces showing at night
Enforcing their will
As they fight
Cody Duvall, Grade 6
Beacon Middle School, DE

With the Power of God

The powers of GOD and Jesus
let us live our lives
the way they are supposed to be lived.

Without sin,
without hatred.

They make life worth living.

They help us love
when we think we can't.

They try to help us believe we are equal,
thought we choose to think it's different.
Alissa Gosselin, Grade 6
Poland Community School, ME

Drug Free

If you are drug free,
It will get you through life.
So be drug free,
And don't ever fight.

If you are drug free,
You will never be drunk.
If you are drug free,
You will not be a punk.

If I am drug free,
I can learn each day,
If I am drug free,
You will hear me say,

Be Drug Free
Kathryn Nielson, Grade 6
Melwood Elementary School, MD

Spirits

Darkness or light
My spirit is bright
and some day I might
Choose who is right
And together we'll sight
A dove in a tree
Just you and me
Hope Simas, Grade 5
Good Shepherd Catholic School, RI

Sister

Never lets anyone get hurt
looks after everybody
helps my family when we need it
caring as our daddy
Learns then understand
tries and accomplishes
smarty pants
smarter than me
puts on a smile on everyone's face
comedian turns a frown upside down
funny as Chris Rock
pretty
beautiful as Tinkerbell
knows and loves it
moves and keeps moving
jumps like crazy
cheerleading is what she is good at
able to talk safe
free to be whatever she wants
she is a *survivor*
Clarrissa Blaine is my SISTER
Brittney Fry, Grade 6
Beacon Middle School, DE

White

White is joyful
White is the color of paper
White reminds me of winter
White is a cloud
White tastes like ice cream
White smells like marshmallows
White sounds like teeth chattering
White looks like snow
White feels like a pillow
White makes me happy
White is fun
David Kiviat, Grade 6
Wakefield Forest Elementary School, VA

The Winter

Winter
Winter
Snow falling down,
Winter
Winter
Snowflake found.
Winter
Winter
Cold and chilly,
Winter
Winter
Dancing snowflakes so silly.
Winter
Winter
Wish I saw,
Winter
Winter
I wish it would always fall.
Katelin Hall, Grade 5
Marley Elementary School, MD

Seaside

A day at the beach
The ocean is flowing
As the wind is blowing
The dolphins are diving
As the sea glass was chiming
The crabs pinching
As seagulls are climbing
Palm trees are swaying
As kids are playing
Emily Dugan, Grade 4
The Pinecroft School, MA

Halloween

The kids are happy
Night is full of fun and fright
Stars shiny and cool
David Fultz, Grade 5
St Joseph School-Fullerton, MD

Lit by Moon

Snowflakes fall on silver lake,
Lit by Moon, the water ripples
Shimmering stars twinkle in the night sky.
But none as bright as Moon.
Moon casts her silvery glow over me,
Comforting and warm.
Pitter, patter, pitter, patter,
The great white beast, winter, comes,
Rearing its shaggy head.
Moon guides me home to where my family awaits.
Winter howls.
Enraged, it sends the winds to find me.
They rip at my clothes, tear at my body,
Throw me into pile after pile of white.
Moon dispels them, light over dark,
And onwards we go.
Winter comes itself.
It tosses me, freezes me, blinds me.
Suddenly, it's over,
Like a bad dream slipping into oblivion.
Thanks to Moon, I am safe.

Henry Kalb, Grade 6
Greenwich Country Day School, CT

Family

Look to your left, look to your right
These are your brothers and sisters

Look to your left, look to your right
These are the people who think about you

Look to your left, look to your right
These are the people who love you

Look to your left, look to your right
These are the people who are always there for you

Look to your left, look to your right
These are the people who care for you

Look to your left, look to your right
This is your family, the most important thing in the world

Elizabeth Jane Addington, Grade 6
St Rita School, VA
*Dedicated to Roger Mainardi

Birches

B orn a sapling
I ncapable of movement
R eaches its branches high in the sky
C arbon Dioxide flows through its trunk up to its leaves
H elps us live by producing oxygen
E nables animals to have homes
S eeds fall off and the cycle happens again

Alexander Laue, Grade 6
St Joseph School-Fullerton, MD

Golden Beach

The sand on the beach is as gold as a sunrise.
The sun is gleaming on the sea.
So dazzling it seems as if it could blind you.
above thousands of seagulls float in the sky like kites.
That's what I see on the golden beach.

Shamima Prianca, Grade 6
Kenmore Middle School, VA

My Grandfather

My Pappy
was kind.
He took
me everywhere.
He made
me happy.
He helped
me do
my homework.
I could talk
to him about
feelings
He made me feel special
by doing
things for me.
That
is what he
did for me
before he had
to die.
Sincerely Zach King

Zachary King, Grade 5
Friendship Valley Elementary School, MD

Who Am I?

Cotton, stretchy,
soft then rough.
If you keep me long,
I'll get tough.
I come in pairs.
We are always twins.
Wear me now.
You will be full of grins.
If I get dirty throw me in the wash.
Flippity flop, flippity flop,
Throw me in the dryer
Hot, hot, hot!!!
After a while I can get holey,
but don't take me to church, Holey Moley!
I slide across the floor as quick as a cat.
Make sure you hold on to your hat!
I protect your tootsies on your footsies.
Who am I?

Connor Ryan, Grade 5
Homeschool Plus, VA

Sunset

The sun is setting
It is quiet and peaceful
The sun is soothing
Warm and tired
Breeze blowing
Leaves rustling in the wind
Will the sun ever come back?
Come back soon!

Brittany Jerome, Grade 5
John J Flynn Elementary School, VT

Blue

Blue is the sky that I can see,
Blue is the tears that fall from me.
Blue is the birds that float,
Blue is the water that is under a boat.

Renée Gallant, Grade 5
Pollard Elementary School, NH

My Nighttime Guardian

above
in the darkness
lies the moon.

quiet and still
watching,
waiting for the morning.

Shining,
sparkling
on the water

slowly
it fades
into the bright sky.

I say goodbye
to my
nighttime guardian.

Taylor Gobeil, Grade 6
Southbrook Academy, MA

My Sister

My sister is a devil
Taking bad to the next level
Kicking, biting
Punching, fighting

My sister is very mean
The biggest ever drama queen
Hitting, smacking
Screaming, whacking

Oh why me

Ethan Epstein, Grade 5
Zervas Elementary School, MA

Fall and Winter

Ode to fall and winter is when the trees go bare.
The leaves fall and when you step on them all you hear is a crunch.
That's not all you better start wearing your winter jacket.
The wind blows faster and we will get more cold fronts.
Try to watch the weather.

Gary Thorstenson, Grade 6
Juliet W Long School, CT

My Nana

If there was a contest of who had the best Nana mine would win.
I don't know what I'd do without her.

She is the most kind, loving, caring person ever.
She will do anything for me.

She will help when needed, and no matter what
I will always love her no matter what.

Zachary Toohey, Grade 6
Graham Middle School, VA

Sorrowful Blues

It's a cold fall morning, and the cool air is carrying wet leaves into the air.
I remember moving far away from my friends to an unknown area.
It is a quiet town and I'm deeply sad.
I miss my friends and my old school.
I'm having sorrowful blues each day at school.
I'm having piling homework from every class, and no one likes me.
The older guy always calls me fresh and beat me up.

Things are tough in my family!
Pop's working at a demanding job, and my mama is homeschooling Junior.
O' sorrowful blues!
With a rata ta ta ta the rain is like spears falling down on the ground.
I'm drowning in my tears.
I'm full of grief!
O' sorrowful blues when will you end!

Myles Cooper, Grade 6
St John Regional Catholic School, MD

Farm Animals

Animals — beautiful, graceful grazing in the fields.
They drink from the stream on hot summer days.
The farmer calls.
They rush to get grain, slop, and hay.
Cream-colored cows love munching in fresh emerald grass.
Horses enjoy frolicking in the pasture.
Pigs roll in the cool mud.
Chickens prefer pecking at the ground catching big, juicy worms.
The sheep get a kick out of just playing and prancing throughout the field.
The meadow looks relaxing with all the daisies.
It's turning darker now.
The moon is getting tired, and so are the animals.
They all doze off.
All you can hear is the soft quiet breathing of the animals.

Keira Goodell, Grade 5
Shaftsbury Elementary School, VT

Words of the Sun

I am up here high in the sky
I am so far no one says hi.

When I am mad I shine my light
When I am sad I look at the moon and wait for night.

Sometimes I'm happy from shining so well
But sometimes I'm sad. Can you tell?

Clouds cover me when I am blue
Or I'll shine my light on you.

Don't stare you can get blind
I am one, and one of a kind.

I am up here high in the sky,
When I see the moon I say goodbye.

Hana Ferrari, Grade 5
Cunningham School, MA

Good Bye Summer Delights

Good bye to summer
Good bye to
Spending days at the beach
And to sleeping in
Good bye to
Playing outside the whole day
And to ice cream for dinner
Good bye to all the great things about summer

Olivia Schmitt, Grade 5
John J Flynn Elementary School, VT

Invisible

I walk through the halls
But no one cares at all
You've known me all these years
Since I'm always ignored, I go home with tears

I'm the one you ignore the most
You might as well walk through me like I'm a ghost
I might as well disappear
No one needs me here

But maybe one day
Somebody might come and say hey
I might talk
I may even just walk

I am always very sad
I may become very glad
I may meet someone like me
Then people will see

Megan Siebenhaar, Grade 6
Graham Middle School, VA

My Blank Is Like a Blank

My mom is like a squirrel,
Chatty and nutty

My dad is like a fox,
Enjoying life and sly

My brother is like a kangaroo
Always hyper and bouncy, wanting to do something more

And most of all I am a shark,
Always wanting more

And all of my friends are something I do not know

Alex Johnson, Grade 6
Main Street Middle School, VT

The Beach the Sea and Me

Come sail away with me
To the beach and the sea
While I come to a stop
I start to feel peaceful cool air
I'm starting to hear seagulls whispering in my ear
When it gets a little dark you see the lighthouse light
Now it is guiding you right to your spot
You land there and see everything you would always want to see
Once you get out you will right away feel the silky sand
And some ucky gushey cocoa sand
While you get out you start to smell icky salty seaweed
You also taste BBQ on the grill
Come to the beach and the sea
I would love you to come with me

Tayla Pingitore, Grade 4
Cranston-Johnston Catholic Regional School, RI

Fall's a Coming

Fall slides in
With pumpkin cookies and leaves soaring
Through the air
On a windy day
Then butterflies and wind blow things around

Alexis Marsh, Grade 4
Dr Charles E Murphy Elementary School, CT

The Buffalo

There is a buffalo in the golden plains
in a field of grass, eating.
The native is creeping up to it
and making no sounds at all, moving swiftly
through the fields.
He waits until his fellow hunter gives him the signal.
He makes the sign and his companion throws a rock.
He hits it in the head.
The buffalo lays motionless on the ground.
It is a terrible sight.

Julian Leiter, Grade 6
Kenmore Middle School, VA

I Am

I am a boy who loves video games
I wonder if I will ever win
I hear the loud noise of the game going "BOOM, BOOM" then the game says "WINNER"
I see the big wooden, hammer swing at me SMACK
I want to reach level ninety-nine and beat the hard difficulty
I am a boy who loves video games

I pretend that I reach 1 on the leader boards
I feel my arms falling off from all the tiring hand movements
I touch the hot, sweaty game controller
I worry about my game freezing so I don't love my progress
I am a boy who loves video games

I understand that I will always try hard
I say "Oh Yeah! I win"
I dream to be in the lead
I try to beat the champion
I hope I will always lead my strong team to hard difficulty
I am a boy who loves video games

Shane Hannagan, Grade 5
Blackrock School, RI

Freedom

Lines marching side by side. Trying hard to fight the wind. Boycotting tea and sugar fighting for freedom. Sons of Liberty by our sides, minutemen too. Fighting for what we stand for, fighting for the truth. Boston massacre straight ahead, but don't go there or you'll be dead!!! Such a racket such a night if only we had a chance to fight. John Adams, Sam Adams get us out of this mess. Let's dump some tea into the harbor, and not confess that we made that mess. There are far too many acts to count. British men you are a snout. The sun was up bright and early. Paul Revere up on his pony. One if by land two if by sea, the secret code is safe with me. Too much smuggling shout the red coats. Let's bring out those rules. So many things that are not fair, if only we had a chance to share.

Emily Clifford, Grade 5
Bethlehem Elementary School, NH

The Worst Birthday

My worst birthday ever was when I was nine somebody left me somebody I loved. I was only nine but I know where he went, to a happier place. He may have smoked. Did the smoke help kill him? Why would such a loving and caring man go the way that he did? A heart attack in the middle of the night and nobody noticed his last glance at earth before he was gone. I couldn't ever understand why he was taken away from me forever, I would never see my favorite grandfather again. I never wanted to say goodbye not right now not today I felt so angry along with sadness bubbling inside me. A chunk of my heart went with him, the part that would always remember all the fun we had, all the times we shared. He was my favorite, the one who cared. He would always be my favorite grandfather I never wanted to say goodbye not right now, not today. I may have only been nine but I know where he went and that was, to a happier place.

Leigha Emerson, Grade 6
Canton Intermediate School, CT

The Tiny Details

Sitting down, leaves crunch. Sitting there idle but not useless as I stare up at the ocean blue sky. A small bird chirps far in the distance. Looking down at the tiny dew drops that have laid themselves ever so carefully on the thin blades of grass. A breeze softly touches my cheek as I sit under the shade-giving tree. A butterfly soars by doing remarkable flips. A bird flies after the butterfly as if it is chasing it. Walking over to the rough wall, looking down at the delicate spider webs that are in tangled designs. Tilting my head towards the sun, it is as bright as a thousand stars. A minty smell comes through the air from a pine tree. Smiling because the small sapling is tiny compared to the huge pine tree. A dragon fly zooms around my head. Walking away from the dragon fly I see another tree, only this one has tiny red berries. I stop walking because a leaf falls on my arm and it a pretty shade of orange. Seeing tall yellow flowers and a tiny ladybug makes me think that it is a gorgeous day!

Kirby Kochanowski, Grade 5
Tenacre Country Day School, MA

A Rain Cloud

Nice, gentle and easy
For plants to thrive.
I am feeling yet so breezy
In the sun I'll take a dive.

Now I'm mad
So unpleased and so upset.
It really is kind of sad
I hope you know this I won't forget.

As I cry I start to think that it wasn't just him it was me
And I am so, so sorry.
It's like I'm drifting along the sea
I must be on a wild safari.

Now I'm tired as can be
I just feel really slow.
The rough part's over can't you see
Let's just forget about ago.

Seth Turnbull, Grade 6
Blue Ridge Middle School, VA

The Calm Forest

What's green with wood, leafy and calm?
Why the woods of course,
With its weeds, trees, and vines,
Why would I not be there.
With it's cool breeze at night,
When the stars twinkle so bright.
Oh how I would want to be there tonight,
Listen to that breeze in the cool, cool night,
While you smell the beautiful nature upon you,
Listen to the water and eat the fresh berries
While sitting under a shady tree.

Monique Lavallee, Grade 6
St Francis Xavier School, VT

Bravery

Color like a shiny silver sword.
Hot like an internal fire.
Cool like a fresh wind blowing through the desert.
Sounds like a majestic French horn sounding through battle.
Tastes like warm caramel on your tongue.
Texture like a smooth path cut in rough mountains.
Moves like a lion bounding down a mountain.
Looks like a flashing lightning storm.

Elizabeth Ludanyi, Grade 6
St Rose School, CT

In the Fall

In fall I see leaves, floating over the town.
They're floating in the air like they're planes in the sky.
They're making the air alive like they're doing a show.
I LOVE watching autumn falling in fall.

Adi Alkalay, Grade 4
Bowen School, MA

Stars and Stripes

Stripes are flashing
Stars are gleaming
Valiant colors flap,
In gusts of wind passing by
Supporting justice and liberty
Stories of history
Embedded in each stitch
Flash pictures in our minds
Fame and victory
are matched with depression and failure
Stories wander
Our flag is strong to represent our country

Calvin Rose, Grade 5
Zervas Elementary School, MA

My Life Is Like a Shark

Don't have anything to fear.
Never to understand or care.
No matter the size or ability to tear.
Never to know not to dare.
Where ever they are, they have nothing to fear.
Some people do dare, but the sharks don't really care.

Ripping, tearing, taking the meat off a fish bone.
Eating anything, but always to stop if there's no taste.
As if tasting the food on the way nothing to waste

Swimming, hunting through the water.
Love to tread the water on the move.
Don't stop to think in the water, might think later.

Must move never stop.
The search for something must go on.
Must move or die from stopping.

Thaddeus Edwards, Grade 6
Blue Ridge Middle School, VA

Halloween

Halloween is fun and scary,
Halloween is spooky, really spooky,
you can get really scared,
You get lots of candy,
When you go trick-or-treating,
People ask for candy,
At your house,
They must be scary.
In their costumes,
They dress as little princesses too,
The parents walk them around,
There are parents to protect their children.
You can do crazy things,
But most of all Halloween is cool!

Allyssa Delgado, Grade 5
Linville-Edom Elementary School, VA

What Is Green???

Green is some froggies
Hopping on lily pads
Green is the taste
Of cupcakes from my dad's.
Green is little lizards
Who climb up the wall
Green is grass shavings
NOT TALL AT ALL!!!
Green is green frosting
On my brother's birthday cake
Green is a cucumber
Which you cannot bake.
You taste the pistachio pudding
You don't like it at all
Green is the sound
Of brushing leaves when they fall.
Green is mint
With flavor blasting power
Green is lime lip gloss
Which stays for an hour.

Rachel Matheson, Grade 4
Wyngate Elementary School, MD

Halloween

Halloween is…
Moaning and groaning monsters
Screaming creatures fright the night
Haunting goblins running to get you
Creeping witches say "Boo!"
Walking hands crawl on me and you
Frightening bats get in your hair
Eating pumpkin pie
Hiding in moonlight shadow's
Halloween is surprising for me and you!

Deserae Hernandez, Grade 4
St Augustine Cathedral School, CT

Serenity

Droplets of rain beat down from above.
In the pond
circle,
followed by circle,
followed by circle
form as rain splashes down.
The frogs leap off their lily pads
and dive for cover.
Momentarily,
all is silent.
No birds sing,
no bugs chirp,
and no frogs ri-bit.
It is only the rain now.
Pitter patter,
pitter patter.

Natalie Lemek, Grade 6
Kenmore Middle School, VA

That Magnificent Castle

Hey, what's that, what do I see?
It's a castle right in front of me!
This colorful, stone building is very enormous.
I could look at it every day, and to get there, I'll take a bus.
This huge house has lots of decorations!
People should build this type of castle all around our nations.
This castle is so wonderful that I want to fetch it and give it to someone I entrust!
Although, it is covered with lots of filth and dust.
It has so many windows, that I can't even count them all!
It makes me very dizzy just looking at it because it's so tall.
This is just such a magnificent house!
Compared to me, I'm as small as a mouse.

Michelle Ostaudelafont, Grade 5
Infant Jesus School, NH

Fall Mornings

I walked outside to be greeted by a foggy fall morning.
I breathe in the fresh air and see the trees.
Leaves are the color of green, orange, yellow and red
With trunks of deep brown.
As I hear birds and crickets chirping, I hear my name called.
I run inside the camping lodge, knowing I'll be outside again soon.
I walk outside again and pull my jacket on tighter,
Thinking it must've gotten chillier while I was inside.
As I stand there, thinking about my morning,
Nothing could ruin this moment.

Jordan Meyerl, Grade 6
St Joseph School-Fullerton, MD

Life

It comes at you fast,
Unexpected things happen.
It's born each moment, as well as lost each second.
It's your most important possession.
When you are living life, trouble always happens.
You will make hard decisions, but it's up to you to live every minute
To the best of your ability.
Never take life for granted,
Because it will end, sooner or later.
Life is a cycle; it comes and it goes.

Edwin Ortiz, Grade 4
Western Middle School, CT

Goodbye Summer Hello Fall

The sun will set the moon will rise early in the day.
The butterflies will fade.
The squirrels will play.
The leaves on the trees turn red and brown falling to the ground.
The wind making the only sounds.
Apple pie cooling inside.
Looking up at stars in the midnight sky.
Goodbye Summer Hello Fall

Anna Gabis, Grade 6
St Patrick School, MA

John Pinckney

John
Kind, friendly, cheerful, loyal
Brother of Tim
Lover of Tim, Harry Potter, video games
Who feels happy, sad, mad
Who needs water, food, more time
Who fears the dark, bees, spiders
Who gives help, presents, love
Who would like to see Tony Hawk,
Harry Potter 5 movie, Harry Potter video games
Resident of Gales Ferry, CT
Pinckney

John Pinckney, Grade 6
Juliet W Long School, CT

The Soldier from the War in Iraq

I turned my back against the war in Iraq
I saw one side and not the other
I was in one place in which I could not change
But then someone came and opened my eyes
He had seen the war
The war in Iraq
He'd seen destruction and happiness
I never thought that was possible
People are asking him to stay
That is not what I hear
We only see the drama
Not what's real
I think differently now
I know the truth
And that is what we should believe
Not what we hear on television
But what he said
And what I write about
Is what you and the people should know
He inspired me to help
Now that I know the truth

Alexa Thomas, Grade 6
Grace Episcopal Day School, MD

My Backpack

Water bottle, sloshing with cold water.
Lunch box, packed with delicious food.
Library book, opening the door to other worlds.
Planner, mapping out my life.
Eraser, the prison for mistakes.
Umbrella, my shield from the rain.
Oboe, poised for beautiful music.
Glue, sticky and stubborn.
Scissors, sharp merciless jaws.
History textbook, a record of the past.
Pencil, the catalyst of all ideas.

Ethan Lowman, Grade 5
Wakefield Forest Elementary School, VA

Raining

it's raining outside and i don't know why
the feeling i have is rather quite strange
i don't like it i hate it the feeling for the urge to cry
i was just fine till the clouds came out
and it gave me the craving to sit and pout
i wish the sun would come out and sing a song
as it dances upon my skin,
i wouldn't be able to help but dance along
but it's raining outside and i don't know why
and i have a sudden urge to cry

Lizzy Closs, Grade 6
Brookville Middle School, VA

What School Means to Me

School to me is fun indeed
There is so much to learn like math, science and history
All I need for school is a brain that works like me
I wish they made an endless school for kids like me
Because when I think of school I'm filled with glee
So let me get back to school
So I won't be a fool.

Severino Guerriero, Grade 6
St John the Evangelist School, CT

My Backpack

Binder clicking tic
Pens jumping while they make noise
Penderwichs saying read me read me
Expo watching out of my zipper
Zippers on my binder zipping and unzipping
Script waiting to say my lines
Recorder bouncing up and down
Word study book reading out my words
Writer's notebook writing my poems
Stamp stamping everything it sees

Rachael Allshouse, Grade 5
Wakefield Forest Elementary School, VA

A Little Ghost That Hurts

There's a certain type of ghost that hurts inside
Not on your skin or in you veins
Or at your muscles or your bones
Not even at your heart
But at your soul
There's a name for this ghost…
It's a bully

Kelly McManus, Grade 6
Thomas Blake Middle School, MA

The Cat and Bat

There once was an old fat cat from hat land
He lived with a mat and a rat
He had a friend bat they were in a spit and a spat
They never got along so now the cat and the bat have scat

Shianne Bradford, Grade 5
McCleary Elementary School, VA

Rotten Rainstorm

I was racing
My bike
And a rotten rainstorm hit.
When I got home
My mom asked me
"Why are you so wet?"
I said "the rain"
In anger we had to pick up
My sister from
School I got into the back seat of the car.
We got there and
She had a big smile
On her face
From how wet I was.
The wipers were going so fast.

Trevon Kyles, Grade 6
Kenmore Middle School, VA

Marlee

My little sister
She cries when she is hungry
She sleeps when she is tired
We hold her when she is awake
we listen to music with her
That sounds like a flow of a lake.
When she wakes up,
she kicks her legs and
swings her arms to stretch.
Really long brown hair,
she fits in my arms,
I like holding her.

Leo Diana, Grade 5
Highland Park School, CT

Outside

I love the outdoors!
I am almost always out!
I love to play out!

Steven Richards, Grade 5
St Joseph School-Fullerton, MD

Spring Enchantments

Birds chirp and deer play,
Horses lay in soft hay,
Flowers blossom once again,
Their petals curl up to the ends,
Squirrels climb the tops of tall trees,
I can feel the wind of a light breeze,
Butterflies fly,
So high up in the sky,
A heavy dew falls upon the grass,
It's finally spring at last!

Gabrielle Manna, Grade 4
Canton Intermediate School, CT

Leaves

Oak leaves float away
Trees change colors in the fall
Leaves of green and brown.

Trey Thomas, Grade 4
St Augustine Cathedral School, CT

Thanksgiving

In the joyful fall
I get a new doll
On the soft leaves
I wear heavy sleeves
I like making ham
I like using pam

Mackenzie Murphy, Grade 4
Brookside Elementary School, MA

Halloween

Halloween spooky trees
Falling leaves
Trick or treat.

Costume buyers
Candy lovers
Ready for the night light fun.

Scary toys
Lots of noise
People running
Some are walking
House to house
Room to room
And witches on their brooms.

The haunted houses
Spook you out
And make you jump
Up and down.

The fun and laughter
The lights that glow
Never ever let you go!!!

Danica Blas, Grade 5
Davenport Ridge School, CT

The Night Sky

I look up at night
To see the moon
Shining so bright.
I see the stars.
It's all such a pretty sight
And it's there every night.
The night sky
Is Earth's night light.

Shannon Harrington, Grade 6
St Augustine School, RI

The Vet

I went to the vet to check my pet
The vet said to take care of my pet
He was as sick as a dog
He coughed out foam
the vet said to give him medicine
He gave me a prescription for my pet
I gave him the medicine
He felt better after that
So we went home
And got a good night's sleep

Gabriel J. Suazo, Grade 4
Marsh Grammar School, MA

Rabbits

They hop and hop.
Jump and bump each other all day.
Hopping home the way they go.

Hopping and hopping
So very fast.
Rum, rum, rum.
Bash, bash, bash.
They go very fast

Diamond Douglas, Grade 5
Melwood Elementary School, MD

Giggles

G iggles
I n class
G iggles to the
G round
L oves to laugh
E specially in
S chool

Taylor Holmes, Grade 6
Ashford School, CT

Love

Everyone no matter who
Has something that is very true
A symbol for it can be a heart
But giving a rose is how it can start.

It's as pretty as a rose
And will start in the finest hour
A beautiful little bird such as a dove
A dove can be a symbol for love.

Under a night sky
Is a great time to let your happiness fly
No matter how you show it
Make sure the one you love knows it.

Anna Kinter, Grade 5
Pasadena Elementary School, MD

My Life

I am from a big TV blaring.
And a soft cuddly couch.
Discussion and decisions from family and friends.
I smell the sweet candles.
Like lilacs in spring.
I am from home — melodies ringing, and chatter so friendly.

I am from children playing and crying.
Old ladies yelling and screaming.
Dogs with wet noses and frightened kittens.
I am from firefighters, nurses, and teachers.
I am with America's finest.

I am from the green, white and gold.
Green fields and mountains so high.
My heritage is Irish so strong and so bold.
A wee cup of tea is always a treat.

I am from courage and strength, my vision is clear.
I want to be a teacher ever so smart,
A family with fun and a big heart.
I want to go to college and live a good life.
Stay in America and become a good wife.

Carrie Doherty, Grade 6
St Brendan Elementary School, MA

Birds

Sitting in a tree,
Blue birds chirping happily,
In the greenest leaves.

Abigail Baukus, Grade 4
Dr Charles E Murphy Elementary School, CT

A Man Almost Got Hit by a Bat!

There was once a man who almost got hit by a bat
Luckily, it only hit his hat
The hat flew through the air
But landed on a nearby hare
Who put the hat back on his mat.

When the hat took flight
It gave everyone a fright
They were so scared
They were unaware
That they would be all right.

Patrick Sanders, Grade 5
Clover Hill Elementary School, VA

Beautiful Day

I see the sun shining through the cracks in the trees
It shines on all of the beautiful flowers and green grass
I look at the tall trees with all the creatures crawling about
The bees are buzzing around looking for honey
What a beautiful day

Tommy Williams, Grade 6
Wakefield Forest Elementary School, VA

Soccer

The big kids tease me because I am short,
but the reason I play is for love of the sport.

I dribble, I juke, down to the goal,
but when he trips me, I land in a roll.

I take the free kick and pass to a friend,
but when they steal it, our journey will end.

Our defense has stopped them dead in their tracks,
I must be on my toes, I cannot relax.

The defense has passed it back up to me,
I am going to take it by myself, you see.

Inside the eighteen, inside the six,
only the goalie left, now here comes my kick.

It's sailing, it's soaring, ripping through the sky,
it went past the goalie, I made it oh my!

We have finished the game, it's all said and done,
the other team is very sad, I can't believe we won.

Andrew Cachiaras, Grade 5
Mountain Christian School, MD

Winter the Best Time of the Year!

Looking out my window, I see sparkling snow
falling gently from fluffy white clouds

Running outside making snow angels,
snow people, and pulling a sled

Can't wait 'til Christmas, the tree up
and decorated

Under the tree presents waiting,
waiting to be opened

Baking cookies smelling so fresh,
and hot chocolate to keep warm after playing in the snow

Winter the best time of year

Emily Thomas, Grade 5
Rosemont Forest Elementary School, VA

In Iraq Fighting

The sound of the shell,
Hitting the tank.
Iraqi tank burst into flames.
The noise of the rocket launcher fills the air.
Smoke fills the air.

Andrew T. Tkalcevic, Grade 4
Dr Charles E Murphy Elementary School, CT

Waves

The waves are crashing
Hitting against the hard rock
How peaceful it is.
Smell the salty sea
The waves are crashing on shore
Let's play in the waves.

Briana Beausoleil, Grade 4
Brookside Elementary School, MA

Leaves

Leaves float to the ground,
leaves change colors in the fall
like colorful gifts.

Oswaldo Rodriguez, Grade 4
St Augustine Cathedral School, CT

Bird

I dreamed
I was a bird
In a tree
Singing with the people
Happily.

Marissa Griffin, Grade 5
Cooper Elementary School, VA

Winter

Winter season is the first
It snows and snows a lot
I dress for the weather
And came out and gave it a shot

The warm sun is hiding
And it won't come out
Until next season
When we come out and shout

The trees have no leaves
Because of the winter breeze
You better have your coats on
Or you will just freeze

Winter is the best
It always will come by
when you feel a breeze
Just look into the sky

Jessica Tran, Grade 6
St Joseph School-Fullerton, MD

Aaron

A lways ready to lend you a helping hand
A chieving each goal within a plan
R espectful to all
O pen to any suggestion when called
N everending lovable person.

Aaron Taylor, Grade 5
Valley View Elementary School, MD

A Peaceful Wish

I wish there was no fighting
I wish there was no war
I wish there were no mean people in the world anymore
I wish there were no vandals or any distressed damsels just like in storyboards
I wish the FBI would take a break and detectives would get off their case.
I wish there was peace in our world once more.

Hayley Jarrett, Grade 6
Juliet W Long School, CT

Touring a Castle

Castles, what a marvelous sight,
But beware, some are quite a fright.
Some are bright and cheery,
But some are dark and dreary.
As you cross the creaking drawbridge,
You see the flowering sage.
As over the mote you walk,
You see the vicious croc!

When you reach the door you knock,
The housekeeper opens the door, and you see the great-grandfather clock.
You proceed down an allure,
Only to pass a minstrel, her voice so pure.
The housekeeper shows you to a scullery,
In the corner is a buttery.
You scrounge around for a bite to eat,
The housekeeper pushes you along, for the tour isn't complete.

She takes you to the tower,
You take in the topography for a hour.
As the sun falls,
You must leave the battlement walls.
The tour is now through, and you must depart with this marvelous sight.

Ethan Michaud, Grade 5
Infant Jesus School, NH

The Sad Toilet

They come day by day, they sit on me.
They put a lot of weight on me.
When they flush me down I have to hold my breath
Because just the thought of getting clogged makes me woozy.
Sometimes people never flush.
When they don't, it hurts my feelings
especially when somebody peeks in and says "eww" or "gross."
When somebody never flushes it stays there for
what seems like hours until the janitor comes.
When he comes, he puts this awful blue liquid in me that really makes me burn.
I really wish I had a better relationship with that guy.
He really seems quite friendly.
I'm so lonely, if only I had one friend then I would be quiet.
So, be sure to say "hi" to the next toilet you see or
I will have all the toilets in the world report you to the toilet police.
(Oh that's right, the toilet police are cemented in the ground
just like…me humph…!!)

Arianna Bacon, Grade 5
Cunningham School, MA

My Dad

My dad is my best friend.
He will be with me 'til the end.
Even though I fail a test,
he still thinks I am the best.
We go everywhere together,
and I know I will love him forever.
We go on big rides, though my dad may get sick.
He goes on the rides then he gets off quick.
Now I am at the end.
Remember my dad is my best friend.

Renee Brien, Grade 5
Good Shepherd Catholic School, RI

Abraham

Abraham is a boy who likes pie,
Abraham is a boy who likes to lie,
One day he ate his mothers pie and well,
He lied and lied and lied,
Abraham is a child who is very wild,
Abraham is a kid who is going to flip his lid,
One day his mother gave him sugar and well,
He's still running.

Asa Pettit, Grade 5
Bethlehem Elementary School, NH

Forgive Me

I have eaten
the last piece of cake
That mother had baked.

Which you
were probably saving
For an after school snack.

Forgive me
but it was so chocolaty,
Creamy, and fresh (besides I was hungry).

Justin Eason, Grade 5
Clover Street School, CT

Christmas

Little children tell Santa their wish,
Others give him a long list.

Santa brings many presents all dressed in red,
Although he will pass if you are not in bed.

At Christmas, houses are decorated with holly,
Everyone celebrates because all are jolly.

Finally, the New Year is here,
When the big ball drops, everyone gives a loud cheer!

Sara Hrdlick, Grade 6
St Joseph School-Fullerton, MD

Exotic

Exotic monkeys fly up in the sky
While bright orange cheetahs fly very high
Lime green elephants wave their long purple hair
As turquoise zebras look down with care
Hot pink alligators lick their lollipops
While scarlet red turtles watch doodle bops
Magenta wombats sit on the sand
As tan rats lend a hand
Sea green deer sent a card
While periwinkle bears worked very hard

Caroline Losure, Grade 4
Mitchell Elementary School, CT

Nature's Arms

Stepping out into the woods,
The cold wind on my face feels good,
The sunlight shining through the trees,
A leaf is riding on the breeze.

My nose is stinging from the cold,
The leaf I see has a delicate fold,
The moss is such a vibrant green,
It's the most magical thing I've ever seen!

The water is moving quickly now,
Some people wonder why and how,
I hear the frogs and birds too,
The sky is turning baby blue.

My camera is ready in my hand,
A pretty finch comes down to land,
What do I want to photograph?
Will it be something that makes me laugh?

Looking at the sky, so blue,
Pictures laid out, it's time to choose,
Not wanting any to be harmed,
Which best describes Nature's Arms?

Ellen Tuttle, Grade 6
Warren Community School, ME

My Shadow, Your Shadow

My shadow, your shadow it's a multidimensional creature.
My shadow, your shadow it's a shaded in feature.
My shadow, your shadow they follow you around.
My shadow, your shadow they stick to the ground.

Connor Duff, Grade 4
Wapping Elementary School, CT

Autumn

Gently swaying,
rustling, crunching, falling
jump in, have a wonderful time
Fall!

Vanessa Evans, Grade 4
Dr Charles E Murphy Elementary School, CT

Dog

I dreamed
I was a dog
In a house
Taking a nap
Peacefully
Verla Campbell, Grade 5
Cooper Elementary School, VA

Frogs

Frogs are nice
They don't give you warts
They are slippery
But not if you are strong and
a good sport

They live in the rainforest
or in a nearby swamp
You can always count on frogs to
romp, romp, romp…

Frogs can be green, blue, spotted or red
They are always hopping because they
never go to bed!
Shawn Parenteau, Grade 5
St Patrick School, MA

Night

The stars gathering;
the moon shining brightly in
the sky above us!
Matthew McDonald, Grade 5
St Joseph School-Fullerton, MD

Seasons

In the spring
There's pollen in the air
In school there are new things
And birds come back to share

The pool fills up
The school closes down
And I grow up
Plus my brain shuts down

The leaves fall
The trees prep for winter
And I start to bawl
Plus I buy cold clothes for winter

The snow falls
Our creek freezes
My body temperature falls
And I feel like I'm freezing
Hunter Perkins, Grade 6
Blue Ridge Middle School, VA

Sun

Sun
Bright, hot
Moving, heating, lighting
Large, big; small, darker
Rotating, spinning, shining
Dark, cold
Moon
Helena Klavin, Grade 5
Wakefield Forest Elementary School, VA

Sundown

As I am walking
I hear birds chirping
I feel exhausted
Soft colors in the air
Why are the clouds changing colors?
I think in my head "amazing"
Pink
Everything is calm
What a colorful night.
Mallory Cross, Grade 5
John J Flynn Elementary School, VT

Autumn

When I look up in the trees
and see those beautiful leaves,
I always wonder how
they get that beautiful color.
Red and green, orange and brown,
several of them go round and round.
Many are different,
many are the same,
But there are so many,
that I could not name.
I wish I could
name them all,
Those are some reasons why I love Fall!
Kyla Rose White, Grade 6
Quashnet School, MA

Lavender

Lavender is calm.
Lavender is sweet.
Lavender is joyous.
Lavender is wondrous.
Lavender tastes like sugar sweet candy.
Lavender smells like flowers.
Lavender sounds like wind chimes.
Lavender feels like silk.
Lavender looks like warm scarves.
Lavender makes me smile.
Lavender is medicine to happiness.
Nguyen Cao, Grade 6
Wakefield Forest Elementary School, VA

The Fall

In the fall
The leaves change color
The leaves fall down
The trees turn bare
Some people harvest crops
It starts to get cold
Animals gather food
Thanksgiving is here.
Shannon Shinault, Grade 6
Graham Middle School, VA

Horses

Horses run free and wild
All throughout the day
Kicking, jumping, romping
This is how they play.

Horses aren't just for riding
There's more to their life you see
Take a look into their eyes
Staring back is personality.

Horses are a special breed
I love them all it's true
My three understand me
Is that something you can do?
Bailee Poe, Grade 6
Graham Middle School, VA

The Paddle Battle

There once was a duck with a paddle
He banged on the door and it rattled
He said, "Where's the pig?
He wanted a fig"
So the pig and the duck had a battle.
Haley Mae Titus, Grade 5
John J Flynn Elementary School, VT

Colors

Blue is wavy but,
is cool and frosty.
Blue makes me feel wet
but, makes me happy.

Red is a strawberry
but, it is a Valentine's heart.
Red is a cherry but, a
great glass of cranberry juice.

Gray is smooth but, is a
soft blanket.
Gray comforts me and
makes me calm.
Micah Ellis Banrey-Chavis, Grade 5
Pemberton Elementary School, VA

Love Your Life

You are dying soon with nowhere to run.
But your happiness has just begun.
You've never realized how important life can be.
Life's a time when you are free.
Never let go of your positive attitude.
Keep the smile on your face.
Let dreams, faith, and strength
Sprinkle onto you!
Never let anyone tell you
Your life is over!
Be yourself and never give up!
It's always your time to
Shine!
Enjoy life while you have it
You never know what might happen if you
Let go!

Bailey Jeffko, Grade 6
Canton Intermediate School, CT

Road to Imagination

When you close your eyes
There should be a road
That road is the road to
Imagination.
My road takes me to a place
A place where frosted trees pose through the seasons
A place where anything good can happen
A place where giraffes and frogs
Roam free and wild
A place that is extraordinary
That place is my place
Because it flows from my
Road to imagination.

Jordan Isabelle Wood, Grade 4
North Star Elementary School, DE

The Sign of Fall

During autumn leaves changing color
And the wind is howling through the night
The sweet smell of apple pies fill the air
Ghost to goblins everywhere
Owls are hooting in the trees
The salty taste of the pumpkin seeds
I see the costumes, what a scare!
I hear the leaves rustling in the distance
These are all the signs of fall.

Guilherme Berthi, Grade 4
Alma E Pagels Elementary School, CT

Thanksgiving

Thanksgiving has food,
And boy there's a ton,
You better be in the mood,
For lots of fun.

Dylan C. Glenny, Grade 6
Floyd T Binns Middle School, VA

Basketball

B asketball is fun.
A nd you have to be athletic
S o you can play.
K ross-over is a good move
E asy and fun
T aking the ball from your opponent.
B asketball is a skilled sport.
A lso shooting the ball is challenging
L ittle hard, you have to have aim.
L et basketball be about fun!

Kyle Pinelli, Grade 5
C Hunter Ritchie Elementary School, VA

My Friend Is a Monkey

I wanted a monkey as a pet very bad
But a monkey stuffed animal was all that I had
Then one day I checked in the mail
Nothing but a big box with a tail!
I looked inside so anxious to see
And guess what I got?
A monkey looking at me!
I took care of him with all of my soul
Eventually he died so I buried him in a hole
And that's the story of my monkey named Jazz
Friendship I think was all that he had

Lisa A. DeMoranville, Grade 4
The Compass School, RI

The Moth

I lay on my bed when a moth flies in.
Attracted by the candle flame,
It folds its wings content in the day.
As night approaches and my candle melts out,
He spreads his wings and flies into the night.
I light my candle again the next day.
Lo and behold;
He comes back again,
And I stroke his wing, content myself.

Noah Goodwin, Grade 6
Kenmore Middle School, VA

Colors

Yellow is the sun shining all day.
Green is the grass on which kids like to play.

Red is the kite that you like to fly.
Blue is the color of the nice summer sky.

Orange is the ball sitting in the yard.
Purple are the flowers that the fence will guard.

What is your favorite color?

Kelley Martin, Grade 5
C Hunter Ritchie Elementary School, VA

An Ode to Lacy

Jumping up to greet people
Your tail is now a blur
Chasing the ball so fast
Sloppy kisses in the morning
A tuck in at night
We go for a walk in the woods
If you come you get a treat
Your ears like velvet fly
As we zoom on the boat
Good job! You high-fived
You swim in the river
And shake to get dry
Your cold nose nudges me
It's time for a run
These are the things about you I love.
Katy Franzone, Grade 6
Juliet W Long School, CT

The Little Pain

I have someone or something
That is a little pain
She's my dog, Chloe
Who is a fur ball and again a pain
She is cute and feisty
And over all strange
But I love her
The little pain
Emily Brashear, Grade 4
Portsmouth Christian Academy, NH

Would You Give Me a Break

I just finished the teepee
but now we have to go.
I wish we could rest a bit.
What's the rush?
The bison are slow.
I know I'm a nomad
but this is ridiculous.
Max Ferlauto, Grade 6
Kenmore Middle School, VA

The Soccer Game

There is a lot of fun
Chewing gum
My friend passes the ball
He stands tall
Then kicks his ball
As hard as he can
It goes to the beach
And hits the sand
The other team is winning
But we do not care
We can win too
Both teams win and celebrate
Ernesto Evans, Grade 5
Perrywood Elementary School, MD

Peaches

An enormous peach hangs from the backyard tree.
Golden yellow fruit droops from it.
White, fluffy clouds move across the blue sky like cotton balls.
A gentle breeze sends them softly in the wind.
Bright summer sunshine casts its yellow shadow on the tremendous fruit.
The red brick house with a black roof stands in front of the peach tree.
Purple curtains hang in the windows.
Red and pink flowers bloom on the windowsill.
Puffs of smoke look like dark, gray clouds coming from the chimney.
On each side of the brown door large stones line the path of marble squares.
A white fence rounds the landscape.
Bright green grass around the pond leads a little stream to the peach tree.
Goldfish swim in the dark navy waters.
The old oak bridge curves across the fish pond like the back of a frightened cat.
A nest with three robin eggs roosts on top of the magnificent peach.
White milkweed pods sway beside the old tree.
The fuzzy stuff inside is carried in the wind.
Abigail Gootee, Grade 5
Home School, VT

Winter

It's winter, wonderful winter
The snow comes down, there and there, everywhere
Christmas is soon
Winter the time of year when merry songs are sung
The cookies are made, the carrots set out
The time of year when the children wait and wait and fall asleep
They open their eyes in the morning
The stockings are full
The presents are grand
They see the carrots and cookies nibbled away
They go and thank their parents and look at each other with glee
Off comes the wrapping paper
Santa had done it again
The children go out and play in the snow
The snowballs and forts are made
The hour comes and snow flies, the mothers call their children home
All this is what makes winter
Lakin Vitton, Grade 6
Greenwich Country Day School, CT

Horses, Foals Everywhere!

Horses, foals, everywhere!
Sun gleams on their coats, as they drink from the pearly blue stream.
Trapped by fences around them.
Shaded by apple trees.
It is relaxing and delicious.
Protected by the large ruby rose barn.
The river empties into a pond, where sits a lemon and coal colored duck.
Hills tumble behind them.
A powdered peacock sky and milky clouds with a gentle breeze drift above them.
Relaxed, they graze or take a drink and soak up the banana colored sun.
MaKenzie Wicks, Grade 5
Shaftsbury Elementary School, VT

Soccer Ball

Soccer Ball
How I wish I was
A foot, kicking around
A soccer ball. But instead I
Am a soccer ball, being kicked around
By a foot. Up down up down the field I roll.
Faster, faster out of control! Once in a while a player
Scores. The crowd screams, and the players
Roar. I am so proud when everyone
Shouts, because I am what they shout
About. And just when I think
Nothing can go wrong
Bam!! I pop!

And then I'm Gone!

JP Panariello, Grade 5
Cunningham School, MA

Dancing 'Till Dark

One day I saw you walking in the meadow
Everything was quiet and everything mellow
So I danced with you in the meadow
The bright sun so yellow.
We had fun dancing in the sun all our dreams come true
So much fun I had dancing with you.
The sun was setting and the moon was coming
And we wished upon a star.
I wished I knew why
When I looked in your eyes
I was sailing the ocean blue.
We kept on dancing 'till it was dark
I loved you with all my heart.
We smiled.
We danced and danced and danced.
Dancing 'till dark

Emily Tetreault, Grade 5
The Pinecroft School, MA

A Dream

Is it imaginary?
Can it be seen?
Is it a thought?
No, a DREAM!

For it has no purpose,
It's just something in your mind,
That occurs every time you close your eyes.

When the sun goes up, it's gone.
Not a trace will be left.
Never to be seen nor imagined again.
For all it was, was a dream in your head.

Alessandra Colapietro, Grade 6
St Rocco School, RI

Billy's Environmental Adventure

They never stood a chance!
Within seconds
That the pollution hit the water,
They were gone.

The Strong, Striped bass was extinct.
Their numbers had decreased to a new low
in recent years.
Eventually the striped bass
were confined to one lake.

Efforts to save them were strong.
Alas the toxic pollution destroyed
the striped bass.
They are extinct.

Billy put away his toy fish set and within seconds,
He dashed off to school.

Charlie Phillips, Grade 6
Kenmore Middle School, VA

Spiders

Spiders are so beautiful!
They make ravishing webs of silver silk.
When it rains, tears of water form on the web.
When it is sunny it glimmers and shines!
When it snows, stars of white fall through the night
and stick to the web of wonder.
The spider is beautiful with eight eyes to see,
eight legs to walk and a beauty of mystery.
Why be scared of these creatures,
for them a person walks over them screaming!
Please don't kill these beautiful spiders,
Mother Nature created this.
Just please don't kill them.
Oh just please!

Michaela Miller, Grade 5
Boonsboro Elementary School, MD

Pop!!

Bubbles are like dreams.
POP!
When they hit the grass of life, they vanish
POP!
Your dreams are gone.
POP!

Emily Schilling, Grade 5
Boonsboro Elementary School, MD

The Sweater

There once was a lady, who knitted a sweater,
The yarn that she used was as light as a feather.
You could wear it in spring, summer, or fall,
Or you could choose not to wear it at all, at all.

Alyson Picard, Grade 5
Good Shepherd Catholic School, RI

I Am a Girl Who Loves Playing Basketball

I am a girl who loves playing basketball.
I wonder if I'll win a trophy
I hear the ball dribbling on the court, the referees whistle, the buzzer buzzing in my ear
I see children running back and forth on the court
I want my team to be able to be in the championship
I am a girl who loves playing basketball.

I pretend that we won even though we didn't
I feel confident when I win a game because I am proud of myself
I touch the floor when running
I worry that I won't get a basket in 4 seconds
I am a girl who loves playing basketball.

I understand that my friend didn't make the team
I say I'm so sorry Lea
I dream I'm a professional basketball player
I try to do my best
I hope that my friend Lea makes the team next year
I am a girl who loves playing basketball.

Kaylyn Pierce, Grade 5
Blackrock School, RI

Fruit Salad

Strawberries,
Juicy and red, sweet to the taste.
Grapes,
Solid and round, spheres of royal purple.
Apples,
Crisp and delightful, skins of red and green.
Banana,
Peel it and eat it, soft and delicious.
Plum,
Deep in color and taste, bitter skin, but surprising inside.

Together, one delicious, delightful, juicy sweet, crisp, surprisingly good mouthful of goodness.

Tasha Kim, Grade 6
Greenwich Country Day School, CT

Dylan

Loving, outgoing, confident

Wishes to act like a star.
Dreams of flying, flying far and fast like a river's current.
Wants to study and be studied like a big book.
Who wonders everything, everyone, everywhere what's beyond the seas
    to what's beyond the stars and ground.
Who fears fear, to fear is to worry and worry does not solve anything.
Who likes people, kids, adults, babies, elders their personality, their uniqueness.
Who believes impossibilities, nothing is impossible, everything is able.
Who loves space and time, the stars, the planets, and the everlasting space.
Who plans to flee not from my home but from Earth any attachments to my soul to the planet.

Dylan…loving, outgoing, confident.

Dylan Cooke, Grade 5
C Hunter Ritchie Elementary School, VA

The Star

I am a star who shines at night
They call me a big fat light
I soar through the sky at night
I fly faster than a hawk at night
I hope you see me at night to grant a wish
Please I'm not a giant starfish
I make constellations with my friend
I hope I could see them again
I shoot through the air
So please give me a stare
And I promise I will see you again

Curtis Brown, Grade 5
Perrywood Elementary School, MD

Snowboarding

Scraping whistling falling snow.
On a snowboard.
Cruising down the mountain.
I love the snow in the morning
Reflecting the sun
Sparkling snow
You go outside and hear the crunching sound
Of your boots meeting the snow
Winter is so much fun
Will it snow?

Nicolas Francis, Grade 4
John J Flynn Elementary School, VT

Crazy, Cool Caddisfly

I am a crazy, cool caddisfly.
Look up, you may see me in the sky.

I have many body parts, well, only three.
Head, abdomen and thorax as you can plainly see.

When eggs are laid they land into streams.
Predators think I'm not there, or that is what it seems.

I stay in the water until I am fully grown.
Then I fly out to make my wings well known.

Sometimes people confuse me with moths they see.
Because they look a lot like me.

So if you see me in the sky
Please remember that I am a caddisfly.

Zackary Langrehr, Grade 6
Immaculate Heart of Mary School, DE

What School Means to Me

School is cool, fun and exciting
You can learn a lot by writing
Getting homework and laughing with friends
School is cool 'til the very end!

Nicole Martin, Grade 6
St John the Evangelist School, CT

Rabbits

Rabbits hop and hop and hop
you think they would never stop
but even though they are the best
they sometimes need to get some rest

Rabbits love to eat juicy carrots
but I'm not sure if they're good for parrots

Rabbits can be a little jumpy
When they get a little scared they can be quite thumpy

Rebecca Lindblom, Grade 4
Center School, CT

The Clam and the Island

The purple clam under the sea,
More of above he wants to see.
Up he goes by hip and hop,
After a while he's at the top.
All he saw was sand and a palm tree,
And the bright, surrounding sea
He realized he couldn't live on the sand
So he left for the underwater land
But a gull came and swooped him up,
and swallowed him with one gulp.
So that's the end of the purple clam,
All he wanted to see was the upper world's glam.

Kyle Whalen, Grade 6
Main Street Middle School, VT

The Bird in Your Heart

Every morning Hope rises with the sun
She spreads her wings with the birds
  Then she flies
She flies to your soul
Engraving her sign
Letting you know Hope is always there
If you don't Hope why live?
You are only hurting you
If you try to break the brick wall
Hope was there
Because to break the wall is like saying a mushroom is a rose
When Hope is in your heart
She sings rain's song
She is the wind that parts the clouds
Revealing a smiling sun
Wouldn't everyone like to see that beauty in themselves?
When Hoping comes naturally
The bird flies away
But only to her nest
So you can always call her and

She will always come

Olivia Pelebach, Grade 6
Canton Intermediate School, CT

Fading

As you glide around town,
You see a new sidewalk,
You've never seen before.
You go down to investigate.
As you explore,
You leave marks with your chalk,
So you won't get lost.
But they almost instantly vanish.
The rainbow you saw earlier,
Begins to go away.
The world,
Along with you,
Is disappearing.

Stephen Lin, Grade 6
Kenmore Middle School, VA

Dogs

Dogs are cute and fun
They are funny and awesome
I love dogs so much

Emily Ross, Grade 5
McCleary Elementary School, VA

Fireworks

Colors, colors, everywhere!
Colors, colors, in the air!
Colors blazing, soaring high,
Colors lighting the night sky.

Colors, colors, every one,
Colors, colors, so much fun!
Scarlet flashes, purple, too,
Golden ones, and, of course, blue.

Colors, colors, almost all,
Colors, colors, hear their call!
Green flares, a silver spark,
Colors brightening up the dark.

Colors, colors, see their shine!
Colors, colors, aren't they fine!
Colors, colors, all of them.
All the colors of fireworks.

Trevor Jennings, Grade 6
Grace Episcopal Day School, MD

Gummie

Gummie
Funny, happy
Loving, caring, smiling
Suffered from horrible cancer
Crying, fighting, losing
Sad, scared
Grandma

Emily Derkosrofian, Grade 6
Charlton Middle School, MA

Self Portrait

My Brother: He is always fun-loving, kind of lazy,
but respectful and musically inclined
My Flute: His fingers fly up and down my body
pressing holes and making music
My Dad: He is constantly reading all day, very forgetful but hardworking
and pounds on my nerves like a sledge hammer
My Mom: He is wonderfully polite and very helpful,
plays hard and works hard on his homework every night
My Soccer Ball: He kicks me hard as a hammer
and runs swiftly towards me to get me before anyone else does
Books: He reads us every day, switching us constantly
and finishing us quickly, while getting his work done every day.
Frisbee: He throws me every day for hours on end
gracefully catching and throwing me in a fluid and swift motion
My Dog: Pet me, come on you do it all the time
and you rub me for hours on end, come on you know you want to
My Bed: He lays down on me, every day at 9:00 p.m.
and breaths heavily and exhausted and breathlessly

Kyle Miller, Grade 6
Middlebrook School, CT

Pieces of Life

Everything I have ever owned is stuffed,
like a Thanksgiving turkey, into a big truck.
My thoughts and memories,
wishes and dreams, all in one small space.
If you look at it, it's odd, everything together
instead of scattered every which way.
Clothes neatly folded in the old chocolate brown bureau.
All the glass dolls in order from smallest to tallest on the white shelf.
Instead they are packed in boxes that stored Christmas ornaments,
and wrapped in newspapers of yester years.
From one place to the other,
pieces that put your life together move.
Bringing with them new stories.

Eleanor Park, Grade 6
Pemetic Elementary School, ME

The Meaning of Life

The meaning of life is a beautiful thing!
It kind of hits you with a ping,

But, what is the meaning of life?
It comes with every husband and wife and every child in the world,

The meaning of life is God put us on this planet for a reason,
To love, to learn from our mistakes, to learn about our history,

I'm so glad he put us on this planet, and you should be too!

And every night when I go to bed, I thank Him,
Because things happen for a reason, like people dying and people crying.

And that is the meaning of life.

Meg Moore, Grade 5
Long Meadow Elementary School, CT

If I Could Put a Curse on You

If I could put a curse on you,
I know exactly what I'd do.

I'd take all of your valuable gold,
I'd exchange it for some mold.

I'd mark your grades down a few points,
I'd make you lose a couple joints.

I'd change your house from wood to worms,
I'd give you the most awful germs…

Oh, dear, I seem to have forgotten,
You're not the kid that was so very rotten!

Jason Frost, Grade 6
Village School, MA

Merry Christmas!

M any smiles and hugs galore
E vergreen trees twinkling in the window
R iding past houses shining in the night
R eindeer flying through the night
Y uletide fires crackling on the hearth

C ookies coming out of the oven
H olly
R inging bells all over the town
I vy
S now flying down from the sky
T alent emerging from every corner
M istletoe
A ngels singing a song of joy
S aint Nicholas

Elizabeth A. Oberley, Grade 5
Rosemont Forest Elementary School, VA

What School Means to Me

What school means to me
I think it means essays, homework, quizzes and tests
Boy can tests be pests!

Yet with all this work comes a great prize
For people will surely sympathize
Your great amount of smartness

So yes, you have to go to school
Unless you enjoy being a fool
All your dreams can come true
If you study through and through

Whether it's Harvard, Boston, or even Yale
Study hard and you cannot fail.

Sage Solomine, Grade 6
St John the Evangelist School, CT

The King of Greece

There once was a man named Maurice.
Who was one named king of great Greece.
One day he escaped and took all his riches,
And then a royal guard made a lot of snitches,
The next day he was caught,
And back to great Greece he was brought.

Jamie Villanueva, Grade 5
Good Shepherd Catholic School, RI

My Princess Self

I look like a princess.
I have diamonds in my braces
like all princesses do.
I have a dog that is a boy
and is as cute as a cat.
My eyes sparkle like one hundred diamonds in the sunlight.
The house that I live in is ten stories
like a library.
My pool is as blue as a sapphire ring.

Abigail O'Connell, Grade 5
Fairfax Collegiate School, VA

The Golden Lion Tamarin

The Golden Lion Tamarin,
A special little monkey with a big, golden heart,
Has an interesting story that is about to start.
It lives in Brazil and has for a while,
Give it some food and it will surely smile.
They became endangered 200 years ago,
The GLT likes the rain better than snow.
The number is growing so don't have a cow,
Don't give up hope or leave and say ciao.
Now there are over 1,000 or so,
They have black fingers and toes.
Their fur is like a peach with long hair and a tail,
But the skin around their eyes is actually quite pale.
The GLT is cuter than the little girl that brings you cookies,
There is so much fur even in the crans and nookies.
They are frightened of snakes and hawks,
And of the cat that stalks.
Wait! There is one more thing,
Hopefully soon they will have themselves a king.
Now it's time to say good-bye,
Do some research, don't be shy!

Maya Hanna, Grade 6
Lyman Moore Middle School, ME

Eagles

E ntertainment
A thletic
G reat
L eague
E nergetic
S coring

Jeremy Cates, Grade 5
C Hunter Ritchie Elementary School, VA

Falling Leaves

Red, orange, yellow falling leaves
Leaves falling here
Leaves falling there
So where are leaves falling
Leaves falling everywhere
Kadija Dukuray, Grade 5
Keene Elementary School, DE

Leaves

The leaves are floating everywhere
They are soaring in the air
The leaves are falling off the trees
They are blowing in the breeze
Now all the leaves are in a pile
They'll only stay there for a while
Alexa Burchill, Grade 5
Pollard Elementary School, NH

One Window Is All I Need

To make a difference in the world
To see what there is to see
To be what I want to be
To think of thoughts unknown
To climb the heights of many sights
To go on the endless journey home
Sophie Martin, Grade 6
St Rose School, CT

A Rainy Day

Today is a rainy day.
I have nothing left to do.
I was planning to go outside today,
But now I'm feeling blue.
I don't feel like playing video games
Or messing with my rocks.
I just need something to do,
At least until the rain stops.
I tried playing with my Hot Wheels cars.
I even played with shuriken stars.
Nothing amused me.
So I sat down and watched TV.
There's nothing good on today.
Hey, look, the rain stopped.
I have to go out and play.
J.D. Pitts, Grade 5
Linville-Edom Elementary School, VA

What Animal Am I?

I slither in the deep grass.
I hunt in the dark night.
I play with my small prey.
I am the yellow-orange glowing snake.
Allison Adams, Grade 4
Greylock School, MA

Spring

Spring is the best time of the year
The kids are having some fun
This season will cause you no fear
And there is beautiful light from the sun
Lori Bezanson, Grade 4
Center School, CT

Flashlight

When I'm on, you see.
When I'm not, you can't.
I'm used to help you see.
When I'm plugged in, I charge,
Then I'm used in the dark,
So people don't bang into trees.
Ian Watkins, Grade 6
Main Street Middle School, VT

Fright Night

My name is Sandy McKay,
I sleep in a pile of hay.
I dreamt one night,
And had a big fright,
I woke and was fine the next day.
Madison Szadis, Grade 4
Brookside Elementary School, MA

The Perfect World

In the perfect world there is no strife,
In the wonderful and perfect life.
There is no weeping or crying,
Because no loved ones dying.
No tragedy or sins lay about
No father or mothers scream and shout,
Or lay about in this perfect world.
But wait there is this one little girl
That lays alone in this cold, cold world.
She's all alone because her parents died,
But she only told one little lie.
Just one little fib can change it all,
Be careful or you too will fall,
Onto the trail of tears and sadness.
Beware of what you say and do,
Or you too will end up like the
Little girl who wept and cried
Even if you tell a little lie.
Emily Butler, Grade 6
Juliet W Long School, CT

Japanese Doll

There's a tune
In my room
Sings a lullaby
With dragonflies
Abigail Wierschem, Grade 4
Home School CHHA, VA

The Lilac Flower

Off-white and dainty,
a scent of lavender
fills the air.
The flower is a beautiful handkerchief
crumpled up on a tree.
The flower is as spongy as a sponge,
Petals fall weightlessly
to the ground in the gentlest breeze.
What a beautiful day!
Mariah Neumaier, Grade 5
Fairfax Collegiate School, VA

Cat

I dreamed
I was a cat
On a sidewalk
Chasing a mouse
Quietly.
Kitana Richards, Grade 5
Cooper Elementary School, VA

The Kitten from Earth

There was a kitten from Earth
And it loved to swim in the surf
He loved the waves
And he went in caves
The kitten was always mirth
Cierra Frango, Grade 5
McCleary Elementary School, VA

The Wild

The eagle, flying toward her nest.
The entire wilderness flies by.
She soared over the great roaring river.
Then she let out a loud screech,
as if she could talk to the river,
telling it to flow miles and miles.
Noah Freeman, Grade 6
Wakefield Forest Elementary School, VA

Butterfly

Butterfly Butterfly
don't fly away.

Butterfly Butterfly
go in a sway.

Butterfly Butterfly
don't make me cry.

Butterfly Butterfly
are you in the sky?
Rashonn Adams, Grade 5
Melwood Elementary School, MD

Song of Myself

I sing of
Baseball, the crack of the bat, the whip of the ball
The bang of the glove, spearmint gum and some fun,
Sports and Red Sox and family.
All a part of my life.

A life that is alive within
I see the navy blue ocean
I smell the gum very strong and minty.
I taste the food, spicy and sweet.
I feel the baseball, smooth and bumpy.
I see the beach clean and cool.
I smell the salt at the beach.
I taste the snow, sweet and cold.
I feel the snow, cold and melty.

A life with sounds I live in
I hear me thinking.
I hear my family talking and laughing.
I hear the seasons.
I hear the baseball games

All, yes, all living sounds
Within my song.

Connor Cossett, Grade 6
Main Street Middle School, VT

Emily

Emily
Funny, smart, good friend
Wishes to go to the swimming finals
Dreams of meeting Jonas brothers or
    Hannah Montana.
Wants to go to a concert of Jonas brothers.
Who wonders how old the Jonas brothers are
Who fears sharks
Who likes opposum pie.
Who believes in the boogy man.
Who loves cats and dogs
Who plans to be a swimmer.

Hannah Preston, Grade 5
C Hunter Ritchie Elementary School, VA

Halloween

Halloween is
— screaming your head off
— running away from terror
— waking up to the door and saying "Trick or Treat"
— groaning goblins
— moaning voices
— hiding from monsters
— scaring people
— haunting houses
— See you next Halloween for a nasty fright.

Xavier Hopkins, Grade 4
St Augustine Cathedral School, CT

Heavenly Forest

I shine the light for nature walkers.
I soar through the sky to get a glimpse of what's waiting for me.
I dive down to land on the soft ground.
I am the amusing, changing foliage.

I wait for my prey to come by to eat.
I slither, fast after my prey.
I sleep and have a dream of catching my food.
I am a calm, hunting snake.

I flow steady and calm through the forest.
I relax the animals in forest.
I curve dodging the trees one by one.
I am the sparkling, glittering stream.

Logan Rumbolt, Grade 4
Greylock School, MA

Serenity

When I die, I will fly
Up to the heavens
In the big blue sky,
I would hope to come back soon to this wonderful place
To this little ball of life
in outer space
But not just yet
I think I will rest for a while
and let my dreams wonder
for miles

Madison Hersam, Grade 6
Main Street Middle School, VT

My Middle Name Ain't Smart

I think my brothers,
are not very smart.
They dare each other to do some
really dumb dares.
One of them,
My brother Daniel calls it the test.
I don't think they know what a danger it is.

Jordan Yauger, Grade 6
Kenmore Middle School, VA

Winter Wonderland

Silent and serene are the trees barren laps,
With all of their branches in snow covered caps!
Fires are burning at hearths in the home,
All children smiley and anxious for the jolly 'ol' plump gnome!

Snow colored beard and a soot covered sack,
Cherry red cheeks and a joyous knack.
Sliding down the chimney with glee,
Comes Santa to boost the Christmas party!

Crosbie Marine, Grade 5
New Canaan Country School, CT

Invisible

Invisible.
That's me.
Un-visible,
The one they don't see.

I'm not here.
They can't see,
So I'm not here,
Not me.

I'm unseen,
Non-visible.
Not keen to be
Visible.

Jennifer Caldwell, Grade 6
Main Street Middle School, VT

Fall Feast

Time for pumpkin pie
Turkeys everywhere
We all join together
To share good food
A time for family
A time for friends
To sit and share the feast.

DenaJah Gray, Grade 4
Alma E Pagels Elementary School, CT

Trees

Green trees in the sun
Turning red, orange, and yellow
Bushes, branches, bees

Samantha White, Grade 4
St Brigid School, ME

Frigid Air

Frigid air blowing,
Trees, plants, leaves are blowing free,
In the frigid air

Chloe Olivia Greene, Grade 5
Pollard Elementary School, NH

Blue

Blue is calm
Blue is the color of my eyes
Blue is the swaying of the sea
Blue is the color meant for me
Blue tastes like blueberries
Blue smells like the ocean air
Blue sounds like the crashing of a wave
Blue feels like a cool crisp breeze
Blue looks like the sky at dusk
Blue makes me happy every day
Blue is the color made for me

John Dolan, Grade 6
Wakefield Forest Elementary School, VA

I Can't Think of Anything to Write About

Today I can't think of anything to write about.
My list is at home. My teacher is mad.
This is not good! What am I to do?
Somebody help!
I can't do this by myself. I need help
That reminds me of a Beatles song. (*Help!*)
I don't know why I said that.
This is hard. How am I going to write something?
That reminds me of another Beatles song. (*Paperback Writer*)
Gosh, I still can't think. This scares me.
Can some one hold my hand?
That reminds me of another Beatles song. (*I Wanna Hold Your Hand*)
Yesterday this was so easy.
Yet another Beatles song. (*Yesterday*)
I wish I was in Russia
Not another Beatles song! (*Back in the U.S.S.R*)
I just wrote something, didn't I?

Wills Green, Grade 6
Grace Episcopal Day School, MD

The Line

The line is something I cannot say.
The line is something I cannot do.
The line is the limit between me and you.
You toss and turn, you think and you think.
You can't get it straight, you go over the brink!
The line is the limit between life and death.
If you go over that limit it won't be for the best.
You won't come back, you won't be forgiven.
Your thoughts will eat away 'til there's nothing left.
Your life will be one big regret.
You have nothing to live for, you have nothing to die for.
The line is the path we walk, the line is the separation of good and evil.
Never cross the line.
Never!

Isaiah Johnson, Grade 6
Windermere School, CT

My Dog, Colby

I have a pet named Colby.
He is a very crazy dog.
One time, he even tried to eat a frog.
But he is really nice.
We had to go to the vet before, because he swallowed two toy mice.
He likes my family lots,
and digging in flower pots.
He is only one and a half years old,
but definitely too big to hold.
Sometimes he chases his tail,
Sometimes he even chews on the mail.
All together though, he is a very good boy,
and he brings my family a lot of joy.

Payton Trivits, Grade 5
North Star Elementary School, DE

The River

There I sit,
Reading my book.
As I stop to look out into the yonder.
there it is,
The huge flowing river
The river is crystal blue,
As it dashes away.

Taylor L. Crews, Grade 4
Dr Charles E Murphy Elementary School, CT

My Big Brother

My big brother likes to fight
He would do it all day and all night
There are times that he won't share
When playing games he isn't fair
He's always eating.
He drinks all he can.
But he plays football and he's a basketball fan!

Although he can be a pain in the neck
If I lost him I'd be a nervous wreck
Because I care about him an awful lot
He is my BIG BROTHER!

Darius Campbell, Grade 5
Valley View Elementary School, MD

Apple

Apple way up high
Juicier and tastier than a pie
Apple way up high
You sit out in the sun and bake until you're dry
Apple way up high
Why are you falling from the sky?
Apple way up high
Let me eat you
Crunch!

Jamie Cuffe, Grade 6
Greenwich Country Day School, CT

Summer

Everyone give a cheer
for summer is finally here
Everyone says yipee
with lots of glee
This is no time for school
No, it's a time to hop in the pool
It's time for lots of fun
until in fall when it's done
Children love to play
when this season comes, they all shout hurray
It's time for summer to come my way
Oh how I wish it was today!

Dylan Abate, Grade 4
Oswegatchie Elementary School, CT

Brussel Sprouts

Oh, I ate my brussel sprouts
I tell my mom with no doubts.
She looked at me, quizzically
But why that look at you sweetie?
So, she checked beneath the couch
Then, sent me a look, I could have said ouch!
She checked my hair, ears, and nose
Then she peeked down the hose.
Finally, she said you win
From coast to coast was my grin
I had won another fight
Now, a hiding place for tomorrow night!

MacKenzie Earl, Grade 5
Mary Walter Elementary School, VA

Then and Now

I used to be in Kindergarten
Sitting on the floor.
But now I'm in fifth grade,
Learning even more.

Lexy Sams, Grade 5
C Hunter Ritchie Elementary School, VA

The Great Blue Ocean

Come sail away to a magnificent place.
The great blue ocean, what a great race.
All kinds of birds, pigeons and hawks.
Everyone likes birds and does not mock.
They're all in the sky, soaring above.
With the eagles and falcons, the chirp is so nice.
Come sail away with me to this magnificent place.
What would be named as the Great Blue Ocean.

Vincent Caruolo, Grade 4
Cranston-Johnston Catholic Regional School, RI

White Snow

A white desolate wonderland
the snow untouched by man.
It's glittering, beaming, shimmering, gleaming,
the light enhances its beauty.
A seal slides out of the water
breaking the frost.
As more still come
to play aloft the ice,
it suddenly cracks.
The seals scatter in all directions
a curious baby seal peers
into the crack
only to find
a fish.
The fish looks up
at the baby seal and
swims away with the seal
in hot pursuit.

Blossom Smith, Grade 6
Kenmore Middle School, VA

Polar Bear

Polar bears running
Across the frozen Arctic
Looking up at the Northern Lights
In the violet sky.
Walking in the frigid snow.
Searching for food.
But all they see is white sparkling snow.
All tall glimmering icebergs.

Amanda Johnston, Grade 5
Pollard Elementary School, NH

Follow the Wind

Follow the wind,
To find your future,
To find where you are going.
Follow the wind
Wherever you are.
But remember that saying
Follow the wind.

Today I followed the wind,
And it led me to my street sign,
So that must mean I belong here.
So follow the wind,
And you will go far.
So remember,
And keep saying,
To yourself,
Follow the wind.

No matter where you are going,
It could bring you down the street,
Or it could lead you across the ocean.
Or even to the other side of the world,
Just follow the wind.

Kaleigh Gordon-Ross, Grade 5
Litwin Elementary School, MA

Thunder

The thunder BOOM cannot be seen
So quick and clean
Lightning CRACKS clouds
Something so loud

Thunder rolls in the break-less night
Everything might
Collapse apart
It scares my heart

Something stirring around the sky
Hear it go by
Like a mixer
BOOM, BOOM thunder

Willow Cobb, Grade 5
Princeton Elementary School, ME

Pizza

I dreamed
I was a pizza
Inside a box
Melting with four types of cheese
Slowly.

Xavier Petway, Grade 5
Cooper Elementary School, VA

The World

The world is sweet.
The world is nice.
It may be as cold as freezing ice.
It is very busy,
Sometimes we get dizzy.
The World is a great place to be,
With you and me.

Harold Prak, Grade 4
Brookside Elementary School, MA

It's Snowing!

I look out the window
when I wake up
and see something cold and white
and hear the wind blow,
hard through the snow
SNOW!!
The first snow is today!
I jump out of bed,
so happy it's snowing on Christmas day!
I run down the stairs
so fast, but so quiet
ready to see my
green stocking
stuffed tight
with candy canes, toys
and of course lots of walnuts,
and a big juicy orange
way at the bottom
There will be no ifs ands or buts
I got what I wanted
for Christmas this year

Josie Slade, Grade 6
Main Street Middle School, VT

Intensity

Ears pound from the bass of the drums
Arms flowing in control
Feet rolling off the sticky surface
Hair swirling with movement
Muscles cramping from intense work
Sweat dripping slowly
This is the feeling of a dancer

Emily Roy, Grade 6
Bethlehem Elementary School, NH

Through Day and Night

Through day and night
the day goes by,
by day it's light
by night it's dark
during the day
people work and play,
during the night
people sleep and dream,
while it's morning
the sun rises
and the moon sets,
while it's night
the sun sets
and the moon rises

Vanessa Contreras, Grade 6
Irving School, CT

A Girl I Do Not Know

The moonlight shone,
like a shining sun.
She drew a deep breath,
but didn't let it out.
She felt as if,
she needed to shout.
She thought with her heart,
but not with her brain.
She cried,
and the tears fell like falling rain.
She thought and thought,
and finally smiled.
It seemed as if,
the smiles were as long as a mile.
This girl of which,
I do not know.
Her eyes looked confused,
her hair was as white as snow.
Even though this girl is gone,
her cries and laughter echo on.

Anna Coulombe, Grade 6
St. Rocco School, RI

Daylight

In the daylight
I hear the birds chirping
I only listen

Joseph McKinney, Grade 6
Thomas Blake Middle School, MA

Leaf

L ovely flying leaves.
E legant bright oak leaves.
A nnounces fall is here.
F lying and floating across the blue sky.

Marly Frederique, Grade 4
St Gregory Elementary School, MA

Card Play

I found them in a boisterous squabble,
When I found my share of playing cards.
The Royal Queen was in a bicker with the Jack,
The sorry guard.

"All right, All right," the King did yell,
As he picked up a club.
"I will settle this if you cannot!
I'll bump you to a nub!"

They bickered and they squabbled;
Oh, what a disgrace!
#1 was boasting on how
He thought he was an ace!

The 10 was acting like some big deal,
And the five just wasn't straight,
On why the seven disliked nine,
The card which whom he eight.

I cannot think,
I just can't play!
Wait…cards can't fight!
Am I okay…

Katherine Mail, Grade 6
Infant Jesus School, NH

Sea of Dreams

Summer days and winter nights
The moon shines without a right
Spirits come from all around
From the sky and from the ground
The wind will make you shiver
That voice will make you quiver
You will fall into a deep sleep
Your little mind will creep
Your imagination will ponder
Your head will wander
Where you will be
You soon will see
The sight you imagine is wet and cold
You think you see some gold
The truth is you will see
For that you are in a sea, a sea of dreams!

Jordan Kinser, Grade 6
Graham Middle School, VA

Bandit

B ad
A nnoying
N ot nice most of the time
D umb dog
I gnorant puppy
T rouble with a capital T!

Madison Boise, Grade 5
C Hunter Ritchie Elementary School, VA

For the Love of Soccer

Cameron Wilson is my name,
And soccer is my game.
I have been playing since I was five,
And when I run, kick, and shoot on the field, I feel so alive.
I represent the BSC Rapids in wearing white and blue,
The position I play is center halfback wearing #32.
My friends Zach, Ryan, Matt, and Vince are all on my team,
And one day playing in high school is my dream.

Cameron Wilson, Grade 6
St Joseph School-Fullerton, MD

Watermelon

My friends and I
Are sitting on my steps
Eating watermelon
It's so yummy!
We keep spitting the seeds
There landing everywhere!!
The neighbors came over to see what we were doing
We told them
Then they asked if they could join us
We said yes
We all sat there eating watermelon
Spitting the seeds everywhere.

Sydney Winkler, Grade 6
Kenmore Middle School, VA

The Great Castle

The castle is 200 feet tall.
It's ten times bigger than the mall.
I would do anything to live in it,
Sleeping in the room with 50 TVs.

The castle has 1000 rooms.
To sweep it, you must need a billion brooms.
The cleaners must be so overwhelmed.
They deserve a humongous raise.

If you look out the window you can see the water.
I even think that I saw an otter.
The castle would be great to live in.
I would have the best time of my life.

Justin McQuarrie, Grade 5
Infant Jesus School, NH

Winter Sun

When morning whispers, night remembers
the teaching of moon and sky.
Flowers sing and stones dream,
The mountains listen on high.
At the end of fall,
A Winter Sun rises calming all.

Rachel Atkinson, Grade 6
River Bend Middle School, VA

Cats and Dogs

Cat
Sneaky, soft
Purring, catching, cuddling
Animal, pet, hunter, sleeper
Barking, running, playing
Fluffy, sleepy
Dog
Alanna Church, Grade 6
Juliet W Long School, CT

Popcorn

Pop, sizzle, crunch,
Munch, munch, munch,
Buttery, salty popcorn,
It's such a treat.
It goes in your mouth,
Not on your feet!
Have popcorn for lunch!
Pop, sizzle, crunch!
Regan Clements, Grade 5
Homeschool Plus, VA

Winter Glory

Winter creeps in,
right after fall.
When here it struts,
the best of them all.
It melts away,
as quick as it came.
Making room for spring,
to play a new game.
Kathryn D'Alessandro, Grade 6
St Rose School, CT

Praying to God

Every night
I turn on my light.
Sit in my chair
And run my hands through my hair.
I start with the sign of the cross.
And then I am lost
To the world.
Everything around me will disappear
And I will be here
In heaven.
Talking to God, praying to God
Everything is lost
When I pray to God.
Our Father, Hail Mary, then a Glory Be.
Then a run-through of the day with me
And God.
Talking to God, praying to God
Everything is lost
When I pray to God.
Nick Pollak, Grade 6
St John Regional Catholic School, MD

Somewhere Over a Rainbow*

S omewhere over the rainbow
O ver the Earth
M y mom
E ventually the angel flew away
W hy did she have to go?
H eaven is the place to be
E verything crashed in my world when I look up I see,
R ed, orange, yellow, green, blue, indigo, violet, all the colors in the rainbow
E ven a pot of gold but no Mom

O ver the rainbow
V ertically over my head
E ven I can't stop her with my
R aging tears, but I can stop the tears, anytime I want

A nd, if I could, I would build a staircase of tears and climb it to see her

R ainbow
A round my head the rainbow quietly waits for someone else
I can't let her go
N ow I understand I have to
B ut
O h I
W ish I didn't have to, but I did

Gabby Rubino, Grade 6
Canton Intermediate School, CT
*In loving memory of my mom

Boa

Death slides slowly, but nonetheless coming...
   Searching...
     Wrestling...
      Choking...
    Devouring...
Glistening fangs dig into the poor bird's flesh...
   Click!
Unhinging its jaws like only a snake can do.
A pit of despair opens up for one more soul to fall into.
Binding the great bird in its 33 foot long body, it is gone in a flash.
Uncovering the nest is a bonus. Dessert is often rare, but good.
   Gloating...
     Hoarding...
      Surrounding...
       Feasting...
No one can escape the steel coils.
I AM DEATH!!!
I AM THE BOA!!!

Andres Ramos, Grade 6
Madison Middle School, CT

Autumn

Pretty leaves all around, many colors can be found.
Orange and brown and sometimes red, my nature craving is fully fed.
Listen round and you will hear, the sounds of fall within your ear.
Lillian Schwab, Grade 6
Kent Gardens Elementary School, VA

Thanksgiving

All the smoke set off the alarm,
It's not our fault we didn't mean any harm.

Most of the boys have root beer,
While we watch the Macy's Parade we usually cheer.

We always make a delicious pumpkin pie,
When people arrive we have to say hi.

Go in the dining room to take a seat,
All of us have some turkey meat.

Katelyn Banta, Grade 4
Dr Charles E Murphy Elementary School, CT

Ode to Harry Potter

Brave, heroic, and smart
Talented with a wand

Survivor of Lord Voldemort,
The century's most powerful wizard
Until he tried to murder Harry Potter

True friends with Ronald Weasley
Hermione Granger and Albus Dumbledore
The headmaster too

Hogwarts school
Witchcraft and wizardry
Friends and families
Professors of all elements of magic
A very talented wizard

Joseph Trahan, Grade 6
Juliet W Long School, CT

My Dog

My dog, my dog, she is so rude,
She drinks from the toilet,
And eats all our food.
Just as we set the food down,
I'm so mad I could scream at her,
When she plays tag really mean!
I took her to school,
She had me in a tizzy,
She was running around and making me dizzy,
Then I took her to Gram's,
I should of known better,
It was supper time,
She ate all the ham!
My dog, my dog, she is so rude,
Hold on! that was me,
I learned that from my dog
Don't you see!

Nateya Murray, Grade 5
Linville-Edom Elementary School, VA

Eyes

Your eyes let you see the Earth,
from the foothills to the mountain tops.
Up to the sky where the sunset takes place,
it looks like a child's finger paints.
To a flower bed of many colors,
and to all of the wonders,
that the Earth has to explore.
You and I can discover together,
life and colors of the Earth with our eyes.

Jill Greenberg, Grade 5
Davenport Ridge School, CT

A Lion's Mane Jellyfish

My life is like the Lion's Mane
Drifting in the sea,
It makes no difference what it gains
And the same is true for me.

It has a very open mind,
And does not possess much might,
But swim near it and you'll find
That you're tangled pretty tight.

While it is mostly transparent,
It's a master of disguise
It may not be apparent,
But don't always trust your eyes.

It doesn't weigh very much,
It isn't very quick.
It is not choosy with food and such,
But its size will really stick.

I share many of these traits,
Not just a fraction.
So while the world moves the jellyfish waits
And then springs into action!

Ann Dunn, Grade 6
Blue Ridge Middle School, VA

Snowboard Feelings

It was a cold and blustery day
With heads under helmets
And bodies under coats.
The sound of snowboards grinding
Against the crisp ice.
Speeding, sliding, scraping, suddenly airborne.
As you fall you feel burning, freezing
And a biting feeling as you hit the ground.
Slopes with shred marks and
Trees with dent marks
Twirling, whirling, and hurling
As you go down the trail.
What a great feeling you get when you snowboard.

Chase Tyler, Grade 6
St John Regional Catholic School, MD

My Life Is Like a Burger

My life is like a…burger, it has different parts
And I don't wait to say that I have different arts

It's a burger because it has different parts I'm very good at sports
But I also have the smarts and my humor is not that short

I am different to my peers I don't care how I look
I don't want to hear about the hobby that I took

My life has a little bit of salt I like the little things
I do a lot of extra stuff that is not my fault and all these little things make me the king

People like how I have some extra sauce all my friends think I'm funny
At school I am the academic boss I don't really care much about money

My life is flamed grilled and exciting I have to find some time for a little golfing practice
With travel baseball is very nail biting trust me, I need some advice

Ian Hildebrand, Grade 6
Blue Ridge Middle School, VA

Rainbow Colors

Let the colors in your heart shine like a never ending lamp. Red, orange, yellow, green, and blue and purple, they are all of the colors of life and combined together they make beautiful planet Earth. The red birds and all of the green trees and the beautiful blue sky on and on the lamp shines forever and ever. Until the Earth stops its violence and hatred is forgotten that is when we will all live happily together with love and peace.

Autumn Crossan, Grade 5
Keene Elementary School, DE

An Ode to Soccer

Shooting the speeding soccer ball toward the net guarded by a wall
As she reflects the ball it goes flying in the sky like a plane gliding past us
There it goes bouncing on the other side of the field
Running as fast as a whizzing rocket, our team gets the ball back as we race to the net dodging the players
We blasted the ball as the goalie jumps for it
The ball reaches the top corner and hits the back of the network
The whistle is blown a goal with six seconds left
The final whistle is blown we have won the match with one goal to zero

Mandy Wong, Grade 6
Juliet W Long School, CT

Remember

Remember the tiny square kitchen, with the wooden chopping block in the middle, making Christmas cookies with each other
Remember playing limbo under the long phone cord that could stretch over to the stove while my mom was cooking
Remember the large porch where humming birds always came on warm sunny days
and drank nectar from the hanging pink petunias
Remember the damp smelly basement that relentlessly made you sneeze, and
continuously on rainy days would create an unhappy pool of water
Remember the landscaped area where the huge rhododendron bush stood high
above all the others, where the secret hole inside it was perfect for hide and seek
Remember sliding down a newly waxed slide, and landing hard right on the ground
Remember the hours spent pumping in and out,
singing songs on the swings with neighborhood friends.

Remembering my old house.

Danny Barrack, Grade 5
Jack Jackter Intermediate School, CT

My Favorite Time of Day

When I wake up in the morning I get in my bathing suit.
I am going to the pool.
It's my favorite time of day.
I get to the pool in a hurry.
It's my favorite time of day.
I jump in the pool.
It's my favorite time of day.
After a while, my thumbs get wrinkly.
It's my favorite time of day.
I hop out and dry myself in my favorite towel.
My favorite time of day is over.

Abigail Cowles, Grade 4
Litchfield Intermediate School, CT

Back to School

Waiting at the bus stop
Rain pours down my face
Children under their parent's umbrella
As the bus comes I get on
All these familiar faces
I'm back to another wonderful year of learning

Francisco Lam, Grade 6
Wakefield Forest Elementary School, VA

On Halloween Night

Halloween the costumes come out
Kids run, scream and shout
Suddenly, there isn't a bit of sunlight
The children will have a great night
Bags overflow with treats
Then everyone heads home to eat their sweets
The clock turns to midnight
All of the kids are out of sight
Skeleton bones rattle everywhere
Ghostly figures would fly through the air
Now everyone is asleep
There isn't a single peep.

Emma Virbickas, Grade 5
The Burnham Elementary School, CT

Project?

I can't believe I have to write a poem for a project!
I really have to object!
I have no idea how to rhyme,
but I do know how to whine!
Why was it me that the teacher had to assign?
And it's a poem that I, yes I, have to design!
It has to be checked,
It has to be signed,
This is making my brain decline!
But hey!
I guess it isn't as hard as that!
Now for my next project…
I really have to object!

Sooren Moosavy, Grade 5
North Star Elementary School, DE

School

School is like a comic strip,
Different squares for a different subject.
In science you could learn about a comet.

In English, you could learn about
declarative and interrogative sentences.
That's what you could learn.

In math, numbers swarm in your head like a bath
You could learn arithmetic or watch a clock tick.

In reading, you could learn about Maniac Magee
and how he flees.

In social studies, you learn about legends
and not bees.
Bees are for recess.

At recess, you run around in joy of success,
it has been an excellent first day!

Josh Hall, Grade 6
St Brigid School, ME

The Winter Clash

Come splash in the freezing water.
Come jump on some rocks.
Come play in the forest,
and have a snowball fight.
Come climb some prickly trees,
and pull some nasty weeds.
Come pick up some brown smooth rocks,
and don't look at the clock.
Come have a blast.
Come explore.
The water is fine.
You'll want to come here all the time.

Dylan DiLibero, Grade 4
Cranston-Johnston Catholic Regional School, RI

Fall

The fall season is finally here,
The time to trick or treat is near,
The leaves are changing, the air is cool,
Here are some things we learned in school:

Pilgrims + Indians = A new way of living,
Now we celebrate each year with turkey on Thanksgiving,
America is the land that Columbus found,
He proved to the world that the Earth is round,

These are some things that happened in fall,
This is why I like fall the best of all!!!

Tyler Thomas, Grade 4
Alma E Pagels Elementary School, CT

Snow

Snow, snow, wonderful snow,
reminds me of Christmas,
reminds me of winter,
as the white flakes fall,
I try to catch them,
what cheer it brings,
that wonderful snow.

Megan Smith, Grade 4
North Star Elementary School, DE

Christmas

Christmas is joy
Christmas is snow
Christmas is wreaths with big, red bows.
Christmas is family
Christmas is white
Christmas is also the birth of Christ.
Christmas is feasting
Christmas is gifts
Christmas was declared December 25th.

Jayla Harrington, Grade 6
Melwood Elementary School, MD

The Squirrel in the Tree

The squirrel in the tree,
Wagging its tail all day long.

Waiting for acorns on the ground,
For itself and friends.

The squirrel in the tree,
Hiding from dogs in sight.

It also stores its acorns in the ground,
Like a mole and gets it during winter.

The squirrel in the tree,
Wagging its tail all day long.

Caezar Dave S. Emmanuel, Grade 5
Marley Elementary School, MD

The Old Lady with a Beard

There once was a lady who was weird,
she would never shave her gray beard,
Her face was scary,
'Cuz her chin was hairy,
That's the tale of the lady with the beard.

Brianna Mortimer, Grade 4
Brookside Elementary School, MA

Nature's Habitat

Birds in a V-shape
The sun is shining brightly
Parallel big trees

Brian Roberts, Grade 5
Pollard Elementary School, NH

I Am

I am respectful.
I wonder if I am a good guitarist.
I hear, "Linkin Park" in my head.
I see my friends and family.
I want to have an electric guitar.
I am respectful.
I pretend I fly a fighter plane.
I feel like someone is watching me.
I touched a live crab.
I worry about the apocalypse.
I cry when someone yells at me.
I am respectful.
I understand Nepali people
I say that there is life on Mars.
I dream that I will discover alien life forms on a different planet.
I tried to fly when I was little.
I hope that we find a second Earth.
I am respectful.

Akash Kunver, Grade 5
Clover Street School, CT

I Am

I am funny and smart
I wonder if my grandparents are going to love each other again
I hear crying in the morning from my little brother
I see birds in the morning sky
I want to go flying around the world
I am the middle child in my family
I pretend that I am singing on stage
I feel that I get my work done in school
I imagined that I touched a million dollars
I worry that my family is ok
I cry when I see a sad show
I am funny and smart
I understand more math than I did before
I say I should not care what other people think of me
I dream that I will be proud of what I will be when I am older
I try to do and be my best in school
I hope I will not live on the streets
I am funny and smart

Jordan Hunter, Grade 5
Clover Street School, CT

Mother Nature

I think Mother Nature is sometimes fickle and sometimes she is not.
She can make blizzards and make it cold.
She can make droughts and make it hot.
When she's happy the sun comes out.
If she's sad it starts to rain.
When Mother Nature feels angry she will make horrible storms.
The weather depends on how Mother Nature feels.
No matter what weather men say.
This is what I think and it won't be changed.
Mother Nature is fickle and sometimes she is not.

Deryk Michel, Grade 6
Irving School, CT

Baseball

I like when it's my team's turn to hit
Since I play first base I don't wear the catcher's mitt.

I love to wear my team's red hat,
Once it flew off when I was at bat.

My friend Devian hit a very high pop
But when he tries to catch the ball, on the base I saw it drop.

Usually you'll find me on first base,
Once I almost got whacked right in the face.

Isaiah Mack, Grade 4
Dr Charles E Murphy Elementary School, CT

Bark But No Bite

My life is like a Maple Tree
My thoughts all scattered round
Moods like colors as you can see
Sometimes they're hard to get off the ground

The roots like my background
They spread in many ways
Going all around
Yet they really show all days

My branches spread too
Like ideas branch out
They may go so far, they touch you
It gets so cluttered sometimes, I need to shout

The trunk like the people around me
Bark but no bite
My life is like a Maple Tree
Sometimes wrong, but never always right

Elizabeth Gauriloff, Grade 6
Blue Ridge Middle School, VA

My Horse

This is my horse.
Beautiful and fast.
She runs like the wind.
And never comes in last.

This is my horse.
Trusting and kind.
We're made for each other.
And think like one mind.

This is my horse.
Muddy and dirty.
But I still love her.
And sometimes she can be quite perty!

Amanda Ward, Grade 5
C Hunter Ritchie Elementary School, VA

Flying

Hi my name is Skye
Someday I hope to fly
I would go on an airplane
I hope I can still be sane
That is my dream, I do not lie

Flying would be very fun
So high I could touch the sun
Soaring above everyone's head
Even the people who are still in bed
I would never stop flying, I would never be done!

Skye Sinyard, Grade 5
Clover Hill Elementary School, VA

The Dragon's Pledge

With wings that could never fly,
My heart, it does,
Still rest in the sky,
For you are who you are,
Remember that.
And think of all the places, in which you have sat,
In thought.
And think of all the things you'll have to do,
To save our world, and
Us too.

Lucia Roach, Grade 4
P.B. Smith Elementary School, VA

Shopping Time!

When I go shopping there's no stopping
we just keep on talking and walking.
We can pick up a Starbucks or a Wetzel's Pretzel too
but there's an 8:30 sale and I need shoes!
We can buy a flat screen TV or a brand new laptop for you
but when it's 8:30 I need to go get those shoes!
Shopping's over and now it's time to pay
when I got up to the cashier she said hello and how is your day?
And I said yeah yeah I just need to pay!
Ok how would you like to pay today?
And I will say well I have a secret it's pretty harsh
just charge it all on my momma's big fat credit card!

Kelsey A. Riegger, Grade 5
Pasadena Elementary School, MD

Ode to Christmas

Oh Christmas!
What a joy!
I love to find each and every toy
Ripping colorful bright paper
Reveals an enjoyable new toy
Bounce and vault
Out of my bed
Rushing to the glowing sparkling tree of joy
Gifts anxiously dawdle to be torn

Nick Lauer, Grade 6
Juliet W Long School, CT

I Am That Girl

I am that girl,
Sitting in the apple tree,
Kicking her feet up and down.

I am that girl,
Splashing in the waves,
Swimming against the current,
Hair in her face.

I am that girl,
Leaning against the tree trunk,
Reading a book,
The wind blowing in her hair.

I am that girl,
Reciting this poem,
Up on stage.

Only to see,
The hundred smiling faces,
Beaming back at me.

I am that girl,
And many more.

Emily Horowitz, Grade 6
Ocean State Montessori School, RI

Football

Touchdowns and tackles
Cheerleading and spirit
Cheers them on

Harley Wolfe, Grade 5
McCleary Elementary School, VA

Clouds

The clouds are white
And in the sky
The clouds are always swooshing by
The clouds have shapes all the time
Each shape is unique
In shape and size
The shapes are white
And sometimes gray
Whether white or gray
I always have a great day!

Angela Dansereau, Grade 5
Good Shepherd Catholic School, RI

Leaves

Finger oak leaves float
In the cold drifting breezes
Like a bird flying.

Jose Tabora, Grade 4
St Augustine Cathedral School, CT

Wind

The wind came through
The clothes line whipping back and forth
There go the sheets
I watch them as they sail

Sarah Mueller, Grade 5
Wakefield Forest Elementary School, VA

Fall

F lickering leaves
A mazing weather
L ovable holidays
L iving a great life

Jordan Murdy, Grade 4
Wapping Elementary School, CT

Video Games

V ery exciting.
I ntelligent creators create them.
D escriptive designs.
E xceptional graphics.
O utstanding sketch drawings.

G amers play the pro games.
A wesome main characters.
M ost do not have glitches.
E pic storyline.
S everal are good for your brain.

Joshua Meek, Grade 6
St Joseph School-Fullerton, MD

Nature Is Rising

Rivers running deep
Leaves are blowing in the wind
Nature is rising.

Amanda D'Amico, Grade 4
The Pinecroft School, MA

The Positive World

We are the people
We are the givers
We are the receivers
We are the keepers
We are the continents
We are the world
We will live as one
We will be here forever and ever.

Tiffany Wilder, Grade 6
Main Street Middle School, VT

Fall Sounds

Leaves blow around the yard
Loud barking, cat's claw on the trees
Breeze blows through the air.

Piper Spellman, Grade 4
Wapping Elementary School, CT

The Loves of Life

I am from cozy pillows and
kids running all around
with the smell of flowers in the air
watching sunsets night to
night

I am from where you hear
the birds chirping and
the cars honk from day to night
The smell of danish
in the air but greasy French Fries
everywhere

I am from the love of Irish people
wearing dark greens and orange
Girls and boys dancing
step to step and all over
you shall see red haired people

I will be a movie star
the star of the century
with college and family
and singing and acting busy and
rich is how it shall go

Erin O'Brien, Grade 6
St Brendan Elementary School, MA

Miami Beach

Come to the beach with
palm trees swaying in the
rainbow sky.
Come with me to chill
in the sounds of seagulls.
We're at the beach where
the ocean is the smell of salt.
Miami Beach.

Angelina Weng, Grade 5
Zervas Elementary School, MA

A Dream

I lay down in my bed
Hearing whispers from the dead
What's that, the lights are dim
Now I see a terrible grim
He is after me I run so fast
What, a witch that I past
Now I see a beam of light
Man, what a terrible fright
Fu, it was just my mother
Oh brother
It was just a dream
It seems

Tori Brown, Grade 6
Graham Middle School, VA

My Bike

This is my bike.
It is all blue and very cool.
I can go off big ramps.
I can go so high, I can go over the school.

This is my bike.
It has flames like a dragon.
I go so fast.
It looks like a flying wagon.

This is my bike.
I landed on a spike.
I had to get stitches.
And I still ride my bike.

Cory McMullan, Grade 5
C Hunter Ritchie Elementary School, VA

In and Out

A silent worm, weaving its way
Through the wet earth, sliding gracefully
In and out

Such is the way a needle weaves a jacket
For a boy who has nothing
Sewing warmth and love into it with every strand
In and out

Such is the way a clever thief winds his way
Through the alleyways of the city
Searching for something worth taking
Trying not to get caught in the act
In and out

A worm, a needle, a thief
All so different, but the same in their differences
All showing the quality of movement
Doing the same thing over and over
Each trying to sustain a simple cause,
To stay alive, to help a soul, and to stay hidden
All following the same rotation
In and out
In and out

Christian Cilley, Grade 6
St Brigid School, ME

Autumn Leaves

I love this time of the year,
When the leaves turn red and gold.
I love to see them dance around,
As the wind begins to blow.
They are happy with what they have done,
By protecting people from the hot sun.
Now, they will be down in piles so deep.
As they settle in for their long deserved sleep.

Paul Paliotta, Grade 6
St Rocco School, RI

Shadows

The leaves outside are a pumpkin orange,
Autumn is the crisp new season.
Jack-o-lanterns light up the thick night sky,
While children go trick-or-treating.
Spooky shadows follow in their footsteps
As Halloween comes again.

The cardinals are staying here,
As other birds are migrating south.
Galloping through crunchy leaves,
I head to a gargantuan coop.

The first frost is on the frozen ground,
As children pile in the house for hot cocoa,
Marshmallows melting as they slide to your stomach.
Santa hopping in his sleigh as the reindeer clippity clop
As they prance on the roof top.
It's already Christmas!

Annie Werdiger, Grade 6
Greenwich Country Day School, CT

Butterfly

Butterflies flutter in the summertime.
They seem to float in the dark blue sky.
Watch the butterfly sit on a yellow sunflower.
They love the nectar because it is sweet like honey.
They always rush to the fields
to sit on the prettiest and biggest yellow sunflower there.
The curious butterfly eats leaves.
They live in woods or meadows.
Butterflies look like a young lady in a blue dress.
Butterflies would like to stay out all year, but they can't.
They have to get their rest so they can continue their life cycle.

Toni Kuzawski, Grade 5
Shaftsbury Elementary School, VT

Winter

The snow on the ground
The laughter of children
The snowmen being made
The smell of hot chocolate in the air!
The warmth of the cozy fire
Winter is a time of sweetness!
The children decorating
Hanging their stockings
Christmas is almost here
Making snow angels
Sledding with laughter
Partying with everyone after!
Having fun catching snowflakes on your tongue
Winter is a time of warmth
Winter is FUN!!

Danielle Ternullo, Grade 6
St Mary of Czestochowa School, CT

Halloween

Halloween knows how to scare
When to go and
Where to go for a nice treat.

You're about to meet his scary feet
But he knows how to sneak
And snarl, groan, and growl

He knows where to scare
A scary, merry, glarey glee.

Bruce Micucci, Grade 6
St Brigid School, ME

Hissy Fit

My sister is having a fit
Not just any fit, a hissy fit
She goes around the house
Kicking and hitting anything in her way
"Waaahh!" she cries.
"Arroooohhh!!!" cries the dog
As she kicks him.
My sis is having a fit.
A very big hissy fit
My mom finally stops her
And calms her down
The hissy fit is OVER!!!

Gabriella Anne Vaccaro, Grade 5
St John Neumann Academy, VA

The Apology

I have to say I am sorry
for not being there for you.
I have to say I am sorry
for making you so blue.

The promises I made
were heartfelt and true.
Situations change.
I hope you understand, too.

When we first met,
the first time I laid eyes on you.
I would have bet
we would be stuck like glue.

Our lives took different paths.
What were we to do?
And looking at the past,
who was hurting whom?

But through the years,
the winds of change blew.
And after all the tears,
can we start anew?

Grayson O'Saile, Grade 6
Graham Middle School, VA

Green

Green is the fern that suffers from harsh winds.
Green is the moss on the tree that soaks up all the water from the heavy clouds.
Green is the whisper from the trees above.
Green is my voice when I sing a high note.
Green is the smooth touch of the Granny Smith apple that I eat.
Green is the ticklish touch of the grass.
Green is the fragile fragrance of a candle that is lit.
Green is the sweet smell of the pine needles on a pine tree.
Green is the taste of lime lemonade.
Green is the taste of a green sour, makes your lips curl up gum ball.

Emma Murphy, Grade 6
Amherst Middle School, NH

I Am A…

R is for rally the Red Sox had in game seven
E is for energy the fans have in the stands
D is for David Ortiz, the designated hitter and one of my favorite players

S is for spirit that we have in the Red Sox
O is for Okajima and his fast pitched he throws from the mound
X is for eXcitement you feel when you catch the ball that is hit into the stands

F is for Fenway Park. The best ball field in the world!
A is for another chance at winning the World Series
N is for NEVER giving up on the Red Sox!

GO SOX!!

Jenny Heller, Grade 5
St Patrick School, MA

What Do You Like Most About the Seasons?

What do you like most about fall?
Do you like the colorful leaves falling from the trees?
Or gathering with family to give thanks after Thanksgiving Eve?
Soon will be Halloween, ghosts and goblins wear spooky green!

What do you like most about winter?
Do you enjoy the holidays, or riding in one horse open sleighs?
Do you like a snowy day, or would you rather be indoors to play?
Would you rather skate on ice, or cook something warm and nice?

What do you like most about spring?
Warm weather is a sign of spring, then the robins start to sing.
Do you prefer rain showers, or beautiful flowers?
Now is April Fools, too cool to swim in any pool.

What do you like most about summer?
Chill at a beach or in a pool, because we have no school!
Do you like to sleep late, or call up a playmate?
The excitement of the Fourth of July is going to come,
Or would you rather just act like a lazy beach bum?

So don't pollute the air, and we can enjoy the four seasons everywhere!
Fall, winter, summer, spring, and all you have to do is this one little thing!

Amanda Gastel, Grade 5
Lincoln Central Elementary School, RI

Safety

Silence.
Blackened night surrounds me.
I lay huddled close to my cream colored fuzz ball.
A smile that resembles a mountain
lights up my face
just as the moon and stars brighten the sky tonight.

His eyes as black as midnight, rimmed with blood red,
peer into mine. Understanding me.
I speak but need — no reply
just the look in his eyes.

My head moves.
My cheek brushes his cold black nose.
Cool ripples of safety run up my spine,
I remember sleeping like this
in my dad's arms.

I gather my fuzz in closer
for even more safety and sigh.
My eyes shut.
My head slowly slides
onto his fuzzy fur.
Now I feel safer than ever.

Emily Grey, Grade 6
Mystic Middle School, CT

A Bead Necklace

One day an Indian named Kolikiwala
Was making a beautiful necklace.
The necklace was made of beautiful beads and feathers.
The beads were the color of the ocean
When the bright sun is shining on it.
The feathers came from a hawk,
The rarest hawk known to man.

Jamie Osorio, Grade 6
Kenmore Middle School, VA

Day Dreaming

I'm stuck in this world
This imaginary world in a
Place where you can do anything

Have you seen the sky
So bright and the grass so green

So beautiful colorful why so
Wonderful

A place where you can keep your
Mind wide open to all the
Possibilities

Nicole Sardi, Grade 5
Friendship Valley Elementary School, MD

What School Is to Me!

School to me is mostly fun
But weekends are my number 1.

For all the different things we do
There are some things I'd like to remove.

The teachers here are quite nice
But sometimes I feel like I'm on thin ice.

With all the things that you have heard
You must be feeling very bored.

But now that my story is done
You can go out and have some fun!

Paige Demas, Grade 6
St John the Evangelist School, CT

Christmas Eve

Decorating the green Christmas tree,
With red and gold leaves.
You saved some pine cones from fall.
Paint them gold, get some string, and drill a hole.
Then put them on the tree.
Next the lights,
Twist them green and red,
Spin the tree round and round,
Now you're at the top,
Time for the star.
Leave out lots of cookies and milk for Santa.
Carrots for the reindeer.
Go to bed, can't sleep
For Christmas is tomorrow!

Benjamin Galli, Grade 5
Highland Park School, CT

Feeling Colors

Blue skies cool the day.
Yellow is as a sour lemon
Pink as a butterfly's wings
Red is as colorful as a rose.
Green is the color of grass and leaves
Brown as the bark of a tree.
Black is dark and absorbs the sun
How do colors make you feel?

Richey Myers, Grade 5
C Hunter Ritchie Elementary School, VA

The Story of the Flag

The 4th of July is my favorite holiday
and it is also my birthday.
I kind of like to hang, although I get so lonely.
I did feel very scared when those mean British soldiers
kept throwing guns and bombs,
but I kept standing tall and strong…forever.

Adam Burkhardt, Grade 5
Old Saybrook Middle School, CT

Trees

T he branches sway in the wind
R eady to provide shelter to animals
    during the frosty winter months
E arth's cleanser
E ndless fun in the fall
S hade on a blazing hot summer day
Abigail Boisvert, Grade 5
Good Shepherd Catholic School, RI

Dancer's Inner Voice

Black out!
The lights turn off.
The music turns on.
My ears start to tingle.
I walk out on stage.
Ten zillion eyes bug out at me.
Are they looking at me or her or her?
I take a breath.
I let the music fill my body.
So much that I can't control myself.
So I start to move.
I start to dance.
Victoria Leone, Grade 4
North Star Elementary School, DE

Batteries

The little
useful cylinder
quite small
they are
but they
emit powerful
energy
they power
certain toys
and machines
so I
say thank you
batteries
for giving
me all
your energy
Monty Bone, Grade 6
Graham Middle School, VA

Charlie

He barks
He licks
He's black
I walk him
I feed him
I play with him
He's my dog Charlie
Brandon Rodriguez, Grade 4
Marsh Grammar School, MA

Sweet Blizzard

As fall leaves were swept away
A snowstorm was on its way.
With biting winds that blow
To bring us a blanket of snow.

Mountain tops covered with sugar
Front yards sprinkled with ice;
Wherever you look around you
It's a sweet-tooth's paradise.
Zachary Brown, Grade 6
Graham Middle School, VA

Daisy the Dog

There was a dog named Daisy,
Daisy was very lazy,
She sat on her butt,
And people called her a mutt,
But then she went out to pick daisies

Daisy got tired and started to sway,
She said "This has been a very bad day!
I sat on my tail,
And fell down the rail,
I guess my month is not May!"
Madelyn Boehnlein, Grade 5
Clover Hill Elementary School, VA

All About Me

M iraculous
A dorable
R esponsible
I ncredible
S poiled
S pecial
A ttentive

Now you can see I am who I am
and who I want to be!
Marissa Knight, Grade 5
Valley View Elementary School, MD

Silent Rainstorm

Drop drop drip drop
Quiet is the rainstorm
Hitting the ground with a steady beat
1 2 3 4, 1 2 3 4, 1 2 3 4, 1 2 3 4
Counting the beat of the this dreary day
I sit quietly waiting
Waiting for the rain to clear up
Boring boring boring boring
Nothing to do but sit and wait
Hooray the silent rainstorm is gone
Tiara Duffy, Grade 6
Beacon Middle School, DE

The Minstrel

The strolling minstrel, far he came
To woo his lady love;
He played upon his violin,
Watching the window above.

He sang of love and how they would
Together forever be.
He hoped she'd see him standing there,
Invite him up for tea.

But to the window not she came,
For down there in the thicket,
No matter just how loud he played,
The minstrel was a cricket!
Jennifer Coleman, Grade 6
Martin Barr Adventist School, MD

Thinking

Lying down in a place
Where I can get away from it all.

I feel the cool breeze
Brush against my face.

Feeling my body
On the soft, green grass.

A peaceful place
Where I can Think.

Think about yesterday
Or think about last year.

Or think about the future
Or think about today.

Or simply watch the sun set
Over the horizon

And watch the sky
Turn from red to black.
Reagan Walker, Grade 6
Tomlinson Middle School, CT

Dreams

As I look up at my bedroom ceiling,
A sea of dreams drifts over me,
And washes upon my head.
But just as I'm enjoying it,
My mom comes in and ruins it,
By saying, "Get those buns out of bed!"
So I emerge reluctantly,
For the waking, I always dread.
Zoe Albion, Grade 4
Berwick Academy, ME

Yoshi

This is my dolphin, Yoshi
She is bluish gray
She is very funny
She loves to play

This is my dolphin, Yoshi
She jumps really high
She's as fast as lightning
She hates when I say bye

This is my dolphin, Yoshi
She's gone in a flash
Loves to do stunts
She's back in a blast

Alex Smith, Grade 5
C Hunter Ritchie Elementary School, VA

I Have Eaten a Piece of Cake

I have eaten a piece of cake.
Which you were probably saving for dessert.

Forgive me for this, but the frosting
was so creamy
and the strawberries inside
were so delicious!!!

Mark Wilson, Grade 5
Clover Street School, CT

Sky

Do you ever get caught up in the sky blue,
It looks so marvelous, it is amazing,
With all of its shades of blue,
It almost looks like it has a mood.
If it is navy, it is mad.
But if it's light blue, it's joyful,
If the blue sky is the head,
What would that make the clouds, then?
I'd consider the clouds to be the eyes
Because when it rains it would cry.
So, just take a second to gaze up there,
I think you'll enjoy it as much as me,
You'll probably have a bunch of fun
Hey, what would this make the sun?

Daniel Coveney, Grade 5
E Ethel Little Elementary School, MA

Webs of Dawn

It's dawn and the sun is rising,
petit spiders dangle from their silk-like webs.
The spiders look like little black beads
thrashing in the wind.
They begin to weave their webs of lace
all around the blooming orchard.
The spiders leave a masterpiece.

Margot Austin, Grade 6
Kenmore Middle School, VA

Soccer

S core goals to win
O ur team plays both outdoor and in,
C ompetition is tough, so you better beware
C ome out and play if you dare,
E asy, this sport is not
R unning, kicking, take a shot

Jude Barlow, Grade 6
St Joseph School-Fullerton, MD

Shadows

Shadows, the people who are with you, though they're not
It's the shadows that are really memories in black suits,
waiting for you.
All I can think of now is
GRAMPA
My favorite memory.

Jonathan Torres, Grade 5
Jack Jackter Intermediate School, CT

A Relaxing Place

Come sail away, to a relaxing place
Where the blue and purple mountains shine
With a white streak like a waterfall so big and tall
I feel just like I'm going to fall.
With trees blowing and fish growing.
Frogs hopping until they drop…
Saying "Ribbit ribbit."
The fresh air is so fresh and clean I don't want to leave…
With the pink flowers and rocks all around
The flowing crystal rivers so peaceful and quiet…
With the sky reflecting on the water so pretty.
The green grass of fields…
You feel so free just to be your own plain self.

Megan Christina Nadeau, Grade 4
Cranston-Johnston Catholic Regional School, RI

Witch's Lake

I swim very rapidly.
I dive down low to build up speed.
I flip so high in the lake.
I am the sparkly dazzling mermaid.

I squeak while the witch opens my door.
I shake when she uses her powers.
I decay because I am so old.
I am the rotting breaking cottage.

I cackle waiting for my spell to work.
I limp while I try to walk.
I curse people swimming and they change
Into mermaids.
I am the mean terrifying witch.

Hannah Levesque, Grade 4
Greylock School, MA

My Puppy

My puppy is crying
She wants me to play
I can't say *no*!
and I can't shoo her away
She's way too cute
She's way too adorable
I can't! I can't! I just can't!

Jessica Harlow, Grade 5
Southbrook Academy, MA

My Bus

Yellow,
Kids ride on school buses.
Donna drives a school bus.
They go slow.
My school bus is very quiet.
Sometimes my school bus is late
They came at 7:25.
I get to school at about 7:40.

Jeffrey A. Kittredge II, Grade 6
Main Street Middle School, VT

Boards, Boards, Boards

Huge boards
Short boards
Short, slow, trick boards
Those are just a few
Puny boards
Mountain boards
Electric, gas, manual boards
Boogey boards too!
Surf boards
And don't forget skate boards.
Last of all
Best of all
I like long boards!

Caile Johnson, Grade 6
Juliet W Long School, CT

Winter's Crown

Through the window
I will see
Winter's snowflakes
Floating free

Falling, floating
Drifting down
Winter's snowflakes
Are winter's crown

On the ground
In the air
Winter's snowflakes
Everywhere!

Theresa Machemer, Grade 5
Pollard Elementary School, NH

Summer

When summer is here we will have fun in the pool and on the slide.
We will throw water balloons at each other.
But it is hard to believe that it is the first day of school.

Laura Feiereisen, Grade 4
Wapping Elementary School, CT

Soft Silky Smooth Sand

Soft Silky Smooth **S** and
Reading on the bea **U** tiful beach
Visiting grandparents on Ji **M** my Pond Lake in Maine
Eating flavored **M** ashed up ice
Bar **E** feet on the crowded Boardwalk
Diving in to the c **R** ystal blue water
T he mucky and beautiful lake
Nice cold lemonade with crystal **I** ce that makes your mouth water
Visiting **M** emorials from History
Eating melty ice cr **E** am

Megan Ryan, Grade 6
Wakefield Forest Elementary School, VA

Summer

Summer is the time of day when you run outside and play,
Swinging high, swinging low, you feel like the day is never going to end.
Going to a pool, lake, or anything!
Having fun and eating hot dogs in a bun.
Coming home with a burnt back, not even caring,
Just going back outside to play.
Loving, caring, sharing, oh my!
You don't want the day to go by!

Hailey Roosa, Grade 4
Mitchell Elementary School, CT

Christmas Is Coming

Christmas is coming,
Can't wait oh dear, Oh dear!

Presents glisten in the light,
Brightly colored paper with fluffy bows.

Santa Claus is coming, he's coming, he's here!
I hear his large footsteps crunch in the snow.

I got some warm milk
and cookies, so here you go.

I hope he likes my cookies,
I made it just for him.

If he comes up to me with his rosy nose.
I'd say hello Mr. Santa Claus
How do you do all the wonderful things?

Because without Mr. Santa Claus there would be less joy at Christmas.
So let's all celebrate the miracles of Christmas!

Amanda Gonzalez, Grade 5
Rosemont Forest Elementary School, VA

I am a Flag

I lie here swinging every day.
People pledge to me every morning.
I'm attached to the wall.
I feel like a swing flying back and forth.
I have fifty white stars because of my country.
I have red and white stripes: 13 stripes to represent the first thirteen states of American history.
Everywhere you go, even to graves, where people have passed away, I will be waving for their freedom.

Alyssa Pasionek, Grade 5
Old Saybrook Middle School, CT

Before You Go

Before you go,
I want you to know that I love you
Before you leave this earth, I want to tell you I'm sorry for all I did
If I ever made you cry, if I ever made you sad, I'm sorry and I take it all back
If you ever come back, I will be better, I promise
Everything I did that was wrong, I wish I could take back
I wish I could redo every day I shared with you, practically my whole life
I only ask three things of you before you leave forever
Please don't remember the times that I yelled at you and disrespected you
Please don't reflect back on the arguments we had
Please don't recall the silences that fell between our disagreements
I'll remember you as a person who loved me, cared for me, cherished me, and held me close
As a person who never shunned me, criticized me, or judged me
Please remember me as a loving daughter
We cared for you, loved you, and only wanted two things
To make you proud, and to be just like you
Although there are many things you always were, always are, and always will be
There are only two that are the most important
My hero, my mother

Before you go, I want you to know that I love you
Because when you're not here anymore I fear you won't know…

Gabrielle DeBartolomeo, Grade 6
St Rose School, CT

John's Anatomy

My hair is as long as a full grown giraffe's neck with its head stretched as high as the sky.
My heart is like a sleigh dog that never stops running on a 12 hour grand race.
My skin as smooth and soft as a flat blanket laid flat out.
My eyes are like pine trees beginning to sprout a trunk in a pot of black soil.

John Erickson, Grade 6
Tolland Middle School, CT

One Last Thing

Before I go
I want you to know that I like you for your funny personality
When I said that the jokes you made were not funny I was just jealous
The things I said that ever hurt you I really did not mean
You really are the best person I've ever met because you never stopped trying to make me laugh
The things I said that scarred you were not deep from the heart
I need you to know before I go that
I take back everything I've said

Brianne Moulder, Grade 6
St Rose School, CT

Christmas

Children around the world
waiting for Christmas Eve
with gifts waiting under
the Christmas tree
the fireplace burns down to flames
but when you get up in the morning
you can have fun and games

Olivia O'Brien, Grade 4
Brookside Elementary School, MA

Halloween

Halloween Is…
— creeping kids down the street
— groaning ghosts scare kids
— buying candy for Halloween
— goblins haunting the streets
— running mummies chase the cats
— eating candy all night long
— howling wolves scare the night
— laughing witches fly in the sky
— And that's what Halloween is.

Natalie Barahona, Grade 4
St Augustine Cathedral School, CT

Tarantula Life

T oo
A wesome
R adical
A ll
N atural made
T arantula
U sually
L azy
A t noon

Jamarius Wallace, Grade 6
Floyd T Binns Middle School, VA

Shadow

I perched by the window
when I saw
through the foggy murkiness,
a shadow.
All of a sudden,
I heard an echo
that tore through my spine
like a saw.
Aaaaaaaaaaaaaah!
Suddenly,
it ceased
and all I could see was a child
plodding out of the woods
that morning.

Josh Inyangson, Grade 6
Kenmore Middle School, VA

Extreme

I can swim across the ocean,
Live beneath the seven seas.
I can stay in water forever
And never have to breathe.
I can crawl across the desert,
With a burning, hot, sand bottom.
I can walk there day and night,
And never need some water.
I can climb Mount Everest,
And never wear my coat and gloves.
I don't care if I get frostbite
Like a man named Jack Frost does.
I can float through outer space;
I'll go to Neptune, Saturn and Mars.
I'll be the first to invent
A super rocket car.
I can do so many things
No one else can do.
I live my life to the extreme.
Do you?

Elena Lloyd, Grade 5
Bethlehem Elementary School, NH

Hounds

Hounds
Strong, fast
White, black, brown
My choice of dog
Hounds

Amanda Dillon, Grade 5
McCleary Elementary School, VA

Autumn Days

Autumn Days are
Warm and loving days.
You can feel the warm
Crisp air and the
Brightly colored
Leaves
Dancing in the wind.
The wonderful smell of your
Mothers fantastic
Pumpkin pie leading
You back home
To be,
In a warm cozy home.
Jumping in the leaves
With joy and happiness.
And now it's time to say goodbye
To the autumn days.
And say hello to winter
For those cold and
Snowy days.

Tiana Dove, Grade 6
Juliet W Long School, CT

Sun and Moon

Sun
Hot, bright
Shining, solar, craters, little gravity
Revolving, reflecting, rotating
Dark, dim
Moon

David Bianculli, Grade 6
Charlton Middle School, MA

Discovered

There was a rush in the
Flowing sea.
The nice chirping
Birds
Created a noise.
The clouds faded
Us at the sea

Kristian Spraggins, Grade 6
Kenmore Middle School, VA

Sharks

Sharks are serious,
And also scary,
They'll scar you badly,
And scare you away.

Their teeth are sharp,
And breath smells.
Your legs will shake,
If you saw one.

They're swift and steady,
They're sure to eat.
The way to scare one,
Is to smack one on the nose.

Tommy Kaminski, Grade 4
Riverfield School, CT

Funky Monkey

Once there was a funky monkey.
Who was quite chunky
He knew how to dance.
But never got a chance
To learn now to dance very funky.

Tomislav Kraljic, Grade 5
John J Flynn Elementary School, VT

Earth

Earth is a wonderful place
It has rivers, oceans, and lakes.
Earth is a planet in space
It has animals such as snakes.

Nathan Swarens, Grade 6
Floyd T Binns Middle School, VA

The Beautiful Rainbow

The blue crab stuck his head out of the muddy brown soil.
Then he saw a delightful rainbow hanging above him.
With the blink of his eyes,
the amazing sight began to fade.
What happened to the rainbow?
Blue crab asked eagerly.
It was such
a beautiful sight.

Mikayla Venson, Grade 6
Kenmore Middle School, VA

Welcome to Fall

The courtyard is bursting with colors like green
My oh my, it's such a scene
The leaves are turning red, it's true
And the sky is a beautiful baby blue
Welcome to fall
With your sweater and all
As the wind whistles through my ears
For right now I have no fears
Fall is great and it is true
I love fall, don't you?

Kristin Gaudreau, Grade 4
Brookside Elementary School, MA

School

The chalkboard is a black hole
That sucks up chalk bit by bit.
The gluesticks are traps
Trapping papers in notebooks and never letting go.
The pencils are like tools
They make everything easier.
My desk is like my home,
Giving me a place of my own.
My report card is like the score in a sport,
It keeps changing and seeing if I'm doing well.

Elliott Brooks, Grade 5
Wakefield Forest Elementary School, VA

The Weatherman's Mistake

I lie under my favorite tree
and gray clouds is all I can see.
The weatherman who looks like a wizard,
predicted an amazing blizzard!
I got my sled, warmed up my bed,
I even bought a new hat for my head!
I'm so excited I jump up and down,
I turn on the TV and then I frown.
I rip off my hat,
I shout "rats!"
My preparing for the blizzard is done.
The weatherman changed the forecast to sun!

Casey Shearns, Grade 5
Millis Middle School, MA

Rainy Day

I was outside
when I noticed
a big dark
storm cloud
over me
then it started to rain.
I shivered
and shacked
and headed home.

Jessie Vormann, Grade 6
Kenmore Middle School, VA

Friday

It's the end,
Yet the beginning,
It's a finish
Yet a start,
It's completed,
Yet it's uncompleted,
It's halted,
Yet it's launched,
It's the limit,
Yet the limited,
It's an introduction,
Yet a conclusion,
It's free, wild, everything!
Everything amazing,
Everything tiring,
Everything extraordinary,
It's the world coming alive,
It's being alive!
It's the glories of the universe
It's the fast beating drum that is your heart
IT'S FRIDAY!

Nicole Gagnon, Grade 5
Jack Jackter Intermediate School, CT

Christmas

It is Christmas day
so say hip hip hooray
Christmas came so swift
there are lots of gifts
some are hard to lift
the birds of Christmas day they just flew away
you see they need some place warm to stay

Julia Zygiel, Grade 5
Southbrook Academy, MA

Christmas Morning

When I came downstairs in the morning, I looked around.
I found presents here, presents there, presents everywhere.
Wow, is that my pile? It looks like a whole file.
Look, I got a book and it came with a nook!
I love Christmas, why can't it be every day? Even in May!!

Kelsie Wood and Caly Farina, Grade 4
Long Meadow Elementary School, CT

Dreams Go a Long Way
As I close my eyes
I hear voices coming from the television.
Soon I drift into a deep sleep.

Wonderful images are popping out in front of me.
I see fields and roses and the shimmering face of the sun.

I am skipping in one of those fields of roses when
suddenly I hear a thunderous beeping noise,
With a startle I wake up.
Allison Reno, Grade 5
Four Seasons Elementary School, MD

Dogs
Dogs are playful,
happy,
and just plain cute!
You play with them
until
they tire you out.
They beg for food
until
you just have to give them a piece
and then you get in trouble.
Take them to compete in a dog show
and yours will win;
and after you'll get a huge grin!
I don't have a dog
but
I think they are the best pet you can get,
way better than other kinds of pets!
Laura Hammer, Grade 4
John Ward Elementary School, MA

Fall
May the grass turn brown,
Let the leaves fall down,
May the groundhog never see its shadow again,
The logs are being loaded into the fireplace,
And the first sip of hot chocolate
is being taken,
I see birds flying south,
Which is so, so sad,
Because fall should last forever.
Abigail Bostley, Grade 6
Village School, MA

The Girl from Florida
There once was a young girl from Florida
Who was named Dora
She lived in a hole
With a mole
He was like a rabbit that couldn't get out of his cage
Travis Welch, Grade 5
McCleary Elementary School, VA

Index

Author Autograph Page

Author Autograph Page

Author Autograph Page

Author Autograph Page

Author Autograph Page

Author Autograph Page